'Don't Call Me Nigger, Whitey'

'Don't Call Me Nigger, Whitey'
Sly Stone & Black Power

Andrew Darlington

Leaky Boot Press

'Don't Call Me Nigger, Whitey': Sly Stone & Black Power
by Andrew Darlington

First published in 2014 by
Leaky Boot Press
http://www.leakyboot.com

Copyright © 2014 Andrew Darlington
All rights reserved

No part of this book may be reproduced or transmitted in any form or by any means, electronic, mechanical, photocopying, recording, or otherwise, without prior written permission of the author.

ISBN: 978-1-909849-05-1

Contents

'A Dance to the Music of Timelessness'	9
'It's a Family Affair'	13
'The Autumn of His Years…'	29
'San Franciscan Nights'	46
'Where Do We Go From Here: Chaos or Community…?'	62
'A Whole New Thing'	82
'From New York… To Detroit'	96
'Dance to the Music'	108
'Everyday People'	125
'Getting Higher at Woodstock'	140
'Different Strokes For Different Folks'	158
'Revolution/Evolution'	174
'The Revolution Will Be Televised'	194
'There's a Riot Goin' On'	214
'Running Away Ha! Ha! Ha!'	228
'Fresh'	242
'Small Talk'	258
'Heard Ya Missed Me…?'	278
'Ain't But the One Way'	296
'Thank You'	313
Discography	333

'sometimes I'm right,
and I can be wrong,
my own beliefs
are in my song...'
(*Everyday People*)

Chapter One
'A Dance to the Music of Timelessness'

'Sly & The Family Stone harnessed all the disparate musical and social trends of the late sixties, creating a wild, ludicrous, incandescent fusion of soul, rock, R&B, psychedelia and funk that smashed down boundaries with brilliant disregard for precedent. The first racially and gender-integrated band, with an integration that beamed out through the music as well as the personnel...'

(*'Lillian Roxon's Rock Encyclopaedia'* Grosset & Dunlap' 1971)

'What is it... Sly & The Family Stone...?'

It's about time. It's about space. It's about ups and downs caused by life in general. But more than anything else, it's about music and it's about people who are obsessed by music...

This particular night was the occasion of his induction into 'The Rock & Roll Hall Of Fame'—the music industry's equivalent of the Oscars or the Golden Globes. Yet here at the New York Waldorf-Astoria on this 12th January 1993 night, the man called Sly Stone had totally vanished from public view. In a red-carpeted air-kissing micro-climate of fragile egos and mirrors-in-the-bathroom, the surviving functioning members of other once-mighty music legends had already gathered to compare their psychological scars. Alongside inductees Cream, Creedence Clearwater Revival, and the Doors, there were all six members of the original Family Stone. But not, it seemed... the reclusive Sly himself. The extraordinary superdude of black music had become the Greta Garbo of Soul. The Syd Barrett and JD Salinger of Funk. Why *should* he turn up? Sightings persist. Before, and since. They've become mythic, the subject of internet debate and discussion. Fans consume vast amounts of bandwidth analysing rumoured sightings which continue to be reported with the regularity of Elvis, or UFO activity over Area 51.

But it was a hall of the self-styled industry aristocracy here to congratulate itself on its own celebrity, lavish with designer tags and hyper-expensive flash, gold awards clearly blinging in their eyes. A rarefied flashbulb-irradiated atmosphere of refined and futile dandies with their arm-candies, beautiful face-lifted people there to be seen being beautiful. Not an audience easily impressed by any presence other than their own. But eventually, after a slow-burn build-up of speeches and presentations, the Family Stone troop up there as George Clinton goes into his introduction spiel. The audience listen as he relates how Sly Stone had been such an immeasurable influence on R&B, Pop, Rock, *and* Hip-Hop. How Sly—more than any other single artist, had irrevocably reconfigured the geography of sixties and seventies Soul music. How, at the same time he'd shown Rock the rhythmic potential of 'funk' when transferred from riffing horns to electric keyboards and wah-wah guitars. How he'd first been influenced by, and had then influenced the funk of James Brown. If James Brown had invented funk, it was Sly who perfected it. Then shaped the production techniques of George Clinton's own Funkadelic, the costume make-over of the Jackson Five, the Rock-guitar excursions of the Isley Brothers, the vocals of the Ohio Players, and the full-frontal assault performances of Earth Wind & Fire. More, Sly Stone was a serious proponent of music as a tool for social change, for confronting, altering, and fine-tuning attitudes. He was influential… *and* funky!

As Clinton stood aside, bass-playing long-term founder-member Larry Graham led the group into a contagious vocal work-out around "Thank You (Falettinme Be Mice Elf Agin)". Then an exhilarating impromptu "Dance To The Music", after which each bandmate stepped up to the podium to accept their awards. Brother Freddie Stewart, respectably bespectacled, and sporting a neat beard. Sister Rose Stone, offering her brief thanks. Then a graceful Cynthia Robinson. Horn-player Jerry Martini. And finally, out from behind the drum-riser, Gregg Errico. Until, just when it seemed it was all done, there was a disturbance that came from the back of the hall, then rippled all the way up to the front, as Sly himself abruptly materialised to gasps and whoops of delighted surprise. The hall spontaneously erupted into thunderous applause as he stepped up to the podium. A moment that transfigured the evening from an orgy of complacent industry self-congratulation, into a fully qualified seismic event. He graciously, almost shyly, received his award, tagging a hasty speech to it. To everyone's surprise, including his former band-mates, he looked up, and closed with a promise to 'see you soon'. It would be another ten years before he'd fulfil that promise. The man they saw on the podium was a strange and beguiling mixture of who he'd become, who he was… and who, if things had worked out differently, he might have been. Then he vanished back into the night, to wherever he'd come from. For something like the next decade, at least…

'When we started out' Martini ruefully confided to *'People'* magazine, 'Sly Stone had the power to control 80,000 people with his eyes, but in '93, he couldn't even look at me.' Maybe loving the Family Stone is a tough love? But it's a forever thing too. Sly Stone hasn't issued any new music in decades. He'd even acquired a tarnished reputation as a functioning human being. But he achieved so much during what might be pedestrianly described as the nine lives of his career that his artistic status can never be questioned. He's a shadow-presence for music historians to argue over. But the commercial and musical monster he created has ensured his place in music history. Pieces written about his work tend to follow set formulaic patterns. How his journey began as a child prodigy performing with his family gospel group in Vallejo, California. How it took him through his key role as DJ, producer and activist with the incandescent social revolutions of San Francisco. Then as singer, songwriter, bandleader, performer and multi-instrumentalist, through the counter-culture's highest zenith of Woodstock, into documenting the corruption of that idealism through the darkening vision of what many consider to be his finest album, 'There's A Riot Goin' On'. Sly Stone is a larger-than-life figure who could fairly claim to have been both blessed and cursed by his early success. But mostly blessed. The curse—when his American dream of fame and unlimited wealth became a burden rather than a blessing, only came later in the arc, as is often the way with precocious talent. Until he eclipsed himself into eventual invisibility. And all the classic script-ingredients for a hack screenplay are there—sex, drugs, violence, pride, self-indulgence, hubris… downslide. But the real Sly Stone story is so much more than that fingernail-image suggests. The arc of his career was played out across the greatest period of convulsive revolution in the American experience. An essentially amiable musician and human being Sly was drawn into that destructive, and liberating process against his most natural inclination. That's the real story. As I hope to indicate in what follows.

To Greil Marcus Sly Stone is one of the great American performers, those who, 'because they take more risks than most, risk artistic disaster'. His other iconic performers include Robert Johnson, Elvis Presley, the Band, and Randy Newman. Artists who are 'more ambitious', because they risk 'the alienation of an audience that can be soothed far more easily than it can be provoked'. Artists who 'dramatise a sense of what it is to be American'. Who 'share unique and public personalities' with 'enough ambition to make even their failures interesting…' To Greil Marcus, Sly possesses a quality he attributes to a Robbie Robertson quote, that 'music should never be harmless'.

Music is littered with burnt-out heroes, beautiful losers and washed-up victims. Some have gone through its worst most extreme ravages, forced to confront the imminence of their own extinction, yet have come out the other side functionally intact sufficient to enjoy a late second-career celebrity, surviving by practising the art of reincarnation without the inconvenient necessity of having to die. Brian Wilson. Arthur Lee. Iggy Pop. Keith Richards—the patron saint of celebrity narco-survival, even Fleetwood

Mac's founder Peter Green. Others are lost forever. Sly is the consummate star. An enigma for who interest will always be high. For Sly, knocked off course by his own personal cocaine blizzard, we can only wait. But despite sporadic unfounded but persistently hopeful rumours, we wait. His music is down-loaded and heard on MTV as the backbeat for hip-hop, as new artists give credit to the originator who laid the foundations for what they're now building on. Even those too young to have experienced his records first-hand, know him through the music he influenced...

There are a million stories that take place within the arc of this narrative. I sometimes feel I've lived the entirety of my own life within them. I've spent many hundreds of hours discussing and teasing out details of that time, both in direct relation to, and around the events within which they occurred. I talked to the late Gene Clark of the Byrds, Grace Slick, Sid Griffin, 'Country' Joe McDonald, Dave Davies of the Kinks, Rick Parfitt and Francis Rossi of Status Quo, Mick Fleetwood, Donovan Leitch, Graham Nash, Sam Moore, and others. Thanks also to David Kerekes for suggesting this project. I'm grateful to Joel Selvin, Vaetta 'Stone' Stewart, and Gene Sculatti for their best wishes and example. To my great regret, I've acceded to the wishes of several other sources who confided first-hand knowledge of personal and musical events, but specifically requested anonymity. However, to such people I'm indebted for their insight and contributions. Textual reference to a person's inclusion or exclusion from a sequence does not necessarily infer that that person has contributed to this book. And loving thanks to my wife, Catherine, for her tolerant patience as I laboured over the laptop she bought me.

I've also conducted research through countless books, magazines and web-sites and have gratefully given credit accordingly. However, I apologise for those instances where I've been unable to correctly attribute quotes, despite my most exhaustive attempts to do so. I invite corrections to such omissions, which will be rectified in future editions.

While Sly's riot is still goin' on...

What it is... Sly & The Family Stone?

Chapter Two
'It's a Family Affair'

'The very next line will blow my mind…'
("I Cannot Make It")

Listen, inevitably, mythologies have sprung up around and about Sly Stone. To the extent that it gets impossible to separate out facts from the multiple fictions that surround him. And lives are too complex things to reduce down into a couple of hundred pages anyway, so how can it possibly show the depths of truth? It can't. But these things are… probably, true. It starts off as a Family Affair. The Stewart family are deeply religious middle-class African-Americans living on Prairie Street in the Texas town of Denton, near Dallas. Parents K.C. and Alpha Stewart unite their nuclear family through the strict doctrines of the Saint Beulah Church of God in Christ, enlivened by its joyous interaction of Hallelujah-preacher and congregation. There are people who claim that this denomination has many of the attributes of cult exclusivity, one comparable to Mormons, or Jehovah's Witnesses. An 1890s offshoot of the Pentecostal 'Holiness' movement, it is strongly based around the concept of 'Baptismal Regeneration'—redemption through spiritual rebirth. 'Speaking in tongues' is another strong part of their culture. Its more extreme adherents even disapprove of the use of musical instruments during worship on the highly debatable grounds that they're never mentioned in the Bible.

Sly was born Sylvester Stewart on the 'Ides of March'—the 15th March 1944, the second of five children, into this large boisterous socially involved family. His eldest sister, Loretta, was the only member of the Stewart brood not to attempt a musical career. And music came early. Young Sylvester was a child prodigy from the start. At the precocious age of four he was already beginning to show an interest—and a prodigious talent, for music and singing gospel in the Church choir. The schism from Gospel cross-over into secular is both a standard part of the black music experience, and a continuing source of its inner torment. Think Aretha Franklin or Sam Cooke. Think Little Richard... or Marvin Gaye.

To understand Sly's family background is vitally important in any attempt at understanding the man. In the phraseology of the time, you have to know where he's coming from to appreciate where he went. But first, there's no suggestion of the regimented parental bullying that scarred the Jackson family into becoming The Jackson Five. For 'Big Daddy' KC was no stern disciplinarian. Unlike Murray Wilson, a bullying belittling frustrated songwriter whose sons—the Wilson brothers, had to achieve as the Beach Boys, what he'd never been capable of. Both the Jackson and the Wilson families endured treatment that took fragile and artistic minds and caused extreme damage and psychological problems in adult life. By contrast, the talents of the Stewart children seem to have been nurtured and encouraged, within a loving tightly-knit family. Indeed, in the wake of the storm and the pain of celebrity, younger brother Freddie would find a new comfort-zone niche performing and preaching as a pastor of the Vallejo, California's Evangelist Temple Fellowship Center. Returning to where he started out. He even markets his own Gospel CD through the website. But then, didn't the wonderfully surreal humour of Lord Buckley once proclaim that 'entertainers are the new clergy'...?

'*Dallas*' is a shiny TV Soap. Dallas is also a staunchly Republican conservative town that never really reconciled itself to Rock 'n' Roll. Perhaps, like Bobby Ewing, Sylvester Stewart may one day wake up in the shower to find out it's all been a dream. All the hits and concerts, the incredible highs and dreadful lows, the albums, 'Woodstock'—and beyond. All a dream. And he's just plain Sylvester Stewart in the Lone Star State's two-bit Denton. If you follow Interstate 35 down to where it forks west for Fort Worth, and a mere thirty-six miles east to Dallas, you arrive in Denton. A more laid-back place than its bigger brasher near-neighbour, with a more active music scene, largely due to the presence of the 'University of North Texas' campus. It had been settled early on by small subsistence farmers who owned very few slaves. It was also sufficiently distanced from the Mexican border—and, despite some cotton-growing, lacked the large agricultural demand for hand-labour, so it had relatively few black or Hispanic residents, at least until the 1980s student influx.

And on the radio in the Stewart's front room there'd be music from the diverse cultural cross-currents of Country 'barn-dance' shows to Bob Wills' Western Swing. From the Grand Ole Opry's 'Yodelling Cowboys' to Doris Day. From fiddles to sermons. From cosy soporific big-bands, to Latin and Zydeco, all with their distinctive regional characteristics. Huddie 'Leadbelly' Ledbetter worked in Dallas. Blind Lemon Jefferson played slide-guitar along the Central railroad track in the Deep Ellum section, the honky-tonk heart of the city's black community. Then… down Highway 20 there's Lubbock, home of Buddy Holly. Janis Joplin came from Port Arthur in south-east Texas, but had to relocate to California to become what she would become. The legendary Doug Sahm comes from San Antonio. And further south, towards the Texas-Mexico border, there's the fiercely independent Tex-Mex Chicano influences that produced renegade Punk Garage classics from Austin's Thirteenth Floor Elevators, Sir Douglas Quintet ("She's About A Mover"), Question Mark & The Mysterians ("96 Tears"), or Cannibal & The Headhunters ("Land Of 1,000 Dances") which fuse Tejano sounds to R&B beats and cheap Farfisa whirling keyboard runs.

But nine months *after* Sylvester's birth, and three months *before* third child Rosemary's arrival (21st March 1945), the Stewart family up and moved from their home state to California, to Chuck Berry's 'Promised Land'. Taking that long overland drive from Texas—accounts vary as to exactly when, leaving some thirty kinfolk behind, calling off at Bakersfield where they also had family connections, then following Highway 80 from Sacramento west towards the coast, direct to the city of Vallejo. Located twenty-five miles north of Oakland on the San Pablo Bay, Solano County is connected by a regular ferry service down the bay to San Francisco. Vallejo wasn't pretty, but it was a rough, friendly, active waterfront suburban sprawl. A community named for its Mexican founder—General Mariano Vallejo in 1844, and pronounced Mexican-style as 'Vallay-ho'. Here, there are tastefully restored Victorian homes and business frontages, with newer affordable housing in the Northgate and Hiddenbrooke developments, its commerce centring long-term on the grimy industrial suburbs surrounding the Mare Island Naval Shipyards which eventually closed in 1996. This was the community in which the Stewart children would grow, and which they would best remember as home. Sly once called Denio Street, on the west-side, 'like a Watts, only with more whites'. But he was never a 'ghetto child', even though—as Hamp 'Bubba' Banks pointed out, it would be a useful fiction to later pretend that he had been.

There's little evidence of extreme financial hardship either. Daddy KC ran a janitorial business. Which means, he cleaned offices. He was also a deacon in the local Pentecostal church. In a later photograph from Vet's archive he is caught about to board an aeroplane, as part of a Family Stone tour package. He's a tall slender dignified man in a Panama hat, white jacket, and red bow-tie. He smiles with pride and natural warmth. He carries a colourful plastic bag, and a guitar. Beside him is Big Momma Alpha, barely inches shorter, more solidly and maternally rounded, in a flowing full-length dress of black and white swirls. Her hair is elaborately teased out into a dark halo around her face. They're both smiling with quiet pride and excitement at their family's great adventure. 'My Momma gave me a song' Sly wrote in 1973. 'Make your Daddy happy, Momma likes it like that.'

Back then 'Big Mama' Alpha was directing the church choir, so it's fairly obvious the children sing there too. It was a family steeped in music. 'We went to church four times a week, I sang in every choir' Sly tells. But they had an uncle who also preached, and the entire brood shared the same raw talent nurtured by those original gospel roots. Younger brother—and fourth Stewart child, Freddie (born 5th June 1946) recalls his father playing violin and washboard (he calls it 'scrub-board'), accompanied by his cousin on piano, with the brothers and sisters singing along. Daddy KC would also invent little tunes and put verses from the Bible to them, as infotainment for the children. 'I started playing music, instruments, when I was very young' recalled Sylvester, 'everybody else had swimming pools, we had drum-sticks'. To fan-interviewer Willem Alkema he adds 'I grew up in a musical family and thought everyone made music. It was just something you did. On the way to the kitchen you came by the piano, so then I stopped for a while and started playing. It was like learning how to talk' (in *Mojo*, March 2010). If music became an integral continuity in their lives, it has to be attributed to this environment in which they grew. Youngest child 'Vet' Vaetta says their music is 'rooted in family'. Momma and Daddy Stewart 'instilled respect and caring in their children. They supported each of their child's dreams and helped any way they could'. According to Vet, there's a posed photo of the children in the family archive. Loretta poised at the piano, fingers at the ready 'seemingly taking direction from the Lord himself'. Sylvester looking 'wise like Solomon'. Rose is 'intense'. Freddie 'even then, spiritually dapper'. With the baby Vaetta with 'her head cocked to the side, ready to sing...'

Freddie began learning to play wind instruments around third grade. He recalls how, 'during his elementary years'—even before 'Little Sister' Vaetta had arrived, the four eldest kids, Sly with sister Loretta, Freddie and Rose were already performing in the family's gospel group, 'The Stewart Four'. Around that time they used to rehearse harmonies in the front room, working out routines, with Sly sometimes beating out rhythm on drums. Then KC and Alpha would transport 'The Stewart Four' from place to place, Momma and Daddy up-front in the car, the kids crammed in the back, to where they could perform in front of audiences. 'We travelled around from church to church, all over California, performing concerts' recalls Vet, 'we thought we were just like any other family. We had no idea.' They played the local 'sanctified' circuit, the church itself getting and keeping a major cut of the money they collected after each performance—nickels, dimes, or the 'quiet cash' that came in note form. And—in 1952, they recorded and released their own 78rpm single through the local Northern California Sunday School Dept. For the 'A'-side, "On The Battlefield For My Lord" was already a Gospel standard. 'I was alone and idle, I was a sinner too' until 'I heard a voice from heaven...' Freddie was only four years old, and exactly how appropriate its message of the 'sinner saved' would be as sung by such a youthful quartet must remain debateable. They chose "Walking In Jesus' Name" for the 'B'-side, Sly singing lead on both. Only Loretta was not there for the recording itself, her place being taken by 'a niece'. Later they got together around the kitchen table to package the red-labelled 'Church Of God In Christ (COGIC)' record themselves, and then sold them through the church network, with Daddy KC transporting some copies in his car, all the way back to Denton. Despite such determined distribution efforts, to all intents and purposes, no copies of the record are known to survive, although a taste can be gained from subsequent versions of the song recorded by the Belleville A Cappella Choir, or The Harmonizing Four.

As the Stewart Family wunderkind became teenagers the sounds in their household tended to be predominantly their own—kids' tongue-twister games such as 'how could a would-not could-not, if a would-not could-not would', or teasing taunts—'you're a cluck-cluck-cluck-cluck chicken', contrasted with the sound of contemporary gospel stars on the radio. But if this were to become a movie—which it well might, for Syl Stewart there's no convenient trigger event to transfigure his life, no key moments of trauma to act as creative catalyst. There's no single crystallising moment, nothing to compare with the infant Ray Charles witnessing the accidental drowning of his brother, followed by the near-Biblical consequence of his subsequent gradual descent into blindness. As it was portrayed in the fine movie 'Ray' (2004). And nothing approaching the kick of guilt and remorse that galvanised young Johnny Cash when *his* brother, Jack, was mortally wounded while cutting fence posts with a circular saw and died eight days later, as portrayed in the movie 'Walk The Line' (2005). When researchers undertake a voyage of ancestral discovery into the Stewart family genealogy, they find there are few skeletons. Alpha—née Haynes, met KC Stewart at a Denton church function. She was still in her teens. She'd never known another man. He doesn't drink. Never swears. And has never smoked a cigarette, or even been tempted to. She has a sister called Omega ('I am Alpha and Omega, the first and the last'—"Book Of Revelations i II'). So much, so clean. Their marriage would last sixty-nine years.

And there's a strong impression that morally-improving religion provided a more important defining point for the family than race ever did. The Stewart's were church, church, church, of the sanctified and holiness variety. Leaving an impression that—for them, 'congregation' underscored their concept of 'community' rather more than colour. If there was an 'us'-and-'them' social dichotomy, what mattered most was the one delineated—not by skin-colour, but by the god-fearing 'saved', versus the unenlightened secular masses. But even within that apparently solid congregation there was a complex increment of belief. Not all of which was a direct influence on *all* members of the congregation, except maybe among the most strictly devout. Material success to some, was in itself suspect. Because material success necessarily involves an element of compromise with worldliness. And that leads to a distancing from spiritual values. From righteousness. From god. There can be no middle ground. You are saved. Or you are damned. Mortal sin presages eternal damnation. And it's unforgiving.

Even if we of a more atheistic disposition find such levels of religiosity difficult to empathise with, it's not difficult to understand how the first cut is the deepest, how those immersed in such intense impressions grow up with an indelibly long-lasting soul-imprint. Or how such close-harmony family-bonding provides the crucible for their overlapping vocal arrangements, and leads to a near-telepathic sibling affinity that will never leave them. Perhaps something of Sly's evangelical 'message' of social unity through the transfiguring power of love can in part be traced to what he absorbed from church? As well as the come-down that follows. The fall from grace. If it's true—as Tolstoy almost epigrammed in *'Anna Karenina'* (1877), that all happy families are alike in their happiness, but unhappy families unique in their own misery, then the Family Stewart have been through both polar extremes.

Although Vallejo was a polyglot racially-mixed kind of blue-collar city, neither it, nor Denton, had a predominantly black demographic. And Sly's friends and Public High School classmates were not predominantly black. Not to say that an awareness of racism wasn't ever-present. No African-American could grow through those turbulent years unaware of the immense social changes and inequalities rupturing the continent. Sylvester absorbed his politics by osmosis. He later told *'Rolling Stone'* that 'I was in race riots when I was in high school in Vallejo, five-hundred people in the student body carrying on, and that was more exciting than anything else…' No-one could write "Don't Call Me Nigger, Whitey"—even with its flippant twist, without having first experienced it. Yet there was an unlikely musical precedent for Sly's kind of racial cross-over. R&B star of the 1950's Johnny Otis was born in Vallejo. Although of Greek parentage he danced across the racial divide to find 'soul', so convincingly he became a legend within black music.

'I had a great childhood as a black youth in Vallejo' he told *Mojo* magazine, 'but you didn't know any better. On Saturday there was swimming for blacks and on Monday night blacks were allowed to skate. There was a school being built for black children. But when that school started competing in sports events, they won every trophy…!' Nevertheless, the route-map to deliverance—for the Stewart family, was still more spiritual than it was a direct-action political concern. It's only when the certainty of those ideas run aground, or prove inadequate, that their limitations show. But there's no angst to grind, not yet. That will only arrive further down their convoluted path along the mighty long road of Rock 'n' Soul—from the congregation at Vallejo, through the hits, the stage at Woodstock… with the obligations of celebrity. And the destabilising psycho-nightmares that follow. The intrusive press interrogations. The intervention of Black Power activists who see Sly as a figurehead ripe for recruitment as a provocational agent of the revolution. Through to their induction at the 1993 'The Rock & Roll Hall Of Fame'.

****

At Vallejo there was just one, mixed-race High School. 'Like, high school was terrible' Sly would later recall. 'It was boring for me 'cause either I was too smart, or too dumb to realise what I could learn. There wasn't enough challenge. In English 1-A, it was such a drag that by the end of the semester I forgot what I learned…' In a *'Rolling Stone'* interview he elaborated, 'in school I didn't read. You know, just spell it like that and there's a test at the end. I really don't understand what's in a book.' Reflectively he admitted 'I used to be ashamed to mention that I didn't read anything. I've tried to read, but the only thing I want to read is on stuff I care about…' From the start, music had the advantage of greater immediacy, 'I mean, I've never heard of anybody getting their minds blown by written media. You don't really know where the idea comes from… in literature, unless I know the person, you read it once or twice and that's it. But you can listen to an album over and over until it wears out. It really seems like music, and that's it…'

Sylvester had already taken to calling himself Sly ever since a spelling-bee anagram in Mr Edwards' fifth-grade class had rearranged his family nickname 'Syl', and it stuck. And while they were at High School both Sylvester and Freddie were involved in a number of music outfits. Music was already their mother language, Sly had music oozing out of him. He learned to play a number of instruments, settling primarily on guitar. His first had been a second-hand store-bought instrument Daddy KC picked up for him when he was nine years old. And KC monitored his progress carefully. To the Stewart brothers, blues was for old men. Jazz was what they played in elevators. But Syl was happy to raunch 'The Top 40 Rock 'n' Roll Hits of the Day' with Joey Piazza & The Continentals—a name so perfect it sounds like a post-modern invention contrived for a *'Happy Days'* walk-on. Yet it was a name immaculately attuned to a genre of *other* bands named after US high-finned gas-guzzling chrome-gleaming autos, and—after all, John F Kennedy *was* gunned down in his Lincoln Continental, in Sly's near-birthplace, Dallas. Another member of the Continentals was Jerry Martini. They became close friends. Sly also hung out with a high-school street-gang called The Cherrybusters—who wore uniform orange jackets, and he was a member of The Royal Aces.

His was already a bi-cultural identity. But did he run with the brothers on the block, as some would prefer to think, hanging out talking trash, swapping jive in odd patois? He may have subsumed and used that identity when it suited him, but he'd already developed an insider-outsider's habit that extended above and beyond that life-style. Sly was something else. He was tight family, but he was independent too. He thought differently. He thought big. And he thought unique. By the time he'd turned sixteen he had already written and scored his own regional hit single with "Long Time Alone" c/w "Help Me With My Broken Heart", recorded as 'Sylvester Stewart' and picked up by the local G&P label. The escalation seems astonishing. And it was. Other families have photo-albums. The Stewart family do too. But from the very beginning, they had sound recordings as well. For the Stewart siblings you track their childhood years through tracks. Punctuated at every stage of their growth there was music. And it was captured on disc at intervals sufficiently regular to form a narrative. Heavy 78rpm shellac. Then 45rpm vinyl minigroove. That's just the way it was. As Miles Davis said, he had 'music all up in my body, and that's what I wanted to hear'. For Sly, it was ultimately this all-consuming time-preoccupation with music that cut him out of the gang thing.

"Long Time Alone" is one of Sly's most accomplished early constructions. It begins as a Platters-style composition, structured around a fashionable epistolary narrative, 'I'm writing this letter to let you know...' while in the background the group chant 'long time alone' in a way reminiscent of the Flamingos "I Only Have Eyes For You". Before going into a big finish—'please come back, I've been a long... (gulp)... time alone'. While flip the record over and Sly is assuming a more Ben E King or Clyde McPhatter guise, his voice descending soul-deep before ascending into falsetto swoops. It's perfectly good Pop soul—with a melody vaguely reminiscent of Tony Orlando's hit "Bless You", a jaunty sax break and typically idiosyncratic Sly lyrics about 'if I had a zipper on my heart, I would look inside, yeh, and I would try to fix it before I die...'

But, smartly dressed, with his hair neatly parted, Sly was equally happy to become lead singer with the Viscaynes, a Frankie Lymon & The Teenagers-style close harmony Doo-Wop group. After all, the example of The Teenagers and their tragic young star was also an early influence on George Clinton. While Bobby Womack lived a few blocks down from the Cleveland Majestic Hotel where he pestered Frankie Lymon and the group while they stayed over there mid-tour. But there's a cautionary tale there too. In 1957 Alan Freed's prime-time nationally televised ABC Rock 'n' Roll show *'The Big Beat'* was abruptly cancelled after Lymon pulled a white girl up out of the studio audience and danced with her onstage—outraging southern sponsors. Race was an incendiary issue. Yet the Viscaynes' history is far from clear—some writers, including Greil Marcus—but not Joel Selvin and the Family Stone website 'Phattadatta', even prefer the alternate group-spelling 'Viscanes'... and what does the word mean anyway? The closest definition, and most likely source, lies in the same automotive vein as the 'Lincoln Continentals', the 'Fleetwoods' or the 'Chevvy Impalas', which would be the Chevrolet Biscayne. Writer Miles Marshall Lewis suggests—in his chatty conversational mini-book *'There's A Riot Goin' On'*, that the group's name came about simply as the result of a typographical error that occurred at the "Yellow Moon" pressing plant—their intended name all along was the Biscaynes. An explanation that sounds eminently reasonable.

Whatever, the groups' chemistry even anticipates something of what was to come, its mix providing a matrix for the Family Stone. There were two girls in the line-up, Charlene Imhoff and Sly's girlfriend Maria Boldway. There was a white guy called Charles Gebhart and his brother Vern, or sometimes Mike Stevens. Then there was Sly, and his Filipino friend Frank Arelano, who were the only non-whites in the six-piece line-up. 'Yes… it was a mixture of man, woman, and different races and that is the way it should be' Sly told interviewer Willem Alkema many years later, 'I never caught on with that discrimination. For me that was normal, in my head. I wanted as much as possible for the band to be a reflection of the soul of different sexes and different skin colours. So that people could see such different people having fun on-stage and have it be an example to them' (in *'Mojo no. 196'*, March 2010). Even allowing for a certain measure of retrospective re-editing, this provides a good example of his continuing mindset.

The Viscaynes worked the clubs and bars of the North Beach, then went to Los Angeles to record a few singles, working with husband-&-wife songwriting team George Motola & Ricky Page. Starting with one called "Stop What You Are Doing", the single achieved a degree of regional popularity. They got to perform it on local TV, on San Francisco's own version of 'Dick Clark', called 'The Dick Stewart Show'. Then the strongest of their singles combines two Sly songs, "Yellow Moon" c/w "Heavenly Angel". "Yellow Moon" takes the tight Platters-style lead with group back-up format, to make a lunar appeal for the 'magic glow' of the moon's 'golden light' to illuminate his way into her affections. Its naïve Pop appeal is even enhanced by a dramatic spoken interlude. "Heavenly Angel" takes a similar Platters big ballad template, opening with cheesy horns, decorated with 'heavenly' chiming girl choruses as Sly's yearning voice rises from 'my heaven', emphasised by repeating 'my heaven', then peaking even higher with a third 'my heaven'. The melody reference-points would have to include recent Pop hits "Devil Or Angel", "Donna", or even "I'll Be Home". An alternate 'B'-side, issued under their alternate Biscaynes identity is even stranger. This time Sly takes his model from the Coasters, with a kind of "Alley-Oop" (Hollywood Argyles) pacing. "Uncle Sam Needs You My Friend" uses martial drums and 'Hup-2-3-4' vocal-effects for a comic novelty take on military conscription—'when Uncle Sam calls, man, you sure gotta go'. His reaction to his call-up papers begin 'I don't think I'd like it in Berlin', through comic falsetto and bass-voice interjections, to a final protest in the fade-out 'I can't go, I got a moustache'!

These are songs redolent of Doo-Wop and fifties chart Pop, artfully-constructed pastiches multi-referencing the full range of innocent cliché, pulling in every carefully-studied technique and vocal trick in the genres' limited vocabulary. 'I learned a little in a lot of places' Sly acknowledges. Yet, precociously preoccupied with his music, it's interesting that Sly chose to avoid raw Rock 'n' Roll or hard R&B in favour of its sweeter more appealing Pop variants—commercial cross-over's which, even then, could make a claim to be racially non-specific. These are the styles he replicates with impressively crafted precision. Noting lyric ideas. Grafting in lines as they came to him, most often from other songs, then reshaping them to fit his equally borrowed melodies. But even when playing it for laughs, he was ambitious to get it right. Less plagiarism, more synthesis. These rare records now form elements of a trove of songs collected, recombined, and reissued in various compilations ever since.

"You're My Only Love" is an up-tempo example of catchy teen-Pop with "Three Steps To Heaven" guitar strum and deep bass-man vocals numbering the way he loves his girl, 'the way you kiss tonight, the way you hold me tight, the way you set my heart and soul on fire' (not 'alight'?). The rhymes might tend to the obvious—'your slightest touch, thrills me much too much', but the talent is unmistakably advanced. "You've Forgotten Me" is an appealing facsimile of a romantic ballad with a heartbroken Sly lamenting 'now I'm alone with a heart that cries' (issued as a single by 'Danny Stewart', it was released again under the alternate title "I'm Just A Fool In Love"), while "Oh! What A Night"—a straight copy of the Dells' version, is a group exercise with a range of contrasting vocal deliveries, demonstrating Sly's already highly-developed skills as arranger. The only ingredient missing from these extraordinary early works is that of the *authentic* Sylvester Stewart himself. Yet many artists have enjoyed respectable degrees of success and long-term careers by remaining firmly within genre limitations, and never evolving a distinctive separate identity even within those cosy confines. So it's easy to imagine how—with national distribution, a little enthusiastic promotion and TV exposure, any of these titles *could* have taken off across the charts, in which case Pop history would have assumed a slightly skewed direction. In that conjectural alternate time-stream, 'Danny Stewart' would have become a teen-idol in much the same way that Frankie Lymon had. And instead of making his big breakthrough with the Family Stone he might already have been touring the nostalgia 'Golden Oldies' circuit by 1970, performing "Heavenly Angel" or "Long Time Alone". But it's also significant that precisely because these singles *were* one-off deals done with small-but-happening independent labels, there was no corporate machine behind them. They were created by the burgeoning talents of Sly, and his teen-accomplices, unaided by A&R manipulation or production meddling.

Sylvester was an uneasy cocktail of self-effacing vulnerability, and ambition. That was fast becoming part of the 'Sly' Stewart style. But at the same time, he was not neglecting his academic development. He was a pretty good student, keeping up with his studies. He got straight 'A's in the subjects where it mattered to him most. Even while he was looking at the clock on the wall—trying not to make it too obvious that his mind was on what he'd be doing later. Then every evening, after he'd finished classes, he'd learn as much from hanging out. Nevertheless, he went on to do three semesters at Solano Community College (it was then called Vallejo Junior College). He sang in the college choir, and attended Music Theory 1A-1B classes where he studied composition, theory, and trumpet. Tutor David Froelich's lectures integrated jazz with elements of Pop and classical music. 'I'd learn more from him than from listening to anybody' Sly later admits to Ben Fong-Torres. And Froelich—who moonlighted as a local jazz pianist, was a tutor Sly would acknowledge as a major inspiration through album liner-note 'thanks'. 'He was the kind of person who never washed his hair, but it was always clean. White and beautiful and long and healthy. He was cool. He had a crazy walk. Now that I look back, he was—whew!' Finally, as the decade tipped over into the early sixties, Sly graduated in music theory while simultaneously playing in several Bay Area bands, again, often with brother Freddie. And listening to the radio. Making plans. Before dropping out of music college. He always believed that 'you could do it, you could do it better, and you could do it in the way you want to'. His remarkable self-confidence and restless energy making him impatient for a more active involvement in diverse areas of music.

For Freddie—two years younger, things were not going quite so smoothly. Families have patterns. And Freddie was a typical middle child—both lacking the natural authority of his three older siblings, while never quite being doted on like Vet, the baby of the family. Loretta was the oldest, so she became the sensible surrogate mother to those who were younger, she was expected to baby-sit and organise her brothers and sisters when required. While Sylvester, as the oldest male child, was musically the first one able to pick out keys and carry the tune, so he was first chosen to be the soloist. Until it often seemed that Freddie never got his fair share of attention, so never developed Sylvester's self-confidence. There's an entire syndrome about being a middle child, because they don't have a really established role within the family. When the attention that should be focused on them, at the last moment, is diverted to the smarter older, or cuter younger sibling. To Sly, 'Freddie does so many things so well, I have to watch him or he will explode'. But for Freddie, each setback he experienced was a grudge to ruminate on. He recalled a long-nurtured hurt that happened when he was seventeen years old and a senior in high school. He already played wind instruments in the Concert Band, as well as upright bass in the school Dance Band, but it occurred to Freddie and another member of the Dance Band to get deeper into the music, so they suggested trying their hand at writing some original music for performance. The instructor granted permission, and they set about writing a small piece each.

Freddie concentrated hard, stayed up late into the night trying to make it as perfect as he could, until he turned it in to the instructor at the appropriate time. But the band didn't play it. He asked the instructor why not. The response—as Freddie recalled to Joel Selvin, was 'I'm not going to let them play that trash!' Words have tremendous power. And although Freddie continued with the music, for many years following that high school experience, there was always the thought in the back of my mind that said 'this is not good enough'. Had he listened to that music instructor, he might have given up. But there were others around him—especially his family, who encouraged him and they let him know that 'you've got everything it takes to make it'. 'I learned that although some people will not recognise your potential, there are always those who will...' Yet he was always the 'little brother', always dependent on Sly. Sly was the achiever. Freddie forever in his shadow. So instead, Freddie developed his own role, he became the family mediator.

Into the fall of 1963 Sly was preoccupied with a new venture, living over in Frisco itself while completing a three-month stint at the 'Chris Borden School Of Modern Broadcasting'. Borden was a jock at KEWB through the early sixties, who also ran radio DJ basics courses from plush red-carpeted studios across from Union Square on Post Street. For their $350 subscription students got access to a UPI wire machine, three trial turntables, plus a crash-course in technique, tips, and tricks. Graduating in October, Sly was immediately talent-spotted, and directly taken on as a tyro disc jockey on Oakland's new R&B/Soul station KSOL-AM. Hired by proprietors Alan Schultz and Les Molloy he was allocated the try-out seven-till-midnight Monday-through-Saturday slot. To close family members Sylvester was always 'Syl', and would remain 'Syl'. But elsewhere he was already known as 'Sly'. Sly as in Sylvester, but also 'sly'—as in cunning, as in 'as a fox'. So when they went off-air for the first time they sat goofing around and began free-associating an airtime surname to go with it—'Sly Sloan' perhaps? No. He didn't like that much. Instead, he became 'Sly Stone'. His call-sign became 'Hi-i, Sly...' And for him, K-SOL became 'K-SOUL'.

Now—when you think DJ, you think 'Superstar DJs' like the Chemical Brothers, Fatboy Slim, Pete Tong or Tim Westwood, anonymously sequencing beats from twin-decks for mass club all-nighters or festival audiences. DJ Sly Stone was *not* like that. Those were different days. Sly became the kind of DJ who announced the records he played, jive-rapped in the gaps between, read 'live' dedications, talked annoyingly over the intros, triggered the station identifier-jingles, and—as it was a commercial station, inserted the ad-bites too. Because it was a local station the adverts promoted local services, stores, franchises and products, so he even contrived his own advertising jingles—'if there was an Ex-Lax commercial, I'd play the sound of a toilet flushing. It would've been boring otherwise'. And he got Freddie to come in to sing for one of them, an on-air promo for jeans. He installed a piano in the studio so he could sing 'happy birthday' to listeners. Sly even read the weather updates, then signed off his slot by singing his version of Jesse Belvin's "Goodnight My Love". The station was based around a play-list of regular black R&B artists, but unlike today there was not the monopoly Top 40 focus-group rigidity. So long as they could hold their audience, DJ's had the freedom to play whatever they liked, or whatever they felt their listeners would like. They were compromised only by the inducements of record-pluggers, and by the obligatory airtime obligations of play-for-pay back-handers. The allegations of 'payola' that led to Senator Harris' 1959 revelations that eventually destroyed Allan Freed's career. Not that Sly ever stooped to such dubious illegalities, surely? Although there's more than a suggestion that that's precisely the reason Sly's future colleagues Tom Donahue and Bobby Mitchell quit Philadelphia in a hurry.

On air, the newly self-styled 'Sly Stone' was a fast hit, developing from imitator to innovator, opening his slot with a loop of Lord Buckley—'Hey, all you cats and kittens'. But within months of Sly's opening radio-cast the nation switched its collective attention to the 'Ed Sullivan Show'—going out live coast to coast on the Sunday-evening of 9th February 1964. The Beatles had just gone to no. 1 with "I Want To Hold Your Hand". Unsmiling Sullivan—a dour Richard Nixon look-alike, had already proved to be the sympathetic Pop host vital in launching Elvis Presley nation-wide. He would later do the same for the Byrds, the Rolling Stones, the Mamas & Papas, and Sly & The Family Stone. But his Beatles shows would go down in history. The first attracted 73-million viewers. Setting off a succession of shock-waves that would reverberate, and permeate down through every level of American music over the months and years that followed. And Sly expanded his airtime accordingly. Perceptive and eager to pick up on what was happening he included 'integration records' by the Beatles, and other mainstream Rock acts too, from Ray Charles to Bob Dylan, from the Rolling Stones, to the Kinks "You Really Got Me". He was soaking up everything he could. 'I was into everyone's records' he explained to *Rolling Stone* much later, 'I'd play Dylan, Hendrix, James Brown, back-to-back, so I didn't get stuck in any one groove'. His playlist was a giant upended jigsaw of music, and for those tired of listening to the programmed schlock of corporate radio, Sly's mixture of brains and eccentricity was a blessing beamed in direct from nirvana. 'Every night I tried something else. I really didn't know what was going on. Everything was just on instinct'.

Sly was a good-looking dude with an easy charm. His 'Shock-Jock' popularity with KSOL listeners meant he eventually graduated from working the graveyard-shift Monday-through-Saturday. Into the afternoon drive-time slot, propelling the audience figures way out ahead of the station's more established soul rival, KDIA—which had twice the watt-power output. In fact, Sly's ratings were so stratospheric that his programme managers were well-wary of hassling him over the revolutionary things he was putting over. The sleeve of a much later Ace compilation—*'Precious Stone: In The Studio With Sly Stone 1963-1965'* catches him on-the-air, sat leaning into a large 1950s style broadcasting mike. He's half-posing for the photo, as if he's confronting a one-man firing squad. Caught awaiting the click. Behind him, Venetian-blinds filter daylight from the street beyond. He glances up into the lens, half serious, just the beginning of a smile curling his mouth. He wears a closely-patterned sports-jacket over a roll-neck top. With a rich mop of hair that might be a failed Little Richard pompadour—what they used to call a 'conk' of straightened hair, only combed forward. A kind of compromise that straddles between styles much as his musical taste was doing, and would continue to do… This is an image that seems to captures a moment of truth. In every sense an exposure, an x-rayed moment. It's as if you're looking directly through his eyes, into his head. Until Sly writes his own autobiography, this is about as close as we can get.

For a while, turn-tabling fired his enormous creative ambitions. And it was radio—proving his wide taste and knowledge of music, that would lead him into the next stage of his career, simultaneously constructing a bridge over the years by providing the parallel role producing records for the indie Autumn label. 'Unlike the average record buyer, a disc jockey gets to hear the enormous output of records that never make the charts' points out Chris Albertson (of *'downbeat'* magazine). 'Each week he receives a staggering number of singles and albums by hopefuls whom the general public—for sadly obvious reasons, never become aware of. There is a lesson to be learned from listening to those records and they can, in one way, become a source of inspiration equal to that of successful efforts. It is, of course, pure conjecture, but hearing such varied fare might well have set Sly's creative wheels rolling.' So, according to this equation, some of it sticks to you, some of it blows right through you, and some of it gets trapped in there. There's art, and there's commerce. And there's the hinterland between. So why does this record work on one level, but not on the other. Is it possible to combine the two? And if so, how? Bobby Womack recalls that while Sly was 'a DJ in Oakland, the story went that he had a piano in the studio and when he gave a record a spin he would play along on the keyboard. Sly would improvise a new opening, middle or end. He'd tell his audience, 'man, this could have been a hit record if only the guy hadn't let it go flat right there'. Then he'd add his little tune to liven things up. People would call in to ask him to do his versions'. In this way, he'd receive the stimuli, it went down into his subconscious, and some of it settled there, some of it didn't. But everything you absorb, you must eventually secrete.

After two-and-a-half years of—according to Vet, 'the best raps on radio' with KSOL, he finally quit in June 1967. He complained on-air 'I haven't had a vacation since I been here'. In the meantime, inbetweentime, he felt he had to go someplace, do something, even if it was wrong. So he listened to the voices in his head. And he dropped out to concentrate on the greater creative possibilities of his own musical ambitions. Briefly, he would later decide to return to radio, by up-switching and hopping wavelengths to the 6-to-9pm slot on the competitor station KDIA. Working his fast-talking, wisecracking show for a two-month stint at 107.7FM broadcasting from across the Bay from October 1967. Programme director Bill Doubleday observes that 'you know how most DJ's put on a whole style when they're 'on'. Sly didn't create an on-air personality. On air, Sly was the same. That *was* Sly Stone'. But this move, lured back behind the radio-mike, would very quickly be curtailed as his own music career took off.

San Francisco was ahead of the game. Always. It is what SF music historian Gene Sculatti calls 'Hip City USA'. Frisco, where fog rolls in across the bay, has long provided a hospitable environment for both bohemian artistic and political radicalism, long before the explosion of 'hippie' culture in its mid-sixties Haight-Ashbury nexus. The 'Go West Young Man' restlessness had taken pioneers all the way to that western Pacific rim, from where they could go no further. In 1944 Woody Guthrie played Berkeley. Lawrence Ferlinghetti's North Beach 'City Lights' bookshop, at 261 Columbus Avenue off Broadway, became the spiritual home of Beat Generation poetry. Jack Kerouac and Neal Cassady hitched west to Frisco. Allen Ginsberg took his sheer bardic energies there too, to read his revolutionary tract *'Howl'* at 'City Lights' and the 'Six Gallery' in October 1955. Then Kenneth Rexroth read his poetry at the Palo Alto Peace Center. Josh White—the 'King of Black Folksingers', was a performer with a strong African-American consciousness at a time when integration and racial equality were first threatening the status quo. He played the earliest years of the sixties when there was a small but flourishing rock underground in the city, but a livelier Folk and jazz music scene in clubs like 'The Purple Onion' or 'The Hungry i' (where the Kingston Trio cut a live album), or in the university centre of Berkeley across the Bay, Palo Alto, or 'The Trident' in Sausalito. According to writer Hank Harrison, a young David Crosby would come up from Sausalito to play folk songs 'to augment his income as a cat burglar'. Lenny Bruce appeared at 'The Jazz Workshop' 4th October 1961, and was arrested for using the word 'cocksucker' onstage. From 1962 and into the year that follows Ron 'Pig-Pen' McKernan was playing with the Zodiacs, Bill Kreutzmann was their sometime drummer, on occasions Jerry Garcia sat in on bass. During 1963 Janis Joplin was there too, living on Page Street. Already it was a forming counter-culture in miniature, defined by attitude and discontent. One alienated by the smugly smiling billboards and TV-sets offering their materialistic cornucopia of consumer goods—a whole roster of crazies hard-wired to blow-up and take everything they considered false and phony down with it, seeking a truer and more communal America.

Sly dug the scene. He invited Freddie to 'come to San Francisco', and he came down from Vallejo too. Meanwhile, another element in the Sly Stone story—Tom Donahue, was gravitating towards this vibrant scene. Known as 'Big Daddy' because of his size and gargantuan appetites, Tom was born 21st May 1928 in South Bend, Indiana. He started out working as a deejay with WTIP in Charleston, Virginia, from where he went on to become Philadelphia's top disc jockey at WBIG in the fifties before setting out for the greener grass of San Francisco in 1961, under dubious circumstances...

Chapter Three
'The Autumn of His Years...'

'The Autumn Stone...'

But listen... in the mid-1960's as BritPop's first tidal wave was decimating the U. S. West Coast, Tom 'Big Daddy' Donahue was an established DJ radio-beaming his shows from KYA-AM—'The Boss Of The Day'. He drove a big Cadillac, strove always to be 'hep' and 'with it', and outmanoeuvred the opposition by the simple strategy of intro'ing records not just from the Top Forty, but the Swingin' Sixty too. According to Michelle Phillips of the Mamas & Papas, Tom—along with the other KYA disc jockey, black-clad Bob 'Mighty Mitch' Mitchell 'came up there and turned the radio station around... they were avant-garde all the way through the sixties' (in her book *'California Dreamin'*, Warner 1986). But they were far more than *just* that. Tom's involvement with the San Francisco music scene was *total*. Later—in mid-summer 1965, he would promote gigs at his own club—'Mothers', featuring such high-flying beat-groups as the Byrds and the Lovin' Spoonful. He would gain kudos as one of the first radio-jocks to spot the potential of "Mr Tambourine Man" after a young David Crosby had personally slipped him a shiny new acetate. By giving it high-rotation air-time he was instrumental in breaking the record along the west coast. From San Francisco it was picked up in Sacramento, Fresno, and into Los Angeles. From there, within three weeks it had become a massive national coast-to-coast hit.

But some considerable time *before* that—in 1964, he was emceeing a cheapo series of spin-off Record Hops. These teen-soirees, again done in hoc with 'Mighty' Mitchell, became so popular it allowed them to add live 'personal appearances' by aspirant vocalists and hopeful groups. Eager for exposure they'd often be so fawningly grateful for the opportunity to lip-sync their wannabe 'hits' into unwired mikes that they'd do so without payment. From there it was an easy step for the radio personalities to further supplement their income by promoting bands themselves. Donahue put Peter Paul & Mary on at the

Masonic Auditorium, then arranged for local star Bobby Freeman to support Chubby Checker at the 18,000-seater 'Cow Palace' in south Frisco. Donahue also happened to be there on hand promotion-wise when the Beatles and the Rolling Stones played that same 'Cow Palace'. Change was in the air. Music industry expectations had been thrown into confusion. And with it, came limitless new opportunities.

So that same year the duo raised their game, raised their aim, and notched their ambitions up the next logical step. They hatched the scheme of setting up their own label—'Autumn' records. First by utilising the KYA studios after-hours to record in, when it was off-air, then creating their own 'Golden State Recorders' studio-space up a steep climb of stairs above an apparel warehouse on Dorman Avenue, a stone's-throw from 101 Freeway. At the time, all the music industry major players were either centred in New York, or increasingly in Los Angeles. For the Bay Area there were only small opportunistic dog-eat-dog independent labels all searching for the 'next big thing', all hunting radio-play air-time and struggling against distribution problems. Across roughly the same years, the most memorable of them was probably 'Fantasy', which released vinyl by Lenny Bruce and Vince Guaraldi. They also issued fine early sides by the Golliwogs from El Cerrito—who later became Rock 'n' Roll Hall of Fame inductees Creedence Clearwater Revival. But there was no shortage of other local Frisco labels too. 'Autumn' would be merely one of many. But what Donahue began as a prospective 'Hit Factory' lacking business experience or a history to lean on, had one edge over its rivals, 'Autumn' had its own access to airtime, and a live appearance promotional network.

All the while Tom continued multi-tasking as promoter and deejay, in which capacity he happened across the burgeoning talent of Sylvester Stewart. "Yellow Moon" c/w "Uncle Sam Needs You My Friend" eventually found its way onto his turn-table. A record made in 1961 by the Biscaynes—Jerry Martini and a guy called John Turk play back-up on the record. But listen, there's this guy—another local radio DJ, who provides lead voice on both sides, the same voice they could hear every day making DJ-waves on KSOL, and hey—they decide, he's pretty damn impressive. 'This guy's good. This guy's got potential. We could use him.' A meeting between Donahue and Sylvester was arranged, following a show at the American Legion Hall. Sly had met many music industry regulars who were content to sit around smoking dope and drinking wine. Big Tom himself was no slouch in that respect, but he had energy, and he was an enabler. While 'Sly' was equally motivated, more intense, bright and animated, with no 'ghetto attitude'. He was a sharp dresser too, in tight black pants and Beatle-boots. A Beatles haircut too, tinted somewhere between red and chestnut-brown, and styled at 'Huff's Fashionette' down on the corner of Fillmore Street & Geary Boulevard, by Bubba Hamps. 'I told him I had some songs' Sly recalls. So he played Donahue his latest batch of dance tunes. Again, Tom was impressed. 'He was very obviously a talented musician' he says, 'and he had some good ideas on arranging.'

For Sly, it wasn't exactly Motown come a-knocking. It wasn't an invite from Jerry Wexler at Atlantic, or Leonard Chess from Chicago either. But to the young Sylvester, the hook-up seemed to offer an opportunity for the big time. A route-map to fame and fortune. Sly was recruited to join the fledgling company as in-house arranger and producer, on a staff-rate of $150 a week, plus use of free studio time. A chance for his first real experience of recording alchemy. Soon he was splitting his days, juggling grooves between dee-jaying on radio while also working the controls for Autumn. It was hardly a hugely impressive set-up. But for a tyro knob-twiddler it was a perfect play-station to test out ideas, experiment with manipulating sounds, overdubs, and developing production skills. For Donahue and Mitchell, they soon realised they thought they'd signed a useful talent, but brought a genius on-board. Adept at writing and arranging, undeniably proficient on guitar, keyboards, drums—in fact, any instrument you cared to mention, Sly was the right guy in the right place. He had a keen ear for detecting imperfections, and the rapidly evolving skill at tweaking them back into line. And Autumn was his audio playground. A lo-fi three-track apology for a sonic romper-room. But one with a deadly serious intent. After all, much grassroots American music had come from similarly primitive lean-to studios with makeshift egg-box soundproofing. 'Sun' was a crude one-room operation in Memphis. Stax was a converted movie-house where they sold the latest singles from what used to be the popcorn concession-stand in the foyer. Link Wray converted his chicken-shack into a ramshackle home studio from where he unleashed several classics of Rock-guitar distortion. And hadn't Ray Charles cut "I Got A Woman" while he was pressured into an Atlanta radio station—unable to hear playbacks because a news announcer was simultaneously broadcasting from the control-room? Sure he had. It was alchemy. But an alchemy that worked.

And the first positive result from Autumn's new arrangement was instantly spectacular. They achieved their first national hit with their Sly-produced and Sly co-written second release—Bobby Freeman's "C'mon And Swim". Bobby Freeman will probably go down in history—if at all, as the first-ever San Francisco rocker. Born there on 13th June 1940, he was a black pianist and vocalist who started out recording with a local group, the Romancers, for the Dootone label, at the age of fourteen. As a solo singer, just three years later, he had a run of memorable Rock 'n' Roll hits for Josie—beginning with the self-penned and frequently revived "Do You Want To Dance" (Josie 835) which entered the chart 26th May 1958, reached no. 5 and stayed listed for seventeen weeks. In the UK angry young rock 'n' roller Cliff Richard twitched his hips and scored a cover-version hit with it. Years later the Mamas & the Papas did their own take on the song, then the Beach-Boys also charted with their royalty-generating interpretation. Meanwhile Bobby's "Betty Lou Got A New Pair Of Shoes" (Josie 841) entered the chart 18th August 1958, but only reached no. 37 for a solitary week. It would be revived in the eighties for an American sneakers TV-commercial. But for now, his brief bright burst of celebrity seemed already to be on the slide. More singles followed. A less successful but equally torrid "Shame On You Miss Johnson", the standard "Ebb Tide", and then "Mess Around". Between 1958 and 1961, he was busy touring and promoting a spread of seven singles in total. He also became a near-fixture on TV's 'American Bandstand', only Frankie Avalon logged more appearances than he did...

Of course, since Chubby Checker jovially set the world gyrating with "The Twist" and "Let's Twist Again" the teeny-pop scene was wide-open to yet another dance-fad. Chubby had ignited an international social phenomenon in which—for the first time, the dancers danced *without* touching their partners, or even necessarily doing it *with* a partner. Jackie Kennedy was photographed dancing the Twist at the 'Peppermint Lounge'. The *'Daily Mirror'* carried its own DIY guide—'you dry your back with an imaginary towel, while stubbing out an imaginary cigarette with your toe'. Knowing what was hot and what was not on the newest dance scene became a big deal. After the Twist came Chubby's own "Pony Time" and "The Popeye", then the Locomotion (Little Eva), the Mashed Potato (Dee-Dee Sharp), the Hully-Gully, The Hitch-Hike, and just about anything that could possibly be contrived into the semblance of dance-moves. Bobby had already tried out with a few dance-craze items himself with "(I Do The) Shimmy Shimmy" (King 5373) which entered the chart 26th September 1960, and stayed for three week... until 'The Swim' gave Bobby Freeman—and Sly, his signature hit.

Bobby claimed to have improvised the 'Swim' in direct competition to Chubby Checker when they did their 'Big Daddy'-promoted 'Cow Palace' concert together. He was gratifyingly encouraged by the spontaneous audience reaction. Then he took a three-week trip to Hawaii, returning to find all the local North Beach Broadway clubs featuring 'Swim' dance contests. He indignantly told *'Rolling Stone'* 'I said 'wait a minute, this is *my* dance". He confided the situation to Donahue. He said 'well, the way to straighten this out is to do a record'. So Donahue and Sly got together to write a song to go with the dance, Sly hastily sketched it out, Tom Donahue contributed lyrically. The result was "C'mon And Swim". According to the established dance-disc template their lyrics provide an easy-to-follow primer for uncertain dancers—this new dance-floor variant is 'kinda like the Monkey, kinda like the Twist, pretend you're in the water and you go like this...' Then the vocalist adds more helpful suggestions that it's 'just like the Dog, but not so low, like the Hully-Gully but not so slow...' There's a swelling Sly-powered Hammond organ break with twangy beach-movie guitars, then a re-immersion in more free-form lyrics inviting the dancer to dog-paddle, back-stroke, and even 'do what you want to, do like you wish, c'mon baby now and swim like a fish.' Finally Sly managed to twist the lyrics in ways that anticipate his playful Family Stone technique of drawing in references from other sources—'shake it up baby, twist and shout, do the swim baby now and work it on out…'

Sly was already working with back-up bands for Donahue's live shows—and Freeman recalled how he'd actually first played on a bill with Sylvester when he was a young hometown musician at a long-ago show in Vallejo. Now Sly assembled a fifteen-piece studio band for the recording, although he played guitar, organ and bass himself on the sessions. He also called in Jerry Martini, and there's a suggestion that even Freddie was there to help out ('Freddy on "Swim"? I don't think so' Joel Selvin tells me). The result of it all turned out right. Although according to one version of events Donahue wasn't immediately convinced. He took it to Warner Brothers A&R instead. They declined to pick up on the option. So the uptown soul of "C'mon And Swim" became Autumn 2, and Bobby Freeman's biggest-ever chart record, easily eclipsing everything he'd done before. Debuting 25th July 1964, it reached a chart high of no. 5—qualified for gold disc status, and stayed listed for ten weeks. 'That was the fastest record I've ever had as far as being a hit' commented Freeman. 'I think it was out two weeks and it just shot up' (to Patrick Sullivan, 14th March 1974).

For Sly, it meant a shiny gold disk for the second of his first two production jobs. A pretty damn good start. And while it might have been the first time Sly's name had figured in the upper echelons on the chart—it was to be far from the last. You've got to hunt for his name on the label, beneath the song-title and artist credit. But it's there. "C'Mon And Swim" also secured a British release on the deep-red Pye label, and although it was drowned in the tidal wave of guitar-toting beat-groups, it was important in that it marked the first glimpse of Sly-product in Europe. And more—the Freeman/Stewart partnership was far from finished with the dance-fad craze they'd created. They followed the hit by hastily concocting a cash-in sequel, Bobby's "S-W-I-M"—a kind of 'let's swim again' recorded in a raucous celebratory party-atmosphere, complete with a burst of proto-Family Stone harmonica from Sly. Bobby's vocals brag 'down with the twist, it's all over now' because the Swim has become 'the no. 1 dance in the USA'. That may well have been true, but even so, 'Bobby's gonna show you how to do the swim' again! Meanwhile, there was a bandwagon still to be jumped. No sooner was Bobby safely placed on the radio playlists, than Sly himself got in on the action with his own "Scat Swim" single, a wild tongue-twisting slow-it-down speed-it-up scat vocal nonsense which he delivers with fluent ease. Unfortunately, neither of the singles got much more than local airplay.

Nevertheless, there was a tie-in album to be made— *'C'Mon And S-W-I-M'* (1964). With a sleeve designed to provide a helpful photo-sequence of how to do the dance-moves. One shot of Bobby himself, alongside six of an attractively gyrating girl. While the vinyl within remains an intriguing time-capsule example of Sly's early work. Obviously leading off with the dance-hits, it quickly follows them with Bobby's cash-in covers of Lee Dorsey's "Ya Ya", the Rufus Thomas hit "Walkin' The Dog", and Berry Gordy's "Money", as well as jazz standard "Work Song". The rest of the album is made up of now-rare original Sly compositions such as "Do The Monkey" and "Speedo (The Monkey Man)". Later, those original twelve songs would be augmented by an Ace-label CD re-issue adding a bonus trove of five previously singles-only tracks plus a generous seven session out-takes. As a result, Sly originals such as "I'll Never Fall In Love Again" can be heard in two versions—first the album take, then the faster single's mix. Academics can compare them with the eventual Family Stone version—with Larry Graham vocals, on the *'Dance To The Music'* album. There are further Sly compositions, the Motown-style "Swing Me", and the more anguished "Honest". While among the out-takes, there's even a first-ever demo of "Every Dog Has Its Day", a song that would eventually appear on vinyl as part of numerous compilations of varying degrees of legitimacy—and a dry-run for the *'A Whole New Thing'* track "Underdog". Of the related material that actually emerged at the time, Sly's own subsequent Autumn singles "I Just Learned How To Swim" and "Temptation Walk" could easily be written off as regulation shots at milking the latest dance craze. But they were the product of sessions storing up skills and techniques for later.

For Bobby Freeman, his renewed celebrity kept him in the public eye well into the 1970s, at which point he adopted a more Soulful emphasis for some Double-Shot label records, until he full-circled back home to Frisco. Those who crossed the black Fillmore district and headed in the rough direction of Fisherman's Wharf, would come to the notorious Broadway strip, where blues clubs rubbed shoulders with sex shows. At the time, riding unprepared through the area after dark could be an unsettling experience as neon signs flashed up one after the other announcing 'TOPLESS', 'NUDE ENCOUNTER GROUPS'... JOHN LEE HOOKER. Some might find such juxtapositions totally disorientating. But Bobby Freeman was soon contentedly working the topless clubs and titty-bar circuit around the Broadway, North Beach area. While for Sly, the Swim-craze had provided a first-time hit, something to add to his career resume. He'd just turned twenty, but he'd already crammed an awful lot into those twenty years. His success meant he could afford to relocate the entire Stewart family into a large rambling house in the south-west Frisco suburbs. Using the money from "C'Mon And Swim" he made the down-payment on 700 Urbano Drive, an Ingleside District house with a lawn. Soon,

Momma Alpha and Daddy KC were occupying the upstairs, while the family, alongside Sylvester's Great Danes, all lived below.

By now, Tom Donahue had sniffed the mother-lode, and he was greedy for more. He sat in the studio, feet up on the console, flipping through *'Billboard'*, checking out the chart-placings for 1st September, the week "C'Mon And Swim" peaked at no. 5. Above Bobby Freeman the old order was still holding firm with sing-along schmaltz from Dean Martin's "Everybody Loves Somebody". At no. 3. The Supremes "Where Did Our Love Go" at no. 2 pushed Motown as the emerging force in black music. But he couldn't fail but notice that it was the Animals "House Of The Rising Sun" there at no. 1. The Dave Clark Five were at no. 4. Gerry & The Pacemakers "How Do You Do It?" at no. 9. And the Beatles latest, "Hard Days Night", finally vacating the top slot, but still dominating the radio-play listings. There were lessons there for the learning. Next time around, he was determined to mastermind his own Beatles. Bob and Tom knew next-to-nothing about running a record company, Sly was painstakingly learning his trade, 'so we all tried to learn together'. At this point, some comparisons can be useful. Isaac Hayes was perfecting his craft for Stax as writer/producer for the likes of Sam & Dave. While Holland Dozier Holland were powering Motown's ascent. With both teams working exclusively within the R&B field. Yet, from the start, Autumn's in-house producer Sly was as familiar with the nuances of white Rock as he was with the proto-Soul of Bobby Freeman. And soon he was to be helming the plaintive acid-tinged harmony-Rock of The Beau Brummels. Then working with a number of other San Franciscan garage and psychedelic bands…

****

'I could be a Beau Brummel, Baby… if you'd just give me half a chance…'

Around the same time, a hooker friend of 'Big Daddy' took him down to San Mateo—the spine of Frisco, to the 'Morocco Room' Club, where a fresh group called the Beau Brummels just happened to be on-stage. For Tom, the connection was immediately obvious, and probably inevitable. Here was a combo of pudding-bowl Mop-Tops who looked like five Brian Jones, or just possibly five Keith 'Yardbird' Relf's. They were also sporting a neat line in twelve-string lead guitar, set to plaintive minor-key harmonies reminiscent of the Searchers—and later the Byrds, or the Stone Roses, all grounded in hard Beat-Boom rhythmic urgency. Hey, their group-name meant they'd even get to sit alongside the Beatles in alphabetised record-store racks! To establish their vaguely cross-Atlantic credentials the Brums had taken that name from a sharp-dressed English Regency Dandy, while second vocalist Declan Mulligan actually came from County Tipperary—although he quit early on and later opted to sue when the hits came. Meanwhile, guitarist Ron Elliot was writing engagingly simple-minded harmonica-edged Folk-Rock songs with titles like "Sad Little Girl". Songs that would help define the emerging scene, even though the group itself was destined to be often overshadowed by those who came after them.

Late summer 1964. An eagerly salivating Donahue promptly hauled the Beau Brummels into the studio, drafting Sly in to produce them. As they trooped in for the first time the five-piece were a little in awe of the occasion. It might be a fairly rudimentary set-up by most standards, but it was already responsible for a million-selling top ten hit. Sly was already well at home there, and he made an effort to put them at their ease. He'd assembled some musicians of his own, just in case they were needed, including brother Fred. As it happened, they weren't required. The band ran through their own material perfectly adequately. Pretty much as they'd played it on-stage. Sly had only to mix and balance. The resulting vinyl—unleashed as 'Autumn 8', fired the opening salvo in America's retaliation to the 'English Invasion', with a sound full of weird intimations of the Californian psychedelic strangeness to come. Two national Top Twenty hits followed. Sal Valentino sings powerful lead on the first—"Laugh Laugh" c/w "Still In Love With You Baby". Opening with melancholy keening harmonica the lyrics mock the proud girl who 'thought she was too good', but is brought down to earth because 'you don't learn everything there is to know at school'. The rattling tambourine-driven mood switches from the driving chorus, moving into a more sympathetic 'lonely—oh so lonely' mid-point harmony section. Finally offering 'take my advice, don't be so smug' or she'll wind up sitting on the shelf. Not—perhaps, an era-defining record, but certainly one with its antennae finely-attuned to the way the times were a-changin'. Accordingly, it rapidly took off, entered the Hot Hundred, and climbed all the way to a US no. 15 in December 1964, later to be collected onto Lenny Kaye's prestigious *'Nuggets'* (1998) box-set.

Its follow-up, the looser, less-structured "Just A Little" c/w "They'll Make You Cry" (Autumn single 10) peaked even higher—no. 8, in the early months of the following year. Both were produced by Sly, who was keen to involve himself in every aspect of the recording. He can be heard playing timbales on the fade of "Just A Little". The titles of all four sides were prominently splashed down the right-hand bar of the cover of the debut album, *'Introducing The Beau Brummels'* (1965). The cover-photo shows them frolicking away from the encroaching waves on the damp sand of the Frisco beach. But the best bits of the band's collective story had already been told, from the soft focus "Don't Talk To Strangers" to the heartbreak 'magic spell' of the "Sad Little Girl" 'walking by the sea' she 'stares at the limb of the driftwood tree/ washed by the waves to a sandy shore.../ she won't be happy any more' with its lonesome harmonica and rhythmic pulse behind its folksy harmonies. The bulk of the material is mostly attractively open, energetic stuff that sometimes anticipates an early naïve Love, or at other times a stripped-down blueprint for the Byrds. *'Crawdaddy'* magazine went so far as to proclaim Sal Valentino 'the best voice in Rock'. But that didn't prevent their next, and last two charting singles—"You Tell Me Why", and a cover of the Lovin' Spoonful's jaunty "Good Time Music", from registering lower and yet lower peak-positions.

With the release of *'Beatles For Sale'*—retitled *'Beatles '65'* in America, in December 1964, flaunting its pastoral sleeve and Dylan influences, the Beatles were perceived to have 'gone folk'. And although the Byrds "Mr Tambourine Man" would most exemplify the scene, all over the Bay area mushroom-cut fringes were becoming longer and guitars janglier. The Rock 'n' Roll sands were shifting. It was another lesson Tom took to heart. Bobby Freeman might have fallen out of favour, the Beau Brummels might be well into decline, but the label's initial success provided the impetus for Big Daddy & The Mighty One to recruit more British invasion-derived bands. Problem was, the would-be entrepreneurs were smart enough to spot the seeds of psychedelia, but lacked the final financial push to break on through. So instead of hits, the rest of their story is made up of early blue-prints and demo's by names destined to score on someone else's plastic. Oddities and curios by curious oddballs, and toe-tappers with the 'for specialists-only' tag still intact. Another problem was that once the duo signed them, they quickly lost interest in their new protégés, leaving them for Sly to coax whatever he could out of their potential. Fortunately, Sly was more than equal to the task.

He went on to hone his remarkable production talents by working with the Vejtables, who Tom had also spotted at the 'Morocco Room'. Formed in San Mateo in 1964 they followed the Beau Brummels twelve-string folkiness while aspiring to an even more convincingly crisp Byrds/Beatles synthesis. Sly produced their single "I Still Love You" c/w "Anything" as Autumn 15, which soon broke out regionally, then went on to scrape into the national Top 100, eventually peaking at no. 84. As it climbed, the group played support to the touring Yardbirds and the Beach Boys, and guested on 'American Bandstand'. Another career high-point occurred on 14th May 1965 when 'KYA' presented a mouth-watering line-up at the Civic Auditorium listing the Rolling Stones, the Byrds, the Beau Brummels… and the Vejtables. Although their career was effectively ruptured by the eventual collapse of Autumn, vocalist Bob Bailey held various line-ups together into 1966, and later name-switched briefly to The Book Of Changes. Guitarist Jim Sawyer went on to join Syndicate Of Sound. The group never managed to record a full album while together, but the valuable archivist label Sundazed eventually scraped together every available track, including rescuing previously unissued tapes from dusty vaults, to compile the CD *'Feel… The Vejtables'* (2001). It includes the Sly-produced 'B'-side, "Anything" with its darker more disturbing intimations of the psychedelia that was to come, plus both sides of their second (probably non-Sly) Autumn single—Tom Paxton's "The Last Thing On My Mind" c/w "Mansions Of Tears", in addition to bonus solo sides recorded by the group's drummer Jan Errico under the alias 'Jan Ashton'.

As photogenically dark-haired as she was musically gifted, Jan was one of the more remarkable presences at Autumn. With the label collapse she switched from the Vejtables to join The Mojo Men. Despite the obvious gender-contradiction of hence becoming, apparently—a 'Mojo Woman'? her voice and talents probably form the strongest asset either band ever enjoyed (she had already written "I Still Love You"). Although the Mojo Men originally came from Miami where they'd been gigging as Jimmy Alaimo & The Valiants they relocated to the West Coast where Donahue renamed them, and as the Mojo Men they became another of Sly's notable production successes. Although too Pop to be totally part of the coming Haight-Ashbury scene, their sudden splurges of fuzz-guitar—as on their Stones-inspired "She's My Baby" ('when she leaves me hanging, / I know I've been hung'), and their ornate baroque production-effects made them equally a little too weird for the more mainstream Mamas & Papas or Association audience. Sly produced three singles for their earlier more garage-punk line-up, Autumn's nos. 11, 19, and 27—all issued during 1965, starting with a rampaging cover of the Rolling Stones "Off The Hook". But, exploiting the sneering guttersnipe swagger of this first group-phase, they hit their greatest response with the second single, "Dance With Me", replete with its Farfisa organ and 'ee-ee' vocal effects. Exclaiming a stoned-dumb 'like, what's happening baby' vocalist Jim Alaimo then irreverently nods at Tom Donahue in the fade with a cheeky 'like, Hiyo Big Daddy'. A further track—"Dance Your Pants Off", issued much later as part of a deceptively mistitled *Sly Stone & The Mojo Men* album, seems to suggest teasing anticipations of Sly's distinctive "Dance To The Music" horn arrangement. Meanwhile, the Mojo Men achieved even greater post-Sly post-Autumn success during their second career-phase. The nucleus of Jim (vocals and bass), Paul Curcio (lead guitar), and Don Metchick (keyboards) remained, but with drummer Dennis DeCarr replaced by Jan Errico, their sound was soon enhanced by the big bucks studio time provided by their major label signing to Reprise. With their sound sweetened more towards impeccably orchestrated Folk-Rock, and the soaring angelic harmonies of the newly-forged vocal alliance of Alaimo and Jan Errico, they took Stephen Stills' "Sit Down I Think I Love You"—symphonically arranged by Brian Wilson's collaborator Van Dyke Parks, into the national Top Forty in March 1967. Jan later joined yet another chart band, We Five, and remained an active part of the Frisco music scene for many years.

But already, the speedy buzz of Sly's attentions were darting elsewhere, faced with argumentative new projects, hot-housing new groups with new songs on a weekly, even daily rota. The chore of shaping their raw material into marketable white-Pop confections meant that Sly's ideas and inventions were forced to become more numerous, on a virtually open-ended basis. Even though Sly's domineering perfectionism could rub some bands up the wrong way, he was negotiating his own untutored path, learning, storing techniques and skills from each encounter. Within this growing catalogue of cool there were sessions with the Chosen Few—recording the much-covered "Nobody But Me" (which eventually charted for the Human Beinz), and the Knight-Riders' mutated 'Louie Louie'-come-Kinks riff "I" with its mad-frantic instrumental break. There were studio try-outs for the proto-acid Charlatans, one of Frisco's earliest pioneer bands, who were destined to remain in cult obscurity. Other tracks were laid down by an early Grateful Dead line-up under the guise of The Emergency Crew in November 1965, during the time they were playing the 'In-Room' in Belmont. They'd first auditioned as the Warlocks, whereupon Donahue told them to 'shove it', and get 'a better education'. So they came back under the fresh aka. Later they considered a further name-change to 'The Hobbits' or 'Vanilla Plumbego', but finally opting for a random I-Ching approach to the Dictionary which resulted in 'Grateful Dead'. The Sly tracks would remain unissued, until they were finally officially incorporated into *'The Birth Of The Dead'* (2003) double-CD.

The next band Sly got to oversee was The Great Society, who gave a grateful world the mesmerising Grace Slick. As the group's vocalist she was both its visual and musical focus. It was Sly's first encounter with a genuine bunch of hippie long-hairs. In the summer of 1965 Tom—wearing his impresario hat, had opened the world's first psychedelic nightclub—'Mothers', a North Beach venue located along the Broadway sin-strip of topless bars, where—with the assistance of the Mighty Mitch, they began promoting gigs by outsider bands. They doubled-up by also using the club to host a series of cost-saving open auditions designed to check out likely Autumn signings. It was there they and Sly first witnessed the Great Society, and subsequently invited them round for a studio try-out. In total, the group were together for little longer than a year—having rehearsed at the 'Fire House', then made their debut at the North Beach 'Coffee Gallery' on 15th October 1965. Yet they left a lasting imprint on the pervasive West Coast folk-psychedelic anti-Pop underground. Alongside the luminous beauty and laser-sharp intelligence of Grace herself there was her then-husband Jerry Slick (drums), his brother Darby Slick (guitar), and David Miner (vocals and guitar), plus Bard DuPont (bass) and Peter van Gelder (saxophone), although the last two would fail to survive the group's full brief duration.

They'd begun by immediately establishing their intellectual credentials through selecting a name—unlike some cutesy misspelling of vegetables or a Blues reference to Muddy Waters' Mojo, by ironically referencing a politician's buzz-phrase. When Lyndon B Johnson described the United States as the

'Great Society'—in his 22nd May 1964 University of Michigan speech, it was the American equivalent of Premier Harold Macmillan complacently telling his British electorate that they'd 'never had it so good'. The band then compounded their cerebral tendency by perpetrating a song in defence of Lenny Bruce. Although subsequently reclaimed as a confrontational satiric-comedy genius, at the time Lenny was still widely denigrated as a potty-mouthed un-American junkie. Or what zoot-suited art critic, jazz singer and *bon viveur* George Melly would perceptively celebrate as 'a sharp-tongued show-biz Yiddish foul-mouthed evangelist, a free-wheeling poet, a revelation'. While Grace was already re-imagining Lewis Carroll's *'Alice In Wonderland'* by sending its characters through the phantasmagorical LSD wormhole of "White Rabbit".

Darby Slick took the precaution of hanging out in the studio to watch the way Sly worked with the Beau Brummels, yet despite gaining a grudging respect for his working methodology, dealing with the Great Society—for Sly, proved to be both stranger, and more problematic. They were more opinionated than the other bands he'd worked with, and less open to suggestion. Eventually Sly dragged Billy Preston in to help out and provide support. Soon, producer and band were working together on an Indian-influenced song called "Free Advice". And another called "Somebody To Love", which had been written by Darby. Sly offered to sit in on the session, but was turned down, so he cajoled them into further efforts that ran to some fifty takes—'it was only fifty-three' Darby Slick insists, despite which the song would not mould itself into a national hit until Grace reworked it a couple of years later as part of Jefferson Airplane (it also proved to be a long-term standard that would be sampled and mashed-up in chart dance-mixes into the next century). Memories diverge. Other accounts of the sessions at Golden State Recorders recall Sly becoming frustrated by the group's failure to deliver what he wanted. Which tended less towards their structured looseness, and more towards the direct statement. Finally, according to Gene Sculatti's sleeve-notes 'he threw up his hands and stomped of the studio. Worlds were colliding' (*'The Autumn Records Story'* Edsel, 1986). Tom Donahue relates his own take on the events to researcher Ben Fong-Torres, 'there was a sense of paranoia on the part of the Great Society about the level of their musicianship. But they also had a hippier-than-thou sort of thing'. Except for Grace, who seemed to Donahue 'too far ahead of the others'.

At the time, only a solitary single emerged from the sessions—"Somebody To Love" c/w "Free Advice" assigned to Autumn's even more modest 'North Beach' subsidiary label—numbered 1001. Subsequently, an even briefer flirtation with Columbia resulted in two separate live Great Society albums— *'Conspicuous Only In Its Absence'* (1968) and *'How It Was'* (1968), repackaged as a double-album in 1971 to cash in on Grace's escalating status—she'd by then replaced Signe Toly Anderson in Jefferson Airplane. Then, a much-later CD compilation returned to collect all of the available material from the Autumn archives, issued as *'Born To Be Burned'* (Sundazed—1995). With tracks such as David Miner's "Double Triptamine Superautomatic Everlovin' Man", and two alternate takes of "Free Advice", which—even in rough demo form, indicate that Great Society were one of the most creative bands the studio had ever played host to. There's also their "Father Bruce"—the Lenny Bruce tribute, given added gravitas by the fact that by then the confrontational comedian had been found and photographed dead on his toilet (3rd August 1966).

Meanwhile, there was growing industry-insider awareness of Sly's work among those who took the trouble to read producer and songwriter credits. Networking through the chart success of Bobby Freeman, the Beau Brummels, and the rest, it was linking to further connections beyond the immediate Bay area. And there was one in particular which proved to be of long-term significance. The friendship he forged with amiable teenage keyboard prodigy Billy Preston. Born William Everett Preston on the 9th September 1946, he was two years Sly's junior, but also a Texan who'd taken that California trip, not from Denton to Vallejo, but from Houston to Los Angeles. Billy had imbibed Gospel sitting on his mother's knee, and while not yet in his teens he'd already played organ on Mahalia Jackson's inspirational "In The Upper Room". He appeared on Hollywood celluloid too, robustly taking the role of the young WC Handy in *'St Louis Blues'* (1958), with Nat King Cole assuming the adult version of the founding father of blues in the same biopic. He was then recruited into Little Richard's 1962 backing band, and as part of the primal rocker's European tour he got to befriend the Beatles during their pre-Fab Four residency at the Hamburg 'Star Club'. On returning to the States he was invited to join the resident house-band for the 'Shindig' TV-show, while building a reputation as an ace session musician. So, barely into double-figures, young Billy was proving his talent with the likes of Ray Charles, and contributing to Sam Cooke's version of "Little Red Rooster"—Sam can clearly be heard exclaiming 'play it Billy' just prior to the rippling instrumental break. Cooke was so impressed that he signed Billy as a solo act for his own SAR label, but Sam was shot dead before any material could be released. Instead, 'Billy's Bag' became hanging out with Sly. He came around to the KSOL studios to provide rhythm tracks for the sound-salad of radio-jingles they improvised together. Sometimes they joshed about forming a band, modelled on Ray Charles—the 'Sons of Ray' perhaps? And for Billy's second album—issued through a Vee Jay contract, he worked closely with Sly. *'The Wildest Organ In Town'* (issued in March 1966) was arranged by Sly, and features three Billy Preston/Sly Stone compositions including one credited on the sleeve as "Advice". The song would later evolve into Sly's 'Woodstock' high-point "I Want To Take You Higher".

While for Sly himself, his close-on three-year stint with Autumn was a highly productive, immensely prolific period. 'I would just get thrown into spots to do stuff, like the bass player here and a vide player next week, so I had to learn how to play vibes in a week just to have a job.' He took advantage of available studio time to record a batch of songs himself under the name 'Sly Stewart', including intriguing Booker T-style instrumental grooves like his own "Buttermilk", and its experimental rebranding "Suki Suki"—which both showed he had an ear cocked towards proto-Funk R&B. But far more work was produced than was ever released during the abbreviated lifetime of the label. Sufficient raw material to compile a fascinating box-set. Accordingly, over the decades since, the Autumn archives have been repeatedly plundered for anything that can remotely be connected to a Sly session. There are salvaged demos, covers, and formative family work-outs of "The Swim" by Sly & Rose or "Dance All Night" by Sly & Freddie. His echoey close-harmony take on the Five Satin's 1956 hit "In The Still Of The Night". The sax-driven Junior Walker-style instrumental "Watermelon Man". His more folk-rockish attempts, including "As I Get Older" written with Mojo Men Steve Alaimo and Paul Curcio. And collectively, they make for intriguing snapshots of wildly eclectic moments. With music that playfully runs the full spectrum of sounds from primitive collisions of soul and Pop, novelty dance songs, and derivative doo-wop, into teen-pop that somehow manages to involve elements of all those genres. The valuable and well-researched Ace compilation *Precious Stone: In The Studio With Sly Stone 1963-1965* assembles previously unissued sessions he produced and wrote for Gloria Scott & The Tonettes—"I Taught Him" and "Don't Say I Didn't Warn You" done in the strident Phil Spector girl-group mode, or George & Teddy—"Fake It" and "Laugh", alongside "The Nerve Of You" by Emile O'Connor, plus out-takes from Bobby Freeman sessions—"That Little Old Heartbreaker Me" and "I'll Never Fall In Love Again", plus "Take My Advice" and "As I Get Older". There are further try-out demos for material that would later be drawn into the Family Stone repertoire, such as Emile O'Connor's take on the Bobby Freeman track "Every Dog Has His Day".

An artist's selection of the songs he covers can provide a revealing Rorschach test, a series of random clues to what he's listening to, what he respects, and what he aspires to. Retrospectively, it's the flux capacitor that allows glimpses through time into his state of mind. So what conclusions are to be drawn from Sly's mock-live versions of Willie Dixon's "The Seventh Son", or Leiber & Stoller's "On Broadway"? "The Seventh Son" portrays the swaggering, bragging, invulnerable ultra-male whose magical voodoo-powers enable him to 'heal the sick, raise the dead, make the little girls talk off their heads'. Here, he's advertising his matchless sexual prowess in a way that's as much a part of the blues tradition as Muddy Waters' "I'm a Man", or as seen through the 'Stagger Lee' archetype. Did Sly see, or even half-see himself in this way? It could be argued that all adolescent males go through something similar. It's to do with testosterone. Or is it just a convenient vehicle for the music, the punching horn-driven 'High Heeled Sneakers'-style repetitions that slam the message home, 'in the whole wide world there's only one, I'm the one, I'm the one, the one they call the seventh son'? By contrast, "On Broadway"—an aching hit for the Drifters voiced by Ben E King, illustrates the hazards of seeking stardom, the hunger and disappointment when you're standing where the neon lights are bright, where there's a magic in the air which you can never reach. Yet the song ends on an upbeat. The doubters who advise him to take the Greyhound bus for home are wrong, 'I know they are, because I can play this here guitar, and I won't stop till I'm a star'. Sly too. Sylvester was obviously aware of the work of its writers, Jerry Leiber & Mike Stoller, so it would be intriguing to hear his take on another of their classics, "Riot In Cell Block No. 9" recorded in 1954 by the Robins (an early Coasters line-up with additional vocal contributions from Richard Berry). Later revived by Dr Feelgood, and the Blues Brothers, the first verse describes how the narrator is sitting in his prison-cell 'on July 2nd 1953', serving time for armed robbery, when the convicts begin to get restless and 'it spreads like fire across the prison floor', leading into the irresistible chorus chant 'there's a riot goin' on, there's a riot goin' on, there's a riot goin' on, in cell-block no. 9'—until the riot is put down by warders armed with tommy-guns and tear-gas. It must have been a song Sly was familiar with, and which he'd deliberately reference much later in his career. Instead, he opts for a Trini Lopez live-party setting of "Searchin'"—another Leiber & Stoller song. Other covers he attempts include "Little Latin Lupe Lu (Medley)"—a version done very much as a Righteous Brothers vocal interplay between Sly and Billy Preston, and the Jimmy Reed's composition "Ain't That Lovin' You Baby".

But it's been guestimated there's a Sly involvement in anything up to ninety percent of all Autumn releases. More than enough to tie potential biographers and Sly completists in knots. With guesses extending out into myths and rumours of other lost sessions with soul stirrer Bertha Tillman, or a solo Dino Valenti—away from his usual band-duties with Quicksilver Messenger Service (there are related stories that Valenti was approached by Sly's eventual manager, David Kapralik, with a management offer, which was turned down). Plus tapes of the rumoured 'lost' *'On Stage With Sly'* album from 1965. But even the slightest oddities, curios and sonic doodles have all been issued and reissued in a bewildering scattershot array of barely-legal compilations. All of them entertaining in a period sort of way, and they provide valuable litmus tests for academics researching the state of Sly's head at this vital period of his evolving creativity. But there's nothing here that remotely resembles the innovations to come, and their inclusion on such eclectic compilation albums must prove confusing to those who stumble across them expecting *'There's A Riot Goin' On'*. This is material for serious collectors only. Sly Stone's history may be a matter of record... but it's not these records.

However, while all this was on-going, for various reasons—mostly financial, Autumn records failed to fulfil its potential as San Fran's first hit factory, and it folded prematurely in 1966. Taking with it any promise of what it may have become. Why did it have to end? perhaps, as Grace Slick sang, 'ask Alice, I think she'll know'. The failure was certainly not due to any deficit on the label's creative side. Rather, Donahue's extravagant appetites were little suited to the disciplines of balancing the financial aspects of an indie label, especially when they were complicated by success, and when anticipated revenues that should have filtered back to him were siphoned off at various stages by distributors better-versed in deviousness than he was. A lot of money got lost on its way from the record stores back to the record company. A situation made more precarious by Donahue's overwhelming predilection for blowing royalty-cheques at the race-course, and to hell with the creditors.

Bob Mitchell died tragically early in 1966 of Hodgkin's Disease. But by that time, Donahue's massive appetites, extravagant mismanagement, and newly-acquired taste for LSD, combined with Autumn's lack of promotional muscle or distribution, to force them into a major label sell-out to pay off debts. Leaving the high points, in among the flawed and the flimsy, and taking what remained of the artist roster—including the Beau Brummels, to L. A. based Warner Brothers. The group failed to prosper through this new arrangement. Hipness of the Brummies' calibre was a rare and fleeting thing, and by then their moment had passed. Drummer John Peterson quit after an ill-advised covers album. He joined another Sly-client quartet, a surf-pop group called the Tikis from Santa Cruz, who became Harpers Bizarre in time to chart with Paul Simon's "Feeling Groovy". The group are probably most notable for featuring Ted Templeman who—among other things, was to produce "Jump" for Van Halen in the eighties. While Sal Valentino and Ron Elliot—a long-time diabetes-sufferer, with bassist Ron Meager hung on for the ambitious Progressive indulgences of their *'Triangle'* (1967) album. After that Ron commenced a career of session-work for Randy Newman, the Everly Brothers, and Little Feat (including *'Sailin' Shoes'* in 1972).

After that final demise, and with the ultimate full-stop placed on the Autumn story in 1968, Tom Donahue quit KYA too. If not as well remembered as Bill Graham, Tom—who died on 28th April 1975, certainly epitomised that early Frisco approach to music. And his involvement in the scene remained as intense during his final years. With Larry Miller, he set up the revolutionary 'underground radio' station KMPX-FM, the first hip FM rock station, the first to champion the sounds of the new West Coast counter-culture. He followed it up with KSAN-FM, and continued to exploit his industry connections by promoting and managing various groups—including Sal Valentino's Brummels' spin-off Stoneground, plus the Fast Bucks and Bad Rice. He even helped negotiate Jefferson Airplane's recording contract with RCA. He also maintained contact with Sly, and would reappear later in his story.

While Sly found himself back on the street. He'd come out of the experience with his fingers seriously burned. He'd master-minded hits. Three national chart hits with tie-in albums. Plus a smattering of regional sellers. So where had all those royalties gone? Sly had come away with enough to make the deposit on the new Stewart-family home, but not enough for the monthly payments. Nevertheless, in the enclosed world of what they used to call 'discdom', there were those on the recording studio side listening out, and there were those on the disc-sales side listening in. As a DJ *and* producer Sly had found himself installed mid-point, with an ear cocked in both directions. As David Froelich observes, Sly 'had a good attitude on life, he never thought he *wouldn't* make it'. These were lessons he would store up for later.

Chapter Four
'San Franciscan Nights'

'In the manner of the very greatest rock 'n' roll, Sly & The Family Stone made music no-one had ever heard before...'

Greil Marcus

'Ladies and Gentlemen, Boys and Girls, Cats and Kitties, Hippies... and Squares...'

Unlike—say, country records out of Nashville, or Grunge from Seattle, San Francisco does not have a trademark 'sound'. If there's a San Francisco sound, it's Babel of disparate voices. San Francisco is more an attitude, a freedom from convention, a slap in the head at commercialism. In the fall of 1964 LSD hit Frisco like a primal detonation. First it came at $7 a dose, but was soon free-falling to a more accessible $2.50. It came on really strong over the following twelve months. Prior to LSD everything was a cruddy black-&-white schmaze, after LSD, everything was in Technicolor. Timothy Leary's IFIF—the International Federation For Internal Freedom was based around that white cube of impregnated sugar. To Hank Harrison 'the real summers of love were to be had in '64, '65 or '66 when people were undetected and unparanoid and mostly cool', the years of 'Autumn' records, the period of going from proto-phase to after-weird in all its Day-Glo destiny. During those years an influx of Topless joints, high rents and pressure from tourists forced the Beatniks out of their traditional haunts, out to Marin County, or the Big Sur, or over to the Haight district—an area named for an otherwise forgotten city-mayor from around 1880, which became the epicentre of the new hip aesthetic, the working psychedelic capital of the hyperverse. An urban sprawl Robin Williams dubbed less an authority, more 'a human game preserve'. The cheap Victorian housing of Haight-Ashbury provided a music laboratory for psychedelia, a magic chemistry set for the acid-freak scene fomenting there. Adapt, and mutate. And those multiple strands flowing from the Haight formed a microcosm for what was soon to go global

In 1962, much of the radical rhetoric had emanated from two dissociated scenes at Berkeley. The music-drug scene, and the political-drug scene, forming two separate personalities feuding within one organism. It was only around 1965 that agitator Jerry Rubin found acid-hedonism a perfect political synthesis of the two, and organised the first 'UC Berkeley' Peace March against Vietnam to celebrate the new unity of purpose. The debut issue of radical pioneering underground magazine *'Berkeley Barb'* appeared that same year, soft-socialist, non-violent, anti-fascist, Trotskyite. By the fall of the year other elements were coming together. Ken Kesey was writing what he still called 'The Cuckoo's Nest Document' while holding his first parties at Perry Lane, while the Pranksters were inaugurating the acid-test Trips Festivals at the Longshoreman's Hall. The 'Family Dog' was giving its historic first dances, Bill Graham's guerrilla theatre Mime Troupe was producing existential plays in an old church on Kapp Street in the Mission District, the Fillmore was giving its Mime Benefits, and the Warlocks were just emerging into what would later be the Grateful Dead, playing in a pizza parlour called 'Magoo's' on Menlo Park. Palo Alto became the crucible of the Dead. They weren't really into achieving anything much, in fact they were doing something close to nothing apart from getting laid, smoking lots of grass, and trying to survive on their music.

The 'Sexual Freedom League' began at 1090 Page where Big Brother & The Holding Company rehearsed. In November '66—the month Ronald Reagan became California Governor as his first step on the White House trail, Lenore Kandel was busted for writing a poem about the pleasures of giving her boyfriend a blow-job. Portrayed as 'Ramona Swartz' in Jack Kerouac's *'Big Sur'* (1962), her *'Love Book'* (1966) became the target of raids on the 'Free Press Bookstore', 'City Lights', and 'The Psychedelic Shop'—perhaps the world's first-ever head-shop, on Haight Street. The Doors promised to play a benefit for her. Ralph Gleason was there to cover the emerging scene—first as liberal columnist of the *'San Francisco Chronicle'*, later to transfer to *'Rolling Stone'*. From summer '66 local promoter Chet Helms had the Avalon Ballroom, while former Mime Troupe member Bill Graham co-opted the musicians' commune occupying the old 'Carousel Ballroom' on Market Street, converting and renaming it into the 'Fillmore West', so creating another showplace for groups with strange and alluring names. Jefferson Airplane made its first appearances as an acoustic Folk group playing at 'The Matrix' at the foot of Fillmore Street, a club founded by Marty Balin with an entrepreneur called Mat Matz. The five-piece Charlatans were back in San Fran from a formative three-month residency at the 'Red Dog Saloon' in Virginia City, Nevada, to become pivotal in the Bay area. They seemed bound for glory… obviously. As it happened, after their 'Autumn' sessions with Sly, they became one of the first regional groups to sign a major label contract, but for a variety of reasons it didn't work out and it was 1969 before their flawed album eventually emerged, by then it was too late, the magic had evaporated.

On October 6th 1966 (666), LSD became illegal. A defiant protest party at the Golden Gate Park was held to celebrate the date. And, in the space of a matter of months, on successive glorious sunny Sundays, the park became the site for free concerts and mass love gatherings called 'Human Be-Ins'. The first 'Gathering Of The Tribes' happened on Saturday 14th January 1967 at the Golden Gate Polo Grounds, among those attending were Timothy Leary, Gary Snyder, the Grateful Dead, Allen Ginsberg, Jerry Rubin, and Quicksilver Messenger Service. Jefferson Airplane played, and LSD was distributed among the crowd when power failure led to a break in their set. David Crosby was there, he wrote a song called "Tribal Gathering" about it—which later appeared on *'The Notorious Byrd Brothers'* (1968) album, he was watching the 'friendly motorcycle angel' who comes 'to sit and talk awhile and share a smoke', and the 'pretty little whirling butterfly' girls who go 'dancing by, caught up in the sound of talking drums', all of them lost 'in the wheel of sound'. It became the defining 'summer of love' moment that not so much ignited what had begun to happen, as the media-event that came to identify and focus on what was already there, what had been evolving through Hank Harrison's "64, '65 or '66 real summers of love'. Thereby unleashing the hippie goldrush. Afterwards, the 'beautiful people' could no longer go 'undetected, unparanoid and merely cool'.

New music was something very much in the air. DJ Sly Stone was playing it. What did such bands have in common? They all broke the mould. They all sounded like nothing else when they first emerged. They were all laboratory experiments that, again the odds, proved successful. But they were all fired in the kiln of diversity and subversion known as 'San Francisco, Wear Some Flowers In Your Hair'. During 1967 this highly localised phenomenon of experimental LSD-fuelled rock bands erupted into an unpredictable international counter-cultural force. With Jefferson Airplane signed to RCA, the Grateful Dead to Warner Brothers, Moby Grape and Janis Joplin's Big Brother & The Holding Company to Columbia, Country Joe & The Fish to Vanguard, and further… as they began to score hit albums, other aspirant musicians mingled in with the thousands of teenage runaways flocking to Frisco to join the 'love generation'. To find a place where 'walls move/ minds do too' according to Eric Burdon, who relocated into what he called 'an American Dream' that 'includes Indians too'. San Francisco was reimagining civilisation into an Aquarian community. But it was more than just 'freak-out music' forging what Gene Sculatti called 'future-sounds made out of chemicals and electricity', it inspired other musicians to experiment within and without an anti-Pop rock framework throughout America, pointing all the way to Woodstock, then Western Europe, until it eventually went global.

And Sly? He was hung up on the street corner. Heat bouncing down, melting the blacktop, releasing its mildly intoxicating shimmer. Something else in the air too. Something even less tangible. A new freer vibe in there every time you inhale. In the language used by stoned freak-journalists to write about it at the time, there were tokes in the park. Black and white dudes dressing down, loosening up. Slouching in together. Nubile chicks looking sweetly decorous. Beautiful freaks. It was buzzing in the ozone, crackling invisibly in the air with the radio-waves. Earthquake weather. New bands. New sounds. New coming-together. Art, anti-art, politics, anti-politics, celebration, squalor and calamity. Stroll for less than ten minutes under the pines and palms of Golden Gate Park and across the Panhandle. That brings you to the beginning of Haight Street. There were dimly-lit incense-scented head-shops that deal in drug paraphernalia, tie-dye tops, radical magazines and hand-strung bead necklaces. Gaudy posters by Mouse or Rick Griffin with art deco tentacles of luminous colour erupting up like avant-garde collages out of least-expected fly-posted windows and drab walls. Speed-reading new titles as you pass the newsstand there's *'Berkeley Barb'* from just around the Bay, ripping up taste alongside the rules of lay-out with its violent art and typographic riots. *'The San Francisco Oracle'* launched by psychedelic entrepreneur Ron Thelin with Allen Cohen in September 1966, first as *'The Love-Haight Ashbury Bush'* then *'The Haight-Ashbury Oracle'*. It promotes the acid-philosophies of Timothy Leary, Allen Ginsberg, Alan Watts and Gary Snyder to whom LSD is a chemical tool with the potential to cleanse the 'doors of perception', expand consciousness, and facilitate a moral leap to match the technological advances of the previous hundred years...

Throughout these happenings Sly was grounded in a rootsy involvement with the Frisco acid-trip, rubbing up against the birthing process of all its freaky vibrancy. He'd been programme-sequencing it into radio-waves through his readiness to mash-up airtime Rock with R&B. While in the 'Autumn' studio he was intimately conspiring with the activists accelerating its hyperactive musical environment. Working closely in the studio with both the Beau Brummels and Great Society on one side, and Bobby Freeman and Billy Preston on the other, the hybrid interconnections already falling into place. Wherever his head was, he was in the right place at the right time, to feed it. But that meant he was a pivotal participant in life-styles totally unlike and distant from the insularity of mainstream ghetto life. While both his radio speed-jiving and his forays into vinyl had already brought him a recognition-factor, and bread enough to invest in a custom-painted purple Jaguar XKE. Sharply-suited, Sly was using his on-going dee-jay celebrity to forge other useful connections too, 'he was working at the Cow Palace in San Francisco, so all the pop acts that came through there, he had access to their charts, so he was familiar with R&B, and with Pop' (George Clinton)—he even got to introduce the James Brown Show live on-stage in Frisco. And the James Brown Show at this time was a revelation.

Sly had already called in session line-ups for 'Autumn' signings. He'd assembled pick-up bands for Tom Donahue's live Record Hop guests and spin-off shows too. He knew all the right phone numbers to call. And soon, taking his cue from 'Big Daddy', he was taking his own roadshow around the clubs and other local landmarks—becoming a regular at the North Beach 'Condor', sweating and structuring a total act with other musicians, but promoting himself as much as the music. Studying and ingesting every influence, to create new collages of sound. Surely it was only a matter of time before—during the few hours of the day he had left, that he formed his own regular band, and just as inevitable that, when he did, it would be no ordinary band. A singing disc-jockey...? Like Big Bopper...? And sure enough—in 1966, he created Sly & The Stoners, as writer Peter Doggett suggests, a 'cute title for the hippie capital of the world'! The basis of his new group was largely derived from blues guitarist Johnny Heartsman's former band, convened on a casual pick-up basis. Although never a major national figure, shaven-headed Heartsman—who died in December 1996, enjoyed a long career as a respected bluesman and session-player in the San Francisco area. But during the period Sly spent with 'Autumn' the line-up of Johnny's band had numbered Sly's old high-school friend John Turk from Vallejo. Although Turk was a former member of the Viscaynes, he had jazz pretensions, in fact he'd been working with LaVern Baker's group in Las Vegas when Sly made the reconnection. And after the Stoners he would remain within Sly's orbit, going on to play back-up for Sly's eventual spin-off project, Little Sister.

Next, Sly recruited sister Rose, and fellow high-school horn-player Cynthia Robinson on trumpet (born 12th January 1946). Sly described Cynthia as simply 'one of the most talented trumpets alive, and that includes guys! Cynthia is bad, bad, bad and by that I mean good, good, good'. They'd first met during the senior high school year that Sly had spent with sister Loretta—in Cynthia's hometown of Sacramento, ninety-minutes inland or so by car from the Bay area. Supposedly Sly had been excluded from Vallejo High, for some unspecified misdemeanour, details of which are blurred. And 'I was in an inspirational all-faith church choir' Cynthia told *'Rolling Stone'*, and playing brass instruments in the school marching band. Since that first meeting she had allied experience to technique as part of house-bands for different nightclubs around the area, including Jimmy Mamoo's Band, where she had to adapt at short notice to the repertoire hits of visiting high-prestige artists such as Lowell Fulsom or Jimmy McCracklin. And playing with 'Big Al's houseband where, during the sudden craze surrounding the Adam West and Burt Ward TV-series, the musicians were persuaded into Batman caped-and-masked outfits. With Cynthia costumed as the only 'Robin'. Then 'we just ran into each other again when I came to Oakland and he was a DJ'. She describes herself as an 'introvert', if such a thing is at all possible within the Family Stone continuum. Except with the Stoners 'I have, on occasion, insisted she sit down because she is workin' just *too* hard' commented Sly. While to Cynthia, Sly initially appeared 'observant, very quiet, mannerful, and respectful. He never said a lot of useless things. He seemed to be very intelligent, and I never saw him act like a crazy teenager'. Not shy, but sly.

Sly was displaying early signs of his characteristic sharp sartorial extravagance, as his energy-levels continued to be intimidating. He'd come off air, speed straight across town to the North Beach in his XKE roadster, showing up around one am, to play a full set with the Stoners. Often, the band would have already started, killing time by jamming around until whenever Sly arrived. Then they'd go into whatever routine they'd worked out with him. At KSOL these live commitments began to interrupt his broadcasting schedule. And vice versa. But the band was proving more of an instant gratification than radio. For Sly, when you get up, you're instantly part of the story. And that upfront immediacy is something that can really become addictive. Sometimes, at 'Little Bo Peeps' in the Mission District, which abuts Haight-Ashbury, they'd share the bill with Freddie's current bar-band—Freddie & The Stone Souls. And although the area is now predominantly Hispanic, the audience then was a more multi-ethnic one. No 'peace & love thang' in the Mission district either, the police station had come under attack so frequently it had been reinforced with bullet-proof windows, heavily-locked doors, and a protective surrounding shield-wall. It would also become the target of a (failed) SLA terrorist attack. But together in this unlikely location, the two bands were becoming extraordinary ambassadors for the new drug and youth-revolution by bringing elements of West Coast white Rock into their versions of regulation soul-fodder, such as "In The Midnight Hour". The Stoners were not destined to survive long. Almost as soon as they'd got together, they were already petering out. Because Sly was impatient to express more advanced musical ideas…

****

'A New Generation, With a New Explanation…'

Sly & The Family Stone happen this way. Before Richard Nixon's presidency, before the Moon Landing, before Elvis' TV Come-Back Special. By routes that evoke the idealistic sensibilities of the Bay Area and its unique combination of musical and spiritual vibes. And they're pieced together from two bands. The Stoners, obviously. But afro-haired brother Freddie 'Stone' had his Stone Souls and, to Sly, 'Freddie will either gas you or scare you!'. Freddie had studied music theory and composition, and acquired impressive skills in wind and string instruments. Then he'd followed Sly down to Frisco. Sly had even helped him out through the KSOL airwaves, sneaking recruitment notices for his brother's projected band into the programming between records. As a result, full-blooded Italian-American 'Funky Drummer' Gregg Errico linked up with Freddie initially at a YMCA, then fitted naturally into Freddie's line-up. He came direct from working with a soul-band called the VIP's, which he'd stepped into when their original drummer fell sick, some time during 1966. According to Sly, Gregg was 'sometimes called 'Handsfeet' because of his clear communication between his mind and his fast, funky hands and feet. Gregg is so good because he plays the best licks, the fastest and the funkiest' (writing on the liner-notes to *'Dance To The Music'* vinyl album). Although Sly had his own place on Ocean Avenue in the residential Sunset District, both bands—Sly's and Freddie's, would rehearse together in adjoining rooms at 700 Urbano. Sly yelling suggestions down the hall. Members bullshitting together with goof-offs extending well into the night whether there was dope or not. But the well-respected Stone Souls were destined to work together for just short of twelve months.

It was bright spring in San Francisco. It was early 1967. It was a time of vibrant new fusions, new freak-mutations opening up new worlds of previously unimaginable possibilities. What's more natural than to take the most gifted players out of their respective line-ups, and fuse the two bands? Because both of them played guitar, multi-instrumentalist Sly suggested that for the projected combined line-up he should move over to concentrate on keyboards, leaving Freddie to assume lead, playing fuzzy Rock-styled guitar lines, while contributing vocals. He would also bring Greg Errico in from the 'Souls'. Sly took the keyboard and vocals role, bringing Cynthia along as one of the core components of the new band, on trumpet and vocals. She'd been on the brink of quitting, until Sly secretively whispered for her to turn up the next day at 700 Urbano. He had something in mind. He couldn't elaborate, not yet. She was still living out at Oakland, but eventually agreed to move in with Rose. More convenient that way.

Together they added dandily bearded Jerry Martini, a mischievous and fun-loving white high-school buddy of Sly's, or 'the best indication of Love & Peace any human being could conceive of', according to Sly. They'd first met around 1959 or '60, during Sly's Viscaynes days, but they'd stayed in touch. Betweentimes, he'd become a well-respected session-player on the San Fran scene, equally dextrous on saxophone, flute, accordion, piano, and clarinet, as well as shaking a mean tambourine. In fact, Jerry had helped out on the "C'mon And Swim" sessions, and he'd made serious inputs into unfolding events beyond that. It had been Jerry who urged Sly to form his own pick-up band for his club roadshows in the first place. And later, it was his suggestion for them to combine the two bands. His striking hepster looks, with his penchant for loose cravats, had also blagged him a minor walk-on part in the haunted-house movie-thriller *'Two On A Guillotine'* (1965). From a Henry Slesar story involving a severed head the drama features blonde popstrel Connie Stevens ('Cricket Blake' from TV's 'Hawaiian Eye') in the dual mother-*and*-daughter roles, with Dean Jones and Cesar Romero ('The Joker' in TV's 'Batman')… and amongst such stars, blink, and you'll miss Jerry. However, he had enjoyed a more rewarding employment playing with Al Lewis & The Modernistics where he'd briefly been paired with guitarist Larry Graham. And he'd already toured Europe, enjoying an eventful club residency at 'Club 84' in Rome as part of a George & Teddy & The Condors package. He hooked up with Sly at KSOL on his return. Jerry 'blows his life thru his saxophone' wrote Sly, 'when you hear him play, I'm sure you'll say 'he couldn't be all bad, as a matter of fact he might be all good'.'

Finally and perhaps most significantly, the line-up was completed with the addition of cousin Larry Graham Junior (born 14th August 1946 in Beaumont, Texas). The textbook narrative tells how Sly hooked up with Larry after he first received a phone-in eulogy of his unique bass-style from a fan of his KSOL show. There's just a suggestion that the 'fan' might have been Larry's mother! Following the radio-lead he stumbled across Larry when Sly—with Cynthia in tow, happened to see him work at a nightspot. Since the age of fifteen Larry had been an integral part of The Dell Graham Trio accompanying his mother, who was a sophisticated lounge-core songstress who sang like Dinah Washington and played piano like Erroll Garner. They played venues such as the 'embassy Club', 'Esther's Orbit Room', or the 'Black Cat' on the Peninsula or around the Bay Area. Due to the limitations of the trio line-up Larry had been forced to make up the deficit by becoming not only adept on bass, but also guitar, harmonica and drums. As Joel Selvin tells me, 'the Dell Graham Trio was playing a club in the Haight when Sly saw them'. Sly promptly invited him into the project. He did not refuse.

Sly and Freddie had been in a position to draw from a wide pool of experienced and skilled musicians. For most of the members involved, there were shared back-stories of bands that stretched all the way to their schooldays. There was a family tree of inter-connections between them that had lapsed, ricocheted and reassembled like complex geometry. As a result, the combined forces of the two Stewart Brothers' bands could now boast musical abilities and an originality of approach that was unrivalled. They were already tight. They were solid. Sure, Sly's compositions were so complex and oddly structured that they demanded a rhythm section just as nimble on its toes, just to hold the thing together. For Sly, being merely 'good' in itself was not good enough. But—according to Martini, even the racial and gender mix of the band was deliberately preconceived, Sly was something of a chemist, fusing human elements together, 'he knew exactly what he was doing—boys, girls, black, white'. It didn't *have* to have been that way. There were technically better musicians around. 'There was a shit-pot full of black drummers that could kick Gregg's ass' as Jerry phrased it, 'and there was a lot of black saxophone players that could kick mine.' But Sly already had it mapped. He didn't fuck around. He had no time for time-wasters, no patience for laziness, and a low tolerance for lack of motivation. Attitude was as important as ability. And mix-ability was as important as attitude.

The newly-minted Family Stone was a special kind of family. Even the group's chosen name was riddled with levels of semi-meanings. To reiterate Peter Doggett's suggestion, it was another 'cute title for the hippie capital of the world'. From the obvious drug reference—'stoned'—through the Family nature of the band-members, to Sylvester's own nickname, which chimed every bit as hip as their music. When initially probed about which band members were genuine 'family' Sly retorted 'we all are'. Yet while family-based bands are hardly unique in music history, each of them involves a unique dynamic. Two loving feuding collaborating brothers are the basis of the Kinks' soap-opera psychodramas, the tabloid sibling sparring of Oasis, and the immaculately attuned harmonies of the Everly Brothers. The biological chemistry of the Family Stone determined that Sly would always be the 'big brother'. After all, as a child, hadn't Freddie worn his brother's hand-me-downs? Sure he had. That pre-existing relationship established an immediate hierarchy. But wouldn't it also store up grudges? Time would tell. Involve further elements from the same gene-pool, and you get the Bee-Gees, the Beach-Boys... or the Jackson Five. The Chambers Brothers from Los Angeles were made up of four black brothers, with a white drummer. Yet for the Stone's there were more 'Family' connections to come.

Sly invited sister Rosemary to join. After all, 'not only is she as beautiful as any woman around' according to Sly, 'she is as talented and as consistent as any other musician around!' But no, 'Rosie' already had a steady daytime job working the checkout till in the 'Sherman & Clay' record store. She was doing all right, she didn't want to risk losing her regular income for the unpredictable vagaries of Pop. Instead, there was Vet. 'Baby' sister Vaetta had been recruited by a gospel outfit called The Heavenly Tones (of The Ephesians Church Of God In Christ in Berkeley, CA). Her school-friends Mary McCreary and Elva Mouton were also members, alongside other names such as Tramaine Hawkins. They all harmonised under the benevolent mentorship of gospel legends Reverend James Cleveland, Shirley Caesar and Albertina Walker. In the States, the Holy Lordy circuit of churches where they speak-in-tongues, testify and are moved by the spirit forms the 'Gospel Highway'. It's also a hugely prosperous enterprise with its own star system and record market. One that engenders fierce loyalties. James Baldwin eloquently writes about the fire and inspiration of Gospel, the leap of grace in gospel music. It's possible not only to thrive comfortably but enjoy major celebrity status within the enclosed realm of its own exclusivity. Encouraged by local congregations and church choirs, Gospel 'family' singers easily evolve into touring attractions through recommendation and exchange visits to other congregations. That kind of thing stays with you. That kind of joyful noise. That kind of churchy blues sound. It gets into the blood.

Occasionally it can even break through into the mainstream. As have such respected acts as the incomparable Staple Singers, the Winans family, or the Edwin Hawkins Singers who scored a global no. 1 in 1969 with the massed choir sound of "Oh Happy Day". But commercial success on that scale, even when still operating within a strictly religious context, can result in serious dissention and disapproval among those of a more austerely puritan persuasion. For stars on the 'Gospel Highway', to 'cross over' entirely into secular music can be interpreted as tantamount to betrayal, heresy, apostasy, or worse. The career of Gospel's first great star, the amazing Sister Rosetta Tharpe (also of the Church Of God In Christ), was brought to a halt when she recorded for the 'Race' market, to the extent that her reputation never recovered. The great Sam Cooke first resorted to recording pop music under aliases to protect his gospel reputation. Others—Aretha Franklin, Solomon Burke, Al Green, continue to maintain an uneasy equilibrium between the two worlds—sacred and secular, alternately pulled in conflicting directions. For Vet, the division seems arbitrary. 'I've always considered Sly to be a chosen person' she later confided, 'people sing songs like "Everyday People" in church! He's always had a message.' For the various Stewart family groups, there seems to have been no great qualms of conscience about Sly's more commercial instincts. And it's significant that following the eventual implosion of the Family Stone, a number of its members would gravitate back into the comforting embrace of the church. Another trait bizarrely, is that not just a talent for close-harmony and very intense singing runs in the family, but a history of recording vinyl evidence of that talent too. The Reverend James Cleveland—the man who later married Bobby Womack to his second wife Regina, produced The Heavenly Tones first album for the renowned Savoy label (1966), distributed around the time that Vet, with the 'Tones', was performing with some of the top names in the gospel community. Cut the Stewart family, they bleed vinyl.

Meanwhile, 'Vet' had just turned fifteen, but she, Mary and Elva now wanted into her brother's new band too. So Sly recruited the three teenagers directly out of high school to become 'Little Sister', the troupe's long-term backing singers. Just like the Ike Turner Band had the Ikettes, or the Ray Charles Band had the Raelettes. But this happened strictly on the proviso that when they toured Daddy KC would, at all times, be close by Vet's side, while Rose would maintain a protective sisterly look-out for her too. And that's the way it worked out. Daddy Stewart travelled across America with the group. It's a Family Affair. Dramatically, Vaetta's role in the band had been seriously threatened, almost before it began. She was struck down by a serious illness with gloomy diagnoses from the Doctors. Yet she rallied after brain surgery, or—in the words of her website, she was 'miraculously healed in a very short time'. Time enough to catch the group's lift-off. Then, within the year—soon after the recording of the *'A Whole New Thing'* album, 'Rosie' was finally sufficiently convinced to commit too. 'Rose is the electric piano player, singer, dancer and anything else I need' Sly explained, 'you see, when Rose joined the group everybody was doing everything on stage, and that was almost a requirement that any new member had to meet'. Fortunately 'my sister found that no problem'. She brought not only her electric piano, churchy Hammond organ and vocals into the already visually distinctive line-up, but also her penchant for wearing a shock blonde-hairpiece. With four Stewart family members now involved, as Sly would write it, 'there's a sister, there's a brother, having fun with each other' ("Fun").

The first number the Family Stone rehearsed together was Sly's horn-based rearrangement of Ray Charles' storming "I Don't Need No Doctor", an early text from the pens of future Motown-team Nickolas Ashford and Valerie Simpson. As Ray had realised, the lyric consists of an extended addiction metaphor, 'I don't need no doctor, 'cos I know what's ailing me', then 'I don't need no doctor, for my prescription to be filled'. Although supposedly addressed to the healing medicinal qualities of the singer's 'Baby', its narcotic code made it an attractively subversive proposition to garage-bands, and it was consequently picked up and recorded by San Jose's Chocolate Watchband. While the Family Stone extended their repertoire by cherry-picking from Wilson Pickett and James Brown specialties. There was "Try A Little Tenderness", Junior Walker's "Shotgun", and Otis Redding's "I Can't Turn You Loose" which would eventually be mangled into the reconfigured shape of the Family Stone track "Turn Me Loose". By now they were living and sleeping the expanding repertoire. But when Sly rehearsed, his attention wasn't only on his fingering, it was on the total sound. On his different kinds of truth. Introducing elements of Rock into Soul, and vice versa. 'We had all this input no-one had ever thrown together before' rationalised Gregg Errico, 'you had R&B, you had white Pop, you had the psychedelic thing and the English thing, mixing together for the first time.' Sly was less interested in crossing racial and musical lines than he was in ripping them to shreds. Of course, like the Grateful Dead, they were also breaking beyond the 2:50-minute song limit. And in the same way that James Brown had horns, Sly had horns.

The first time they played to a live audience—16th December 1966, was at the 'Winchester Cathedral', a predominantly white after-hours teenage hangout—formerly 'Tin Pan Alley', but opportunistically renamed after the trans-Atlantic New Vaudeville Band novelty no. 1 hit. Located in Redwood

City among the sprawling suburb towns of the El Camino peninsula, on the 101 highway to San Francisco airport, an hour's drive—and far removed from the city's psychedelic ballrooms, it was nevertheless a venue more used to hosting white garage-punk bands such as the aforementioned Chocolate Watchband or Strawberry Alarm Clock. But, playing Friday and Saturday every weekend for five months, the Family Stone sets soon began attracting the car-crowds. Two bands alternated, with the 6/8th Paradox on at 2am to 2:45am, then Sly from 3am to 4am, 6/8th Paradox again from 4am to 4:45am, and the Family Stone from 5:00 until… whenever. The club's owner was Rich Romanello, who—in a small-world web of interconnections, also ran the 'Morocco Room' where 'Big Daddy' Tom Donahue first talent-spotted the Beau Brummels, who Romanello had briefly managed. Now he became the Family Stone's first manager too, sort-of. He kind-of, informally, looked out for their interests. Nothing as uncool as what the straight world would recognise as a contract. But they began picking up knock-on bookings at other after-hours clubs in the 'burbs, rowdy joints and bars in San Jose, blue-collar Hayward, around Oakland—Frisco's darker twin brooding on the opposite side of the bay, and 'Wayne Manor' back in the Mission. Freddie recalls 'we'd play places like 'Frenchy's' in Hayward and 'The Losers' in San Jose six nights a week, then on weekends drive to the 'Winchester' to play all night'.

Their set would count-in with Gregg Errico coming up to his drum-array first, and setting up a steady rhythmic dum-dum pulse. Then each member, one-by-one would get up to join him, often fording through the audience, to add their own solos. Collectively it built and extended into an eight-minute segmented jazz-riffing piece, largely built up improvisationally. The chemistry lay in the way they were playing off each other, everybody playing above themselves, almost from the start, playing what the audience saw as 'weird hip shit'. Their communication was already operating on an altogether intuitive level, a step above the dull and flat-footed form of verbal communication most of us have to get by on, speaking out direct from the body, through the instrument, to each other, and only then to the audience. From that point on the groove never stopped, with no gap between numbers, and scarcely space to draw breath. Each band-member took solo spots. Larry would do material in the Lou Rawls vein—"Tobacco Road" or "The Shadow Of Your Smile". Freddie would emote Otis Redding's aching "Try A Little Tenderness". Cynthia took lead for "St. James' Infirmary", then Jerry followed-up with a raucous "Shotgun". But no matter what the provenance of the material—be it covers of Wilson Pickett, Otis Redding, the Spencer Davis Group hit "Gimme Some Lovin'", or titles such as "What's It Got To Do With Me", it was remade, remodelled into something new and original.

Understand this, even at the starting point of their journey—before the genre had had chance to fully take shape, there were few precedents for Sly &

The Family Stone. Essentially a Soul Revue, it was funkadelia before they'd had time to invent a name for it. The world had never heard music *quite* like this before. It was all so delightfully confusing. Already herbally-enhanced the Family Stone were paying their dues in places where the septet's colour-blind multiracialism crossed virtually unheard-of cultural boundaries. Pulverising polarities, smashing stereotypes with a grab-bag of audacious eclecticism—from the James Brown body-bending proto-funk pulse, through the hippie-acceptable acid head-trip, into sing-along Broadway show-tunes. The decimating blasts of stylistic promiscuity fired by Larry's supercharged plucked bass, took them to places even more distinctive than the area's numerous Love Generation dope-head bands. Music that didn't exist, until they played it... until the set drew to a close with Greg pounding out the final solo, his eyes closed in concentration, piledriving down into a slowing plod, until he lets the sticks fall for the last time...

Grok this and grok it good, not only do they *sound* different, they *look* different too, retuning the collective eye and ear of the cool and the switched-on. The collective entity they've assembled forms an outlandish multiculturalism, rejecting all stylistic boundaries, a melting-pot of different racial backgrounds, ethnic and gender identities. Caucasian *and* Afro-American—just four short years after the repeal of the segregation laws. Black, white, and brown. And the girls were there as musicians, they play instruments onstage rather than merely adding ooh-aaah shooby-doo-wah vocals or serving as eye-candy visual decoration. A stone-free example of independence for African-American women. Sly's stomping grooves drew from across a socio-political spectrum, exemplifying racial harmony, ethnic diversity, and communal affirmation with their interacting voices blending and assimilating gospel anthemics, straight-up R&B jive, and funk-horn innovations. Plus just about anything else he cared to toy with. Consigning physical differences to the garbage-skip, the Family Stone were socking it to them 'as you would have them sock it to you' ("Fun"). Inter-racial, inter-gender, and into-drugs. Was there a gay in the set-up to cover all bases in its diversity? Wait, on the management side, there would be. Meanwhile, Sly took advantage of Cynthia's way with brash vocal ad-libs when the only people she orders to 'go home'... are the squares! Freaks unite. Squares, fuck off !!!

Soon the Family Stone were becoming a regional Bay Area phenomenon, a super-bad psychedelia capturing the prevailing spirit of those heady times. Their after-hours 'Winchester' sets—playing to predominantly white audiences, were developing a large following with an electrifying underground 'buzz'. With a fusion of cultures all conspiring to lift it higher. Music that could lift the spirit faster and more effectively than the latest street drug. In the hippie's dictionary of cool, you hear colours, black and red. You see sounds that fill your head. Altered states, as different from the Grateful Dead's slow builds and meandering guitar improvisations as it was from just about everything else on the scene. And there, in the audience, was an impressed Mickey Hart from the Dead itself. More specifically, whereas those white bands were effectively drawing on folk or country roots, the Family Stone represented a thoughtful continuation of what had been happening in black music, crossing social faultlines—bringing James Brown to the pan-cultural Love-in. Of course, the Family Stone were liberated by the same new attitudes, but their music bore little relation to the loose stoned guitar-jams of the acid rockers.

Also, like Bill Graham and Jan Wenner, Sly had a commercial instinct that was not necessarily in contradiction to such idealism. That didn't make them any less real. The Grateful Dead were not trying to win anything. So how could they lose? Sly and the extended Family were different. They had objectives. They may have been fuzzy-logic objectives. The career stuff and ego trips would mutate from these beginnings. But that doesn't invalidate its core values. They were young. They were—what Bobby Womack later called, 'cooking some dope-fuelled shit for a while'. They were having fun. Even the most acid-addled member of the flower-power crowd could pick up on that. If Sly—and probably Sly alone, harboured ambitions of taking it way-further, he could have had little sense of just how far that way-further would take them.

Yet there were already destabilising elements that would later take on relevance. As the shows became more intense, Sly recruited James Vernon 'JB' Brown, and Hamp 'Bubba' Banks as enforcers, minders, security goons, and club bouncers. Bubba was useful to have around. In fact, he'd been 'around' at least since 1964 when Sly had been best man when Bubba married Lillian Scott at Saint Dominic's. Although not necessarily a big super-sized guy, his sheer physical presence could add gravitas to Sly's argument with club owners who were less than enthusiastic about parting with the door-money they owed. And there are some unscrupulous promoters out there. He could be a useful appendage to the band in other ways too. Sly's lyric might taunt 'you might think you talk just like a player' ("Colour Me True"), but sometime-Marine Bubba *was* a player. He had the street-wise awareness of a shakedown artist, something that Sly conspicuously lacked. When Sly was old enough to drive, he got his own car—a light green Chevy Buick '53 with its trunk painted a darker 'booty' green. Bubba—by contrast, had fought for what he'd got, he'd been immersed in the kind of *real* ghetto-life that exerted a dark fascination over Sly. After all, the bad guys always seem more exciting. And Bubba openly bragged of living the pimping and dealing thug-life.

Sly was in thrall to the outsider romance that Bubba seemed to embody, the lure of the socially excluded 'guiltless outlaw'. This 'badness' is what Greil Marcus meant when he selected Sly to represent the mythic 'Stagger Lee', the distinctively black twist on the trait, the transgressor on the mean streets thrown back on the speed of his wits and his fringe-legal inner-resources. The lone good-for-nothin' out there on the shadow-margin, alienated, at odds with conformity living on the edge, surviving by his nerve-ends. As Bobby Womack comments, 'Sly had a little gangsta thing going on. I don't know why, because Sly was definitely no tough guy'. Perhaps, because Sly was specifically *not* a ghetto street-kid, he was able to view its hard-knocks romance with a distanced perspective. Seeing its vitality, its cool poses, its vital culture, more in a second-hand way… more in the way that a white kid would? But this isn't just R&B archaeology, it's also part of the mainstream of American myth from Jesse James, through James Cagney's Hollywood gangsterism, through Bonnie & Clyde and John Wesley Hardin(g)… into 'Easy Rider'. Further refined by Iceberg Slim's Chicago-based autobiographical novel *'Pimp'* (1969)—its defining text. In the next decade Hollywood assimilated and subsequently helped make the pimp stereotype iconic, until no blaxploitation movie was complete without a flamboyant Mack Daddy reeling from scene to scene. The black no-good-nik chancer recognisable clear through to the Rapper's ghetto poses. British record-buyers may have first become acquainted with "Stagger Lee" through the wonderful February 1959 hit single by Lloyd Price, but by then the character was already an outlaw archetype, at least since Mississippi John Hurt's "Stack O' Lee" recorded for Okeh 28th December 1928, and Frank Hutchison's definitive 1927 version "Stackalee".

It was the same dichotomy Michael Jackson embodied in the extended seventeen-minute full-length video—directed by Martin Scorsese, for "B.A.D". The shy bookish kid who dreams of becoming the respected street-wise gang-leader clad in warrior black leather throwing all the right moves. Not that Sly was ever shy and bookish. Far from it. But only so far as the analogy holds. Bubba could make up for Sly's credibility-deficit merely by them hanging out together. He could make the street-connection Sly needed. Wearing hip shit, acting like the baddest bad-ass mother on the block. Bubba had already contributed voice-over raps to Sly's radio shows, investing it with authentic jive-smart qualities. Through Bubba, Sly could reinvent his own back-story. And as late as the *'Fresh'* album liner-notes Sly would thank Bubba in the same type-size and bracketed into the same acknowledgement phrase as 'Bro Fred'. Sister Rose was immediately attracted to Bubba. Sly warned her off. He's 'bad'. Inevitably, she ignored his advice. For now, however, Bubba's association with the band would be prematurely curtailed. He euphemistically 'went away' for a period, and would not reappear in the story until his penitentiary release around the time of the 'Coldwater Canyon' events

Meanwhile, 'Autumn' was no longer an operational concern—that was last summer's scene, so the unwieldy aggregation began working around a small private studio owned by Leo Kulka. There, they worked on Sly songs "Life Of Fortune And Fame"—his impassioned vocals imploring 'I hope it's not your fate / to stand in my shoes…' (a later bootleg album salvages no less than twenty rehearsal takes of the song), and "Take My Advice" which, although fairly crude in comparison to what was to come, show startling quivers of originality. They cut demos of these and other songs that were then licensed to Kulka as a payment-in-kind trade-off for the studio time they'd gobbled up. Leo astutely made the most of what he had, capitalising on what soon constituted a valuable property. The tracks have appeared under the guise of numerous fly-by-night labels ever since. And resulted in the first Sly & The Family Stone single, the tight horn-based "I Ain't Got Nobody"—backed by their unorthodox bump-and-grind cover of Otis Redding's "I Can't Turn You Loose", which became an instant regional micro-seller for the local Loadstone label.

It all constituted a parallel-universe sideways-switch from conventional show-biz. In fact, any resemblance between the two definitions was purely coincidental. Sly Stone was special. Accepted strictures no longer applied to him. The Family Stone was more than a band, it was an ideal of a band. Located at the sharp end of the racial interface, they had become a physical demonstration that the ideas of racial co-mingling were not only possible, but that they could do extraordinary things together. It even lets you hear what it all sounds like when racial lines dissolve before your ears. A sound that shook all preconceptions just as surely as a San Andreas fault tremor could shake the Bay Area.

The Family Stone have a special chemistry. Unfortunately, they also have special chemicals...

Chapter Five
'Where Do We Go From Here: Chaos or Community...?'

'You love me, you hate me, you know me and then, you can't figure out the bag I'm in...'

("Everyday People")

'Music For the Human Race...'

New. Yet dragging enough baggage to fill the capacious interior of both Fillmore's. It's time for some necessary background detail. A little cultural, and sub-cultural history. If you just want the fun Pop-stuff you can skip direct to Chapter Six. But without all of *this*, there wouldn't be any of *that*. The austerity angst of the fifties has retrospectively been effectively made-over into an all-singing all-dancing 'Grease'/'Happy Days' costume situation-comedy. In the same way, in Pop-culture mythology the sixties is the party decade. If you play its years like the newsreel sequence in *'Citizen Kane'* (1941), you see it all flashing before your eyes. Mods on multi-mirrored scooters, and Mary Quant mini-skirts in Brigit Riley Op-Art grids. Hippies in bells-&-kaftan silliness. Fey hippiechicks with hippy-dippy flowery-powery blossoms in their hair. The 'Woodstock' nation. The Isle of Wight Festival.

This is only partly true. It was more than that. To understand the decade, understand these three things. First, this is also a time framed by what Bob Dylan termed 'the worst fear that's ever been hurled'. He teasingly denied that "A Hard Rains A-Gonna Fall" specifically targets atomic war, he dissembled that its 'pellets of poison' were not necessarily radioactive, but the fact that they were universally interpreted as such tapped into the pervasive paranoia of MAD—Mutually Assured Destruction, in which two rival antagonistic super-powers bridged the Atlantic with an arsenal of enough ICBMs—Intercontinental Ballistic warheads, to eradicate all life of Earth many time over, in a matter of seconds. Since Hiroshima, the world had existed on a time-fuse. Sylvester Stewart was born precisely as World War II raged to its climax, the month American troops landed at Anzio and US warships began shelling the Japanese home island of Paramishu. Then, when he was just seventeen-months-old, American A-bombs vaporised Hiroshima and Nagasaki, closing down the war, and opening a new era of terror. Shock-waves trembled the world, all the way to Denton, Texas. The atmospheric radiation levels took a hike, from which they'd never recover.

Those too young to recall the Berlin blockade might be familiar with the Cuba Crisis. Sylvester Stewart was eighteen-&-a-half during October 1962, when a U2 spy-plane spotted Soviet missiles on Cuban soil, and John F Kennedy confronted Premier Khrushchev by announcing his naval blockade. The world held its breath, and the USSR had the good grace to 'blink first' and back down before the button was pushed. The Cuba missile crisis was not only the most dangerous moment in the Cold War, but also the most dangerous moment in the whole of human history. Because the antagonists were technically tooled-up to annihilate the planet in 'the roar of a wave that could drown the whole world'. So that, even when not consciously there, instant annihilation was a constant subtext to the decade's excesses.

Second, in SE Asia the Cold War was incandescing into a napalm white heat as the two rival ideological systems sought to physically blitz each other back into the Stone Age, masked through the ciphers of puppet regimes. In July 1965 there were 100,000 US GI's active in Vietnam. By the end of that year, the number doubled. Over the following year it doubled again. Vietnam became the first media-beamed war, with TV-sets spewing atrocity into your front-room on a nightly basis from that escalating war-zone. You flip channels, but it's just the same, its still there. Provoking mass protest and agitation fuelled as much on visceral repulsion as on political principle. Acting in turn as a catalyst for further social protests. During Spring 1967 100,000 protesters rallied in New York, led by Martin Luther King. That same October—the month the Family Stone's debut album emerged, there were co-ordinated anti-war rallies clear across the States from Boston to Atlanta to Washington. In Oakland, forty 'Stop The Draft' protesters were arrested—including Joan Baez, for blockading the military induction centre. In LA Florence Beaumont deliberately torched herself to death outside the Federal Building. Yet as the scale and fury of the protests intensified, so did the sense of futility. So much rage. No-one listening. 400,000 US troops in Vietnam at the onset of 1967, a number that swelled to half-a-million by the year's close. Hundreds of GI's were being slaughtered on a weekly basis, many more maimed or wounded. For the Vietnamese it was incalculably worse. The supposed 'Summer of Love' was 'a fabulous euphoria in the middle of a deluded un-winnable war', coming up hard against reality, and was failing to withstand its onslaught.

While third-equal, the civil rights struggle was incrementally transfiguring LBJ's 'Great Society', a campaign fought from the dawn of the decade into long after its close. A gathering wave of revulsion that reverberated down through the years demanding 'Which Side Are You On?' revealing the rifts underlying the patriotic complacency on which the nation's aspirational dream was built. Each hard fought-for gain was resisted with appalling violence. Despite the truth that 'all men are born equal' deemed 'self-evident' by the republic's founding fathers, a century had passed since the abolition of slavery, yet restaurants, hotels, night clubs, public facilities, transport and the schools system were stubbornly oppressed by social apartheid. There were white's-only diners and toilets, white's-only water-fountains alongside black's-only water-fountains although—as Bo Diddley pointed out, the water came from the same pipe. The front of the bus was for whites, the rear-half for blacks. Systematic discrimination meant that job opportunities were ruthlessly slanted in the white majority's favour. Big Bill Broonzy wrote his lyric 'if you was white, you's alright, / if you was brown, stick around, / but it you's black, oh brother, get back, get back, get back' in 1949, it took him two years before it was allowed out on vinyl. Many organisations had been created to promote the goals of racial justice and equality by working through the system to affect change. Groups such as the NAACP—'National Association For The Advancement Of Coloured People' formed in 1909 by WEB DuBois, CORE—the 'Congress Of Racial Equality', and Baptist Minister Dr Martin Luther King's SCLC—the 'Southern Christian Leadership Council'. All of which advocated peaceful methods through litigation, legislation, and education, on the basis—like the English 'Fabian' socialists, of the 'inevitability of gradualism'. But progress was painfully slow.

It was not until the sixties that a hundred years of effort began to seriously force the pace of change. Throughout the years Sylvester Stewart was growing into maturity the issue of race was inescapable, and the forces for social transformation that would determine the arc of his career were gaining momentum. In February 1960—when he was fifteen, four young African-Americans began a student sit-in at a racially-segregated Woolworth's lunch counter in Greensboro, North Carolina. Their example led to the formation of the SNCC (the Student Non-Violent Co-ordinating Committee), intended as the direct agent of change, to recruit, enthuse, and empower. And the further radicalisation of the earlier SDS (Students For A Democratic Society)—founded in Chicago as early as 1962, which stayed active on campuses throughout the decade. Taking inspiration equally from Ghandi and socialism, they were careful not to associate themselves *too* closely with known communists. The broad African-American community consisted of a disenfranchised minority, and as such they by necessity depended on the support of white sympathisers, and on prodding the conscience of those caught up in the spirit of the 'changin' times'. Yet activists such as Pete Seeger found themselves accused of being the 'Communist fellow-travellers' that J Edgar Hoover attacked as a subversive 'red front'. The legacy of paranoid-obsessive anti-red Senator Joe McCarthy's was still insidiously pervasive—as George Clooney's 2006 movie *'Goodnight, & Good Luck'* recreates. Yet the origins of the Folk revival, which did much to connect white audiences into the Blues, and the Civil Rights movement was, to a large extent, a reaction to the stultifying conformity of the McCarthyite era.

Bob Dylan's first protest song—premiered in February 1962, was "The Death Of Emmett Till". Till, from Chicago, was fourteen years old—just three years older than his near-contemporary Sylvester Stewart, when he 'went down to Mississippi in 1955 and whistled at a white lady… he didn't know he wasn't supposed to wolf-whistle. That earned him a death sentence' narrates Bobby Womack. 'The rednecks beat him to a pulp. Cut off his tongue. Cut off his balls. Knocked his right eye out of its socket, his left eye into oblivion. Knocked out most of his teeth. Cut off an ear and took an axe to what remained of his head'. Miles Davis recounts how 'they threw his body in the river. When they found him and pulled him out he was all bloated. They took pictures of him and put them in the papers. Man, that shit was horrible and shocked everyone. I won't forget them pictures of that young boy as long as I live'. A lesson for the learning by every young black kid who saw those photos, all the way from Mississippi, to Vallejo. Emmett Till's mother insisted the body was left untouched, face up, in an open casket at the funeral. 'It just let black people know once again just how most white people in this country thought of them' emphasises Davis. Bob Dylan was born the same year as Till—as was Muhammad Ali.

Race was a movement with global dimensions too. On Monday, 21st March 1960—a week after Sly's 16th birthday, in a black township suburb of Johannesburg in apartheid South Africa, police opened fire on a peaceful protest against the hated Pass Laws requiring them to carry ID papers at all times. The fusillade murdered sixty-nine and wounded 180 more. The 'Sharpeville Massacre' sent warning shock-waves around the world. The old order was changing. During the summer of 1963 US TV-screens were awash with images from Birmingham, Alabama (where Dr Martin Luther King Jr. kicked his stylish heels in a jail cell), as a march by 4,000 black children was brutally assaulted by police with dogs and fire hoses. Throughout the segregated south of the 'Jim Crow Laws' it ignited 758 demonstrations, marches, rallies, strikes, riots and violent confrontations resulting in 14,733 arrests in 186 cities, forcing grudging concessions from the white authorities. The 21-year-old Dylan had written "Blowin' In The Wind" soon time earlier—it first appeared in print in *'Broadside no. 6'*, so it was already familiar in civil rights circles. But it had to wait until that June 1963 for the clean harmonies of Peter Paul & Mary to carry it high into the charts—selling 300,000 in just two weeks. The lyric 'how many times can a man turn his head and pretend that the just doesn't see' inescapably tied into those telescreened events.

But it was "We Shall Overcome"—derived from Charles Tindley's turn-of-the-century gospel song "I'll Overcome Some Day", which became *the* movement's anthem, sung on the front lines of the struggle to express both endurance and ultimate vindication. Following an historic 1957 'Brown vs. Board of Education' ruling by the US Supreme Court that school segregation was unconstitutional, nine black 14-15-year-olds were confronted by white mobs backed up by the Arkansas National Guard when they attempted to attend Little Rock Central High School. They had to be given an escort provided by the 101st Airborne ordered in by President Eisenhower to enable them to claim those rights, heroically running a gauntlet of abusive hatred. The scenes were front-paged around the world at a time when Sylvester Stewart was an impressionable thirteen. The 'Little Rock Nine'—Elizabeth Eckford, Melba Patillo, Minnijean Brown, Carlotta Walls, Jefferson Thomas, Gloria Ray, Terrence Roberts, Thelma Mothershed and Ernest Green would eventually be invited to attend Barack Obama's Presidential inauguration. Yet in late-'62 there were white riots in Oxford Town when black student James Meredith enrolled at the University of Mississippi. It's a vast state of more than 48,000 square miles, and close-on three million inhabitants. The Governor—Ross Barnett, rabble-roused several thousand reactionary white college boys to obstruct and intimidate Meredith, until the Kennedy administration was pressured to send in 23,000 troopers to enforce the law. And on 12th June 1963—when Sly had just turned nineteen, NAACP activist Medgar Evers was murdered by 'a bullet from the back of a bush'—as Bob Dylan wrote, in Jackson Mississippi. It was only in February 1994 that his racist assassin—Byron de la Beckwith, was finally brought to justice and given life for the crime. By then the incidents were on-screen as part of the Woopi Goldberg movie *'Ghosts Of Mississippi'* (1996). Phil Ochs eloquent "Too Many Martyrs" references both Emmett Till and Medgar Evers.

The Civil Rights Act itself, which John F Kennedy announced, would not have been passed had Martin Luther King not led his 'March for Jobs and Freedom' on 28th August 1963, the greatest mass mobilisation of African-Americans ever seen, 250,000 people gathering in Washington DC to hear Odetta, Joan Baez, and a tousled 22-year-old Bob Dylan sing… and to hear Dr King share his inspirational 'dream' in front of the Lincoln Memorial. Some events lodge in the collective memory. People recognise those significant moments, incidents they keep returning to within their personal memory bank. This was such a moment, caught in 'the fierce urgency of now', whether you viewed it live, on television, in New York, Liverpool… or Vallejo. The Lincoln Memorial is included, in a perhaps ironic reference to the event, as part of the inner-sleeve collage of *'There's A Riot Goin' On'*. There were critical voices, Malcolm X described the gathering as being 'run by whites in front of a statue of a president who has been dead for a hundred years and who didn't like us when he was alive'. For others, the people gathered there, and the many thousands more watching on TV, it seemed as though limitless possibilities were but a breath away. On a rising tide of expectations, the Civil Rights Act of 1964 effectively outlawed most forms of segregation, followed a year later by the second bill eliminating discrimination in voting, giving millions of southern blacks access to the vote for the first time. Yet in 1964, despite these victories, only 5% of the eligible blacks in the state of Mississippi were permitted to vote.

The bigoted god-botherers of the redneck states, with their white supremacist reactionary institutions retaliated with shootings, arson attacks and beatings, supported by the police and with the full complicity of the law. And the brutality of their crimes is shocking. Men, women and children were shot, stabbed, bombed or beaten to death, murdered in broad daylight and cold blood. Bodies were mutilated and hidden. Often murders were never investigated by local police forces which were either complicit in the crimes or deliberately ignored them. When suspects *were* charged in cases of crimes perpetrated by whites against blacks, rigged all-white juries mocked justice by simply acquitting their fellow whites, no matter what the evidence. In one notorious case, a civil rights activist, the Reverend George Lee, was found dead in his crashed car in the Mississippi town of Belzoni. The sheriff declared the death a traffic accident and claimed that the shotgun pellets coroners picked out of Lee's head were 'dental fillings'. In 1963 Andrew Anderson was accused by a white woman in Arkansas of molesting her daughter. He was beaten to death by a white mob in a bean field. His death was ruled 'justifiable homicide' by the local authorities. FBI agents sent into Mississippi devoted more time to investigating civil rights activists than they did to hunting down white racist killers. While 'uppity' blacks continued to be lynched (between 1889 and 1940 3,833 people were lynched according to figures supplied by Alabama's all-black Tuskegee Institute). While white 'Freedom Rider' who headed south to help them were 'disappeared'. The disturbing 1988 movie *'Mississippi Burning'* recreates the circumstances surrounding the murder of three civil rights activists by the White Knights of the Ku Klux Klan in Philadelphia, Mississippi on 2nd June 1964. They were Michael Schwerner, head of the Congress of Racial Equality's local office, and volunteer Andrew Goodman—both white Jewish students from the north, plus twenty-one year-old volunteer James Chaney. They were arrested by deputy Cecil Price and other officers who turned out to be, like Sheriff Lawrence Rainey, members of the local Klan. Held in jail for six hours and severely beaten, reportedly with chains, they were then handed over to a lynch mob, taken to a swamp, shot and buried in a newly built earth dam. At first there was an official refusal to accept that murders had even taken place. It was even maintained that their 'disappearance' was faked to attract attention and funding. Eventually nineteen men were put on trial—not for murder, but for depriving the victims of their civil rights. The judges' attempts to dismiss all but two of the charges was overruled by the Supreme Court, yet only seven of the defendants were found guilty, and were sentenced to between three and five years. It was not until 2005 that Chaney's mother, Fannie Lee, was able to give evidence in the trial that levied Edgar Killen, a preacher who had masterminded the murders, a sixty-year prison sentence.

This was no liberal 'not-in-my-name' detachment. This was placing your life—very literally, on the line for what you believed. To oppose the monstrous evil of America's greatest historical scar. The 'Mississippi Freedom Summer' was an incandescent concoction of anger and revolutionary change, fuelled by music and the tantalising lure of new freedoms. Music was 'a weapon in the ceaseless battle against white terror that had to be waged town by town throughout the south' (says Mike Marqusee in *'Chimes Of Freedom'*). A music both echoing the activism on the streets, and capable of galvanising consciousness-raising radicalism. A music that carried the weight of those hopes and dreams, aspirations and anger. Nina Simone's "Mississippi Goddam" was wrought from the pain and anger provoked by a vile redneck bombing of a 16th Street Baptist Church in Birmingham—15th September 1963, in which four African-American girls were murdered (commemorated by Spike Lee as *'4 Little Girls'* (1997), while, a nine-year-old Condoleezza Rice recalls hearing the explosion as 'a sound I will never forget'). She followed it with "Backlash Blues" from lyrics supplied to her by author Langston Hughes. And turned yet another song—"Ain't Got No/ I Got Life", into a celebration of black pride and enduring defiance. Although not strictly hers, it was originally written for the hippie-musical *'Hair'*, from the first note—regardless of its provenance, she makes it her own. As her spellbinding performance at the 1969 Harlem Music Festival proves. Then she delivered the stirring "Four Women"—an impassioned protest against oppression that relates how 'I'm awfully bitter these days / because my parents were slaves'. Evoking echoes all the way back to Billie Holiday's haunting "Strange Fruit" which had been provoked by lynchings, and which Billie recorded for the indie Commodore Records label when John Hammond refused to risk such uncompromisingly inflammatory material with Columbia. The song was derived from a poem written by Abel Meeropol—as 'Lewis Allan', published in the January 1937 issue of the *'New York School Teacher'* union magazine.

On the 7th March 1965 a thousand demonstrators set out from Selma to walk the fifty-four miles to Montgomery, the Alabama State Capitol. The march was viciously broken up by local police and state troopers at the Pettus Bridge spanning the Alabama River. And TV viewers across America gawped in disbelief at them beating, clubbing and kicking men, women and children, dispersing the crowds with water-cannons and attack-dogs. A second march of 3,000, this time involving Martin Luther King, followed three days later, only to be turned back again. Now the District Judge was forced to issue a 'permit and protect' order and the National Guard were called out to preserve the peace. King finally presented a petition of black grievances on the steps of the state Capitol at the head of 25,000 marchers. After the Kennedy assassination LB Johnson confronted the reactionary atrocity of the KKK as a 'hooded society of bigots', and delivered a commencement address to the Howard University declaring his administration's determination 'to shatter forever not only the barriers of law and public practice, but the walls which bound the condition of many by the colour of his skin' (4th June 1965). Instead, freedom was a shot away. As the forces of reaction struck back. The white backlash, endorsed by the benign neglect of the law, combining with the social inertia drag-factors.

If change was gonna come, it was taking way too long…

****

Hipness is black. Hipness has always been black. The story of twentieth-century music is that of successive waves of black, or Afro-American music-styles spreading to inundate first what James Baldwin called these 'yet-to-be-United States', and then to globalise the world beyond. Freeing up and liberating social restrictions. Without enslaved people there would be no significant African presence in America. Then there would be no Blues, Jazz, R&B, Rock 'n' Roll, Reggae, Funk, or Hip-hop. Whether the one balances out the other… I don't know. Try explaining the moral equation to the poor wretch chained into the slave ship. But I get the impression that some hypothetical alternative slavery-free time-continuum—lacking those cultural inputs, isn't much fun. Hipness goes from 'Nick' La Rocca's Original Dixieland Jass Band studiously replicating the sounds of black New Orleans, thereby extending the world's introduction to the jazz record. From the young Bix Beiderbecke slouched on the banks of the Mississippi drawn away from strict adherence to his family's German Marching Band tradition by the luring sounds of jazz syncopations drifting in across the water from the riverboats. Teaching whitey to dance. Tracing down the black genealogy, first it was Dixieland, Storyville, Ragtime, Stride, Boogie-Woogie, and Swing. From the minority communities of New Orleans up the Mississippi igniting Chicago, Detroit, New York. Then London, Liverpool, Paris. Looting the detritus of European culture to add to its own, arriving at something wholly original and yet still somehow black. Forever restless, just as soon as it solidified into one style, it was renovating into Bebop, purposefully turning its back on its audience, who followed it anyway. And when it sophisticated away from mainstream audiences it electrified itself into R&B and reconquered the world. It's impossible to be moved by twentieth century music without acknowledging its black roots. Because, even before it fragmented into Rave or Dance Culture, Trip-Hop, House, Drum & Base, or Grime, its influences are everywhere.

Exuberant band-leader Cab Calloway had already crossed-over to mass celebrity and become a household name by the 1930s and beyond, using a twice-weekly national NBC-radio 'Live At The Cotton Club' show to leap the colour barrier. He sang and danced like no other performer of his time, tall, good-looking, and resplendent in a white zoot-suit, his stage presence was electric. Like Sly he utilised vocal histrionics, and wildly extrovert visuals to create a music that succeeded in being funny, energetic and subversive all at the same time, his audience call-and-response anticipating Ray Charles' "What'd I Say" routine by clear decades. He'd given up law school and turned down an offer to join the Harlem Globetrotters basketball team, instead he grabbed a passing dance-craze, popularising a variant of the Lindy-hop he called 'Jitterbug', sneaking sly narcotic subtexts into his songs that could be decoded only by those familiar with his hipster dictionary. 'Kicking the gong around' refers to smoking opium in a song called "Smokey Joe", or more explicitly there's "Reefer Man". His biggest hit, "Minnie The Moocher" happened in early 1931, first introduced during a live radio broadcast from Harlem's 'Cotton Club' where—to disguise the fact that he'd forgotten the lyrics, he improvised 'Hi-de-hi-de-hi-de-ho, Ho-de-ho-de-ho-de-hee'. In his autobiography *Of Minnie The Moocher And Me'* (1976) he recalls 'I asked the audience to join in, they hollered back and nearly brought the roof down'. It went on to become jazz's first million-seller, assisted by using three-minute film 'soundies' screened as cinema bonus-features as a promotional strategy to reach yet-wider pre-TV audiences, presaging the pop-video by decades. The much-repeated anecdote of his firing Bop-visionary Dizzy Gillespie from the band for playing 'Chinese notes' has less to do with musical reactionary tendencies, and more to do with prankster Dizzy pulling a knife and wounding him during a violent spat. By 1967 a now-sixty-year-old Cab Calloway was still around, joining Pearl Bailey as part of an all-black cast for a Broadway revival of 'Hello Dolly'. By then Sylvester Stewart had just turned 23. It'd be interesting to conjure a meeting between the two…? In 1980 Calloway introduced "Minnie The Moocher" to a new generational audience in the hit movie *'The Blues Brothers'*.

Then there was intergalactic visionary Sun Ra, connecting Africa to Chicago via NASA, by way of Saturn. An impeccably disciplined musician and avant-garde composer, by turn both spectacular and preposterous, his was a music that stayed barely within Earth's gravitational pull. Not only out on a limb, but suspended in space. Fiercely independent, his albums in their hand-painted sleeves were released through his own indie Saturn label and distributed by band-members after each performance, standing as an example of both community self-sufficiency and black entrepreneurialism. An early adopter of moog synthesiser with atmospheric compositions based around percussive textures, the solid band leading abilities and improvisational skills he co-ordinated for his 'Solar Arkestra' were light-years ahead of their time, laying the blueprints for those who followed, his startlingly visual space-robed showmanship and cosmic pretensions predating those of George Clinton by decades.

James Brown formed another vital cornerstone. His *'Live At The Apollo'* (1963) remains the live album by which all others are measured, and is still the best delineation of the raw power of primal soul. It propelled Mr Brown—with soloists of the calibre of trombonist Fred Wesley, sax-player Maceo Parker, and rhythm guitarists Jimmy Nolen and Phelps Collins, into the mainstream, paving the way for a string of propulsive breakthrough cross-over hits. "Papa's Got A Brand New Bag" (1965) took a giant step forward by shifting the beat from R&B's usual upbeat 'one-TWO-three-four' to Funk's downbeat 'ONE-two-free-four'. An evolution further refined on "Cold Sweat", (1967), "I'm Black And I'm Proud" (1968), and beyond. The message was encoded into its very rhythms, as a weapon to wake up America. A message that reclaimed the terms of blackness as a way of asserting identity even more powerfully than Martin Luther King. The year King was assassinated he went to Africa for the first time, stopped straightening his hair, and began buying up radio stations in an attempt to control how his message was heard. Yet his 'Apollo' album also formed a catalyst for many great soul stylists, from Otis Redding… to Sly Stone, while providing an early lesson in dynamics for a young Michael Jackson. As a black entrepreneur his take on civil rights was just as characteristically forthright and individualist—'I don't want nobody to give me nothing, open the door, I'll get it myself'.

Music evolves by creating new styles which are then picked up and developed by other musicians, provoked by new rhythmic possibilities, technologies or culture-clashes that then define what is and what is not a part of that genre. Without Cab Calloway or Sun Ra, what followed would not have been possible. Without Louis Jordan, Little Richard, Screaming Jay Hawkins, and Bo Diddley, there would be no Sly Stone. Just as without Sly Stone, much of the music that came later would not have happened. Of course, Funk grew out of R&B and Soul. Which in turn had come out of Gospel and Blues. It was part of an on-going tradition traceable clear back to the start of the century. Some academics trace it back even further, to Dahomean drum-choirs in a continuing dialogue back to Africa… so, Thank You For Talkin' To Me Africa!

The British Beat-Boom was powered by the primal energies of R&B. The highest compliment you could pay them was to say they 'sounded black'. From Cyril Davies, Alexis Korner, John Mayall, Long John Baldry, Eric Burdon, Stevie Winwood, they were all wiggas—'white niggas', striving to achieve 'black' authenticity. What Norman Mailer termed 'The White Negro'. Those bands would come back from touring the States enthusing how black radio stations were playing their records in the mistaken belief that they were black artists. During their earliest American tours the Rolling Stones even sought out the original source of their sound, the legendary Chess Studios to record in. One factor in the Stones remarkable longevity is their constant cleaving close to their default-setting of blackness—from selecting support acts, such as Ike & Tina Turner, to guest musicians Merry Clayton or Billy Preston on their records, or just down to the street-setting for the "Waiting For A Friend" promo-video. Jean-Luc Godard's film of the Rolling Stones' *'One + One'* (*'Sympathy For The Devil'*, 1968) includes scripted sequences posing an interview with black militants. 'What is the link between Communism and Black Power?' enquires the interviewer. 'Same old question' he sighs, before conceding 'the existence of Black Power is asking the same question'.

When Be-bop drummer Max Roach released his uncompromising *'Freedom Now Suite'* as early as 1960, his demands were unambiguously clear. Now Martin Luther King's book-title *'Where Do We Go From Here: Chaos Or Community?'* (Harper & Row, 1967, London, Penguin 1969) posed a more complex equation. Malcolm X's speech 'The Ballot Or The Bullet' posed it even better. As the decade accelerated, the flaws in King's pacifist gradualism were becoming more apparent. His eloquent 'Dream', the belief that once racism had been effectively broken down, everyone would become 'colour-blind' and blacks would be fully assimilated into US society, seemed ever more unobtainable. 'What films are recognised as the greatest works of American cinema?' asked director Spike Lee. '*'The Birth Of A Nation'*, *'Gone With The Wind'*. How do those films portray African-Americans—as eyes-rolling comic step 'n' fetchits? Hattie McDaniel, who played the bustling maid in *'Gone With The Wind'*, had the quote—'better to play a maid than be one'. That's true. But we're still living with those hurtful, stereotypical images'.

Against such social drag-factors, Civil Rights, anti-Segregation, and voter registration had only recently—and grudgingly, been enforced by law. They'd delivered all they could, too little and too late, leaving those supposedly freed still mired in poverty and second-class citizenship. The contradictions stayed just as entrenched—the gots and the ain't-gots, the included and excluded, insiders and outsiders, alienated and the privileged. What happens when your way forward runs up against a brick-wall?—you gotta shove harder. And 'Keep on Pushing'. Soon, frustrated by this impasse, reacting to the turmoil spreading across the land, the liberal-gradualists and the radical-militants arrived at a parting of the ways. A new generation of more impatient groups began advocating more extreme measures to achieve their goals of social empowerment, full justice and equality. Rejecting non-violence, it marked a paradigm shift from pacifist pathfinder into armed resistance. Students for a Democratic Society, the Weather Underground, and the Yippies advocated various degrees of retaliatory action. George Jackson coolly observed that 'the concept of non-violence is a false ideal. It presupposes the existence of compassion and a sense of justice on the part of one's adversary. When this adversary has everything to lose and nothing to gain by exercising justice and compassion, his reaction can only be negative'. Vigilante racists showed no qualms about using violence to wage war against black aspirations. Why should their response be limited to non-violence? James Brown caught the mood of the time with 'we'd rather die on our feet / than be livin' on our knees' (in "Say It Loud, I'm Black And I'm Proud").

The evolving black ideologies of the time coalesced into strands of cultural nationalism. This gets complicated. Stick with it. Marcus Garvey, promoting an eventual return to Africa, and Booker T Washington advocating a separate socio-economic system for blacks, both laid the foundations. The Nation of Islam and the Black Nationalist Movement declared that because all black men were already equal, the white man was the enemy. Even with full desegregation blacks would still be dominated by whites so long as they were part of a majority white nation. The only way to achieve full racial equality was through self-determination—armed insurrection leading to the separation of races and the formation of an independent black state, one perhaps located in the southern 'black zone' where a marginal black majority already existed. It called for African-Americans to make the conscious choice of nurturing and promoting their own ethnic values rather than looking to others to validate them. To identify with their own historical struggle, and use it to help themselves. As James Brown—again, advocates, 'now we demand a chance to do things for yourself / we're tired of beatin' our head against the wall'. To 'assimilate' into white society as King proposed, would equate to the dilution of black culture, loss of Afrocentric heritage and of a distinctive black identity. To them, integration was a betrayal of black pride. LeRoi Jones had already built a formidable reputation as one of the more influential Greenwich Village Beat Generation poets and writers, then as a leader of the Harlem black arts movement, and editor of the *'Cricket'* lit-mag. By the mid-sixties he no longer felt able to associate with whites, took the Muslim name Amiri Baraka—more in keeping with his separatist ideals, and extended the racial severance to include his white wife Hettie, and their children. Why Islam? Because it was a voice speaking out in clear opposition to the materialist western hegemony. And if it wasn't actually black, at least it was non-white. The only other oppositional world-voice was Communism, and black militants took selectively from that too, especially its spray-painted Maoist strand which stressed the role of a revolutionary guerrilla elite moving through the oppressor culture 'like fish through water', supported by their sympathetic sub-class. Baraka's writing assumed a more militant black Marxist perspective with incendiary essays titled "Black is a Country" and "What Does Non-Violence Mean?"

What had germinated in the simple collective unity of singing "We Shall Overcome" had taken on unexpected complications, with converging and frequently opposing strands. Factions such as African Internationalism, National Black Assembly, Congress of African Peoples (CAP), Black United Front and the Marxist Revolutionary Action Movement (RAM) all had their own agendas. They tended to wear African dress and learn Swahili, even though it was increasingly difficult for black Americans to make any special claim to African cultural orientation. Any more than Irish-Americans were still Irish, or Italian-Americans still Italian. When Alex Haley took his ancestral roots-journey back to Africa he wasn't welcomed as a trans-Atlantic long-lost cousin. All they saw was another well-heeled American tourist ripe for fleecing. Africa was the ancestral homeland that was no longer home. But after all, it was black labour that helped build the United States in the first place, so weren't they entitled to an inclusive share of its material rewards? It was into this theoretical quagmire that the Black Panthers party roared, to form the vanguard of the movement.

The Panther story largely orbits one man—Dr Huey Percy Newton, the seventh son of a Louisiana sharecropper transplanted to Oakland. Bobby Seale first met him when Newton, then aged about 23, was haranguing a street corner gathering during the Cuba Crisis. He was young, lean, handsome and extremely dangerous. Other connections were also being fused during those days of tension. Angela Davis encountered New Left theorist Herbert Mercuse during a rally, and became his student. Huey Newton was attending Oakland City College while struggling to master Mao, Frantz Fanon, Malcolm X, Che Guevara, and Plato. Over the next few years of shared political development Bobby Seale gradually got to know him better. What particularly impressed his younger acolyte—and California was full of bullshit artists, was the way Newton would construct arguments in concrete ways by seldom deviating from hard facts. His was the rare leadership ability of expressing complex ideas with a simplicity that anyone could understand. Newton had managed to become an intellectual without ever losing contact with ordinary people, a way of retaining a kind of solidarity with them. Slowly he developed an enviable double reputation of being both someone for the West Coast black movement to take seriously, and also a man who the 'brothers' on the block would have to reckon with personally if they crossed him. 'The bad cats terrorised the community—and Huey terrorised the bad cats'. He had a prison record for assault to prove it.

Simultaneously, Malcolm 'X' Little made the 'hajj' pilgrimage to Mecca on 19th April 1964, and split from the Nation of Islam. A confrontationist of frightening intensity, he was born mixed-race in Omaha in 1925. He later claimed to hate 'every drop of that white rapist's blood that is in me'—the genetic legacy that had bequeathed his hair its reddish tinge. He grew up in foster-homes, and worked as a shoe-shiner at the 'Lindy Hop' club where he once shined for Duke Ellington. He used prison-time to study voraciously in the penitentiary library, so that on emerging after serving time for drug-dealing and burglary he became El-Hajj Malik El-Shabazz, and subscribed to the ideology of black pride, economic self-reliance, and black cultural nationalism. Soon, his fiery oratorical skills, organisational abilities and tireless work began attracting attention. From people like Huey Newton.

The one thing most people think they know about the Black Panthers is that they despise white people. The Truth is that the Party was founded on a split from the nationalists on exactly that question. Huey Newton knew it was illogical to hate white people for simply being white. Influenced by RAM's 'revolutionary cadre' he concluded there was no great difference between a white capitalist and a black one, and that the problem was primarily one of class, not race. For Black Panthers this meant the realignment of American economic policies to benefit everyone—including other races, all those who were being crushed beneath the weight of big-business capitalism. Newton knew those things not so much from RAM's Marxist or Maoist agitation, but from his own experience. Just as he knew that the brothers on the block were not going to be impressed by African robes and lectures on black history. 'Power for the people doesn't grow out of the sleeve of a dashiki' decided Panther Fred Hampton, 'political power flows from the barrel of a gun'. He was part-quoting Mao. But it was over the issue of guns that the final break came.

Stokely Carmichael was going through a similar ideological shift. He'd first gained national prominence as populariser of the 'Black Power' slogan while president of the SNCC. He'd participated in the 220-mile 'March Against Fear' through Mississippi in the summer of 1966. Organised by James Meredith—who was shot by a sniper on its second day, Carmichael aroused the marchers at a rally in Greenwood by seizing the moment proclaiming 'What we need is black power'. The chant was taken up as the platform shouted 'What do you want?' and the crowd roared back 'BLACK POWER' again and again until it reached fever pitch. If there was a moment marking the shift in the black freedom struggle, the tactical split, this was it. Following 1966, Stokely Carmichael became active in organising Freedom Rides and voter-registration campaigns in the south (including the Lowndes County drive)… but just a year later he quit to join the Black Panther Party, where he eventually rose to become its 'Prime Minister' and to eventually assume a new identity as Kwame Ture.

Stokely Carmichael is the man most associated with the term 'Black Power'. But he did not originate it. That was writer Robert F Williams. Publisher of the influential militant periodical *'The Crusader'*, Williams was a NAACP activist who had disseminated the manifesto *'Negroes With Guns'* as early as 1962, recounting the history of armed struggle against the Klan, articulating the principle of retaliatory self-defence. Although by then Williams was on the run in Cuba and China following the kidnapping of a KK Klansman, Stokely Carmichael's posture of armed militancy was a conscious reflection of that vision. 'Power' he said, is the 'only thing respected in this world'. When he called for 'black people… to unite, to recognise their heritage, to build a sense of community… to define their goals, to lead their own organisations, and to support those organisations… a call to reject the racist institutions and values of this society' (*'Black Power: The Politics of Liberation in America'*, Vintage Books, 1967), he was echoing Robert Williams. Huey Newton was also reading the tract, and found its argument irrefutable. Finding strength and confirmation—as well as political justification there, he put the policy of armed response to the group they belonged to, every member but one—Bobby Seale, rejected it. So the two of them split away, and the Black Panther Party was launched. 'And that's how it happened' explained Seale, 'the college boys—the cultural nationalists, all that bullshit, jiving dudes who articulate bullshit all the time and don't ever want to get into the real practice of revolutionary struggle, the black liberation struggle in this country—Huey'd say 'well, later for them. We'll go to the streets'. And I'd say 'Huey, I'm with you, brother. Let's go on and do it'. So we went on out into the streets, and that was it'.

Malcolm X was another who acknowledged a debt to Williams' tract. The 20th March 1964 issue of *'Life'* ran an iconic image of him brandishing an M1 Carbine in his right hand while pulling back the curtains with the other, peering out the window into the street. An image interpreted as evidence of his readiness to use armed resistance. He'd started out by reiterating that the black community had the right to defend itself—'the time for you and me to allow ourselves to be brutalised non-violently has passed. Be non-violent only with those who are non-violent to you', supplying much of the rhetoric, style and attitude of Black Power, yet later he revised those views and split off to form the more conciliatory Organisation of Afro-American Unity (OAAU). In the internecine struggle that followed he was gunned down on stage in the Washington Heights 'Audubon Ballroom' on 21st February 1965. He was shot sixteen times. Three members of the Nation of Islam were convicted—supposedly acting on behalf of Elijah Muhammad who Malcolm had denounced, although the inevitable conspiracy theorists began accusing government agencies. Amiri Baraka commemorated his death with the essay *'The Legacy of Malcolm X & The Coming of the Black Nation'*. Spike Lee made the movie *'Malcolm X'* in 1992, with Denzel Washington taking the title role.

Meanwhile, Seale (Chairman) and Newton (Minister of Defence), with David Hilliard, Richard Aoki, Earl Anthony, and a skeletal core of allies, founded the 'Black Panther Party For Self-Defence' in October 1966 in the wake of massive black urban uprisings in the LA Watts ghetto. Even the name they chose was far from random—the black panther had proved a powerful visual symbol for the short-lived Alabama voter-registration Lowndes County Freedom Organisation. While the image itself carried the subliminal warning—this beast is dangerous, when attacked—it defends itself! And it happened in Oakland, the black ghetto suburb of San Francisco strategically situated next door to the University of California at Berkeley—itself a community of some 35,000, which had already been convulsively radicalised by the 1964 Free Speech Movement. In fact Berkeley was renowned as the fountainhead of the student rebellion and campus uprisings of the sixties, a haven for radicals and revolutionaries, a hotbed of communism, Marxism, socialism and whatever other ism might be current at the moment.

While around the same time, a little way across the city, The Family Stone were rehearsing at Leo Kulka's 'Loadstone' studio, plotting a different—but related kind of direct action. Bobby Seale's *'Seize The Time: The Story Of The Black Panther Party'* (Arrow Books, 1970, Random House 1971, Baltimore Black Classic Press 1991) was vigorously reviewed by Clive Goodwin in the December issue of *'Oz no. 31'*. Seale talked his book straight into a tape recorder, with the prose emerging hot and fresh, an angry but eloquent critique direct from the streets. It explains how Oakland became the scene of some of the Panther's first and most violent student struggles, until they carried campaign-scars from many different conflict-zones. Their ten-point programme was drawn up, and—financed by reselling Mao's book to Berkeley students. And they started buying guns. But first 'Huey studied those law books, backwards, forwards, sideways, and catty-corners, everything on gun laws. And I was right there with him, trying to study them too, run them down, and understand them'. Such research indicated to them that according to the California Penal Code it was legal—even for a black man!, to bear arms, to walk the streets carrying a loaded gun. They proceeded to put that discovery to the test.

From a small Oakland-based group, the Panthers built chapters throughout the country. Eldridge Cleaver, originally from Arkansas but brought up in LA, had also been politicised by reading Malcolm X while serving time for drug-dealing and rape (he later justified the rape of white women as 'an insurrectionary act'). Once released he joined the Oakland Panthers in 1966 where, encouraged by the success of his *'Soul on Ice'* (1968)—essays he'd written in jail distinguished by the same energy as Bobby Seale's *'Seize The Time'* (1970), and the enthusiastic support of white liberals as well as the black community, he worked his way up the hierarchy. With Cleaver as their 'Minister of Information', the Panthers' oriented around a kind of community-based self-help black autonomy that involved the right to control the schools, medical centres, welfare programmes, and police system in poor black areas—'Survival

Programs: Pending Revolution'. They initiated 'liberation schools', health-care clinics in poor areas, plus a Free Breakfast programme for children, which began in the Fillmore district and spread to some forty-eight States. For through it all, in and around the words, Seale's book is not all shoot-outs and dramatic gestures. A lot of it is concerned with the day-to-day grind of organisation, education and agitation. That is the way revolutionary parties are built.

But this eminently sensible community-approach sounded too much like socialism to the McCarthy-tuned sensitivities of the great and the good. The FBI denounced the Black Panther Party as communists bent on overthrowing the US government. They were especially unnerved by the add-on bits about the right to bear arms for self-protection. That, combined with their demand for exemption from military service—and their strident anti-war activities designed to discourage Afro-Americans from supporting the Vietnam war. The reasoning went that Civil Rights weren't merely a struggle of black against white, so much as a struggle for common humanity. So far so obvious, until Vietnam. Was Vietnam also a war for common humanity, or was it the common struggle of oppressed 'peoples of colour' against white oppressors—whether it occurred in SE Asia, or Oakland? Miles Davis saw it as 'they sent us to war to fight and die for them over there, killed us like nothing over here. And it's still like that today. Now, ain't that a bitch!' According to Huey's 'Intercommunalism' analysis, American blacks and the Vietnamese people were comrades-in-arms waging a struggle against the same enemy—the US government. As race-riots spread across America in the summers between 1964 and 1968, RAM mobilised local underground cells to politicise the spontaneous actions into urban rebellions. It was this that would lead to confrontations with the police, to shootings and arrests. When Cassius Clay converted to the Nation of Islam under the influence of Malcolm X, rejecting his 'slave name' to become Muhammad Ali, he refused the draft —'hell no, I won't go', because he 'had no argument' with those people overseas. By doing so he was showing his solidarity with the Panther's step-by-step programme. Athletes Tommie Smith and bronze-winner John Carlos too, they gave the black-gloved raised-fist Black Power salute at the 1968 Mexico Summer Olympics. Placing it firmly at the centre of the national agenda (although in his autobiography Tommie argued it as a 'human rights salute')…

The confrontations that followed are a part of cultural, and subcultural history. One of the first and most famous confrontations happened outside the 'Ramparts' office when the Panthers were providing a guard for Malcolm X's widow. 'One of the brothers had his back turned on the pigs and I guess Huey saw the cops pulling the straps off the hammers all of a sudden, so Huey says 'turn around. Don't turn your back on those back-shooting mother-fuckers!' Just like that. We all turned around. I turned around, Little Joe turned around, Little Bobby turned around, and Huey goes 'Spread!' and jacks a shell off into the chamber of his gun...' The action-drama unfolds like a western. And that was the point. It was a kind of street theatre with a political lesson every Afro-American could understand. 'If you live in a ghetto surrounded by armed white troopers any one of whom can shoot you down and think little of it, then you can get so used to living with fear, it becomes so much a part of you, that you don't even recognise it. But when Huey Newton stood up with a gun in his hand he stood up for every black man. When he made those swaggering racist motherfucking cops back down he walked into history by creating the heroic myth that all revolutions need'. Of course, they could have shot him immediately. But he did something that millions had only ever dreamed of doing, and he lived.

According to media-guru Marshall McLuhan, 'the media is the message'. And the Panthers were playing the media-game expertly. Every conservative bigot's nightmare, they soon claimed a membership numbering 5000. Exploiting white liberal guilt they had celebrity and society hosts falling over themselves to associate with them in what became known as 'radical chic'. Tom Wolfe coined the term in an essay about Leonard Bernstein hosting an evening for the Panthers. For a white woman to engage in sex with a Panther—the more 'street' the better, could be intellectualised as an act of reparation, an expiation of racial guilt for the institutionalised rape of slavery. Something the 'brothers' took full advantage of. In 1972 novelist John Berger donated the prize-money from his 'Booker Award'-winning 'G' to the Black Panthers. Long before then the authorities realised their mistake. It seemed they were appearing in the Panther's combustible games, instead of writing their own. It was time they took back the initiative, which began a war which continued...

****

All very intriguing—but what's it got to do with Sylvester Stewart and his jive-assed band? Everything. It has to, otherwise the whole story makes no sense. Precisely at the time that the Family Stone's upward arc was nearing its point of critical mass, so was the continent. So was the world beyond. Suddenly, the sky was no limit at all. For the first time in human history people were orbiting the Earth outside of that sky. With one hand reaching for the moon, and the other teeter-circling the Armageddon nuclear-button a touch away from global extinction, all—or nothing was possible. While race-war smouldered on the brink of igniting the United States in an inferno of riot-torched cities, shocking the complacency of American society all the way down to its roots, and all the way up to its ruling class. It was intellectually exciting—if scary, to be at the epicentre of such fundamental changes, to have mass uprisings radiating out of your own neighbourhood. The Panthers seemed to represent the sole progressive organisation in the long history of the war against slavery and oppression, one that was armed and promoting a revolutionary agenda, initiating the final epic thrust for racial equality, justice and freedom. It was impossible not to be touched by it. As a black artist, there was no middle ground. As a successful black artist, there could be no neutral zone. As an Afro-American, there could be no opt-out. As the bumper-sticker says, you are part of the disease, or you are part of the cure.

Larry Neal wrote in his 'Visions Of A Liberated Future', 'the political values inherent in the Black Power Concept are now finding concrete expression in the aesthetics of Afro-American dramatists, poets, choreographers, musicians and novelists'. Artists express the consciousness of the movement. Sly's songs deal with racial issues. There was no way he could have avoided dealing with them. To brother Freddie, 'Sly is a thinker. He is very much concerned about what's going on with the world right now'. But even if he'd not made that concern lyrically explicit—which he did, the make-up of the band itself was a racial provocation. By its very nature it took a stance on the issue of assimilation, and against separatism. Soon, he'd be called to task because of it. *'Rolling Stone'* magazine was quick to point out that Sly & The Family Stone were 'the first McLuhan soul group…' And initially, while the black media largely approved of the Family Stone, it was already finding them impossible to pigeonhole. Just as its white equivalent was.

Sly & The Family Stone were infused with the beautifully confusing new-dawn vibes reverberating from Haight-Ashbury, but they were also taking it further. As Charles Shaar Murray pointed out 'Santana, Sly and the Electric Flag… weren't really bracketed with the others. Geographically, they were just as San Francisco as anybody else, but presumably they weren't psychedelic enough to enter the magic circle' (*'New Musical Express'* 15th June 1974). In fact, if the Frisco bands constituted a very white scene, Sly was filling a vacuum. They were augmenting those new-dawn vibes in ways that the other bands could not, by providing a music to work out the counter-culture's racial contradiction. Uniting factions even beyond the anti-establishment kaleidoscopic hippie sprawl, by also riding the almost inconceivable degrees of hope wrapped up in the civil rights movement. Together, it was a utopian wave that seemed on the event-horizon of transfiguring the continent into a more vibrant, more aware, more inclusive place. Could the world have ever held that much hope, that much innocent belief that things could only get better? Yes, it could. Lillian Roxon, the sharp *'New York Sunday News'* writer recognised what was going on, 'Sly & The Family Stone are probably the first example of what might eventually become a whole new movement—psychedelic soul, the almost inevitable fate, come to think of it, for anyone young, lively and impressionable singing soul in psychedelic San Francisco'.

From the white hippie perspective, racial separation in the counter-culture was never an issue. Their Bop-crazy Beatnik heritage would have none of that. The question was once posed to me about the first great wave of Rock 'n' Roll, were the black performers—Little Richard, Larry Williams, Chuck Berry, Frankie Lymon, viewed differently to their white counterparts—Elvis Presley, Jerry Lee Lewis or Buddy Holly? And it's not as straightforward a question as it appears. Of course there are differences, each artist and each record they make is different, and you love them for different reasons. But on racial lines? It's impossible to compare and contrast one against the other. No-one could do Little Richard like the godlike Mr Penniman himself. Not even Elvis could come close when he attempted "Long Tall Sally" or "Tutti Frutti". But the real answer is no, what is most important is that we were all on the same side, they were one of us against the common foe, which was the dull grey conformist world of morally uptight squaredom. Same for Sly. All the sixties bands were different. But they inhabited the same biosphere, they were part of us, up against the repressive conventional straight world. I felt closer—in attitude, to Sly, than I did to my own parents. We were on the same side, beyond whatever apparent divisions. Until Black Power started preaching separation.

Chapter Six
'A Whole New Thing'

'A fantastic mixture of rock, blues, jazz—and yes, baby, tons and tons of Soul'

New York DJ Al Gee on Sly & The Family Stone

'Groovy People, How Do You Do...?'
("Are You Ready?")

But artists need not only creativity and skill, they also need access to the tools of production, they need studios, mixing desks... mass distribution outlets. Record labels had a stranglehold on the industry, there was no internet file-sharing, no download sales, no music videos either. As Sly had discovered to his cost with 'Autumn', if you have no major-label deal, you have no record career. Clive Davis—a former lawyer, was in his first year as president of Columbia Records (CBS in the UK), a long-established easy-listening middle-of-the-road company specialising in the fifties balladry of Andy Williams, Percy Faith, Ray Conniff, and Doris Day. The label's tired fortunes had been partially rejuvenated through John Hammond's off-centre signing of Bob Dylan in 1962—dubbed 'Hammond's Folly' by the sniffily conservative label suits, then the Byrds, Simon & Garfunkel, and Paul Revere & The Raiders. But then Clive took a trip to the Monterey Pop Festival. And once there, sitting beneath the psychedelic spell in perfect sunshine, he saw a shining vision of Rock's future. He took to wearing love beads and a Nehru jacket, and began waving the corporate cheque-book. Across a few years of frenzied recruiting he acquired Big Brother & The Holding Company (with Janis Joplin), Laura Nyro, Blood Sweat & Tears, and Johnny Winter. Amplified by contagious PR rumour, this was where the CBS hit machine tuned in and turned on. And the cash expectations of groups hunting record deals took off with the kind of escape-velocity acceleration that was blasting

Mercury astronauts into orbit. The programme was keyed into high-profile ad-campaigns proclaiming 'The Rock Machine Turns You On', 'The Man Can't Bust Our Music', and a seductive invitation to 'Join The Revolution'. As a result of this burst of subversive activity by 1969 the company had achieved well-balanced and extremely profitable year-end figures…

David Kapralik was embedded deep within the CBS corporate entity, as head of Columbia/Epic A&R (Artist and Repertoire). By his own definition he was a 'middle-class New York-born humanist liberal Jewish prince'. A neurotic 5'6" gay over-forties entrepreneur with a ten-year career more concerned with comfortable lounge-core artists than cutting-edge Rock. He'd overseen the signing of Barbra Streisand, Dino Valenti, and Andy Williams to the label. He also signed Cassius Clay. But he had experience of working alongside John Hammond too, the man who signed Aretha Franklin, and was a major force in bringing Robert Johnson's *'King Of The Delta Blues Singers'* onto the catalogue in 1961. It was Kapralik who introduced Bob Dylan to producer Tom Wilson in time for them to collaborate on the 1962-'63 *'Freewheeling'* sessions. He also encountered a band called The Sparrow by way of their manager Stanton J Freeman, and was sufficiently impressed to get them a Columbia deal in mid-1966. Although they failed to break through, a subsequent name-change to Steppenwolf elevated them into the big-time.

Briefly Kapralik dropped out—or was 'horizontaled out' of, the label to kick-start his own management, production and publishing company, starting out by representing sweet chart-soul duo Peaches & Herb. But he rejoined Columbia's Epic subsidiary soon after at Clive Davis' invitation, while retaining his own 'stable' of artists—Peaches & Herb, the Spellbinders… and then Sly Stone. Word trickled down. This 'interesting' potential signing had first been spotted by San Francisco promotions man Chuck Gregory. The term 'promotions man', perhaps unfairly, brings to mind the Rolling Stones' 'Under Assistant West Coast Promotion Man', the 'necessary talent behind every Rock 'n' Roll band', the man with the corvette and the seersucker suit who promo's bands when they come into town. Nevertheless, it was he who enthusiastically communicated his find to Kapralik. David's curiosity was sufficiently intrigued to hop a westbound flight, and follow-up on the lead. He followed it all the way to the 'Winchester Cathedral' Club, where he instantly discovered he'd walked into a vibrantly celebratory environment, high on energy but with none of the threatening East Coast heavy vibes. The place was jam-packed. No space for dancing. Standing room only. He was blown away by what he saw. If he'd had a seat, he'd have been sat on the edge of it.

After the gig Chuck, Sly, and Kapralik adjourned to a nearby 'International House of Pancakes', sitting in the 'IHOP' booth warily checking each other out. At the time, Rich Romanello was still acting as the group's manager. Kapralik extended his stay to a week, hanging out day-to-day with Sly, sitting in on his radio show. Sly had a college student named Bill Lacy acting as unpaid chauffeur, picking him up from KDIA in Oakland, driving him to Sly's apartment on Haight Street—between Gough and Laguna, then on to the precipitous streets of North Beach or wherever the band was playing. Soon David knew everything there was to know about Sly's ahead-of-the-curve track record as hit producer. And he was itching to sign him. 'Have you ever in your life had those people you met who you just had an inner knowledge about? Your intuition was beyond language, beyond physiognomy, beyond characteristics?' Kapralik was talking money, a whole lot of money, real money—he told Sly 'I know I can help you make all your dreams come true', so things were getting to sound good. And they duly inked. With Sly & The Family Stone added to the Epic roster, the older, more sophisticated Kapralik also became not only the group's manager, but also Sly's partner and co-conspirator. But if David saw this as being a smart move, the experience of overseeing the burgeoning career of his new charges would take the elfish one-time Columbia executive drop-out into many strange new unexpected, and not altogether healthy dimensions.

So was David Kapralik about to become to the Family Stone what Brian Epstein had been to the Beatles, or Colonel Tom Parker had been to Elvis Presley? No. Nothing could be further from the truth. It was always Sly who called the shots. Sly was nobody's fool. Nobody's man. When you negotiate with Sly & The Family Stone, you talk to Sly. And to no-one else. He's the decision-maker. And that's a tendency that would become more pronounced. He was the ringleader exerting absolute control over every aspect of the music from writing and producing, all the way to the performance. He controlled the image. There were management attempts to 'glam-up' the girls from slacks into gowns. They didn't like the idea. Sly backed them against the label. Brian Epstein may have redesigned his potty-mouthed leather-clad protégés into cuddly loveable mop-tops. But when Clive Davis once took Sly aside and pointed out to him that their lurex and satin stage apparel might detract from their reputation as serious musicians, that it might deter plays on underground FM radio, Sly carefully considered his comments. Then decided to ignore them, and the outfits became even more extravagant. Sly didn't do *nothing* halfway. If he was going to be outrageous, he was going to do it better than anybody else ever did. 'When you're dealing with a pathfinder, you allow that genius to unfold' shrugs Clive Davis. It was Sly's decision to make. For Kapralik, managing Sly was 'managing the unmanageable'.

There was just one input Sly needed, and one only. He'd been burned by his first experience with the industry, with 'Autumn'. He was determined he would never let that happen again. What he needed was someone on his side, a buffer at the corporate interface, someone to translate the contractual and accounting aspects of the deal, to work through the small details of marketing and touring. An industry insider, one of the fancy suits, but a fancy suit working on their behalf. A tame suit. This was to be David's role. Sly could do the rest. As it turned out, Kapralik would become much more than just that. He was the perfect foil. A level-headed, knowledgeable, business-smart, computing-brain who was one-hundred-percent behind, ahead of, and on top of just about everything there was to do with the group's career. With the Epic contract pocketed, with Kapralik working on their behalf, the Family Stone rapidly upgraded from appearances at venues such as 'Lil' Bo Peeps' in San Francisco's Excelsior—a club in which Bubba had an interest, or regular 'Winchester Cathedral' weekenders, to a Las Vegas residency. Right up to this point, Sly was still DJ-ing from KDIA, 'but Sly was always itching to move' station co-manager Bill Doubleday grumbles, as he waved goodbye. 'He didn't want a full-time job. He wanted time for his band. Finally, around Christmas of '67, he went to Las Vegas, and that did it…' The end of Sly's radio-DJ career. From now on he'd be making the records, not spinning them.

To Kapralik, all that was necessary now was for the Family Stone to be seen, and to be heard. Surely, once exposed, it would be obvious to everyone that here was a band with an unrivalled stage presence and charisma. Those fortunate enough to see them, and hip enough to know what they were seeing, *must* recognise that this is the band to turn Pop on its head, they must realise that this *has* to be the future of Rock 'n' Soul. Because it sounds like nothing else you're ever likely to hear on the radio. His game-plan forecast a journey ahead that would begin with Vegas, then move clear across the continent to New York, and beyond. But it was never going to be quite the even-paced or straightforward path he envisaged for them. It was not to be a mapped-out world. The three-month residency at the Las Vegas 'Pussycat á Go-Go' casino-cum-disco was their first major out-of-Frisco engagement. And the stint began with a gaudy Family Stone motorcade cruising through the 'Sin City' limits and down the central strip, past 'Caesar's Palace' where the neon madmen climb. Sly first, driving his 1957 purple Thunderbird with its paisley top. Next came Freddie also in a 1957 T-Bird, only his was pink with a white top. Then Larry's. His was a turquoise 1955 model with a paisley top.

Las Vegas is a city where show-biz flows in its life-blood. But was its glossy superficiality right for a unit like the Family Stone? What other Frisco group could have played Vegas? None of them. Kapralik's intention was to get his new signings noticed. And—unique to the city, the 'Pussycat' *did* have a policy of featuring rock acts. Gary Puckett & Union Gap, Stark Naked & The Car Thieves, and the Enemys—featuring future Three Dog Night vocalist Cory Wells, all played there. Ike & Tina Turner headlined there prior to Sly, separated only by a month's residency by the Boogie Kings. But the Family Stone were different. Their costumes, their razzmatazz, they had cabaret impact. Their Soul was a psychedelic sun-splash bursting with joy and invention, bright with melodies and kaleidoscopic arrangements, inextricably intertwined vocal and instrumental interplay over deft fast rhythms. Bill Doubleday acknowledged 'the Family Stone always had a showmanship most other local bands couldn't muster'. While—although his stilted prose-style succeeds in missing the point, an early review in the British colour Pop weekly *'Record Mirror'* observes that 'let's be fair… there's no room for delicacy of touch when this outfit is on the move. They go for a party atmosphere and really hammer into everything in sight. Good for dancing, strong on the ear, but relentless in the way they whack into tough numbers'. The unnamed journalist closed by admitting 'sometimes I felt like begging for a little subtlety, but then the Family Stone are merciless, musically' (January 1969). By Vegas, the major part of the Family Stone's 'merciless' set was made up of originals. They did some crowd-pleasing covers—from Sam & Dave to "Land Of A Thousand Dances", but they were done the band's way.

Kapralik's strategy worked to the extent that word was soon getting around town. Located at 3255 South Las Vegas Blvd the club, showcasing its mini-skirted go-go dancers, stayed open for business till late, with bands performing for the revellers until 6am. Hence it tended to attract after-hours clientele from other Vegas fun-palaces. The bored waitresses out to score some good times, the night-owl showgirls, tired bar-tenders, the more hyper-aware tourists, and post-show performers from the strip itself. James Brown and his entourage called in to check them out. After all, the Godfather had encountered Sly in his DJ/MC guise in Frisco. And Mr Brown knew upstart talent when he saw it. On "Pappa's Got A Brand New Bag", he'd already boasted on record 'I can dig that new breed, Babe' (US no. 8 in August 1965). And something about Sly Stone's latest incarnation said that *this* was that new breed, the genuine real deal. Then Nino Tempo—Phil Spector alumni with his own duo chart-toppers with April Stevens, sat in with the Family Stone, joining in with his fluent alto. Bobby Darin was also working the Strip, cabaret slick—but with a beating heart of social awareness, he brought a bunch of people around. He was suitably impressed. Fifth Dimension dropped by to say 'hello'. Rose would sneak a line from their June 1967 hit "Up, Up And Away" into "Music Lover" on the *'Dance To The Music'* album, by way of acknowledgement. But while the bosses, the show-girls and the middle-class dealers were living out on the city's Hoover Dam side, the luminous Strip concealed the slum on the north side—where the Family Stone were holed up in the El Rancho, a motel for tourists seeking Vegas-on-a-budget, stumbling out of the air-conditioning system direct into the god-awful 120-degrees Nevada desert-heat. Dust infesting everything. And from where, at night, the towers of the city could be seen glowing from miles out.

There were other distractions, and some fear and loathing in Las Vegas too. Sly met Anita ('Nita) who worked the club. And they fell in lust. He was really into her. She was the white ex-girlfriend of the club's owner. She was what Jerry Martini described as 'cute, but a spoiled little bitch… a real pretty, high maintenance chick'. It was Las Vegas 1967, an adult theme-park with neon flashing and one-armed bandits crashing, fortunes won and lost on every deal—Elvis Presley had married Priscilla Beaulieu at the 'Aladdin Hotel' there only a few months previous (1st May 1967), but it was still a straight racially uptight town. Jim Morrison was arrested outside the 'Pussycat' on the pretext of brawling and public drunkenness after his mixed-race group of friends had been thrown out of the club, but that was 28th January 1968, by then the Family Stone were long-gone. The club owner threatened to fire Nita because he disapproved of her 'going out' with a black man. Sly got into a verbal confrontation with him in the back room. It got increasingly physical. The club owner pulled a gun, brandished it, and gave the band two hours to get out of Vegas. Sly wasn't having none of that. He said he'd quit anyway, and 'I'm taking my band with me'. So the residency ended with the gaudy Family Stone motorcade cruising down the central strip and winding its way out through the city-limits back towards Frisco. Only this time Sly was taking Nita with him…

****

This is the story of Sylvester Stewart. Which makes it also the story of 'Sly Stone', Sylvester's more extrovert invention. The alter-ego persona he could assume when and as required, the deliberate exaggeration that he could take off after the show. A whole new personality to play with, but one that would eventually consume and destroy him. Since the Vallejo days, people had found themselves intrigued by the charm Sly could so easily switch on, speaking from the very bottom of his richly subterranean basso-profundo radio-voice. In person, he came on as a beautiful young dude, smooth-skinned, wiry, surprisingly willowy, with endless legs and long slender fingers. Never less than hip, he moved so sinuously and so into his music that he even walked in tempo. Zero in closer, the mystique re-centred on his eyes, as dark brown and liquid as his voice. Sometime later he'd take to wearing big floppy 'Sly Stone' hats, and aviator wrap-around hipster shades occluding those eyes. He was a whirligig of ego, a dervish of energy and appetites—both for music and for less lofty vices, a creature of acute artistic restlessness. But beneath the red rhinestone suits and electrified Afro like a frothing mutation of the scalp, the skimpy tank-tops, diamante flares and proto-Glam platform boots, you sensed there still lurked a fine 'Sylvester' sensitivity. While there was something else in the mischievous half-angelic half-amoral curl to the lips, something of the clever, wilful child about him, a feeling of spirited malice that he got away with because his inventive patter was so humorously engaging. He may flirt with neon-gangster imagery and confrontational issues, allied to his increasingly assertive and keen competitive streak, but there was also an engaging vulnerability to his profile, an in-touch-with-his-feminine-side that rendered any supposed arrogance ludicrous. He liked games, he could be a put-on artist who delighted in testing people out. But even his cruelties and toughnesses had a dandyish feyness about them. 'I'm so hip' he announces across the dialogue play-in to "I Cannot Make It", barely tongue-in-cheek. But for all the flashy 'Sly Stone' artifice of a rising star, he retained an elusive quality of smiling aliveness that would have been just as resonant if he was just Sylvester Stewart sat beneath the shade of a tree by the railroad track in a patched old pair of Levi's, strumming to the rhythm that the drivers made. Women found it an irresistible combination.

Then there's his &-ampersand connection to the Family Stone, the other integral part of the story. The two cannot be considered apart. And as the months accelerate on towards year's end the inter-relationships within and around the band were becoming increasingly complicated. There are important considerations—other than purely musical ones, that go into making up a band. There has to be personal synergy. There has to be bonding sufficient to survive the enforced close proximity. 'The concept behind Sly & The Stone' Sly explained to *Rolling Stone*, is 'I wanted it to be able for everyone to get a chance to sweat. By that I mean… if there was anything to be happy about, then everybody'd be happy about it. If there was a lot of money to be made, for anyone to make a lot of money. If there were a lot of songs to sing, then everybody got to sing. That's the way it is now. Then, if we have something to suffer or a cross to bear—we bear it together'. Not to state it too highly, Sly saw the band as the means by which each member found his—or her voice. The group was a collective form of liberation, a shared vision. There was already spirit going on between them. Together, they were something above whatever they'd been apart. A sum that was greater than its parts. Through the incident in Las Vegas, and then in New York, they were in the process of going beyond that, and becoming genuine 'family', with strong group loyalties. When Jerry and Cynthia reported to Sly that they'd been racially abused and threatened for walking together on the New York street, he got the 'fellas' together and went to beat out retribution on the culprits. Sly didn't take no shit from no-one. The incident was also evidence of Sly's increasing push. He had no need to look outside of the group he'd created. It was now a self-enclosed entity. They are members of a close family. Even those who were, strictly, not family. The Family Stone formed its own gravitational system, and the lives that pass through it never quite achieve sufficient escape velocity to ever detach completely. The early Stewart Four quartet formed its nucleus, so Sly's 'big brother' role easily extended into its Family Stone continuation, after all, 'blood's thicker than mud.' Then, add to it the near-family continuity of two other powerful long-term collaborators in Cynthia Robinson, and Larry Graham. Both were drawn into the family gang's orbit, and became inescapably snared by its powerful black-hole gravitation. Their contribution is never less than mighty.

Born in Beaumont, Texas, but raised in Oakland, Sly described Larry as 'funky as nine cans of wet magic shave'. While still attending college he was already gaining wide experience as an inventive bassist serving as support-musician to visiting John Lee Hooker, Jackie Wilson, Jimmy Reed, and the Drifters. To Sly, Larry 'constantly adds the correct ingredients of bottom whether it be on stage, in the studio, or swappin' fives on a street corner. Larry can sing anything, play anything and do anything'. But he is most significantly credited with inventing the percussive 'slapping' bass guitar technique, which rapidly expanded the instrument's tonal palette. Funk tended to incorporate the same extended chords as found in jazz. And although in the jazz-zone the stand-up double-bass had been granted virtuoso solo status in the dextrous hands of the intimidatingly gifted Charlie Mingus—in Rock Bands musicians more usually got relegated to solid-body bass if they weren't good enough to make lead guitar. There, tied to the drummer as part of the rhythm section, they'd etch out the structure of the beat, and little more. People like Jack Bruce, from a jazz-Blues background, were breaking free from such limitations, with Cream. But Larry Graham, for sure, was never likely to settle for such a reduced role.

Bassists for many years before, back to the very origins of the instrument, had learned how to 'slap' the strings with the right thumb, while using a rotation of the wrist to modify the tonality. Larry took it further. By doing it differently, he pioneered the art of slap-POP, a style that would subsequently become the default setting for the funk electric bass. He achieved it with a percussive thumping thumb-slap on the lower bass-strings coupled with an aggressive finger-snap on the higher ones, often in a rhythmic alternating pattern, so that the string collides with the frets, to produce a metallic 'clunk' at the beginning of the note. Larry claimed he developed this 'thump' trick out of necessity, to compensate while playing in the 'Dell Graham Trio' without a drummer, using the string-'pluck' to replicate the missing snare-drum backbeat. For mid-period Family Stone singles—"Everyday People" and the revolutionary "Thank You (Falettinme Be Mice Elf Agin)", he would push if further still, expanding and evolving the technique to incorporate a complementary 'pull' or 'pop' component. Variously described as 'thumping' and 'plucking', or 'slapping' and 'popping', he managed to incorporate a large ratio of mute/ghost tones to normal tones. Whatever the technical terminology—it worked. Building from such a humble beginning, until a million bassists learned how to 'slap', and it had become a new musical genre unto itself. Subsequent 'machine-gun bass' practitioners—Level 42's Mark King, Red Hot Chili Pepper's Flea, Stanley Clarke, Alex 'Dirk Lance' Katunich of Incubus, all rely on what Larry began. Marcus Miller, bass rhythmatist for Miles Davis and Luther Vandross was also a Larry disciple. And when it came to defining the sound of the Family Stone, setting its controls for the heart of the funk, no other individual—apart from Sly himself, was of greater importance than Larry Graham. Coupled to the further duo of Gregg and Jerry. This was a band that carried no passengers.

But like Fleetwood Mac around the time of their *'Rumours'* (1977) album, or the internal sexual politics that disrupted The Mamas & The Papas, or Human League… or Abba, the gender-mix of the Family Stone would also lead to emotional and sexual attractions, jealousies and fallings-out. Sly had had white girlfriends since Maria Boldway from his Viscaynes days. Celebrity as a DJ, and as a hot musician, meant there was never any shortage of admiring available 'ladies'. Now, Sly was with Nita. Gregg Errico was married. Jerry was also married, with three kids. Larry was getting close-up and personal with Rose. While Cynthia and Freddie were sharing a room. He was already married and had a son. But touring threw them together, and… well, things tend to develop. The band that sleeps together, keeps together… well, maybe. The newly developing relationships also presented a test for Daddy KC's control over his family's increasingly unstable behaviour. When KC called in on them at their New York hotel Cynthia and Freddie strove to be discrete, but the sleeping arrangements were fairly obvious. KC kept his silence. There was no censure from the patriarch of the Stewart family.

And while—within the group, progress might seem torturously slow, to others outside its magic circle, the Family Stone suddenly appear as rising stars. Their increasing visibility offering the 'contact-high' chance of a life to be lived beyond the 'hood', a no-limits fantasy for people trapped by too many limiting social constraints, if only you could attach yourself to the gaudy coat-tails of its entourage. As the incidents in Vegas had indicated, they were already exerting their magnetism across a travelling circus of other musicians, dope-dealers, artists, hangers-on. And there were the predatory groupies 'making whoopee'. With the band's reputation in the ascendant, the 'star-fuckers', the band-rats, became more persistently available… as Sly illustrates in the scenario of 'Jane the Groupee'. Hanging out after the show, Jane might have no idea what their songs were about, but she's 'got a thing for guys in the band'. She wants to take the drummer home. She wants to 'get it on' with Larry. She seductively purrs to Freddie 'I'd like to go around with you'. Then invites Sly, 'you can write your songs upon my knee'…

****

'Sly & The Family Stone are opening the door to a whole new era in soul music…'

(Barry Hansen reviewing *Life* in *Rolling Stone*)

Sly & The Family Stone. For those not old enough to remember, it's difficult to pinpoint the exact place they occupy in that long-vanished world. Yet this was the unwieldy, unlikely ensemble that had inked to Epic. Would they have fared better with a more sympathetic Stax? Or Motown? Epic was an untypical label, in that it was significantly *not* a company associated with Soul or R&B. But that was probably a deliberate calculation too. Record-buyers look out for a new title on Motown, or Stax, because they're known brands. As such, genre expectation provides an easy introduction to new names. But by avoiding such genre expectations, the Family Stone were simultaneously not confined by its limitations. Auspiciously, their first major-label single came in the form of "Underdog", announced by Jerry Martini's attention-grabbing slow horn-fanfare of "Frére Jacques". Why "Frére Jacques"? Well, the Beatles had opened "All You Need Is Love" with a similar Franco-blast just three months earlier "The Marseillaise", which the Pop-savvy Sly can't fail to have been aware of. English Popstrel Jess Conrad once had a dance almost-hit with "Twist My Wrist" which lifts from that same French traditional tune, but it's doubtful if that ever featured strongly on Sly Stewart's play-list. Whatever, Sly knew all about the advantages of complementing different music forms. The snatched minor-key brass-arrangement introducing the seven-inch vinyl has little obviously to do with the punchy rhythms blasted out by soul-regulation Stax-style unison horns that follow, but it's a radio attention-grabber. Would the conservative suits at Motown have been open to such a display of individuality? At this stage in the game, it's doubtful. While it's worth noting that with the ambitiously determined vocal-line—'I know how it feels to be the underdog', the racial content is present in Sly & The Family Stone from the start. From the first track, on the first album. Yet equally, it's already uplifted by the defiant declaration that, hey—that's alright, it just means 'you've got to be twice as good'. It was a street-guise, a challenge, and a twinkly-eyed declaration of hip intent, all in one. In a crowded record-market it constituted an unlikely debut from an unexpected source, but the parting kick 'don't underestimate me' is a promise that Sly Stone would fulfil multifold.

Larry had a basset-hound called Underdog. Some might recall that 'Underdog' was also the title of a Saturday morning TV cartoon show popular at the time! Others might make a connection with the powerful Charlie Mingus autobiography *'Beneath The Underdog'* (1971) with its bragging sexuality and racial subtext… Whatever, this full-frontal single also opened the soon-following debut long-player *'Whole New Thing'* (October 1967). Recording time had been snatched from break-periods during their Las Vegas engagement. There, the band played from nine through to two am. But they took Mondays off, caught a flight down to the Los Angeles Gower Street studios to record, and spent the full twenty-four hours there. The CBS facilities were not exactly high-tech, even *then*. Obviously no computers, no sampling, no magic Pro-Tools for ironing out imperfections. But it *was* a step up from 'Autumn', and from every other studio they'd ever used before. The album was entirely recorded on four-track machines, the maximum available, which meant that the sessions were completed virtually live, drawing on the material they'd already worked out and perfected by playing intensively to club-audiences.

As on stage, the twelve tracks make maximum use of the full available instrumental range, with players constantly altering their function in and out of the rhythm and lead sections, then throwing in pass-around vocals for contrast, their different textures traded off against each other in endless fascinating permutations of high/low, male/female and solo/chorus. In fact, it's almost a Family Stone Revue album, with the nucleus of the band providing the setting for a sequence of featured soloists. As the band history progressed into the future, album-by-album, this aspect would become less and less true, as the focus narrowed down onto Sly himself. There's freshness too, in the album's melodic strengths, in Sly's seemingly offhand lyrics, and in the relentless jostling stop-start rhythm section. He seems to be drawing across the full palette of his DJ record collection of influences, testing out the water, charting a superabundance of potential directions, each of which could have led to fruitful careers. There's a strong riffing Stax/Volt input, showing some obvious Motown, a dollop of sixties-style studio experiment, tangled up in some polka-dot dashes. Or—as Peter Doggett observes, 'the album sounded as if Frank Zappa, the Fifth Dimension and Otis Redding had swapped their molecules around'. A theoretically impossible, but ultimately ingenious style-fusion.

The album also highlights Sly's most conventionally soulful material. Coming most directly from that matrix Larry takes lead vocals on "Let Me Hear It From You". Recorded in the 'wee-small hours' of the morning, it falls strongly into the preachy soul-pleading ballad tradition, with its gospel roots laid bare. Larry's intense Brook Benton-rich voice rides a churchy-deep swelling organ reminiscent of Otis Redding's slow-paced classic "I've Been Loving You Too Long", or Percy Sledge "Warm And Tender Love". A track echoed in Prince's "The Cross" almost two decades later. "That Kind Of Person" is another plaintive soul ballad about the decay of romance, passing the microphone to Freddie who delivers it in near-talking intimacy. Then "Turn Me Loose" accelerates the pace, building layer by layer into a hand-clap driven 1.54-minute tight Otis Redding re-construction based around their "I Can't Turn You Loose" blueprint for Loadstone. It's a parody, played for laughs, complete with its hoarse 'got-to got-to gotta keep on moving' exhortation. With only the breathless 'phew! turn me loose, Pheeeew!' gasped into the fade to add light relief. The exhalation would later be sampled by Public Enemy for "Power to The People" on their 1989 *Fear Of A Black Planet* album.

"I Hate To Love Her" alters the form into high group harmonics counter-pointed by deep bass voice, somewhere around the vicinity of the Four Tops' "Baby I Need Your Lovin'". Then, "If This Room Could Talk" elaborates the range further with cascading horns and exaggerated melismatic phrasing that extends a simple 'I would be less than a man' into the convoluted roller-coaster of 'I would be less than a... woo-woo, woowoooowoo... less than a man'. The track playfully requisitions the Rock cliché 'I want you, I need you, I love you'—familiar at least since Elvis, and later to be punned by Meatloaf, into a precociously post-modern 'I need you, I want you, and furthermore I've got to have you'. All of which is enclosed within a strong haunting narrative that leaves the hanging question, what *really* happened in this room—a fight? or something darker? Its boom-a-boom-boom scat play-out anticipates "Dance To The Music" and—to writer Miles Marshall Lewis, 'prefigures beatboxing' too. Skip the tracks further, there's "Advice" which fuses harmony vocals with sharp break-beats, while "Bad Risk" is a straightforward 'mean deceiver' song, with Larry singing about a heartbreaker. And all the while, so far, Sly has stayed safely within the soul template, even while he's nudging its limits.

But he'd paid his dues in the Autumn studios, he knew all the techniques, how to transfer a 'live' ambience to vinyl, the knack of creating appealing hooks resembling those he'd spun on his radio shows. All he had to do was upgrade those skills incrementally to achieve a 'gorgeous mosaic' of voices. Little Sister were on hand to add vocals—Tiny, Vet, and Mary. Rose was there too. This becomes more apparent on two stranger songs that, in different guise, could have operated as singles for the kind of white acid-garage-punk bands he'd liaised with at 'Autumn'. "Run Run Run" introduces sweet ripples of vibraphone, involved doo-wop Swingle Singers' vocal gymnastics, and a curious wind-instrument breakdown mid-point in what could otherwise be a white Pop song of a more complex guise. There's even a direct lyric-reference to the Rolling Stones satiric attack on the ad-driven Madison Avenue 'hidden persuaders' of "Satisfaction", with Sly slyly interjecting 'then the commercial comes on to tell me what I ought to be smokin"—a flashback to Sly's 11pm nightly KSOL 'integration record' when he featured "Satisfaction" for a straight month. But the shocks don't stop there. Sly was ransacking black—*and* white musical heritages, for in Sly's mind, there had never been much of a chasm there to bridge, churning a potpourri of get-down soul into banshee psychedelia. With the main thrust of the lyrics more concerned with a different, and then more-marketable social division than race. Instead, he was exploiting the straight mainstream mindset of the 'squares', versus the hippie-mentality. Coming down firmly on the hippie's side. 'They don't like what we're thinking' Sly sneers, adding 'they don't like what we're wearing'. The 'we', in this instance, are the cool, the hyper-aware, beyond race or gender. A 'we' defined in opposition to the attitudes he dismisses with 'don't try to figure out what's happening inside *their* heads'. They don't matter, because there 'ain't too much going on inside the head of the dead'. Sentiments then being played out with less wit and perception by any number of pouting long-haired white garage bands, all vying for radio-play.

Then there's "Trip To Your Heart"—which operates on one level as a conventional love song, yet opens (and closes) with Zappaesque "Help, I'm A

Rock"-style screams blended into a disjointed chaos of raw sounds suggesting the 'trip' in question is more than merely a romantic excursion, with bizarre quasi-operatic quavering voices mixed low down into the background. Part acid fantasy, part 'Hammer'-horror mutation, it's a track memorable enough to be singled out many years later by producer Marley Marl to provide the sample forming the basis of LL Cool J's 1990 hit "Mama Said Knock You Out", and then again by Skinnyman. A Whole New Thing? Undeniably—yes, but there's yet another standout, the loping rhythms and Freddie's 'blow your mind' hipness of "I Cannot Make It". A track that perhaps anticipates Sly's own vanishing-point into extreme idiosyncrasy by neatly fingering his eventual problem right from the start, taking a more balanced downbeat 'if I make it till tomorrow / I'll be surprised', before fading into a 'psychedelic' wind-down.

In its totality, as an album, it might not consistently be the 'Whole New Thing' its title brags for it, yet from the lift-off 'Frére Jacques' fanfare of "Underdog", to its book-ending closing answer—"Dog", it still sounds remarkably fresh. 'Every dog has its day' Sly declares, colluded by Cynthia's shout-back dialogue—lyrically arcing back to "Underdog", that 'I'm going to see that you get yours', which can be interpreted as both a promise... or a threat. *'Rolling Stone no. 3'* was unconvinced, calling the album 'interesting, but not entirely effective'. Later, Sly explained to them 'see, the concept was to be able to conceive all kinds of music... whatever was contemporary, and not necessarily in terms of being commercial—whatever meant 'whatever'. Like today—things like censorship, and the black people/white people thing. That's on my mind. So we just like to perform the things that are on our mind'. He means the Family Stone were making music—not soul or Pop, R&B or Rock, just whatever happened to be on his mind. And almost incidentally, that promiscuous mixing of distinct styles ignited a new genre of their own. From the very start—and this album represents *the* very start for the band, such music is on speaking terms with greatness.

Yet, on its initial release, the 'New Thing' stiffed. The reasons *why* it didn't register as perhaps it should are difficult to decipher. Sly was really trying, shoving his versatility to the limits by creating a showcase of his mastery across a range of styles. Each track is individual. Each track is a separate entity. Perhaps it's this very diversity that makes it too rich a concoction for its time—offering no easy simple identifying handle? For 1967, there was no unique point-of-marketing shorthand. Perhaps it's an album best viewed as an investment for future development, better appreciated retrospectively? As re-issue sleeve-writer Chris Albertson (of *'downbeat'* magazine) phrases it, 'their trendsetting ideas were not acted upon at first, but the spark that this album ignited soon exploded into a veritable avalanche in Sly's proposed direction, and even that influential tide of inspiration flowing from Detroit was reversed as his ideas gave the famous Motown sound new directions'.

And yes—as an announcement of intentions, you hear future-echoes of the coming Tower of Power horns, and the horns-within-the-group likes of Blood Sweat & Tears and the Chicago Transit Authority (later CTA, and then just 'Chicago') in its grooves. Sly's sound, the sound of the band, was mashing up marginal genres into a form that was to have universal relevancies… in other hands too, in future-glimpses all the way to Michael Jackson, Africa Bambaataa, Prince, and beyond.

But at the time, another reason for its commercial failure has got to be the intense release schedule gobbling up and spitting out outrageous new bands at breakneck speed, all competing for the attention of hip record-buyers during that vital first month of release. Grabbing all the headlines was The Beatles' *'Magical Mystery Tour'*, The Rolling Stones *'Their Satanic Majesties Request'*, The Monkees *'Pisces, Aquarius, Capricorn & Jones Ltd'*, Cream's *'Disraeli Gears'*, and Jefferson Airplane's *'After Bathing At Baxters'*, as well as more esoteric offerings such as The Velvet Underground's *'White Light/ White Heat'*, Love's *'Forever Changes'*, Frank Zappa's *'Lumpy Gravy'*… enough vinyl-product on the Rock shelf already to keep the aware music fan in a state of high excitation without further complications. Before you even get to the singles by the Beatles ("Hello Goodbye" c/w "I Am The Walrus"), The Who ("I Can See For Miles"), Small Faces ("Itchycoo Park"), Monkees ("Daydream Believer"), Lemon Pipers ("Green Tambourine"), Strawberry Alarm Clock ("Incense And Peppermint")…

Chapter Seven
'From New York... To Detroit'

'Flamin' eyes of people fear, burnin' into you, many men are missin' much, hatin' what they do.
Youth and Truth are makin' love, dig it for a starter...'
("Thank you falettinme be mice elf... agin")

'Don't Burn Baby, Burn...'

Let me tell you about Sylvester Stewart. He was a great bunch of people. And each of them excelled. The writer. The musician. The DJ. The artist. The producer. The bandleader. All coming together as the Soul Package that was 'Sly Stone'. A marvel of self-invention, a construction that was part-showman, part-shaman, charlatan, slick-genius, egomaniac, careerist, ringmaster, magician. A wobbly mix of toughness and vulnerability, laid-back cool and self-doubt. You thought it was a crowd... until it reduced velocity sufficient to see, it was only Sly. Was Sly career-minded? Naw—not exactly. He was a music-minded workaholic. And music was his career. He put music ahead of most everything, and when celebrity became an incidental part of that, then he'd take that too. He was smart, if not yet famous.

America is big. It's quite possible to enjoy a rewarding career as a regional celebrity, known, and working regularly locally, yet virtually unknown outside of your State. Such people are famous, if not quite stars, jobbing musicians who work hard and make a good living. Equally, in the segregated America of the fifties and early sixties you could be a huge 'Race Records' star, yet never cross over into the mainstream, even though the songs and arrangements you create might be 'covered' in marginally more acceptable forms by more photogenic white entertainers. Your song could then achieve sales figures you could only dream of. Hitting the R&B chart was fine, but it only represented 2-300,000 sales. To capture that elusive young, white middle-class demographic, enriched by its high weekly allowances—in your own right, was another matter entirely. Nat 'King' Cole had done it. Johnny Mathis too. But to do it without dilution was an equation few could manage. Only the changing face of cool meant that what you could get away with was less a fixed condition as it was a gradual process. Chuck Berry and Little Richard made it big by first having their songs familiarised through the Elvis catalyst. Or worse still, the Pat Boone catalyst. Chuck Berry, Little Richard, Bo Diddley, Howlin' Wolf, Motown and John Lee Hooker made it big by having their template replicated and universalised by the Rolling Stones, the Beatles, the Animals and the Kinks. Only then was it sold back to America.

So—with one album down, what was it Sly had achieved? He cut out that catalyst-stage. Without dilution. Things were changing, and he'd sensed the change in the times. The Family Stone was a *group*. A self-contained band. That, in itself, was far from the norm for black music. Think Drifters, Four Tops, Coasters, Miracles. A row of four—or maybe five guys, in matching tuxedos doing identical dance-steps and close harmonies. The Family Stone were not like that. What they were doing was an innovation that had percolated down from the British invasion. The same evolution that Bob Marley would provoke by moving Reggae away from DJ-toasters and sound-systems into a moveable gigging entity. Chances are if Sly hadn't done all that, someone else would've done something pretty much the same. That's a given. There was the amazing Arthur Lee blowing his mind with LA's Love into indefinable unmapped musical terrain. 'Forever Changes'. It was in the air. The Chambers Brothers' Afro-psychedelic-Rock was making waves with "Time Has Come Today" (a US no. 11 in September 1968), extending beyond its eleven album minutes to twenty or thirty in live performance, with screaming electric guitars—and an African cowbell.

There was James Marshall Hendrix, who once played back-up for Little Richard, and was noodling his solos away from set riffs while playing with the Isley Brothers. Until he became Jimi Hendrix—the man to whom Sly would initially be most directly compared, flanked by his two pale white-boy toys. Hendrix who had also rejected the restrictions of Soul—with 'I don't gotta-gotta-gotta, 'cos I don't hafta-hafta-hafta', and matching the velocity of Dylan's methadrine-surrealistic word-flow for his own compositions. As writer David Dalton points out 'Jimi Hendrix was the first black to play acid rock, but he remained a black musician playing to white audiences, he did not get played on black radio stations' ('Cooper Square Books' reissue, 1999). Miles Davis was also perceptive enough to recognise that 'very few young blacks had heard of (Jimi Hendrix), because for them he was too far over into white Rock. Black kids were listening to Sly Stone, James Brown, Aretha Franklin, and all them other great black groups at Motown'. This despite the fact that Hendrix's music was firmly based in Blues, finding new routes through old roots—which made it 'blacker' than Motown. He had to come to England to find a receptive constituency sufficiently free of genre preconceptions to listen to, and appreciate, what he was doing. Sly was an artist with power of crossover assimilation, like the Hendrix Experience, but unlike Hendrix, he was able to do so without losing the base Black audience. His canvas was bigger. His palette was wider.

Sly Stone, the Delegate from Hip City USA, had proved himself a musician of sharp originality who achieved his quick-smart ascendancy on his own terms. Not that he was ever colour-blind, nor blind to ethnicity. 'Jerry's white because he's not any other colour' he argued, 'Larry's black because he's not white. You know what I mean?' Yes—it's no big deal. So what? But by taking that attitude, he was taking chances, standing right out in front. He could play exclusively to black audiences, as was pointed out on his Mike Douglas Show appearance, and his response was certain to be big. But by playing to integrated audiences, he would be even BIGGER. Yet incidentally, by doing what they were doing, the Family Stone's diverse make-up was also unwrapping another hidden layer of the Soul agenda. Soul was black music—of course it was black music, but Soul was also a *synthesis* of formerly segregated genres, a meltdown in which white elements served as a not-insignificant ingredient. The Stax house-band, Booker T & The MGs, was also racially integrated.

Albums don't care who plays them. Or whether their subtexts are fully understood. If Sly hadn't done it, surely it would have happened anyway. But the fact is, it didn't. It's the old Elvis Presley argument. If Elvis hadn't taken Country music, and given it a raw R&B back-beat, someone else would've done. It was in the air too. Hank Williams and Rockabilly on one side. Fats Domino in New Orleans on the other. Little Richard washing dishes. Ike Turner recording "Rocket 88". Chuck Berry fantasising about the sweet little sixteen-year-old white girl's market. It would have happened. Fact is, it didn't, not until Elvis cut "That's Alright Mama" at Sam Phillips' Sun Studios in Memphis. Same with splash-artist Jackson Pollock. It's kid's paint-dribbles. Anyone could do it. Yes, but they didn't. Not until he did it. So what was it Sly had achieved? He created the correct era-defining fusions at precisely the right time. That's enough. That's more than enough. In terms of cool and its variants, Sly signified almost everything worth signifying. As Miles Davis ruefully observes from a jazz perspective, 'compared to what my records used to sell, when you put them besides what Bob Dylan or Sly Stone sold, it was no contest. Their sales had gone through the roof'.

So how had the Family Stone contrived such results? Strategies must surely have been a matter of protracted deliberation and calculation, with a heightened attention to detail? Surely Sly must have constantly adjusted his style, his scale, his aesthetics, calculating trends with almost ruthless precision? Yet it seems so effortless. Like he was moving without premeditation. So it more intuitive than planned, unfolding as a long journey unfolds? Was Sly composing and revising in his notebook at night, rarely going to bed until dawn, staying up late dreaming up strange new rhythms, and devising how to construct them in the studio? He was integral to the band's synergy. Their fills and dynamics provide the templates, it was their interaction that was rendering traditional assumptions concerning the separate roles of band and vocals obsolete. But it was Sly alone who determined the final shapes, hallucinatory spaces, and beat-progressions. As Don Was pointed out in *'Rolling Stone'* (no. 946, 15th April 2004), 'Sly orchestrated those early records in very advanced ways—a little guitar thing here would trigger the next part, that would trigger the next part. Then, as time went on, Sly started using some more dissonant colours. He became like the Cézanne of funk. It's like he took those traditional James Brown groove elements and started putting orange into the picture'. The whole band was his palette, the personalities of its members were his colours, deploying their improvisational breaks or throwaway phrases as textures to be blended into the whole. While Sly himself told *'Rolling Stone'*, 'what I write is people's music' with a shrug that says it's almost too obvious to have to explain.

The sleeve of the 2003 digitally-remastered double-CD *'The Essential Sly & The Family Stone'* shows a Gulliver-size Sly with his Lilliputian band standing casually in the palm of his hand—it's actually an old promo shot, the same one that would inspire the Red Hot Chili Peppers' *'Mother Milk'* (1989) CD cover-art. Sly is looking down at his band, a benevolent ruler. That's pretty much the way the thing operated. A democracy… of sorts. But very much with Sly as the Great Helmsman. He's the player. And he's the umpire. There are two ways of achieving that level of control. There's the megalomaniac fire-eater way, those who throw a sneering, violent, malevolent strop when they don't get what they want. There is any number of artists like that in the Rock industry. Or you can do it the way Sly did it, and bowl people over with your enthusiasms, directing the studio engineer while conducting the musicians over the control room pa. 'See, if you could put some more bottom on your bass, 'cause when you hit the fuzz without the bottom, it's like a guitar'. Or to the drummer 'Gregg, are your skins real tight on your snares? You need something heavy on it…', seeking a drum-sound he defined as 'sloppy-tight and raggedy-clean'. Make no mistake, Sylvester Stewart was no musical naïve. He'd paid his academic dues, as well as his street-dues. He knew that Duke Ellington (with Billy Strayhorn) and Count Basie were the real geniuses at arranging American music. But he was also ranging further, studying *'Orchestration'* from a book of that title by composer, theorist and Harvard Professor Walter Hamor Piston (WW Norton & Co, New York 1955, ISBN 0-3930-97404). Born in 1894 Piston was a contemporary of Aaron Copeland. A young Leonard Bernstein was among his students, and his own compositions run to eight symphonies, as well as concertos and work for strings and piano. The influences he drew from include the intellectually heavyweight chromatic twelve-tone techniques of Arnold Schoenberg, apparent in his most famous work, the ballet score "The Incredible Flautist" performed for CBS by the Boston Symphony Orchestra. And his four influential books are not easy reads, they're academic, relying heavily on examples from the core classical repertoire with few concessions to the dabbler.

Miles Davis had gone to Julliard. 'I have never understood why black people didn't take advantage of all the shit that they can' he said. 'It's like a ghetto mentality telling people that they aren't supposed to do certain things, that those things are only reserved for white people'. But while he was raiding the shelves of the NY Public library to borrow scores by Stravinsky, Alban Berg and Prokofiev, Miles was simultaneously learning by listening to Charlie 'Bird' Parker, Dizzy Gillespie, and Thelonius Monk. And he retained healthy reservations about the effects of *too* much learned technique. He acknowledges that although Jimi Hendrix could not read music 'there are a lot of great musicians who don't read music—black and white, that I have known and respected and played with. So I didn't think less of Jimi because of that. Jimi was a great, natural musician—self-taught… a guy like Jimi Hendrix or Sly or Prince, might not do what they have done if they had known all the rest of that technical stuff because it might have gotten in their way, and they might have done something else had they known all that other stuff'. But Sly Stone was serious. He studied Professor Piston's book, recommended it as a tutorial to others, and attempted to apply its harmonic principles to his own work… 'in music, there's notes—a C-chord makes you go 'ahh', a minor chord makes you sad. A C-major implies happiness. Something changes every minute. But with music, I can pinpoint it, who did it. Right or wrong…' Sly was neither Rock boffin nor strutting funk god, although simultaneously something of both. Part evangelical preacher, part mad scientist, while projecting it all through the medium of the collective. Sly was nominal leader. It is his name. It is his 'Family Stone'. As the eldest son, in a family with three girls, he was used to being the centre of attention, and convivially assumed that role naturally. But it had not yet become a control-freak situation. Unlike—say, James Brown who famously fined band-members for bad behaviour, the Family Stone was more an attempted collective. A more idealistic, but a more problematic solution.

'I wouldn't trade my group for all the tea in Mexico.' That was Sly talking about his 'Family'. A weird dynamic. He needed them around him. Yet it was Sly who carried the ultimate responsibility. They were his songs. But he never appeared to dominate the tracks, instead, his voice was balanced in a harmonic dialogue with the other vocal elements of the group. Like Brian Wilson directing and arranging the Beach-Boys' complex multi-layering. The ensemble playing is so consistently superb that individual efforts tend to go unnoticed. But it was Sly apportioning the balance, determining the ratios.

The Beatles had George Martin to produce everything they did. The Rolling Stones had Andrew Loog Oldham, then Jimmy Miller. For musicians, the producer is the semi-detached outside eye who fills out the band's technical inadequacies, who reigns in their more self-indulgent tendencies, who edits and adds the final gloss to the recording process. Motown had its 'finishing school', rigorously disciplining its artists not only in stage-moves, between-song dialogue and sartorial style, but in posture and attitude too. Raising their assurance and self-image. Taking girls from the projects and giving them the confidence to perform at the White House, if that was where it led. For the Family Stone, Sly alone provided all these functions. And not only was he not operating within the traditional producer restrictions, he had the ability to be simultaneously mainstream *and* underground.

By now, the name was out there. It was in-crowd. But it was still a cognoscente's thing. Until—as the album was emerging, they were engaged by former William Morris agent turned impresario Jerry Brandt for their first major East Coast exposure. So they packed up their stuff and headed out across the continent. Sly took his first trip to the Big Apple—and he took a big bite. They deplaned at JFK—renamed from Idlewild in 1963 one month after the Kennedy assassination, the place where—in February 1964, the Beatles had first set foot on American blacktop to conquer. From there they travelled through Queens and across the Brooklyn Bridge into Manhattan to play the 'Electric Circus' in the East Village. Located between Second and Third Avenues at 19-25 St Marks Place, the club was billed as 'The Ultimate Legal Entertainment Experience'. Promoter Brandt owned the venue between 1967 and September 1971, during which it became the premier hip hangout for the grooviest of people. Originally known as the Arlington Hall, it had become the Polish National Home—a regular bar-restaurant known by an abbreviation of its Polish name as 'The Dom'. Then, as a Disco, it was frequented by, and at one time owned by Andy Warhol. He used it to launch the Velvet Underground through the 'Exploding Plastic Inevitable' happenings during May 1966, using the walls to screen his movies, *'Kiss'* (1963) and *'empire'* (1964) as the band played and Nico sang. Briefly it was also known as the Balloon Farm.

As the 'Electric Circus' it consisted of a cavernous ballroom with a balcony overlooking the crazy psychedelic light shows, while there were multimedia multiple-projections and pink cubicles inset around the dance-floor. Also, in keeping with its name, there were circus acts, acrobats, sword-swallowers, fire-eaters and trapeze artists performing as the guest bands played. The air was… well, electric. And the Family Stone fitted perfectly into its freaky ambience. The venue was crammed with dancers. Sly couldn't afford to blow this opportunity. And he didn't. He had to put up or shut up, there was no in-between. He'd never been scared of venturing new things. It's all up there on his radar. But he knew that for this freak-out he had to keep his shit together. He also knew he *was* going to do just that. He was confident his band could stack up against just about anybody. If they wanted a high-wire act without a safety net, Sly was pretty much doing that himself. A precarious high. A long way to fall. A balance to maintain between human fallibility, and gravity. Sly already had live wires sparking where his nerve-ends should be.

Unsane. Unsanity. Unlikely visionaries. On stage, seeing Sly & The Family Stone in their live setting was to be impacted by a multi-sensory detonation. As life-enhancing as defibrillator blasts. When they played, the club was transformed into a space of infinite movement by the light-show, spun-light stinging their eyes. Weird, and loud with the slam of rhythm, they were playing essentially their regular set, highlighted by what were now their album tracks, but tightened up and played more intensely, re-charged with East Coast energies. Arrangements ingeniously embedded in unexpected group-vocal detours, swapping lines at the most unexpected moment through a wildly varying dynamic range, dropping into flash-scatting as agile as Lambert/Hendricks/Ross, rammed with musical shocks too, syncopated rhythms, punchy horns topped off by ridiculously-irresistible pop melody-hooks. And just as an auto needs something to grip on to propel it forward, some gritty bass from Larry Graham under the wheels of the band provided powerful forward impetus. Siring an iconoclastic collision of heavy soul, funk, jazz, rock and anarchic humour, which was soon tagged 'psychedelic soul', a uniqueness of sound that the word 'funky' seems to have been invented for. The Family Stone was a self-contained continuum. Allied to a kookier-than-thou pimped-up show-offery, sartorially signified with wild costumes and self-styled choreography—even their facial expressions seemed to work on some inner synchronisation, delivered with a humour and showmanship that put most hip-shaking, foot-shuffling soul groups to shame. But it was never style over content. More style fused so tight to content they'd become one. If the attitude was 'Fuck Art: Let's Dance', that's only because the art underlying it all was a given.

'Start the Music: Stop the Racism'. Spoken with a passion and conviction so intense its reverberations instantly reached out from beyond the confines of the 'Electric Circus' into the drabber less turned-on world outside. And the media was on it in a heartbeat, providing a lubrication of giddy press write-ups. The album was moving… if slowly. It was in the record shop flip-racks, alphabetically filed between 'Sam & Dave' and 'Supremes'. Radio-play was selective and limited. It was picking up respectful attention from other musicians—Mose Allison, jazzer Teo Macero and others, if not necessarily from the broad record-buying public. George Clinton, still largely unknown, recalls being at the 'Electric Circus' and 'when I heard Sly doing "Underdog", it was like, holy shit! Who the fuck is this?' Betty Mabry—the woman featured on the cover of Miles Davis' exquisite album *'Filles De*

Kilimanjaro' (1968) was introducing the famous 'Man With The Horn' to the new Rock-influenced black music. In his revealing *'Miles: The Autobiography'* (1989) he wrote about this 'new group who had just come out' led by Sly Stone from San Francisco, and 'the shit he was doing was badder than a motherfucker, had all kinds of funky shit up in it'. The groove may well have been in the heart, but the Family Stone were now extending their following well beyond Frisco's emergent psychedelic ghetto. Sly strove harder than most other stars of the time to realize that hippie dream of universal love. But their inter-connections went everywhere.

They were intense times. Hard days. As for accommodation, for this first sojourn in New York the band were allocated rooms in the squalid Albert Hotel. 'Gregg and I (recalls Jerry Martini) were room-mates, and listened to the rats crawling along the wall—it was filthy and dirty, terrible. We heard people getting killed. It was a fucking nightmare'. Sly protested loudly. He made all the right emphatic noises. And they were moved uptown to mid-Manhattan's Park Sheraton Hotel at 870 Seventh Street, where they were also treated as vaguely suspect hippie degenerates. Sly and Nita shared one room. Jerry and Gregg in another, Freddie and Cynthia in a third. There was overspill at the Gorham. They got around on the subway, sitting watching people, and being watched, gulping in filthy city exhaust. Walking uptown to Central Park. Living on rice, upending cans of soup over it for added nutrition. There was a little kitchenette with space enough to fry chicken, and no money to eat out. But the group were unified. They were doing it together. They were part of a band that was happening. Protected by one another. Learning to lean on each other. Secured by one another. A self-enclosed community. And they were going places. This was a band that was going to set the world ablaze. Sure enough, their profile was steadily ramping up. The William Morris Agency lined up a string of bookings for them, and from NYC, they set out into the vastness of the Midwest.

For the most part they travelled in a rented tour-coach. Or sometimes Daddy KC would drive the band in a station-wagon while Sly and Jerry rode shotgun in a van carrying the gear. It's a condition that's part of Rock mythology. Confined together for long tedious periods of time as the freeway unravels through an endless no-place, bands contrive bizarre collective games, incomprehensible to those outside the circle. For the Family Stone, dogs became a kind of group-craze, something to counter tour-boredom. Sly had Stoner, the Great Dane that stayed back in Frisco with Momma Alpha. Now he got another, an English bulldog called Max. Larry had Underdog. And the stable of dogs expanded—up to twenty-eight at one point, Gregg had one, Rose, Jerry and Cynthia had two each, Freddie and Larry had three apiece, Sly had five. 'I read dog books' Sly told *'Rolling Stone'*—especially *'The Treasury Of Dogs'* reference book... there were other lighter moments too. Miles Davis recalls that during their first meeting Sly 'gave me that album of Rudy Ray Moore's, who was a real funny comedian back then, raunchy, you know, out there.' Sly's favourite laughter-track—Rudy Ray Moore, was known as the 'King of the Party Records'. Starting out with some Little Richard-style singles in the 1950's, he released a series of stand-up proto-rap albums through the 1960's and into the 1970s. Albums including *'Below The Belt'* (1959), *'Beatnik Scene'* (1962) and *'Let's Come Together'*—recorded live in 1967 but not issued until 1970, which developed an enduring fan-base—including members of the Family Stone. The style was way ruder and more explicit than contemporaries Redd Foxx or Richard Pryor, and plugged directly into Sly's 'Stagger Lee' ghetto-chic taste. Although the under-the-counter confrontational nature of such material effectively barred him from working on TV, Moore eventually broke through into movies as 'Dolemite', the uniquely articulate pimp alter-ego he'd developed on his records ('… rappin' and tappin' is my game!'). He co-wrote and starred in *'Dolemite'* (1975) and its blaxploitation sequel *'The Human Tornado'* (1976). His career on album and in movies continued, even the 2-Live-Crew incorporated Rudy Ray Moore samples on their early hip-hop albums. But for the Family Stone, for every comedy high, there was a dramatic low.

They got snarled up in a viciously scary scene in Detroit. On their way to an engagement, they were forced to pull off the Ohio Turnpike hunting a gas-station, into the city of Motown, and into the middle of a riot! The streets were dark. Buildings along the silhouette skyline looked to be on fire. There were cops with bad attitude, in vizored-down helmets and riot-shields patrolling every intersection. Their trigger-fingers were twitchy. This was the latest in a series of 'long hot summers'. There had already been violent disturbances in Harlem in 1964 and shock-headline riots in the LA Watts area a year later. In the black ghettoes, the aspirations and political consciousness engendered by the civil rights movement impacted against the daily frustrations of poverty, unemployment, poor housing, corrupt public services, brutal policing, and lethal absence of hope. The federal government that had failed them in the south was now drafting them to die in Vietnam. Newark, New Jersey burned from 13th July 1966 in six days of race-rioting that left twenty-six dead and 1500 injured. Following rumours that white policemen beat-up a black taxi driver, mobs targeted white-owned businesses, and the inner-city was burnt to a shell, bringing National Guard out onto the street. LeRoi Jones (now called Amiri Baraka) was there, and stayed through the aftermath, working through black community-based initiatives to help relieve wretched housing conditions, failing schools and obstructions to black economic opportunities.

Then the summer of 1967 was a season of insurrection, violence and death. In a reflection of what Martin Luther King had called 'this sweltering summer of the negro's legitimate discontent' it was a summer that saw blazing disorder in fifty-eight cities, including Detroit. The city had the highest population of southern-born blacks, part of the northern migration who had responded to the lure of jobs and big money to be made in the auto industry which made the city into motor-town, or mo'town. Yet it was only during July 1967—a sultry 'hotter than July' summer, that the city exploded. A black prostitute was shot dead. Soon, stories began to circulate. She'd been shot by two plain-clothes vice-squad officers. Within weeks there was a police raid on an illegal after-hours club, a raid that began at 03:45 sharp Sunday 23rd. The clients fought back. Eighty-two arrests were made despite the police being pelted with bottles and other missiles. What began as a spontaneous protest in the face of heavy-handed policing, with probable racist undertones, rapidly expanded. It escalated into a four-day orgy of anarchy, window-smashing, random looting, bombings, arson, indiscriminate shooting and attacks of white-owned businesses. A 'Panic In Detroit', as David Bowie would later phrase it. The first victim was clubbed to death in the street by looters in clear view of onlookers. His killing was followed by a 45-year-old white male shot dead by a store-owner for looting. Then a 23-year-old white woman. Copycat riots flared in neighbouring towns, Grand Rapids, Pontiac, Saginaw and Toledo. A state of emergency was declared. State Governor George Romney mobilised 7400 National Guardsmen to lock the city down tight.

There was a curfew. And it was 03:00 as the Family Stone's van, with the band—and Nita in the back, was cheerfully unsuspectingly progressing down Grand River Drive directly into the heart of it. Inevitably they were flagged down, by a convergence of half-a-dozen National Guard jeeps. Daddy KC was good in tight situations. Unlike the rest of the crew he didn't look freaky. He was respectably well-dressed, with a cool and conciliatory manner. Sly was more confrontational, scowling insanely from beneath a woollen tea-cosy of a hat, he added pressure when needed, he took control, stood for no harassment. Sly don't take no shit off nobody. They talked, Sly talked back. And he talked back in a way that came so close to provoking a trigger-happy response that it got scary. It got heavy. Would they let them leave? Unless they were complete assholes…? Eventually… they did let them leave. Together, between them, Sly and Daddy KC had managed to extricate themselves through a combination of luck, swift thinking and bare-faced effrontery, and they high-tailed out of that town in a hurry.

Meanwhile LBJ went further, eventually sending in federal troops with tanks and machine-guns to finally end the chaos. The full total was forty-three dead, 2250 injured and 4000 arrested, 1300 buildings razed or gutted and 2700 businesses stripped clean of consumer goods by looters. Much of inner-city Detroit was never rebuilt. In the wake of the storm accusations and recriminations flew in every-which-way directions. Although it had initially been claimed that a National Guardsman had shot and killed an alleged sniper, the official enquiry established there had been no sniper. The police had actually been fired upon by confused and inexperienced National Guardsmen! Amiri Baraka claimed to see the incidents as an ideological insurrection, a revolutionary act of defiance against the oppressive state, despite its obviously opportunistic and random nature. Martin Luther King disagreed, his contradictory condemnation accused the African-Americans involved of simply harming themselves and their own cause. Inevitably the names of Black Power agitators Stokely Carmichael and H Rap Brown were invoked and dragged into the on-going argument.

Afterwards, for the Family Stone, the incident seemed like it must have been a warning. The great adventure wasn't working out as it should. Despite touring heavily and playing hard, the album wasn't achieving to expectations. Columbia hadn't even pulled an 'A'-side single from it, biding their time for Sly to deliver "(I Want To Take You) Higher" from his second batch of sessions. At this stage, the song still fell far short of the anthem it would become at Woodstock, and the single failed to make much of an impact. Kapralik's other clients—sweet-soul duo Peaches & Herb (Marlene Mack and Herb Fame), were even bankrolling the group's extravagances. For Sly this was a real fork-in-the-road moment. He began to wonder whether perhaps it wasn't time to quit. Return to Frisco where they were reassuringly well-known and guaranteed a good reception. Where, if things didn't work out, he could always pick up on the leads of his neglected DJ career. But despite such occasional lapses into uncertainty, he still suspected that it must all fall into place. Eventually.

Then, 18:01pm 4th April 1968, a single shot rang out in the Memphis sky, and Martin Luther King was assassinated on the Room 306 balcony of the Lorraine Motel, in the name of love, once more in the name of love. Only the day before, he'd declared 'I've seen the promised land. I may not get there with you...' Now, to Eldridge Cleaver, the shot was the sound of 'chickens come home to roost'. The only possible outcome for the path of non-violence. To George Jackson, thirty-nine-year-old King 'was out of place, out of season, too naïve, too innocent, too cultured, too civil for these times. That is why his end was so predictable'. Elsewhere, there was a feeling that the time of opportunity, of possibility… of King's dream, the modest aim of liberating the world, was unravelling. 125 cities were torched in retaliation, exploding simultaneously in America's biggest riot-wave, leaving forty-six people dead, 2,600 injured, and 21,000 arrested. City after city burst into flames. We're still living with the repercussions of those lost illusions. But first, James Brown stepped in, made a live-broadcast through WGBH from the Boston 'Garden' concert-stage urging restraint, then broadcast live on his own stations in Baltimore and Knoxville, followed by a TV-appeal in Washington DC—'be calm, stay home, don't terrorise, organise', talking up more constructive ways of venting that justified rage. His persuasion helped restore calm, to such effect that Vice President Hubert Humphrey bestowed his official thanks. An event that grew into a cornerstone of the 'godfather's legend. The most Soulful of peace activists had now become a White House confidante. Yet despite the commendation of the state, people knew that Mr Brown had 'paid the cost to be the boss'. That he'd fought his way out of a deprived South Carolina background. Poverty had been constant throughout his childhood, abandoned by his mother and then his father, raised by an aunt at the brothel she ran in Augusta, he hustled, shined shoes, picked cotton, and was once sent home from school for 'insufficient clothes'. At fifteen he broke into a car and was sentenced to eight-to-sixteen years in jail, which is where he started singing in gospel combos. He'd achieved the classic American dream through his own talent and abilities. And above and beyond the establishment's official recognition, he'd assumed a giant's stature, looked up to as a figurehead of black consciousness.

Since the earliest months of the year, the war in Vietnam had been taking a sharp downturn. Illusions of American gains shattered by the communist Tet Offensive which maintained a sustained assaults across several fronts, from Saigon in the south to recapturing Hue in the north. Robert F Kennedy announced his late intention to run for the presidency after winning the California Primary. But on the night of 5th June—barely two months after King's assassination, he took a short cut through the kitchens of LA's 'Ambassador Hotel', and—at 12:15am precisely, he was shot to death, point blank, in the head, by Palestinian-American Sirhan Sirhan. His death presciently preceded by his speech about 'no martyr's cause has ever been stilled by an assassin's bullet…'

Then, 'I just looked around, and he was gone…'

Chapter Eight
'Dance to the Music'

'dyin' young is hard to take, sellin' out is harder...'
("Thank you falettinme be mice elf... agin")

'I Want to Take You Higher...'

Major record labels can be harsh and capricious mistresses. When a band first climbs into bed with them, the label promises the big romance—sun, moon and stardom. But if that first album doesn't instantly sell by the platinum planeload they'll just as swiftly fuck you—or stop fucking with you, as the case may be. And that can be as creatively devastating. Things were a little easier in the late-sixties. There was tolerance for what was termed 'artist development'. Although that tolerance had limits, the same principle applied.

It's not that David Kapralik and Clive Davis were unhappy with Sly & The Family Stone's commercial progress. Because they weren't. It's just that—he tells Sly, there's some potential for more. Much more. You have to back-pedal some on the innovation-thing for the folks in Smallsville USA, because they can't handle all that funky-ass chord-thing. Confuse the public, and they'll stay away. If Sly was to *simplify* the sound of their next record? All the band needs is a hit. Sly knows all about hit singles, right? He was the former boy-wonder producer who had crafted a few big ones already, Bobby Freeman, the Beau Brummels. He could do it again, couldn't he? Sly was not convinced, after all 'dyin' young is hard to take, / sellin' out is harder'. No, there was no question of coercion. There were no heavy threats of the label terminating their contract. What Clive Davis was saying was merely intended as a helpful recommendation. Such a move would provide an introduction to wider audiences, a Trojan horse, a viral strategy of insinuating into national playlists. Again, Sly gave thought to the suggestion.

So why not? This time he could see the advantages. Sly alone had the contractual right to select which tracks would become singles. Something most artists did not have. Only he could make it happen, or not happen. So it happened—to the extent that the result of the dialogue was realised with the issue of a classic dance single in November 1967. The gloriously up-lifting life-affirming three-minute project-statement that is "Dance To The Music". Recalling Bobby Freeman, Sly took his muse back to the dance-floor. Then stripped it still further back to the sparse and literally self-referential 'introduction' theme. So that the single had no other subject than the band itself, to the extent that it was imaginatively built around the kind of stage-routine in which each musician steps forward to demonstrate their proficiency with a flash instrumental flourish. An ingeniously high-fiving 'hello' to a yet-wider audience. Less than six months earlier, King Curtis had done something vaguely similar with his sax-led Top Ten hit "Memphis Soul Stew", which introduced each element as an instrumental ingredient of the musical 'recipe'. It's possible Sly had been taking notes. Nevertheless, the idea was not an immediately popular choice within the band. Even Jerry Martini expressed doubts about what he called the record's 'glorified Motown beats'. He saw it as 'such an unhip thing for us to do'. Does "Dance To The Music" make a cheap play for the listener's emotions? Does it flaunt with the conventions of what constitutes good taste? Is it dumbing-down? Who else builds an entire record on a single dynamic crescendo? To 'Rolling Stone' it was simply 'unique. The rhythm section played too hard and the arrangement and recording were too clean for it to be Soul music, but the vocals sounded too soulful for it to be Pop'. Ultimately, such questions never get answered, because there aren't any answers, there's no rational explanation for the way people feel moved by a sequence of notes, or a progression of chords. You make your music, and you shake your butt. In the final analysis, that magic must remain something transcendent, revelatory. But surely there's a qualitative difference between music that comes direct from the soul of the artist, and music that comes direct from the marketing department? Of course there is. But that doesn't mean that commercial music is entirely lacking in merit. "Dance To The Music" is 'just Sly Stone being his natural crazy self'.

On the up-tick, the Family Stone played 'The Kaleidoscope' 4-5 July, a club located on Sunset Boulevard just east of Vine, operated by Skip Taylor—Canned Heat's manager, in partnership with Gary Essert. They shared the bill with Canned Heat, and by all accounts were incandescent, returning for a 9-11 July session. They were unlikely contestants on NBC-TV's summer 'Talent Search: Showcase '68', tying with Jazz singer Joe Lee Wilson in the final round. While "Dance To The Music" did precisely what it was created to do. Primed like a Kalashnikov and aimed at the feet, it broke them into earshot. This was the watershed moment. The point at which Sly declared 'I started to become successful'. Never mind those plans for seeping gradually into awareness, getting snuck in under the air-play radar, this whip-sharp slam of calculated psychedelic-Soul 'n' Roll was first picked up by DJ Lucky 'The Baron of Bounce' Cordell at Chicago's WVON, from there it spread station-to-station city-to-city until soon it was deluging the radio-waves, AM and FM. This exuberant burst of polyrhythmic dancefloor-friendly party-Pop, this ultimate message for affirmation and togetherness, first took the band to the top of the R&B charts, then rose to peak at a US Billboard Pop no. 8. Blink… and they were adorning the covers of every heavyweight music journal across the nation.

And could a band's manifesto ever have been more crisply enshrined in one song than it was in "Dance To The Music"? I doubt it. It opens with Rose exhorting you to 'Get up and dance to the music! Get on up and dance to the funky music' until the whole band punch out the chorus, 'Dance to the music, dance to the music'. Freddie opens with 'Hey Gregg!', Drummer Gregg responds 'what?'. Freddie suggests 'all we need is a drummer, for people who only need a beat, I'm gonna add a little gee-tar and make it easy to move your feet'. Then Larry's cavernous baritone—as deep as San Pablo Bay, leaps in 'I'm gonna add some bottom, so that the dancers just won't hide'. Sly himself contributes 'you might like to hear my organ, playing 'Ride Sally Ride''—which he proceeds to do with a cutting Hammond B3 insert, then 'you might like to hear the horns blowin', Cynthia on the throne, yeah! Cynthia and Jerry got a message, they're sayin'' with Rose ad-lib responding 'all the squares, go home!' The vocals are bounced around like pinballs, as if they're playing some game of catch, male to female, falsetto to bass, until the full band are chanting into the fade, 'dance to the music, dance to the music…'

The soloing, ensemble sections, and even a scat acapella passage all conspire seamlessly into each other in a mosaic of an arrangement that is both unusual and revolutionary. The 'boom-boom' refrain had evolved much earlier when Sly missed his lines during rehearsals, and filled in, each of the band playfully mimicking his lead in precise harmony as the verse came around again. Just as Cab Calloway had disguised the fact that *he'd* forgotten the lyrics by improvising 'Hi-de-hi-de-hi-de-ho, Ho-de-ho-de-ho-de-hee'. For naturally, "Dance To The Music" was a piece of electrifying trivia crafted by Sly—he was producer, song-writer *and* lead singer, yet it was structured as a band-dialogue with improvisational space built into it for each soloist—in the way that Duke Ellington contrived to compose with the talents of specific soloists in mind, leaving deliberately missing passages to be fleshed out by them. George Clinton explains how Sly 'wrote the bass lines out for Larry Graham—even though Larry delivered them unlike anybody else in the world, Sly wrote the parts up. He was an arranger.' With lines for each of the Family Stone's four lead singers to trade off each other. It takes a particular kind of skill to concoct a three-minute dose of melodic crack so addictive that one taste has you hooked. Such compositions can be rays of sonic sunshine to brighten the planet.

****

'Music Is Love, Grab Hold, Wake Up...!'
(Columbia Records advertising slogan run in the underground press November 1968)

"Dance To The Music" was a preconceived project—and it worked spectacularly. The beat was on. It flung open all the doors. It reached bubblegum teenyboppers in the schoolyard, revellers in neon Discos and night-life clubbers, the Brothers & Sisters of the Panthers, hardcore freaks, middle-class desperate housewives, as well as GI's napalming peasant villages in Vietnam. This time there could be no ignoring Sly. With the air-waves secured, even through the subterfuge of toning the sound's radical edge down for the pop audiences, the full visual phantasmagoria could now be unleashed. Sights *and* sounds. The earliest surviving 'studio/promo' clip of the Family Stone performing "Dance To The Music" shows them in almost conventional clothes and hairstyles. The soon-to-follow album-cover also shows the seven-piece group quite soberly attired by comparison with what was to come. Sly sitting to the fore in red patterned open-neck shirt, with sensibly short hair. The band ranged out around him, smart-casual. On the original *'A Whole New Thing'* album sleeve Jerry even commits the fashion faux pas of wearing socks with his sandals! But if you want to be treated like a star, you have to behave like a star—think big to be big, so from that moment on they sharply up-shift into a presentation as purposefully freaky as they could contrive. Freddie's Stone Souls had always been more sartorially adventurous. Now the Family Stone took it further. There was to be no uniform for the Family Stone. Unlike the 'look' that other bands adopted. That was a conscious decision. No uniform—but there was to be a co-ordinating 'theme'. Red, white and black, in a diverse thematic continuity (in a kind of future-echo of White Stripes' uniform colours). They would buy at 'North Beach Leather', or at thrift stores. Not that Sly necessarily had much time for the austere ideological rejections of glitzy superficiality, or the dressing-down anti-consumerism of hip youth culture. He merely wanted in on the party. Yet—when Pop-Artist Richard Hamilton's 1957 manifesto declared that art should be 'popular, transient, low-cost, mass-produced, young, witty, sexy, gimmicky, glamorous, big-business', Sly & The Family Stone tick every box.

The full rainbow-collision was flourished coast-to-coast when the single's success grabbed them their first nationally-networked TV exposure. They performed their hit live on NBC's variety show 'Kraft Music Hall' (21st

August 1968), then on Dick Clark's 'Happening '68' Saturday afternoon show, lip-synching "Life" (31st August). Finally they made the legendary 'Ed Sullivan Show' (28th December 1968) opening with "Life" and "Everyday People". Broadcasting to upwards of twenty-million viewers this was the show that had launched Elvis Presley and the Beatles as national phenomena, and where the Rolling Stones, the Doors, and The Mamas & The Papas had all reached massive new audiences. For the show's exacting requirements the featured songs had to be compressed within precise time-limitations. So to achieve maximum impact within those parameters—as part of a two-song set made up of "Dance To The Music / Music Lover", Sly departed from the script by moving the band off-stage and trooping out into the audience-tiers. With the group's energetically choreographed, onstage routines, combined with the Family Stone's outlandish appearance, they were opening further doors into the mainstream.

As his music developed, from playing colleges and larger ballrooms to capacity venues booked at both Bill Graham's Fillmore's East *and* West, the Family Stone were reaching black *and* white demographics in a kind of kaleidoscopic transcendence. And, accordingly, cross-country touring became more frenetic. Their name in a constellation of lights over the marquee. Performing live—*LOOK!*—all sharped-up… well, maybe. The acme of cool it wasn't. More sweat, glitter and flesh, yet in concert there was tangible electricity surrounding their brash 'dig-*THIS*' retro-futuristic pyrotechnics. An appeal calculated to ripple out way beyond the confines of the Soul and R&B hardcore, to Rock and Pop audiences. An absurd overkill that radiated out from Sly—tall and skinny, in tight gold lurex, legs spread wide, swaying back and forth centre-stage at his Hammond B-3. His Black Power Afro-hair descending into muttonchop sideboards, beneath a huge floppy cowboy hat sequined to within an inch of its life, or a glitter-encrusted tam that sparks like lasers in the stage-lights, down to tight leather trousers and vinyl boots and a huge belt-buckle that spells out 'S-L-Y'. Or assorted crocheted hats with goggles, leather jackets with dangling buckskin fringes worn over suede tie-dye vests, and velvet stack-heel boots. Dancing, measuring every twitch, shrug, and dirty laugh. People who never lived through these times might suspect that reports of his charisma have been exaggerated by nostalgia, and by the poetic hubris of his decline. Not so. On stage Sly flames so fiercely he's in danger of spontaneous combustion.

And he's far from a stand-alone concern, he's flanked by his well-drilled and devastatingly assured Family moving in their category-smashing, devilishly eclectic, sexy choreography, while injecting counterpoint, choruses and hooks in exquisite staccato. Rose in fantastic blonde wigs and go-go dresses. Larry in flowing robes, or capes part-enveloping Edwardian ruffled shirts and fur-lined boots. And Freddie in appliquéd overalls. A mix-matched mishmash with jumpsuits and rhinestone-studded tops, gold lamé shirts with flower-print pants, all with diamond-encrusted accoutrements, brooches and name rings. Jerry might appear in a poncho, modified by Sly armed with a rug-cutter. Cynthia with Afro hair-do, enhanced by smocks in dazzling psychedelic-swirls. Errico in leopard-skin print outfits. Fame had remade the Family into extraterrestrial entities. Alien, years before David Bowie made androgyny vogue. Supernaturally improbable beings, eye-strafingly shiny, both sexually *and* racially ambiguous. Could George Clinton have appeared so extravagantly garbed or funked-up without the Family Stone having first paved the way? This freakiest and foxiest extremism worked on more than one level, to provoke a range of contrasting responses across demographics. From 'how camp' to 'that's so weird it's cool, man'. From a stoned '*WOW*' to the more visceral knee-jerk disgust. And this heightened theatricality of the Family Stone's frenzied on-stage presence used every aspect of the media effectively to provoke attention. Sly's songs and the raps between them were exhortations for people to 'Get on up—and *dance* to the music!' out of their seats, out of their bodies, out of their skins, out of their heads. Sly preferred not to play to restrained audiences. He resented looking out to see a uniformed barrier of badged rent-a-cops between the Family Stone and the audience. He even had a clause written into his concert contracts prohibiting armed cops. 'I don't care if they rush the stage' he announced, 'we love it'.

Decades later—in December 2001, "Dance To The Music" would be recognised by the 'Rock 'n' Roll Hall of Fame' as one of the '500 Songs ThatShaped Rock 'n' Roll'. But meanwhile—Sly was not finished with it yet. Epic helped stoke the buzz by circulating DJ-only instrumental promos of the track, which would later turn up as hot properties on the Northern Soul Scene (and would feature on SRT's dance-compilation LP *'The Right Track'*). And towards the end of the year Sly released a playful novelty French-language version under the 'French Fries' alternate group-name—as "Dance A La Musique", with the vocals accelerated into something resembling Ray Stevens' 'Strawberry & The Short-Cakes'. Real Gonesville! and a prescient anticipation of its animated simulacra added to the 2001 *'Shrek'* DVD-edition as part of the 'Shrek In The Swamp Karaoke Dance Party' bonus-feature.

Meanwhile, there were concentrated sessions at the Columbia Records studios on New York's West 52nd Street, with engineer Don Puluse (who would stay with them across three albums). Until—in May, the resulting same-name tie-in album finally took The Family Stone inside the national LP chart, reaching US no. 142. In its totality, this is an album that takes a calculated step back from the one it followed. Even when spiced with a generous dose of what New York DJ Al Gee called 'the *real* ESP—Exceptional Soul perception'. With *'A Whole New Thing'* Sly had pulled out all the stops, confident that he could dazzle the audience by striving for only the best that he could achieve. This time there was a conscious retrenchment, he was safely playing and replaying to the distinguishing strengths and commercial identifiers of the break-through single, a theme restated, directly or indirectly through most of the material. Deliberately restricting himself to exactly the same go-go chord-progression formula on—count 'em, no less than five of the tracks. The title-listing for *'Dance To The Music'* opens with the first of the album's strengths, "Are You Ready" with its churchy organ intro and Freddie's confident greeting to the world 'groovy people, how do you do? let me dedicate my fuzz to you'. There's minimalist choppy guitar as Rosie takes the strong lead voice, punching out the title in gospel-exhortation style, with the tolerant 'don't hate the black, don't hate the white' line, leading into a stoic 'if you get bitten, just take the bite' moral. Following the title track, there's "Higher"—the gradually evolving piece that had its origins in "Advice", the song Sly had originally co-written and arranged for Billy Preston's 1966 album *'The Wildest Organ In Town'*. Further clues to its genealogy are suggested by the opening organ riff which unerringly recalls Jackie Wilson's "Your Love Keeps Lifting Me Higher", a track Jackie recorded with the Motown house band and took all the way up to a US no. 6 the previous September (there'd been an even earlier version by the Dells).

Among the remaining material, "I Ain't Got Nobody (For Real)" is based around a Motown-beat, its essential conventional content only slightly offset by the absurdist lyric 'she don't have to wear a wig, / she don't have to be too big'. "Ride The Rhythm" carries the kind of 'you might start with the Boogaloo, or you can do anything you want to do' dance instructions that might have spun loose from some old Bobby Freeman session. Then the funky "Colour Me True" is lifted by the smart observational 'do you laugh at the bosses jokes when they ain't funny...?'—with Sly perhaps glancing over his shoulder at making nice to former KSOL co-manager Alan Shultz? Something of the debut album's experimentation is finally allowed to resurface into "Don't Burn Baby", which is carried on a vaguely Doors-like backbeat complete with an even more vaguely Doors-like guitar-break. And again, the message is up-beat. But such adventurousness is swiftly cancelled out by Larry's soulful heartbreak ballad "I'll Never Fall In Love Again", an evocative soft-Soul ballad addressed to the sixteen-year-old girl who'd just torn his heart apart. It was also a song done originally on those long-ago Bobby Freeman sessions for 'Autumn'.

The album running time is all rounded out with a cannily-crafted "Dance To The Medley" which is a 12:12-minute tour-de-force non-stop party track extending through "Music is Alive", "Dance In" and "Music Lover", while taking the "Higher" chant towards the even more elevated "I Want To Take You Higher" along the way. From its psych-distortion and backward-phased drum-roll lead-in, all the way to its repetitive distorted backward-tapes electronic fade reminiscent of the Beatles' "Baby You're A Rich Man", it's an extended work-out elaborating the themes presented by the hit single. Taking its vitality and friendliness, then either extracting all variations—or milking all possibilities from the source? There's a recurrence of the trademark 'Listen to the voices' 'boom-boom boom-boom' scat-breaks. While each band-member gets to reprise their introductions—with variations. First 'I am sister Rose, jumping with the crowd'. Then 'Ready Freddie on guitar'. While 'Lazy Larry on bass' is there 'adding bottom to your fun', only to return with 'music for the human race, I'm going to add some funky bass', then yet again he's 'going to add some bottom to your groove'. Within the band, it proved to be a less than popular concept. But despite Jerry's derisive 'dance to the shmedley' put-down, there's a viable argument to suggest that it's a track that forms the kind of imaginative jam linking themes in the way the group might have improvised it on stage at the 'Winchester'. A showcase in which the repetition of motifs would seamlessly fade into each other as they played, with an irresistible call to the hips to swivel. Perhaps Jerry's downer attitude was at least in part tinged by the memory of contributing his B-flat clarinet part during sessions for the 'Medley' caught up in the middle of a freezing New York snow-storm.

As an album, Rosie's stridently assertive voice adds considerable distinguishing power to the mix. But there's a spread of four co-lead singers in total covering a range from gull-scream falsetto to a deep-rumble bass with the jarring resonance of a subway train passing beneath you. There are Rock-derived guitar riffs from Freddie. Funk basslines from Larry. Gregg's syncopated drum tracks. Sly's own gospel-styled organ lines. Punched out by Jerry and Cynthia's horns. Yet Sly's definitely in the driving seat here, even to the extent of purposefully scaling the melodic range back in favour of recognisable funk riffs and repeated refrains. But he gets away with it. Even the bonus track included on the eventual CD re-release—"Soul Clappin'", forms yet another 'time for the horns to start' "Dance To The Music" variant, opening playfully with Sly reprising his old Lord Buckley DJ call-sign 'Ladies and Gentlemen, Boys and Girls, Cats and Kitties, Hippies… and Squares'.

The sleeve-notes predict 'I know that in short time the name SLY AND THE FAMILY STONE will become as common to you as salt and pepper'. And sure, as the album first emerged in March 1968 they were playing the college-circuit through into the Spring semester. But as the album moved up the chart they upgraded accordingly to larger ballroom venues, playing a four-date engagement at the East Village 'Fillmore East' on 105 Second Avenue, as 'special guests' to a headlining Jimi Hendrix (10th May 1968). Following his incendiary performance at the Monterey Festival Hendrix was an unassailable rock-god. There was no way they could compete with the supernatural aura of such a stratospheric reputation. But Sly was gonna try. A bootleg recording, *'Sly & The Family Stone: Live At The Fillmore East'*, forms a valuable but low-fi historical document of the evening's performance, for which he devised a show-stopping audience-participation set-climax where Sly, Freddie and Larry took a series of flying leaps down off the stage while the rest of the band kept the beat pumping. Then, urging and cajoling the audience up out of their seats, they led them in a triple-pronged gyrating procession down the aisles, hand-clapping foot-stomping like some crazed dance revivalist meeting, all the way out into the auditorium, snaking in and out of the exits, then back into the ballroom again and back to their seats. People called the routine the 'hambone', an old schoolyard minstrelsy ploy (names as diverse as Red Saunders and Bo Diddley had benefited from doing it). Whatever, the show was a triumph. A tipping point in their climb to recognition. From New York they took the show to the Electric Ballroom, to 'The Sugar Shack' and Boston's 'Tea Party' where their outrageous long-haired hippie-weirdness got them thrown out of the city hotels and they had to sleep over in neighbouring Cambridge, then to the Chicago 'Aragon Ballroom', the Detroit 'Grande Ballroom'—no riot this time, and eventually back in triumph to the west coast, to LA, the 'Winterland' and the Fillmore West.

Despite which, the powerful follow-up double-'A' single "Life" c/w "M'Lady" incredibly failed to capitalise on its predecessor's success, managing to peak only as high as US no. 93. Despite the promotional launch-slot on Dick Clark's TV 'Happening '68', and despite both sides being impressively strong. From "Life's Barnum & Bailey carnival-barker hurdy-gurdy lead-in— the same device Smokey Robinson uses on "Tears Of A Clown", into its 'you don't have to die before you live' argument against passive conformity, urging instead 'get your living now'. The lyric utilises the trendy 'tell it like it is' hook, adding 'you might be scared of something / look at Mr Stewart! / he's the only person he has to fear'. In the light of the group's unfolding narrative, this would prove to be an unsettlingly prophetic statement. While flip the vinyl over, and its co-lead—"M'Lady", opens with exploding drumshots into a structure that part-reprises "Dance To The Music" sufficient to establish brand-recognition, yet with a manic scribbling alto figure which the vocals mimic, fuzz-tone guitar, little jazzy horn-fills, and eccentric non-verbal vocal effects to add strengths. Across both pop and soul markets sales were… healthy, if not yet earth-shaking. Perhaps airtime was divided, undecided which side to playlist, and so losing focus? Perhaps Sly had listened to too much unwise advice? Creating a Pop hit had done all they said it would, it had taken them into national prominence, and upped their gate-money, but had it also detracted from their reputation as serious musicians? Making money was the easy part, the trick would be discovering the secret of holding on for the full ride. Were they doomed to be remembered as gaudy good-time one-hit wonders who'd briefly brought people together in the discotheques of the world?

Meanwhile "Dance To The Music" itself was furthering its mission of introducing the band, and name-checking its members around the world. It had earned Sly Stone a platform. Pause here… the first time I became aware of Sly & The Family Stone, it must be around mid-July and I caught it on the radio. I was twenty-and-months. Naturally, I took note. It was as thrilling a sound to listen to, as it obviously had been for the band to make. It was almost indecently immediate. I was well-into R&B and Soul. Hell, to be into sixties Rock, loving black music was obligatory. I worshipped at the shrine of Chuck Berry and Bo Diddley. Otis Redding and Wilson Pickett. Marvin Gaye and Smoky Robinson. Aretha Franklin and Ronnie Spector. But in some ways, Sly Stone didn't exactly fit into any of those established constellations. The beat was quasi-Motown, but nothing that came from the motor-city ever sounded quite like *this*. As a dance record, just thirty seconds into the mix there's the first acapella break, and how do you *dance* to that? And isn't that a fuzzed-up Fender bass in the mix?—on a *soul* record? We knew that Muddy Waters and Howlin' Wolf led the listener directly into the entire Chess stable. Otis Redding, Booker T, and Sam & Dave link you into the extended Stax family. The Miracles, Temptations and Stevie Wonder plug you into the Tamla-Motown factory. Aretha into the mighty Atlantic roster. Yet Sly leads into the Family Stone… and stays there. It takes you nowhere else. The Family Stone was, at least for now, its own self-contained continuum. It's an irresistibly fun record. It's impossible not to react to it. But there seems to be no cultural network to provide convenient family-tree links to other bands, other musicians, other happening scenes.

Even their UK label—'Direction', lacked the heavy Soul-Boy prestige of a Stax, Tamla-Motown-Gordy, or Atlantic. And the label had always been important. These were days when the label was seen as an expression of a singular passion and vision, before corporate mergers and the bureaucraticisation of the music business put paid to such presumptions. Blue Note—under the enlightened guidance of Alfred Lion & Francis Wolff, defined the whole world of post-bop cool. Ahmet Ertegun & Jerry Wexler's Atlantic provided a guarantee of soul quality. In the earlier sixties, Columbia signed Aretha Franklin—but didn't know what to do with her. It was only after she'd left and gone to Atlantic that she began selling records. And that's before you even get to the label founded by Berry Gordy Jr. It was difficult to think of 'Direction' in quite the same way (in fact, to further complicate matters, a slightly different mix of "Dance To The Music"—now the rarest of collectables, had initially been issued on Columbia, before it was hastily replaced by the launch of Direction). The most visible air-play connection to Soul or R&B on the Direction roster came in the form of sweet dance-hit "Breakin' Down The Walls Of Heartache" by Johnny Johnson & The Bandwagon. Hardly essential stuff. It was too easy to similarly dismiss "Dance To The Music" as a novelty hit, a catchy well-structured one-off without the hard relevance of other more vital stuff in the racks. Later, Direction would compile its own self-congratulatory 'greatest hits' album, a label-showcase of 'sixteen tracks, specially picked for their groovy sounds by Derek Everett'. *'Groovy Baby'* (Direction 8-63452) featured 'hit-makers' Sly & The Family Stone (with "Dance To The Music" and "M'Lady"), plus the aforementioned Johnny Johnson hit (plus his "Baby Make Your Own Sweet Music"), with other tracks from Donnie Elbert ("Get Ready"), Bettye Swann ("Make Me Yours"), Cliff Nobles & Co. ("The Horse"), the Chambers Brothers ("Time Has Come Today"), Inez & Charlie Foxx ("Count The Days"), and Kapralik's *other* band—Peaches & Herb ("Love Is Strange")... in fact, enough strong material to retrospectively indicate that, yes, just perhaps they *did* have something to brag about.

But for now, each Sly beat has the potential to act like the dunked Madeleine that set Marcel Proust reeling back the decades. I was there, watching "Dance To The Music" debut at no. 27 (17th July 1968 in the *'Record Mirror'*), as oddly, the chart was topped by another defiantly mixed-race band, led by an equally strong writer—the Equals' "Baby Come Back". Eddie Grant would also take it on from this hook-driven Pop-friendly hit into deeper relevance. On the same chart The Rolling Stones' "Jumping Jack Flash" dropped from five to nine. Simon & Garfunkel's *'The Graduate'* movie-theme "Mrs Robinson" was the highest entry, in at no. 17. The Small Faces' wonderfully strange "Universal" and Donovan's psychedelic opus "Hurdy Gurdy Man" were also inside the thirty. Alongside Pop fluff by comedian Des O'Connor. By the following week, watch, Sly had climbed up to 23. Then 14, and 12. *'Record Mirror'* ran an uncredited interview feature to announce the new chart act in a slightly patronising way— 'it's not every group that can boast a girl trumpeter, but Sly & The Family Stone can—and do'. Finally—14th August, with The Crazy World Of Arthur Brown's "Fire" displacing the Equals up there at no. 1—igniting his head on *'Top Of The Pops'*, Sly peaked at no. 7. That was—no. 7 on the charts compiled by the *'Record Retailer'*, the charts which are now used for the various 'Guinness' *'British Hit Singles'* volumes. But not on the rival *'New Musical Express'* chart. There, it only peaked at no. 10 (17th August). But over the following weeks it would fall to ten for two weeks, down to 13, then to 20... as, that same week, of the 11th September 1968, the full band were jetting into London to commence its first UK tour. Meanwhile, I watched as the record's chart career continued at 23, 31 and for a final showing for two weeks at 37.

London, September 1968. For the Family Stone, these were to be their first major foreign engagements. For them all, it was a big deal. There was a lot of excited anticipation. But the promotional tour was doomed to be a brief one. Arriving at the Airport like strange gods, they check-in at customs, only for a zealous Heathrow bag-searcher to discover a cannabis stash concealed in Larry Graham's luggage. Allegedly it was a spliff Jerry Martini was about to bin, which Larry retrieved. Whatever, as a result, the oh-so-sensitive BBC-TV cancelled the band's scheduled appearance on the prestigious *'Top Of The Pops'*, following which there were disagreements with concert promoters.

Don Arden—of 'Galaxy Entertainments', was less than sympathetic. Despite his reassuring sandy-coloured mohair suit, he was a strong-arm impresario with a long 'twenty years of rough and tumble' history. He was the hardheaded kind of guy who knew where all the Brit-Rock skeletons were buried. Starting off in the 1950s as a singer-comedian he'd found his niche as compére of the first UK Gene Vincent tour, so later—when Gene relocated to Europe, he became the Rocker's manager. Until the acrimonious end of their arrangement. From there he'd switched his attention to promoting home-grown talent, acting as agent for the Animals, the Nashville Teens, and Amen Corner, then was ruthlessly involved in the irresistible rise of the Small Faces. Including chart-fixing for them. When the Faces eventually sued him for unpaid royalties he used protracted contractual litigation to delay settlement for a full decade—until 1977! Peter Grant—Led Zeppelin's heavyweight manager, learned his trade in Arden's employ with the Move and subsequently the Electric Light Orchestra. Aggressive, short-tempered, and fiercely independent, rumours of Arden's mafia connections were perhaps exaggerated, but sawn-off shotguns, and the use of armed bodyguards to intimidate rivals with threats of physical violence was not. In an incident high in the folk-lore of sixties management, the bullying 'Al Capone of Pop' used well-muscled rent-a-thugs to discourage approaches made by Robert Stigwood. They frog-marched him to the balcony, dangled him precariously from the open fourth-floor window over Hanover Square below, and threatened to drop him. In a separate entrepreneurial feud over the Move he had Clifford Davis—Fleetwood Mac's manager, beaten up over a misunderstanding. It was supposed to be Peter Walsh! As a footnote to the story, Don Arden's daughter Sharon married another of his clients—Ozzie Osbourne, to embark on a celebrity career of her own.

For Sly, there were problems with amps and equipment, creating tremendous backstage tension. Demonstrating steely obstinacy, Sly refused to compromise on rented gear. Don Arden's people were already in threatening mood, with Kapralik's diplomacy attempting to arbitrate between Sly's rock and their hard place. Arden was not a man to mess with, but neither was Sly. He dug his glitter wedge-heels in, and refused. Eventually, a grudging compromise resulted in the briefest of impromptu a-cappella sets, with Sly himself defusing the situation. He grabbed the microphone, speaking directly to the audience, fielding catcalls and heckles. A week later the band were back on the plane, quitting British shores without having once performed a full set. It was a downer, but as slight compensation, "M'Lady" edged its way up to a UK no. 32 in October.

Larry had been careless. But hey, it was only marijuana, it had been part of the deal from the very start. Surely the original group-name—the 'Stoners', must have been something of give-away? Jerry and Sly had tried cocaine as early as 1967 at the 700 Urbano Street house. But not Freddie, not yet. Drugs were no big deal. More a fun indulgence. A bonding ritual. It only started to get more serious in New York, which was their recording base of operations for some six months with the band staying over at the Gorham Hotel on 125 West 55th. They had a shady Manhattan Dentist who wrote 'scripts' for prescription drugs—downers, uppers, barbiturates. And pharmaceutical cocaine. It was part of an underbelly of sophisticated sleaze. William S Burroughs describes the same process operating decades earlier. The secret codes communicated by the narcotic underground community to identify 'soft' targets. Doctor Do-Good's who would write scripts as a low-cost alternative to the dealer. For Sly, a dental appointment did not necessarily involve treatment to his teeth. For Freddie, it was during the party the night after the Fillmore East gig with Hendrix that he took his first toot of cocaine…

Meanwhile, as their career took off, David Kapralik ejected from Epic—again, this time to manage the Family Stone full-time, although he continued to also represent Peaches & Herb. First of all he set about rationalising the sprawling out-of-control tax and legal situation complicated by their sudden commercial expansion. He set up Daedalus Productions—which would evolve into 'Stone Flower Productions', as an in-house production unit guaranteeing Sly a considerable cash-yield. Then there was Daly City Music, which acted as the band's publishing brand. With ownership split between Kapralik and Sly, it further concentrated the power-structure, with the group receiving only performance royalties. David retained Barbara Bacchus as his New York secretary, but also engaged Stephani Swanigan as a dedicated personal assistant for Sly himself. Efficient and intelligent, she was more used to working with smooth Capitol Records artists Tennessee Ernie Ford—who'd had hits with "Give Me Your Word" and "The Ballad Of Davy Crockett"!, and balladeer Nat King Cole. Sly was nothing like that. For her, it would be a learning curve into strangeness.

The Family Stone's spectacular first arc of changes drew to a close with the album *'Life'* (issued July 1968), deluged in more pulsating fusions of wah-wah guitar, undulating well-greased bass rhythms, complex changes and fine chanted vocal harmonies. The meanest, slinkiest, baddest asses of 'em all are having fun. And they'll seldom sound quite so playful, or be so much pure good-timey fun again. It starts with the sleeve figuratively asking, is this the show… or is this life? Multiple images of the band sit in audience-rows looking up expectantly at where the stage should be… but, in fact, they are looking out into the camera… by reversing the usual audience/band relationship, they're looking out at the observer. One of the Freddie's turns to confide something to one of the Rose's. Three Sly's sit in a row. There's a scattering of Larry's. Various Jerry's look cool in beard and shades. And the Gregg's watch back at you in green striped shirt and tie.

For its UK release the album was hopefully reconfigured as *'M'Lady'*—

to capitalise on the modest radio-play the single had received, with a different sleeve made up to resemble a collector's display unit subdivided down into shapes for miniature band members to be framed within, alternating with the kind of white heads used by phrenologists to explain the functions of the cerebellum. Each box also carried a song-title. It was given the bonus celebrity endorsement of sleeve-notes penned by maverick former-pirate DJ Emperor Rosko, by then broadcasting through a Saturday lunchtime Radio One slot. 'So, you wanna take a mind excursion, baby?' he invites, 'wanna little diversion—a hip trip—the return to the reality of what positive soul is all about?' Then he describes the sound of the album as 'psychedelicate, i.e. It delicately balances the psyche'. Despite such hyperbole, an unimpressed *'Record Mirror'* sniffily commented that 'one gathers he (Rosko) is rather in favour of the all-out attacking music of this violent group'.

Ground-breaking, in a genre that prefers its ground solidly intact, it remains one of my favourite Family Stone albums. And incredibly, it's their *third* LP in the space of a year. Sly had made the commercial concession, and been rewarded with the promised chart breakthrough. OK—that was great, now could he do it again? And more, it was time to *build* on what he'd achieved. He was impatient not only to consolidate, but also to expand that audience. Taking the thesis-experimentalism of *'Whole New Thing'*—trying to retain that playful adventurousness, while simultaneously fusing it to the antithesis, which was the commercial edge of *'Dance To The Music'*. Forming a synthesis that worked in both zones. As a result, the album might constitute only an uncertain advance on what he'd already done, but this time there's a more conscious attempt to integrate the original R&B base with the wordplay and sonic eclecticism of white Rock. With varying degrees of success. Having absorbed such disparate influences along the eccentric route of his career, Sly found himself located in a place somewhere in between— and capable of taking advantage of both the tighter, conventional song-structures of Pop, and the looser more free-form improvisations which give each participant their head. Here, on the lumbering subdued funk of the experimental "Into My Own Thing", each member of the band, it suggests, are into 'their own thing', and the dialogue teases responses from them. Invited to 'get to the bottom of *that*', Larry responds with a line of stinging fuzz-bass, 'then the drummer', and Gregg adds a shimmer of cymbals. Jerry's sax-line response would later be sampled by Fatboy Slim as a motif for his 2000 "Weapons Of Choice". Then the tighter title-track "Life" with its amusing production touches of circus clown-horns, leads into the rocking "Love City" with its ghostly vocals set back in the mix, suggesting bizarrely that 'you just might even see Harry Truman groovin' with the squares'. And the alternate title-track "M'Lady" which clings to the secure familiarity of another "Dance To The Music" chord variant.

Although this elision of divisions forms the dominant theme, the stronger tracks might be the ones that ride closest to Sly's sources. The blaring demon fuzz-guitar of "Dynamite" winds James Brown tightly into the Quicksilver Messenger Service, an alchemist's elixir propelled by propulsive clapping. Gregg's thundering drums punch out its paean to 'Miss Clean', yet—to be safe, it closes with the 'boom-boom boom-boom' refrain—which is repeated for emphasis from "M'Lady", and then—into the fade, it even quotes directly from "Dance To The Music" with laughter, in much the same way that John Lennon quotes "She Loves You" in the extended fade of "All You Need Is Love". But like the best of the cuts, "Dynamite" up-fronts a more aggressive, heavily-distorted guitar style than previously heard. And if the track had been any more compressed it would surely have dissolved back into petroleum in your fingers.

There's plenty of solid up-beat fun to be had in the funky-Stax hybrids "Fun" and "Harmony". The latter suggests 'you can be you, let me be me… that's harmony', pointing out that—as the Jackson Five would later reiterate, it's 'simple as 1,2,3, easy as ABC', but extends it beyond racial into gender tolerance as Rose interjects an acerbic 'do you like me for who I am, or who you want me to be?' Unexpectedly the track then closes by breaking into a tempo-switch three-quarter waltz-time—predating Jimi Hendrix' similar innovation on his "Little Miss Strange". And while the satiric "Plastic Jim" teasingly references the Bar-Kays recent Stax hit "Soul Finger"—its 'cellophane smile' which 'cannot be degraded' uses the cellophane-reference in the way that "Lucy In The Sky With Diamonds" does, and the 'p'-word as a metaphor for the worst excesses of consumer society. In the same generic way that the Kinks' "Plastic Man" would do, as an all-purpose put-down aimed at everything that's most phoney and artificial. It more firmly shows Sly setting his sights on where he was headed, another stab at exploiting the straight mainstream mindset of the 'squares', versus the hippie-mentality. Again, coming down firmly on the more-marketable hippie's side. On the Zappaesque counter-culture parody "Jane Is A Groupee" Sly's target is even more clearly the world of rock 'n' roll. One by one the male group-members add their line to the tale—relating how to each of them Jane is his 'biggest fan'. And Groupiedom, after all, is a rock subject. 'In case anyone hadn't noticed the fact' *'Record Collector'* magazine points out, 'he covered the song in fuzz guitar' (April 1993).

Elsewhere there's even more random cartoon silliness, on the strutting pecking "Chicken" or the infectious fun of "I'm An Animal", which provides an excuse for further gratuitous animal noises, snuffles and chimp-whoops, plus 'monkey-around' puns. Yes, they're animals, but of 'the thinking kind', a sentiment that can sound clumsy when racked up against Zappa's sharp crisp edits, except the Family Stone benefit from some cool-jazz inserts. And even the fact of drawing comparisons with Zappa rather than, say, James Brown, is surely a signifier in itself. Yet oddly, despite such a wealth of irresistible dance-funk material, the album failed to climb any higher than a US no. 195 in December, and it neglected to spawn the expected hit singles too. In retrospect, this seems barely believable. After all, it's an album which delivers the same incredible buzz that their live reputation was unleashing. It's as though the world at large needed time to catch up with what they were doing. Sly was striving towards some full-blown blizzard of deranged acid-funk that he could visualise, but the mass-public was not yet ready for, it was still thinking in terms of tight boxes—white Rock does this, R&B does that. Sly felt the compulsion to keep pushing towards it anyway. Towards the precisely-balanced Family Stone formula they would deliver so spectacularly, next time around.

There were, however, receptive media voices out there listening. It was hailed by *'Rolling Stone's* Barry Hansen as 'easily the most radical soul album ever issued'. And *'New York Sunday News'* writer Lillian Roxon commented that 'the group specializes in surprises… its members are male *and* female, black *and* white, soulful *and* freaky'. She goes on to observe that 'four people sing lead, and the switch from tenor to bass can happen just about mid-sentence, and again to soprano a second later. Musical puns abound—snatches of old hits, theirs and others, weave in and out of the arrangements. Three bars of "Eleanor Rigby" pop up in a song about plastics—'all the plastic people, what *do* they all come for?" Interestingly—as Roxon point out, "Plastic Jim" starts by referencing "Eleanor Rigby"—which was then barely two years old, then closes with what Miles Marshall Lewis detects as a quote from "Mary Had A Little Lamb", which would also become a 1972 Paul McCartney Wings hit single! Then she focuses in on 'a song called "Chicken", which is not about poultry at all, voices cluck like ruffled hens in an overcrowded barnyard'—or tease like a schoolyard taunt, don't be a cluck-cluck-cluck-chicken. 'Every song crackles with puns, jokes and mad flashes, loopy beats, witty lyrics, and off-centre vocalisations. So far, each album in turn has demonstrated a more polished version of the Family Stone. Now, the whole new-soul apparatus is there—designed to 'knock the corners off the squares', but once that framework is defined, everything else is ingenious new-rock madness, especially Sly's snide lyrics which deal with such non-soul subjects as groupies.'

'Non-soul', 'new-rock', so was it still R&B? It's not Motown, that's for sure. Or Stax either. So what the hell was it? According to authority-figure Charlie Gillett, the difference between R&B and Rock 'n' Roll is that the former was made by black people for black people, while the latter was made by black people for everyone. But it was more than that. A way of dragging James Brown into the next decade? Sly & The Family Stone were unexpected, natural, unexplained, weird, wise, fully-formed, and infused with a spark of unreasonable joy in a world of their own creation. With Sly as never less than the focal point of it all. He's setting the mood and atmosphere as well as chord-progression and riff. Both the abstraction that defined the group, and the hard rhythmic edge of its reality. He was an illusionist, teasing audiences with his freakish control. People wanted to be around him. They wanted to be his friend. As 1968 reached its end, it was obvious it had been a bizarre year of highs and lows. One major chart hit. Would that be all it amounted to? A one-hit wonder? Sales of *'Life'* might have been down on the previous album, but Sly & The Family Stone had become highly influential way beyond the *ker-ching* terminology of cash-registers. Even though the message of the hedonistic "Fun"—'when I party, I party hearty', would prove to have its downside...

Chapter Nine
'Everyday People'

'I'm a songwriter, a poet.
And the things I flash on everyday, they all reflect in what I say.
I'm a songwriter, I'm a poet...'

("Poet")

'Sing a Simple Song...'

January of 1969, and Sly's new single "Everyday People" was a masterstroke, one that abruptly switched the group's mercurial fortunes back around again. Whipping up a hurricane-force of stuttering juicily-kinetic beats it effortlessly topped the R&B chart. Then it went on to unseat Tommy James & The Shondells shuddering reverberating "Crimson And Clover" from the peak of the Billboard US Pop chart, to rule there for no less than five weeks from 15th February to 15th March. This time there was no possibility of ignoring Sly & The Family Stone—or dismissing them as a lightweight one-hit dance frivolity. More than any other number, it established Sly as an artist with a mass following among both young blacks, and young whites. He'd not only won the game, he'd made up his own rules. He had it both ways, Pop stations and R&B stations were equally at war over who could programme it on highest rotation. Even the 'B'-side—"Sing A Simple Song" charted as high as no. 89 in its own right, and would itself later be covered by The Jackson Five, The Commodores, The Temptations, and Diana Ross & The Supremes. Jazz organist Charlie Earland translated his version across genres onto his 1970 LP *'Black Drops'*. While Gregg's drum-breaks would make it the most sampled of all Family Stone tracks, with numerous hip-hop artists such as 2Pac, Public Enemy, and Digital Underground borrowing from it. Prince performed his own version of the song during his 2007 European tour, including his prestige 'secret' gig at Camden's 'Koko' Club.

Meanwhile, in March—just as Sly was entering his twenty-fifth year on the planet, "Everyday People" returned the Family Stone to the UK chart too, hitting a high of no. 36. And it remains a stunning two-minute-twenty-one-seconds of sublime Pop-friendly vinyl with Sly at his most revelationary, singing the main mid-tempo verse at his most slyly inventive. Then, listen as Rose takes that na-na-nee-na-na girl-chorus bridging-structure that goes 'there is a blue one who can't accept the green one, for living with a fat one trying to be a skinny one'… it has the naggingly memorable ear-worm quality of a school-yard taunt or a skipping song. Before the full four-piece vocal line-up of Sly, Rose, Larry and Freddie return to emphasise the title-chorus. 'It is this familiar chant that gives the disc its commercial appeal' explains the *NME* reviewer helpfully, while adding that 'this isn't quite as good as "Dance To The Music" (which was a hit), but considerably better than "M'Lady" (which wasn't)'! Well—maybe.

The lyric-call is a gently persuasive argument for racial tolerance across multiple skin-tones. A sentiment first euphemised through that absurdist guise of the 'blue one' and 'green one' in preference to 'black' and 'white'. But the meaning that comes through is impossible to hide from—that each member of the group, and by extension, everyone listening to it, should consider themselves less members of small factions, more part of the collective whole of humanity. Later, dropping such evasion, the recitation extends more openly to 'there is a yellow one that won't accept the black one, that won't accept the red one that won't accept the white one'. Sly—an Afro-American who had spent years producing white garage bands, then extends the chant still further, to cover prejudice against the counter-culture. As writer Peter Shapiro observes, the catchphrase 'different strokes for different folks… applied the libertarian axioms of Haight-Ashbury's privileged white bohemia to the struggle for civil rights and turned hippiedom's spoiled-brat consumerism into a fully fledged political statement'. The lines Sly writes 'there is a long hair that doesn't like the short hair, for being such a rich one that will not help the poor one' strikes a chord with the spirit of the times. Its exhortation 'ooh-sha-sha, we got-to live together…' works as precisely as an agit-prop advertising slogan. And most everything else on the radio-waves bleaches to grey beside it.

The equilibrium was precisely refined for the needs of the time. Some claim music is the universal language, right?—well, until we're able to hop a ride with Captain Kirk to the rim of the galaxy, we can't tell *just* how universal it is. Others claim that at its most basic level, music itself *is* a form of integration. Every musician who plays two notes, who includes dynamics, tone and pitch, is engaged in an act of integration. But to reach an audience in January 1969, it's necessary to go beyond rarefied theory, firstly—you have to be *heard*. Sales depend on radio play, so the song must be commercially viable. If it's too preachy it will incur radio programming displeasure, and no-one will get to hear it. Too much left-leaning politics, rage or anger will alienate advertisers and sponsors. Even the diverse system of largely autonomous local stations that then constituted the American broadcasting system were dependent on their advertising revenue-flow, and were hence unwilling to risk any controversy that would provoke adverse listener reactions. So it made perfect sense to record sentiments the station would be eager to play-list. And fuzzy logic platitudes about love, peace, tolerance and understanding are unlikely to ruffle feathers. Few could take exception to Stevie Wonder's bland "Ebony & Ivory" duet with Paul McCartney, or Michael Jackson's shallow if well-intentioned "Black Or White". Or, for that matter, Sly's "Everyday People". In a sense, Sly's rainbow-coalition message was going with the flow. But it was a complex simplicity. Underneath it all, there's the subtle infiltration of quite subversively radical ideas 'I am no better and neither are you, we are the same whatever we do'. A simple statement of the obvious, yet there were still plenty of reactionary racist segregationalists out there to whom the suggestion was incendiary, even as they found themselves tapping a toe to its contagious rhythm.

Eventually, the sublime "Everyday People" would graduate into the standard Soul repertoire, with a version by Aretha Franklin, soon followed by the Supremes & Four Tops. Later Joan Jett, Pearl Jam and Belle & Sebastian would reinterpret the song their way. Christian star Nicole C Mullen made it the title track of her 2004 CD, and the Arrested Development collective would use "Everyday People" as the basis for their 1992 hip-hop hit "People Everyday". What the Family Stone had begun would be taken further, and stated more explicitly by other voices, by other hands. There would be the Last Poets. Then Niggers With Attitude—including both Dr. Dre ("Fuck The Police") and Ice Cube ("Cop Killer"), who's work would be described as the 'revenge fantasy of the disempowered'. Public Enemy's "Don't Believe The Hype" would openly name-check Nation of Islam's Louis Farrakhan, while Chuck D's "Fight The Power" (written for Spike Lee's 1989 *'Do The Right Thing'*) reduces Elvis' iconic status to an irrelevance. Was there a direct causal connection to Sly? Perhaps not. But all were undeniably part of the same evolution. The nine-strong Wu-Tang Clan—out of 'Shaolin', Staten Island, would crib warrior-chic and eastern-mysticism from their favourite king-fu movies to accelerate the rage and articulate it with violently confrontational language never before deemed possible. Like a mutant ninja boy-band each Wu assumed his own persona—RZA, Ghostface Killah, Method Man, Ol' Dirty Bastard, allowing for infinite franchising, but while they rapped about hip-hop's enduring affair with gangsta bling and smackhead drugs, they did it in elliptical and consistently dazzling ways. But significantly, they did not have to rely on airplay. They were able to by-pass the radio networks and infiltrate through underground wavelengths not yet in existence for Sly & The Family Stone. If—with this song, Sly represents what the Panthers dismissively call 'a safe negro', with a more easily digestible form of blackness, then it's important to bear in mind that he had to work within the system. Or not work at all.

But first, with the Family Stone working about as good as it would ever get, there was the 3:08-minute "Stand!". A follow-up single that bursts into life with a fanfare of martial snare-drums, then rises through a series of structured crescendo's—'stand', ascending higher to 'STAND', then to the peak of a still higher '*STAND!*', while developing its inspirationally reassuring message along the way, 'stand for the things you know are right', because 'all the things you want are real'. Everyone with ears, everyone who cares about music, has a song that first altered the trajectory of their life. That touched them, and changed the way they view the world. For some it would be Elvis Presley's "Heartbreak Hotel", Bob Dylan's "Like A Rolling Stone", or maybe the Rolling Stones' "Gimmie Shelter". The Beatles "Tomorrow Never Knows", or the Byrds' "Eight Miles High". Other people have other 'consciousness-raising' numbers. And "Stand!" is exactly that kind of song. One that implores you to 'stand' proud, fulfil your potential. In life there will be problems and opposition, 'they will try to make you crawl' and 'there's a cross for you to bear' but 'in the end you'll still be you'. Ultimately—says Sly, it's less important whether you win or not, because the very fact of standing tall for what you believe will set you free. It's a message that can relate either to the individual—or in the wider context, to the community. And all of that reasoned positivism is contained in one concise Pop song. Sly at his best, demonstrating exactly what his chosen medium can aspire to.

However, the evolution of the track shows him at his most cautiously meticulous, using an original mix in the way that movies are now given test-screenings, and adjusted accordingly. Sly took a test-pressing acetate of the first mix down to the 'Rickshaw', a San Francisco discotheque, and got the DJ to spin it. Disappointed with the reaction it received, he took it back into the studio to refocus it, re-recording the final section entirely. As most of the original Family Stone were unavailable, he augmented the regular line-up by falling back on the talents of session players for the final fevered gospel-infused break. Recorded at the Pacific High studios in San Francisco—a few blocks from the Fillmore West, Sly distributed music-charts to the musicians to indicate his exact requirements. This tack-on end-section has been compared to the Beatles' 'hey-la hey hey-lo-ha' fade-back reprise on "Hello Goodbye", while—like "Surfer Girl", the first single Brian Wilson recorded on his own, using session musicians instead of the Beach Boys, the single also formed another watershed in Sly's career. It proved beyond doubt that he was perfectly capable of creating 'Family Stone' music by himself, without the involvement of the Family Stone. That was an important lesson.

The renovated "Stand!" single made it as high as US no. 22 in May, while its 5:23-minute anthemic 'B'-side, "I Want To Take You Higher" also made it up to no. 60. Already an upbeat re-make, of sorts, of the track "Higher" on the *'Dance To The Music'* album—itself based on the Sly/Billy Preston song "Advice", *'Rolling Stone'* called "I Want To Take You Higher" 'possibly the greatest one-chord song of the sixties'. It would return to prominence with a vengeance after its spectacular exposure in the *'Woodstock'* (1970) movie. In its original studio form it stays tighter and cleaner, a group-ensemble performance with Sly, Rose, Freddie and Larry taking lead while everyone else joins in for background vocals. Although many prefer the looser unparalleled energy of the in-concert suite which captures 'the towering power of his music machine'— and where its imperfections are erased by the real emotion which wells up all over it. Its inclusion as part of the live-sequence on the spin-off triple-album also makes it part of the only legal live recording of the Family Stone in existence. Demonstrating just how much audience response is vital to the very nature of the song. It already had a long evolution, and the song would have far-reaching echoes—even U2's "Elevation" is its distant cousin. Meanwhile, as trailers, these singles were making promises and building high anticipations that the breakthrough success of the album was more than capable of living up to. Ominously, *'Stand!* was issued 3rd May 1969, just as a ten-day riot-siege was enveloping nearby Berkeley, with the National Guard tear-gassing crowds and shooting one student dead in the battle for 'People's Park'.

Sly had calculated that once people recognised and accepted the brand's sweet seduction, they'd be prepared to listen to something a little more extreme. Accordingly, now that they *were* all over the radio, he'd force the outer limits of what was acceptable even further. While still playfully testing out those limits. His growing confidence brought polish to *'Stand!'*, bringing a new melodic sophistication to the dance blueprint. With its sleeve made up of a collage of colour-drenched stills of the band in performance, this is the album on which Mr High Energy has finally 'done all he'd set out to do'. Something has coalesced. Things have fallen into place, and they've pulled off an act that music-physicists would previously have deemed impossible. It's an album packed with powerful standout hits that zap you with five bang-bang-bang tracks before you've had time to digest the first. It's almost a stand-alone greatest hits package in itself. In fact, a total of five of its eight tracks would soon be collected onto their *'Greatest Hits'* anthology. Later still, the double-CD *'The Essential Sly & The Family Stone'* would include no less than seven of its eight tracks. One of its problems is precisely these strengths. It's difficult to restrain "Everyday People" as part of an album. It's almost too powerful to be considered as anything but its own self. And that is also true of the tracks that surround it. As an album it's an embarrassment of riches. An album of amazing diversity. No two tracks are alike. Blending highly melodic songcraft with a sonic ambition that seeps through the album like pure adrenaline and makes all things seem possible. What Peter Shapiro calls 'the joyful noise of the American dream realised, a fully integrated micro-society.' Yet it's an album assembled with the eye of a master film editor so that it sequences into a definitive whole that exceeds the strength of its parts. One that hangs together allowing the songs to bloom in context. Invigorated by all of Sly's freaky-deaky earlier influences, it adds an extra fresh flip, flop and fly in the art of direct hits and socking one-liners. Its clarity of purpose rigorously controlled, yet never less than rhythmically fluid.

Leading into the album there's the title track with its teasing racial metaphor 'there's a midget standing tall, and a giant beside him, about to fall', followed by the less ambiguous "Don't Call Me Nigger, Whitey"—a turbulent vortex of mordant distorted vocals nudging six minutes. Over-freakified perhaps, but the message is unmistakeably clear. Freddie's talking guitar constructs its own dialogue with scat nonsense vocal fills, suggesting whatever you want it to mean. The radio stations stayed well-clear. Not so with the apocalyptic openly manipulative "I Want To Take You Higher" with its simple repetitions that build and build, Cynthia's high stabs of horn effortlessly riding the jostling stratospheric rhythm like electrifying darts. The sweeter, but sweetly insidious "Somebody's Watching You" is a tightly structured conversation between female voices and male responses, a dialogue between Sly and Little Sister—with the surreal image 'shady as a lady in a moustache', underscored by Sly's burbling Hammond. "Sing A Simple Song" has Rosie's raucous but perfectly right harangue, shouting out the 'Do-Rae-Me' instructions like an impatient school marm. This is the track that practically invented the wah-wah pedal as a funk instrument, with a main riff that would be appropriated wholesale by Miles Davis for "Jack Johnson". Then there's "Everyday People"—the highest point of this first career-phase. Critics might carp about the album being themed around its occasionally overused production tendencies. Sly had developed an affinity for dual-tracking the bass, fuzzing the sound through one channel, while leaving the other clean. It could be argued he inserts it too frequently. There are phased drums too. A weakness very much 'of its time'. Yet such are the album's wide-ranging algorithms that it also needs continuity. And "You Can Make It If You Try" rounds-out the album with a reiteration of its title-track's message of positivity and positive-action. An 'accentuate the positive, eliminate the negative, don't mess with Mr Inbetween' that feeds strongly into 'The Power Of Positive Thinking' culture—its precision-tuned instrumental interjections etched out by Sly overdubbing bass, not Larry. Lines later sampled by the Jungle Brothers for their 1988 "Because I Got It Like That".

Two tracks break out beyond the singles' length-restriction. "Don't Call Me Nigger, Whitey"—about which more later, and the freeform wilfulness of the grinding wordless jam that is "Sex Machine", an endearingly rambunctious work-out running to 13:45 minutes. Built around a deep-down dirty Blues riff paired to walking bass, it swaggers with what sounds like submerged indecipherable treated sub-vocal noises to suggest all manner of deviant behaviour, from snuffling to blurred grunts. There's a sensually-paced Freddie guitar passage—acclaimed as his 'best recorded performance on a Family Stone album', then a raw sax-break swimming through an accelerating and decelerating drum solo. In total, it showcases an assured group dexterity derived from their free-form 'Winchester Cathedral' jazz-riffing, with the band finding its groove and mining all of its aspects, determined to stretch out and interact with seductive fluidity. With a title that would be 'borrowed' by James Brown for another funk classic the following year, the track had been built up in the studio, with Gregg Errico finally re-dubbing his drums over the completed track to take into account the way accents and rhythmic grids had evolved unpredictably through the process. Almost any of the album's tracks could have been effortlessly extended. Only this one is allowed to flex its groove and demonstrate its chops. At the end of Gregg's final play-out, where the drum solo slows to a barely registering post-coital pulse, there's the sound of spontaneous group laughter.

It's obvious that on this album Sly is allowing himself to have fun in ways he would seldom do again. As though he's enjoying himself, even as 'beneath the music's blissful surface (there) was a coded, sardonic humour that mocked everything, especially Sly himself' (as writer Peter Shapiro points out). Riding his highest visibility and greatest acclaim yet, he was simultaneously luxuriating in new opportunities to be provocative, something that would prove to be increasingly problematic. But it was always to a serious purpose. Sly was a complex amalgam of charming toughness, tungsten and soft-soap. The laughter that closes "Sex Machine" indicates the session's level of informality. Sly had fun doing what he was doing, but he was never less than tightly focussed, absolutely serious about his music. Sly knows it all and controls it all, yet wears it lightly. He works best as an ensemble player, a musician who prefers to surround his own voice with an answering chorus, a musician who likes to bounce off percussionists and other instrumentalists. Even when the title-track's additional instrumentation had been provided by L.A. studio musicians to fatten out the sound, the musicianship was never less than crisp and snappy (as Africa Bambaataa's sample taken from it proves). To the musicians Sly worked with there was a sense that they were in the presence of someone alive to entire dimensions of music they were scarcely even aware of. He could be exhausting to be around. And demanding in his work. Face-to-face, he had a tendency to wax enigmatic, with a sinful glint in his eyes. He wanted to be liked and accepted as a musician, although later, he would firmly turn his back on what people thought too. But for now, there's such a playfulness and humour about this album that it's entirely possible to miss its underlying darkness.

With *'Stand!'* on the hi-fi, even the way you walk to the fridge is different. You can't help but get down to it. This is a record that's near-perfect in its execution, an album of shifting textures, building towards ecstatic will-to-power climaxes, locking into hypnotic grooves. A frantic, dazzling chemical experience from top-to-bottom that constitutes a high watermark in the history of black music. It re-wrote the story, in a way that makes it key to any understanding of the period. The culmination of four album's work recorded at warp-speed, glistening with an accumulated command of studio technology rare at the time, it stood perfectly poised at the intersection of numerous musical, social, and political crossroads. A revelation in which music's of the recent past were re-energised to create the signature style of an exciting new brand, while in the process sounding a wake-up call that resonated across genres. A danceable solution to teenage revolution, nimble light-years ahead of its leaden-footed funk competitors. A fun-vibe so contagious it made crossover appeal seem like a political utopia. For there was no white band capable of approaching the Family Stone's brassy ensemble sound. Although it peaked no higher than the US album-chart no. 13, it stayed listed for over a hundred weeks, to inevitably become the group's first genuine hit album, its three-million sales qualifying it for certified gold disk status.

Even the British press was overwhelmingly affirmative, with *'New Musical Express'* adopting what we'd now consider a curiously staid formality, but which was then their default prose-style, to announce 'here is the hard rock group which weaves not only exciting instrumental patterns but vocal ones as well, between lead vocalist Sly Stone and the girls Rose and Cynthia, who surround him'. It's significant that the journalist 'AE' refers to them as 'hard rock' rather than R&B or Soul. He goes on to commend 'one of the numbers, done with a mock 'threatening-voice'—a sort of distortion to make it sound fiercer. He's referring to "Don't Call Me Nigger, Whitey", which gives the album gravitas by bringing 'the race-relations out into the open'. The reviewer qualifies such praise by protesting the track 'goes on' for 'almost six minutes', while conceding that there are 'some fascinating instrumental passages in it'. Finally 'AE' awards 'full marks for improvisation and experimentation' for "Sex Machine", which 'is another essay in ever-more-intense distorted sounds, which are most effective'.

This is the album that constitutes Sly's first-phase artistic career peak in what was already a wild and privileged adventure. With the dual worlds of black and white music at his feet, it was a creative feast, and a halcyon high-point for the band. It seemed impossible to believe the party would ever end. A cache of film-clips from the time, preserved on-line, convey the sheer energy of the Family Stone in performance, the contagious joy their stage-presence communicates. There's an NBC film-sequence salvaged from the summer 1968 'Ohio State Fair'. Jerry wears a ruffled shirt. Sly sporting extravagant sideboards and rhinestones, while indulging his taste for huge floppy cowboy hats in garish colours. He leaves off "M'Lady" mid-point to lead a spontaneous pantomime shout-back of 'L-O-V-E', with the audience roaring its response to each letter. Freddie and Larry are weaving in co-ordinated dance-steps, offset by Sly and Rose with their own simultaneous but different moves. It's not rigid choreography drilled through repetition and discipline. That much is obvious. No, it's music with a radiant happy grin on its face. At the close of the set the excitable show-compére comes out to present them with a $10,000 cheque, a 'groovy cash' award in recognition of their most-promising band of the year status. An almost-surreal moment.

In another concert clip "Stand" is taken without the rousing drumroll, but as a slow—and revealingly tuneful ballad that gradually builds to a powerful rock-funk group crescendo. An interpretation he'll recreate in Las Vegas as late as 2007, explaining 'I just felt like doing it like that, so everybody could really hear it properly'. Later, a TV-clip from a 1973 'In Concert' features the band playing beneath the huge arch of a studio-rainbow, with Sly taking guitar for "Thank You (Falettinme Be Mice Elf Agin)", adding a convoluted scat passage as Rose takes keyboard. George Clinton—talking to researcher John Reed, describes how it seemed the Family Stone 'was more of a pop group on record' but 'when we saw him (Sly) live—live they was a *funky* band' (to *'Record Collector no. 164'* April 1993). More eloquently Ben Fong-Torres enthuses 'Sly can look animalistic sometimes… since his hits, and concerts and TV shows, he's looked by turn ferocious, babyish, pompous, joyous. Sometimes handsome, devilishly, on stage on the rampage, he can look moon-faced, crinkly eyes, outsized shades, muttonchops, nose and mouth all blended into a voodoo mask, topped with over-flowing hair, attacking you with song, through white walls of teeth'. And the full-on showmanship, the spontaneous choreography and choreographed spontaneity, provoked instant theatre-audience responses. After the first song—or, on a slow night, after the second or third number, the sit-down crowd were up off their seats, dancing in the aisles or stood atop their seats gyrating. Kapralik even found in necessary to buy space for a full-page apology in the trade-press to a Cleveland auditorium manager for the thousands of upholstered seats found stomped to shreds after a Family Stone show there. An apology, and a timely warning-shot to the managements of future venues, for impending concerts, of what they had in store. Stardom had started out an abstract thing. An idea made of dream stuff. Sly was born wired to lead a soul-band—he was a hungry, excited, big-mouthed dude, with the necessary talent and confidence. Even in the grand tradition of divaish Rock frontman, he was extraordinary. But when stardom turned 'rill', overwhelmed by his public persona, he would find it a vertigo thing, an impossible state to reconcile with.

But he'd already developed a long way, and *'Stand'* was more developed than most. It was also the album that marked the most overt emergence of the political aspects of his writing. "Don't Call Me Nigger, Whitey" hits all the racial hot-buttons. Vet would later claim it was written for Dr Martin Luther King. Maybe it was. Whatever, it forms the equivalent of the electrically-charged moment when black cop Sidney Poitier demands 'call me *Mr* Tibbs' to redneck racist cop Rod Steiger in *'The Heat Of The Night'* (1967). And a future-echo of Eddie Murphy's 'I'm your worst nightmare, a nigga with a badge!' The word 'nigger' was even more incendiary then than it is now, as it had yet to be 'reclaimed' or rehabilitated as an ironically defiant self-identification usage. There might have been no such thing as 'political correctness', but using the appropriate euphemism was something equally vitally important. And as the racial status quo incrementally shifted, so did the terminology. Where it was once commendable to say 'negro', it became 'coloured', before it was permissible for James Brown to proclaim 'Say It Loud, I'm Black And I'm Proud', and the 'Black Is Beautiful' bumper-stickers began to be glimpsed. Or for Curtis Mayfield to establish the uneasy ratio between 'mighty mighty, Spade and Whitey'. But 'nigger'... even in the darkly humorous jokily play-taunting endlessly repeating way Sly uses it here, is a word you don't use without inviting slap-back repercussions.

"Don't Call Me Nigger, Whitey" is a 5:54-minute race-riot of a record. With barely audible treated vocal-lines that conspire incoherently, yet knowingly, in an unknowable sort of way. A production-effect gimmick of scat-singing through what sounds like a wah-wah'ed megaphone. Yet to maintain the movie analogies, at this point in his career Sly Stone was also Bart, the black sheriff—played by African-American actor Cleavon Little, in Mel Brooks race comedy *'Blazing Saddles'* (1974). Better-dressed, better-looking, and way-smarter than the simple white rednecks who oppose him, he runs playful rings around them, outwits and baffles them at every turn with a secret mischievous 'Oh baby, you are *so* talented, and they're so *dumb*' twinkle in his eye. Confronted by an angry mob, Sheriff Bart holds his gun to his own head and warns 'Hold it. The next man makes a move, the nigger gets it... drop it! I swear, I'll blow this nigger's head all over this town', then—play-acting out both roles, he adopts the 'nigger's' plaintive cry, 'Oh Lordy-lord, he's desperate. Do what he say, do what he say'. The confused rednecks back down. 'Do as he says, I think he means it' cautions the leading hick, outsmarted by the cunning ruse. Not to diminish the skill or artistry inherent in what he was doing, Sly was perpetrating exactly the same strategy, ridiculing, mocking, and effortlessly besting his opponents.

Perhaps Sly Stone's right-here right-now strategies could only have happened at this precise moment. When he challenged 'whitey's to stop calling people 'niggers'—while at the same time challenging 'niggers' to stop calling people 'whitey's', he changed the nature of the conversation. The defensive accusation goes back and forth in a repetitive dialogue of the deaf, leading nowhere. Which is Sly's intention. Beneath its jive artifice he was suggesting, wouldn't it be cool to go beyond that deadlock, for different races to show some consideration towards each other, and guess what?—maybe the time was right, because—as the sales-figures indicate, he was carrying a sizeable audience along with him. In a rare moment of candour he explained to Ben Fong-Tores that 'you can't scream that because you are a 'colour' you are anything. You are black—you are black, that's all. You are among people who've been mistreated a lot. But it doesn't necessarily mean a white person next door is responsible. His grandfather may have killed your grandfather, but he himself may love you. It's simple… either everything's fair or nothing's fair. Either everybody gets a chance to do what he wants, or… you know what I mean?' Yes, we know what he means. Is it fair to blame Sly because that dream didn't prevail? In the landscape of today's post-affirmative-action America the equality of its constituent racial minorities is no longer such a burning issue. The theme running through Sly's entire career has been neglected by a society that never needed its message more. At what other time in American history would anybody have even bothered to listen to his message?

To Sly, 'I didn't look at my job in terms of black'. He told writer Al Aronowitz how 'when I was a disc jockey, the first station I ever worked for, I got the best slot. I have no idea why, except I could write and I could read and I had a nice speaking voice and the girls liked me. I blew the station's whole format, but the ratings were fifty-eight to seven. Put that down, that's good for my ego. I played Lord Buckley, the Beatles, Bob Dylan, the Rolling Stones and Lenny Bruce on an R&B station. I had all these black cats callin' up and sayin', 'why you playin' whiteys, man?'. 'I explained to 'em that there ain't no black and there ain't no white and if it comes down to that, there ain't nobody blacker than me. There ain't nobody blacker than Syl'. Chris Albertson, framing the first CD re-issue of *'A Whole New Thing'*, sums it up rather quaintly, 'just as black people of the twenties were able to identify with the songs of the great blues singers, so today's fans find personal relevance in Sly's lyrics. Sly, however, has the advantage of changing times, which enables him to reach a much wider and more disparate audience. The message of his songs is aimed accordingly.'

****

'Space Family Stone' (*aka* 'The Rolling Stones')
—title of a 1952 novel by Robert Heinlein

So was Sylvester Stewart—as he'd later claim, a 'Poet'? The thing we call poetry takes many forms. There are as many kinds of poetry as there are poets writing it. But poems are not songs. Songs are not poems. The two devices operate on separate logics. A Bob Dylan verse is not—in itself, a poem. Just as a Keats ode does not necessarily lend itself to adaptation as a song-lyric. Yet there are sufficient hooks of contact that allow them to feed off each other with fascinating and often satisfying results. Lyrically, for the Family Stone, there's never the idealised cosmic metaphysical shit that some of the other Frisco bands were coming up with, but then again—if you happened to be part of the Family Stone, ordinary life could be pretty complex stuff. Sly's penmanship was seldom as honeyed as the intricate poetic flow of Smokey Robinson—'just like Pagliarchi did, / I've got to keep my sadness hid'. And, although Sly's lyrics were daringly underscored by deft wordmanship born of his scrupulous study of Bob Dylan, he never crafted anything with the metaphorical power of Sam Cooke's "A Change Is Gonna Come"—itself an answer to Bob Dylan's "Blowin' In The Wind". Instead, Sly could sometimes write directly, so simply, so absolutely crystal-clear, that the meanings need no deciphering. What Sly wants, what makes him happy, is what's right. He seldom extends that into defining what *is* right. After all, he expresses that through the songs. Dancing is right. Togetherness is right. Getting higher is right. Family is right. Music is right. Yet he never 'says it loud' as bluntly or as directly as James Brown's anti-drugs campaigning either. At this phase of his career at least, Sly worked best in terms of prankster agit-prop slogans. A more 'physical' street-poetry. Repeatedly riffing incendiary phrases. John Lennon refined the technique down to a deliberate manifesto through his Plastic Ono Band and *Some Time In New York'* (1972) double-album, "Give Peace A Chance", "Power To The People", "War Is Over"—explaining his motivations and technique in consciousness-raising stunts and interviews as part of a political process of social change. This, also, is poetry.

Sly Stone had already worked that out. The exuberant joie de vivre cheer-leading of 'Different Strokes For Different Folks' gets into your head. Whether he picked it up as an overheard phrase from street-slang, or even if he coined it himself, you sing along to its funk vamp whether you initially believe in its sentiment or not. Repeat it enough times, you might even come around to his way of thinking. It started as a song. It entered the lexicon, became a national catch phrase, one that took on a life of its own when it vaulted into the ratings as the title of a TV sit-com—NBC's *'Diff'rent Strokes'* which ran from 1978 to 1986, starring Gary Coleman as 'Arnold Drummond'. To *'Rolling Stone'*, it's a song that provides evidence of Sly's ability to create 'messages that take clichés and make them work'. He's also capable of coining near-perfect couplets that combine the raw energy of graffiti with the catchy concision of a Madison Avenue adverting slogan. On "Stand" he can define his stance as 'don't you know you are free, / at least, in your mind, if you want to be'. A lyric as tightly coiled as a haiku, and as potent as propaganda. In relation to the slavery heritage, to Sly—it's not where you're from, it's where you're at. When he writes 'I am no better and neither are you / we are the same whatever we do' ("Everyday People") he was linking directly into Martin Luther King's American Dream of 'when the sons of former slaves and former slave-owners will be able to sit down together at a table of brotherhood'. Literary Poets were writing protest-poems in small-press mimeo magazines. Higher-profile poets like Allen Ginsberg, Thom Gunn, Ed Sanders or Adrian Mitchell were reaching wider audiences through exposure in the underground press. Sly was not only fusing Beat imagery with surrealist insight, but he was getting his message across from the very top of the Pop charts.

'Burn, Baby Burn' was a street-chant used as rioters torched autos and watched them burn, or incinerated white businesses and watched them collapse in flames. Sly snatched that—and neatly reversed it. His lyrics for "Don't Burn Baby" urge 'learn baby learn', advocating the path the Black Power movement had dismissively labelled 'assimilation'. Even though it was the same integrationist message James Brown had urged on "Don't Be A Drop-out", his contribution to the US 'Stay in School' campaign (in November 1966). Sly goes on to playfully advise 'learn', or else 'you'll be sitting around like the underdog'. It might be a sly 'I-told-you-so' reference back to the song on the first album where, marginalised by his refusal to stoop to familiar dance clichés, Sly's innovative flights of fancy had drawn a mostly baffled response from the black community. Then, his attempts to emancipate R&B from its dead-end had yielded only cool responses. Now, during his December 1968 appearance on the 'Ed Sullivan Show' Sly deliberately recited lyrics from "Are You Ready"—'don't hate the black, don't hate the white, / if you get bitten, just blame the bite'. Effortlessly persuasive, irrefutably true, perfectly rhymed, in just four brief lines, avoiding the usual trap of triteness, while hinting at the complex web of relationships existing between individual, race, and society.

Bob Dylan in widely acknowledged as integrating articulate lyric-content into Pop songs. And certainly there was a two-way respect from Sly to Bob Dylan, and back again. To Miles Marshall Lewis Sly 'considers them to be peers of the pen'. As a DJ, Sly had put Dylan records on high-rotation, and as late as a 1986 *'Spin'* interview with journalist Edward Kiersh, Sly expressed a wish to duet with Dylan, in much the same way that Johnny Cash had. Yet literary attempts to evaluate lyrics as poetry are flawed. The academic spat comparing Bob Dylan to John Keats is a nonsense. Sure, Dylan's songs lack the technical precision of a Keats poem, but Keats couldn't create an album like *'Blonde On Blonde'* (1966) either. After all, to Greil Marcus the poetry question not only has 'to do with how a writer uses language', because 'his music will be part of his language', an integral part of the way he makes 'words do things they ordinarily do not do'. Lyrics must work additionally as the integral part of a song. A song tends to operate on circular repetitions returning through a verse-by-verse process to a memorable chorus. Sometimes poems can too.

But when the poem structure too rigidly determines the melodic shape of the song, it can restrict its scope for fluidity. *'There's A Riot Goin' On'* would use a greater degree of layered lyrical ambiguity, constituting more of a rock aesthetic at work, while never to the extent that Hendrix subsumed Dylan's 'skipping reels of rhyme' surreal word-play.

But direct comparisons only go so far, before they founder. Beyond the remit of lyric-poets, Sly never neglects the more physical aspects of human nature, using it instead to speak a unique new dialect within Rock culture. For every infiltration of subliminal politics, there's the development of the hard-edged, improvisational funk of a "Sex Machine" which hews a more carnal groove. "Don't Call Me Nigger, Whitey" says a very great deal, while lyrically consisting of very little. Instead, it artfully conflates liberal politics with the poetry of Dance. *'Stand!'* stands at the pinnacle of Sly's career as a sloganeer. And as he went on, the writing sophisticated. One critic points out, 'Sly can move his audience—to frenzy and riot, but he cannot move them to sit and weep'. Maybe so, at least… not yet. He would move into less defined, more abstract lyrical realms. As Richard Williams, reviewing a later album, illustrates. When he quotes the lines 'you have turned into a prayer / I can feel I'm almost there' (from "Let Me Have It All") he describes it as 'but one of a number of possible examples of Sly writing words which are intelligent, carry meaning, yet still function perfectly within the music, complementing the melodic and rhythmic elements' (*'Melody Maker'* 12th May 1973). Was Sly a poet? a sample from his "Poet" forms the base for De La Soul's "Description", on their *'Three Feet High And Rising'* (1989) album, going places that more formal verse would never venture. So yes, Sly's a poet, you better know it… hope he don't blow it! While, as far as literature is concerned his interests were ranging in unexpected directions. 'I worry about my not reading' he admitted to *'Rolling Stone'*, 'about whether I'm valid'. He revealed he was wading through a book, 'The Art Of Writing' (surely not the Robert Louis Stevenson book of that title?), as a rehearsal for more ambitious projects. The suggestion being that musical theatre was somewhere on the agenda. Or at least that he'd toyed with the idea, in passing. 'I will be a part of it, in the near future, something in the written media that will have contact with people. But before that, I've got to appreciate the potency of the written media…'

Certainly, by 1969, the times were ripe for the seizing. Vietnam was getting uglier and more pointless—spiking napalm atrocity nightly into your front room from your TV set, as the internal US war between the paranoia of the 'straight' system and those outside the power structure, in the ghetto was deteriorating towards flashpoint. What was left of the hippie idyll was crumbling, and the narco-anarcho counter-culture was in an insurrectionary mood. Bill Graham was a big-time promoter, and there was even less of a specifically San Francisco 'sound' as its music up-shifted to become big business. The successful San Francisco bands were setting their sights on wider horizons. It had become generic 'underground music', and it had taken on global significance. Then, on 20th January 1969, despite Medicaid and the Social Security Act, despite advances in Civil Rights and his 'War on Poverty', LBJ's Vietnam Policy finally did for him, ending the Democrats incumbency. Innocence and optimism... impacting straight into Richard Milhous Nixon's ascendancy to the White House....

Chapter Ten
'Getting Higher at Woodstock'

'Tell the truth, to the youth...'
("Babies Making Babies")

'And so on and so on and scooby dooby doo-bee...'
("Everyday People")

First, some facts. There had been festivals before. But never a festival like 'Woodstock'. Even *'Time'* magazine was forced to salute it as 'history's largest happening... one of the significant political and social events of the age'. It spawned a charting triple-album and a follow-up double-set. There was a movie—*'Woodstock: Three Days Of Peace & Music'* (1970), which took it around the world. And it established the benchmark by which all subsequent festivals had to stand. When festival goers frolic in Glastonbury mud, slip-sliding and mud play-wrestling they're consciously, or perhaps unconsciously enacting out some generational race-memory from 'Woodstock' footage. The movie imprinted the Who and Hendrix into the US consciousness, it broke Crosby Stills & Nash as counter-culture gods, made Arlo Guthrie into a marketable cult hero, and absurdly resurrected a confused and bemused Country Joe & The Fish's already overlooked "Feel Like I'm Fixin' To Die" into the UK Top 20 a fistful of years after its initial release. From the stage John Sebastian, fresh out of a run of hits with Lovin' Spoonful, dressed in his folksy granny-glasses and tie-dye denims, oozes 'you're a whole city, and it's so groooovy'. With music itself rapidly metamorphosing into what Ian Carr terms 'Elastic Rock', there was even wide-open space for the oddball stuff. Sha-Na-Na became sudden retro-stars by bursting the festival's heavy tribal intensity with their spontaneous fifties doo-wop replications. There was Santana. And—of course, there was Sly & The Family Stone...

Part of the legend is mythical, but that myth is legendary, amplified by the movie, elaborated by fallible memories and hearsay. The festival anthem was written by Joni Mitchell—who was not there, uniting imagery from the latest cosmological theory that human molecular structure is composed of star-stuff, with Voltaire's *'Candide'* (1759) wish-recommendation to leave the city and 'get ourselves back to the garden'. The UK hit version of her "Woodstock" was by Matthews Southern Comfort—who weren't there either. But part of it is hard historical. It was the first event of its kind. Before 'Woodstock', there was Bob Dylan turning the electric amplification all the way up to eleven at the Newport Folk Festival. Otis Redding had stormed at Monterey—the event that first introduced Jimi Hendrix and the Who to America, on a disparate bill that also included Ravi Shankar. Then there was had been 'Jazz On A Summer Day'. George Wein's long-established Rhode Island Newport Jazz Festival which—for the first time in its long and distinguished arc, was forced to concede that purely jazz was no longer where it's at, and there was a place for that angry young upstart Rock music. Running across the weekend of 3rd-6th July 1969, Led Zeppelin and Frank Zappa played there alongside Art Blakey and BB King, James Brown too—and Sly & The Family Stone. But it was Sly's appearance on the drizzling Saturday afternoon that sparked a near-riot, resulting in the trashing of their tour-bus. And it was the Family Stone's set that was singled out for attention in a disapproving *'New York Times'* report. Through such incidents they were quirkily becoming known as one of the most exciting live bands of the era.

Three weeks before they played Newport, and two before Woodstock they broke another important psychological barrier. As a mixed-race band, they were scheduled to appear at the legendary Apollo Theatre—performing three spots on the 29th June. Located at 253 West 125th Street, The Apollo was 'the heartbeat of Harlem', a club almost exclusively associated with African-American performers—from Swing and Bebop, Gospel, Rhythm & Blues, Dance, Comedy, and Modern Jazz. It had begun back in the 1930s, when segregation was rigidly in place, and the then-owner—Frank Shipman, known as 'the Jewish Brother', turned things around. He began by inviting black performers onstage. 'Amateur Night' was born—a talent contest where dud acts were expelled to the sound of a wailing klaxon, or brushed away by an 'executioner' who came onstage with a broom to sweep up the 'garbage'. It was 'Amateur Night' at the Apollo in 1934 that kick-started a career for Ella Fitzgerald that would last more than fifty years. Everybody who is anybody in black culture had been blooded on this stage. This was the place James Brown had recorded *'Live At The Apollo'* (1963), crumpling to the floor seemingly spent, then screaming, jumping up only to hydroplane across the stage imploring 'please, please, please' as the packed house erupted. The moment captured on the live album by which all others are measured. It would also be the place he chose to finally 'lie in state' after his death on Christmas Day 2006. This was the place 'where stars are born and legends are made'. Its marquee had carried names such as Sarah Vaughan, old-time vaudeville favourites such as Stepin Fetchit and Dewey 'Pigmeat' Markham, then jazzers Coleman Hawkins and a fragile Billie Holiday, and R&B pioneers The Orioles, through to Gladys Knight, The Jackson Five, and Lauryn Hill.

Could the Family Stone measure up? They had already established serious beach-heads into white music. But had they done that at the expense of losing the respect of their black audience? There were narrow-minded critics who saw playing to the Pop market as 'Uncle Tom-ing', as watering down the pure spirit of black music for universal consumption. Now, even Sly had uncharacteristic doubts. It was a large old-style venue with its distinctive big red-and-yellow neon sign. A draughty, sometimes dirty and often smelly venue, sitting in the heart of the most important black community in the centre of America's greatest city. To Bobby Womack 'the neighbourhood was a trip. There were burned-out cars, burned-out apartments and burned-out people. Hustlers, hookers, boosters, freaks, users, boozers'. To Malcolm X, Harlem was a 'Technicolor bazaar', where soul food restaurants served up fried-chicken-&-biscuits as a culinary memory of the south for the descendents of black migrants who'd made the trek north for a better life. New York, New York, if they can make it here, they can make it anywhere! Co-headlining was raunchy Harlem nightclub comedian Redd Foxx. A some-time associate of Malcolm X, his edgy humour on live 'adult' albums paved the way for Richard Pryor, Eddie Murphy and Chris Rock , though it would not be until he appeared in the later US version of *'Steptoe & Son'* that he achieved his own TV stardom. He then used his influence through the sit-com to help revive the fortunes of Ruth Brown, one of Atlantic's founding artists. The Family Stone would also reconnect with Redd Foxx some time later, at his club on La Cienega, where Sly christened him 'hose-nose' in recognition of his huge appetite for coke.

Redd did his set, improvising material and delving into his reserve of late-night blue material when he'd exhausted his regular routines, to cover up for the Family Stone's lateness. Then it began with Gregg coming on-stage and mounting his drum-kit, followed by each member of the troupe, one-by-one getting up to join him, adding their own contribution into a relentless groove that never stopped. This format for the Family Stone set had stayed essentially unchanged since their 'Winchester Cathedral' show. It's good, and it worked. Why change it? But for Gregg, getting up alone on the stage in such a fortress of black culture was intimidating. Those were moments to stress and test out a musician's own limits. But at the Apollo, once it hit its stride, the uncertainty was over. The audience was massively won over. For Jerry Martini, the band's acceptance there was 'one of the highlights of my life'.

Simultaneously, another Apollo programme was also reaching its highest high, with Neil Armstrong's first small step for a man onto the surface of the

Sea of Tranquillity at 02.56 GMT 21st July. And within a month (August) the Family Stone were galvanising the vast audience onto its feet into a different kind of spaced-out experience, at Woodstock, to be widely hailed as one of the festival's peak-moments. Despite a mixing-desk technology of flashing winking electronic defences, like NASA's control room mocked-up from curly-leads and gaffa-tape by a geeky Robert Crumb bedroom obsessive, the scheduling was typically and purposefully chaotic. The entire festival itself was a kind of experimental community. What lifts and shapes it all is that you can't reduce it down to just polemic, music, or social issues any more than you could define its impossible dream. And if those elements were hard to catch, that's because they're so satisfyingly complex. These shabby Rock 'n' Roll gipsies were Homo Ludens, the New Breed, the Coming Race, rampaging through the relics of a lost and irrelevant civilisation with its outmoded values suddenly preserved between quotation marks, marooned to obsolescence by its museum-culture. Briefly, before it was extinguished, this was a microcosm of some utopian future where artful playing, sensuous free-loving, and hedonistic hallucination was all that matters.

Nothing on this scale had happened before. With no turn left unstoned. Columns of hippie-chicks and cosmic roughrider refugees flooded all access routes towards Bethel in up-state New York, bringing traffic to a halt. As the event exerted the gravitational force of a hippie-devouring black hole, circling cop-copters declared it a disaster zone. Systems crack up and break down. The rain comes down-pouring from ravening slate-grey clouds… and passes. There's bad acid circulating. But nothing can halt the celebratory power of this vast tribal gathering. We've become dulled, immune-by-repetition to this stuff, in the wake of 'Woodstock' there would be other equally chaotic counter-culture parties at the Isle of Wight. 'Woodstock' itself was reprised, after a two-decade pause, by which time festivals had become part of the social calendar. Something you do.

Jefferson Airplane preceded them, opening the day. With the same Grace Slick who'd worked with Sly at Autumn Records, now co-fronting one of the biggest bands in America. The two bands sharing the same stage book-ending the day, looking out over that same sea of disembodied heads. The Airplane's mighty "Volunteers" was omitted from the festival-movie. Something to do with lighting. But in the gap between bands, Max Yasgur was ushered onto the stage—the event's 'Michael Eavis', the same guy hymned on Joni Mitchell's anthem. He announced 'I'm a Farmer', to thunderous applause. Somewhere overhead, escalating right out of the frame, B52s riding shotgun in the sky must have been turning into butterflies at that very moment. Then the Family Stone pounced in from the darkness of night, into the rainy early-morning hours of Saturday 16th August, and there's no better antidote to three days of liquid-chocolate mud, rain, and dysentery than Sly's ecstatic exuberance.

Intent on taking the event 'Higher', they did exactly that. According to Vet, they took a helicopter ride into Yasgar's Farm, or—according to Jerry Martini, they were driven in by limousines. Originally scheduled to play between eight or ten, they waited. And waited. Until 03:30am the following morning.

Then, the dense dark mass of heads was suddenly backlit with the opalescent thunder-flash of a lighting-rig halo. The stage swirling with blue light. And—somewhere in the tense play-off between light and dark, horns-up, they exploded in with the devastating fusillade of "M'Lady". A compact scrawl of colour dressed outrageously, Cynthia in emerald blouse, Larry in plumed cavalier hat, Rose's blonde wig, Sly in a near-phosphorescent white-and-mauve fringed outfit, with a silver chain around his neck and mauve shades. A super-fly Sly whipping the audience up to a peak of excitement which stops just on the right side of hysteria. Flakes of gold electric light shimmer in bright-reflected traces across the darkening field, as they start powering into "Sing A Simple Song". It was a scene that feels both real and ideal, vividly authentic, and half-imagined. As a showman, Sly rose to the occasion, overcoming fatigue. Feeding on the positive audience energies he was inciting, and building on it, in an energy-feedback loop. The set continued with "You Can Make It If You Try", "Stand", and "Love City". "Dance To The Music" was carried on smacking drums, choppy guitar, and Rose's screeched exhortations. Vet banging tambourine, singing her heart out. It was an elegant draughtsmanship of dark and knotted rhythms that sustain and magnify the theatricality. Almost seamlessly you realise they've shifted into something else. "Music Lover", 'and on and on and etc'.

Now it's the play-in to "I Want To Take You Higher", with Sly urging 'what we'd like to do is sing a song together. Most of us need to get approval from our neighbours before we can let it all hang down. And what is happening here is we wanna do a 'sing-along'. Now, a lot of people don't like to do it because they feel that it might be old-fashioned. But you must dig that it is not a fashion in the first place. It is a feeling. And if it was good in the past, it's still good. We would like to sing a song called "Higher".' Lights freeze the figures on-stage, until they're delineated by and so artfully animated and synchronised they might be engraved. But it wakes people up, gets tired rain-sodden hippies climbing out of their sleeping bags and off their mud-caked hippie butts, onto their feet and dancing. A feat no other band this night can achieve. The 'BOOM-shakalacka-boom' euphoria is literally heart-shaped, 'the beat is getting stronger', pulsing as it bursts in the air over the washed-out crepuscular landscape. Sly, his raised arms dripping white suede fringes, flashes peace signs. Voices soaring into the night, exhortations to 'throw out those peace-signs', rousing the masses to ram the message home into the call-and-response of that 'old-fashioned sing-along'. In an impatient frantic contagion of energies, Sly is urging 'I'm gonna get you higher—

HIGHER...! higher—HIGHER!!' The band chanting 'I Want To Take You HIGHER!' behind him, and it works beautifully, with some 400,000 voices hurling back 'HIGHER!!!' like some mass gospel-soul chorus hooked into an infinite reciprocation, throwing their arms into the air in unison. Lifting way above the boundaries of the empty pop-culture construct or a stoner joke, into a moment of pure transcendence.

A volume-level so loud they could wear it. The sheer physical sensation of being deliriously drowned in volume is difficult to articulate. On paper it's easy to analyse lyrics, and there are themes, riffs and chorus-construction to intellectualise and play around with. But there's more than just pleasure in the sensory experience of being deluged in the ear-splitting mind-warping strength of pure undiluted sound, intense enough to curdle your earwax. Yet here it's integral to communicating the experience. When the Family Stone flew its freak-flag at Woodstock, they took everyone higher. The rhythms are primal, the wailing horns, Blues harp and thudding fuzz bass competing for space. Its power makes Hurricane Katrina feel like a mild blustery squall. It extends exhaustively, hypnotically into something like a primal ritual, a quasi-mystical thing inducing a trance-state that's near-transcendental. Anthemic, both in the spiritual *and* the narcotic sense, in an extreme stream-of-consciousness. With an energy that is eternally delightful. Whatever it is they're on, they're on fire.

The climax of the Family Stone's set takes up a solid 13:16-minutes of music across the majority of side five of the gatefold triple album. And then it's caught in the frames of the movie. Watch it now, in triple split-screen. The Sly Stone sequence starts at the temperature that Santana ended with… and climbs from there to boiling point. An extended sequence that builds into a visual and aural poem as Sly and the audience hurl the words back at each other across a human tidal wave—'let me see you throw the peace sign in the air! It'll do you no harm!'. The camera focuses in as Sly histrionically lifts his arms in slow motion until they reach an apogee… then the frame freezes, and the chant goes on and on until it fades to a whisper. Time is caught in a bubble. And suspended. Surely, nothing can be the same for Sly Stone ever again, nothing will have one-hundredth the significance of the power and the glory that was 'Woodstock'. To provoke a hundred-thousand people thrusting peace-signs into the air and chanting 'HIGHER' is power such as few men in the world are privileged to wield. Once you've had an audience of 500,000 in the palm of your hand, everything else must surely turn out to be a letdown?… the movie cuts to Janis Joplin.

Jimi Hendrix was originally slated to usher the 'three-day nation' to a close with a set pencilled in for the evening of Sunday, 17th August. Moodily unpredictable weather and a contagion of production hassles plagued the already haphazard organisation, so that—like Sly's, Jimi's slot was shoved back and shoved back further into the morning of the Monday. The mass-audience was already fragmenting and drifting away, down from the estimated peak of a near-500,000, to less than 25,000 when Jimi finally got to mount the stage beneath the scaffolding and lazy pennants. His newly expanded line-up was renamed Gypsy Sun & Rainbows, taking Jimi and long-time drummer Mitch Mitchell from the original trio, but adding drummer Billy Cox, rhythm guitarist Larry Lee and percussionists Jerry Velez and Juma Sultan. Near the close of their already inflammatory set Jimi seamlessly downshifted from a furiously extemporised slight return to "Voodoo Chile" into his incendiary mangling of "Star Spangled Banner". Mitch's drumming swerving manically behind him, 'to keep his hands warm' as he later admits. Even on Michael Wadleigh's docufilm, even across the arc of years, this moment still stands as a peak-experience. For Hendrix—like igniting his guitar at the Monterey Pop Festival, it is an image that will forever be seared into his legend, crystallised as an enduring symbol of his awesome talent. Within the squall of noise coaxed from his white guitar you hear napalm incinerating Vietnamese villages. You hear the shot that took Martin Luther King's life. The race riots in the street. The electric flash of acid. Beautiful violence. It's all in there.

But it's also a defining moment in the slow unravelling of the counter-culture. A moment never to be equalled. Ever. A sense of community never to be duplicated. Ever. Like Newport, like Monterey, the Woodstock of legend was not merely an aggregate of docile consumers. It was a participatory community. A vision of controlled anarchy. And revolution...? Perhaps not. To Andy Warhol, peering through his opaque shades, 'it was ugly, like the Nuremberg Rally, with drugs'. On the event's second night Yippie-activist Abbie Hoffman staggered on stage to harangue a manifesto-appeal in support of jailed self-styled White Panther John Sinclair. Whereupon an unsympathetic Pete Townshend promptly batted him off-stage in mid-rant with his well-aimed Gibson.

Instead, ironically, the merchandising of the event would help identify a new record-buying constituency. What had begun as the hippies' revolt against the fetishism of consumerism, merely entangled them more deeply within it. Dissent—the festival industry said, could be profitably marketed into a passive politically-castrated commodity. And in doing so, it laid the groundwork for the construction of the twenty-first century corporate media global music industry. To Mike Marqusee 'Puritanism had been replaced by hedonism, immediacy was preferred to history. Woodstock posed the question that radicals had been debating since the mid-sixties, was the new Rock audience... a living community with a political ethic, or was it just a new consumer demographic, united by nothing but the music? Was Woodstock itself a moment of collective self-discovery, the self-identification of a new social body, or was it merely the identification—by capital, of an audience ripe for exploitation?' ('*Chimes Of Freedom: The Politics O Bob Dylan's Art*', The New Press 2003, ISBN 1-56584-825-X). Of course, it was something of each.

Otis Redding had represented black America at Monterey two years earlier, insinuating soul into the Love Generation. Now Sly and Jimi conquered at Woodstock, sanctifying that Arcadian hippiedom as its twin acknowledgements of black America. But if it was all about egalitarianism, why were the people on-stage suddenly made of more golden stardust than those out-front wallowing in the mud? Their appearance, and the movie that documented it, massively expanded their fan-base. It was the tipping-point moment for the Family Stone, a paradigm-shift that took them from one level of success and acceptance way up to some newer zone in which everything was possible and nothing was beyond reach. To writer Nick Kent 'Sly's finest hour as Good Humour man cum Seventh-Son-Of-A-Seventh-Son mojo navigator for that particular gathering more than quadrupled the number of converts to the Family Stone's irresistible high-energy walls-of-Jericho demolition work'.

But even as he was reaching his summit… Sly was tipping into his descent.

****

The Family Stone spent the major part of 1969 touring on the back of the massive breakthrough of '*Stand*', its success extended by the post-'Woodstock' effect. Barely a fortnight later they were playing an identical power-set—alongside fellow-'Woodstock' stand-out stars Santana, at the 'Texas International Pop Festival' held on the 30th at Dallas International Motor Speedway, in Lewisville. Sly was spinning pell-mell through history with reality shifting around him at bewildering speed. Music depends on the bicycle theory—move forward, or you fall over. Even if you aren't sure which direction 'forward' is. Sly was good at making audiences feel good about themselves, while he was not necessarily feeling great about himself. His stomach was convulsed by bleeding ulcers, caused at least in part by the crushing stress. He began gulping down prescription placidyls to deal with the condition. And his escalating reliance on the artificial energies of his drug intake was having detrimental effects on both his personal demeanour, and his reliability. As Kapralik related to '*Rolling Stone*'s Timothy Crouse, 'that poor kid was torn apart. And when you are torn apart that means a lot of pain. And one of the clinical ways to ease the pain is cocaine'.

And there was a further looming dark side to Sly's waxing moon. The Jekyll & Hyde dualism of Sly & Sylvester had already been remarked upon, and perceptively diagnosed in print in a '*Rolling Stone*' feature. By David Kapralik no less—who was close enough to know. The 'good Syl—representative of everything that is life-affirming and healthful in our society' and the 'bad Sly—the street cat, the hustler, the pimp, the conniver, sly as a fox and cold as a stone', a split personality, two walking contradictions coexisting in the same host-form, inhabiting the self-same body. Writer Nick Kent defined it as, 'there was Sylvester, prodigal son of the tightly-knit Stewart family from downtown Vallejo—a prodigious talent, Mrs Stewart's pride and joy, feet firm on Jacob's ladder, the Gospel road. In touch with Natural Harmony and all that jazz. And then when night fell, this Johnny Appleseed superspade would suddenly metamorphose into Sly Stone—black on black—a bona fide funkified bad-ass Lucifer badass, harbinger of all manner of amoral mischief, and as alarming as he was incorrigible' (*'New Musical Express'* 19th June 1976).

Naturally, it was a dichotomy Sly himself immediately denied. Sure, he was a Pisces. Sure, the astrological symbol for Pisces is two fish swimming in opposite directions, to represent contradictory impulses in permanent opposition. But Kapralik's analysis took it way-further than just that. To him, there was this 'other Sly', a psychological 'beast in the basement' to which the earlier Sylvester Stewart's amiable sunniness was merely a tissue draped across a psychic disaster waiting to happen. From the beginning, even in obscurity, he had been assembling a myth. 'Sly' was the alter-ego derived from a schoolfriend's misspelling of his first name, and it had steadily inflated into an entirely separate personality. 'No', says Sly, 'right or wrong, good or bad, Sylvester Stewart and Sly Stone are the same person. Sometimes they give you two names, your real one and your 'also-known-as'. But we're the same people—Sly, Sylvester and the whole Family Stone. We're all one, you got that?' Yes, we've got it, and maybe that dichotomy was all a cunning ploy dreamt up by Kapralik. The greatest publicity stratagem of its time, and the perfect cop-out to hurl at angry promoters. 'Sylvester, the delicate poet, wanted to come, man, but Sly, the gum-chewing gangsta-punk wouldn't let him.' Yet it seems such a perfect fit, too convenient a theory to ignore. Even Bobby Womack concurs, 'Sly was two people' he suggests, 'first, there was Sylvester Stewart, who was pretty cool, generous, creative, a genius musician. Then there was Sly Stone. He was the destructive character. Sly was the kind of guy who liked to start fights just to see people go crazy and get tripped out.'

Then there was the pressure Sylvester Stewart was putting on himself to *be* 'Sly Stone'. Later he would twin the album credits by registering 'all songs written, arranged and produced by Sylvester Stewart and Sly Stone'. One word that seems to cover it all is 'Manichean'. A term used to define the near-schizophrenic dualism of the Persian prophet Mani, who taught that there are two rival creations. One bright and good. The other gloomy and immitigably evil. Kapralik was the first to pose that critical question. To ask where the demarcation line was drawn between Sly's attempt to create his own larger-than-life narrative, the guise through which to project his own fable, and the suspicion that he'd actually begun to believe it himself? That Sylvester was taking the Sly character off stage with him. Becoming 'him'. Hiding behind 'him'. Who actually was the 'myself' he was thanking us for letting him be—Sylvester, or Sly? Perhaps even he no longer knew. Certainly Sly Stone's ascending star legitimised—encouraged, even *demanded* behaviour that Sylvester Stewart—the gentle poet, would never have dared. The more cautious 'Sylvester' was still in there, as the critical conscience that urged him to mistrust the success. But 'Sly' was a character he could assume. It was his more arrogant less controllable twin. One assembled item by item along with the outrageous stage outfits, and the attitude that went with it. 'Sly' could make demands, and get results, that would be unacceptable if they'd come from Sylvester. Naturally… the ideal tuning would have depended on establishing some kind of equilibrium between the creative aspects of the personality, and the looming black superstud persona with which he'd been endowed…? But that's not easy.

It may have begun as a useful and amusing guise to assume. But fame is a trip. It opens up your range of possibilities. People give you drugs. You get laid. When you first begin reaping big moollah it's easy to eat, drink, party, and snort all the conspicuous spoils of your new wealth—bam! Bam! BAM!! Why not? You've worked hard to reach this elevation, haven't you? You deserve the rewards. It's your right. After all, to the victors… blahdy-blahdy-blah. It's time to do some resting on those laurels. Tranquilise your mind. Just for a little while. You can always resume work later, soon, tomorrow… whenever. Soft drugs get harder. And his oblique sense of illogic could be inventively surreal. For a party in the New York Hilton he turned up wearing a crocheted green wool cap and a zippered green leather jacket to match. The jacket came emblazoned with multicoloured leather panels on the front and back enhanced with styling in the zigzag form of a thunderbolt. He told a journalist 'this is my Elvis Presley jacket'. When the journalist retorted 'Elvis would never wear a jacket like that', without a pause—and with irrefutable logic he responded 'No. But he would if he was me'. Yet as the two Syl/Sly characters became increasingly fused and indistinguishable, they were becoming more problematical. Until it was impossible to isolate Sylvester Stewart the person, from Sly Stone the fiction. They'd become adjunct personalities of one another.

Press reports were already rife with suggestions that several members of The Family Stone were prone to drug complications. Press stories were networking trade rumours that they'd begun to acquire a reputation for unpredictability, tales of arriving late for concerts in last-minute helicopter dashes, or frequently failing to show at scheduled gigs entirely, citing mysterious ailments and dubious illnesses. The man who provided inspiration through the positive messages of his hit singles, now seemed to be methodically and systematically eroding the reputation he'd worked so hard to build. A band turning up, complete and on time, to their own gig wouldn't normally be—*shouldn't* normally be—a cause for celebration. But suddenly such rules no longer apply in the case of Sly &

The Family Stone. Booking the band had become a hazardous gamble. The funkified concerts that were once meticulously delivered with the fervour of an electric church were now starting hours late, if at all, inspiring vilification and even violence among their dissatisfied audiences. The band's immense success in the wake of *'Stand'* and 'Woodstock', poised potentially on the trajectory of even greater rewards, was instead being severely damaged by those frequent gig no-shows. In fact, the Family Stone failed to carry out close on a *third* of their scheduled concerts for 1970. For a February 15th concert at the Washington DC Constitution Hall the band arrived a full five hours late, too late to avoid violent disruptive protests from angry fans. Following eighteen arrests, the ultra-conservative Daughters Of The American Revolution imposed a ban on subsequent Rock events at the venue. 'I cannot condone disorder or riotous behaviour' protested their spokesperson, citing 'smashed windows, corridors littered with trash, whiskey bottles stashed in corners… and evidence that someone tried to start a fire in the orchestra pit'.

It was a precarious ratio that understandably had an adverse effect on their ability to command up-front money for future bookings. TV appearances and interview-slots also suffered—vital promotional vehicles for any band. The Family Stone were streamed onto a flurry of high-profile network shows such as 'Soul Train' and Don Kirshner's 'In Concert'. They returned to 'The Ed Sullivan Show'—doing "Love City" and "Stand" (March 1969), then promptly flew out to Frankfurt to mime "Everyday People" for 'Beat Club'. The programmes passed by unpredictably. Ben Fong-Torres covered the back-stage activities at Hollywood's Studio C when the Family Stone played ABC's 'Music Scene' show in October '69 (for a major *'Rolling Stone'* feature). Before the tele-shoot Sly was already resplendent in gold velvet shirt cut off at the midriff, with long black fringes brushing down against his leopard-skin pants, which were encased in tall black fur boots. The ensemble set off by huge violet-tinted shades framed on a head that's bursting with hair. Only slightly less flash Freddie is in light violet shirt and black coveralls. Rose in a yellow satin pantsuit, gold-chain cap and silvered hair. While Larry is regal in full black musketeers outfit, with cavalier hat and flowing cape over brushed velvet pants.

They hung around, killing time, as producer Ken Fritz oversaw repeated takes of lame comedy sketches and the taping of music-inserts from the mighty Bo Diddley and a delicate Buffy St Marie beneath harsh studio Kleig lighting, in front of an audience of some 250 kids. The Family Stone backing tracks had been pre-recorded the previous night at Columbia, the vocals would be done live. Eventually 'Sly, a vision in black and pink and fringes, sits at his organ, looks around, groggy/alert, a boxer in his corner ready for the bell. And lined up behind him, the Family, fussing over a piano, sax, trumpet, bass, guitar, and drums that won't be recorded. All of a sudden, four stomps on the black fur boots and Sly & The Family Stone are into "Higher"—Cynthia, pale, with her high, rouged Indian cheekbones, holding her horn high, away from her, screeching her clarion call. Her cousin Larry Graham crooning his melodic bass reply, as he always does, then Freddie, the middleman between Larry's bottom and Sly's elephant roar, carrying it down the line to his brother Sly. Sister Rose is counterpointing him, a serious musician at work on the piano. By now they're all stomping, saxophonist Jerry Martini pumping his hips along with his instrument, his cousin Gregg Errico flailing away at drums above and behind him. Sly is itching to leave his chair, and he jumps out, laughing, clapping hands, roaring coarsely, stamping the stage floor like a tribal chief, thoroughly digging the music he'd spent four hours putting together, in at least two dozen takes, the night before…' The medley they were now well into playing included "Don't Call Me Nigger, Whitey", which Kapralik had had premonitions of trouble about. He'd deliberately ensured the ABC executives were kept in the dark about it, allowing them no time to react to its lyric-content. He watched nervously from the sidelines, then, just as quickly, they were segueing into "Hot Fun In The Summertime", to close with Rose leading into a rousing "Dance To The Music". At Sly's insistence they do a retake, this time encouraging the audience to even greater enthusiasm.

Other telecasts worked out less successfully. During one interview Sly voiced some bitter comments about the unimaginative programming policies of black radio stations—'Soul' or 'R&B' radio is wrong he declared, 'I think there shouldn't be 'black radio'. Just radio', a forthrightness that led to Family Stone records being boycotted for a while in protest. Then Sly was featured on 'The Mike Douglas Show', a networked chat-show hosted by a former big-band crooner. Mike Douglas was accustomed to eccentric confrontations—he also played host to Ray Charles, Malcolm X, Aretha Franklin, and Angela Davis. When John & Yoko appeared on his show they selected Jerry Rubin as their 'guest celebrity'. But Mike Douglas had never interviewed anyone quite like Sly Stone. Then there was an amazingly shambolic three-minute Sly Stone interview appearance on 'The Dick Cavett Show'. It seems Sly didn't feel the need to explain anything to anyone. So he didn't. The Family Stone walked the walk, that was enough, even without talking the talk.

While all this was going on, there was contractually supposed to be a new album. But work-in-progress was sporadic. So in the meantime, a stopgap single was advanced from the on-going sessions, the lovely and lilting "Hot Fun In The Summertime" (stretching back to *'Life'* for its 'B'-side, "Fun"). A sweetly balmy warm breeze of a record, with a summery shimmering poppy glow, its slick groove came in sharp contrast to the anthemic drive of their previous hits. And energetically promoted by veteran PR man Stephen Topley, it first broke on Detroit's CKLW—significantly, a Top 40 station, *not* an R&B station. Soon it was ubiquitous, it drenched the airwaves, hitting no. 2 on the national chart in October. It was a hot-wheelin' with the top-down with the scent of melting asphalt in your face record. A hotter than black vinyl upholstery on a hot summer day record. *'Rolling Stone'* found its close-harmonies 'something akin to a hard version of the Lettermen', with the voices of Rose, Freddie, and Larry, allied to the first use of Sly's trademark throaty growl. Together, they celebrate being 'out of school', with a breathy splendour that anticipates the Isley Brother's 1974 "Summer Breeze". The alternating voices provide the key to its dynamics, infusing the record with its flavour. The mixed-down horns lending support. There's no sub-text, no subversion—unless it's intended to be read as an ironic commentary on America's long hot summer of racial unrest, in which case, almost no-one got the joke! And as the last great summer single of the sixties, the song became an obvious target for other artists to cover, charting in 1982 for funketeers Dayton. Most bizarrely the Beach Boys recorded their interpretation for their less than successful 1992 album *'Summer In Paradise'*, then Manhattan Transfer took it in yet another direction, assisted by guest vocalist Chaka Khan.

Next, for Sly Stone, there was the stunning sucker-punch that is "Thank You (Falettinme Be Mice Elf Agin)" c/w "Everybody Is A Star". The last recorded Family Stone product to emerge from the sixties, it hit US no. 1—first unseating Shocking Blue's "Venus" from the top slot on Valentine's Day, only to be then dethroned by Simon & Garfunkel's "Bridge Over Troubled Water". It went on to achieve double-gold status in the February of 1970. And what a strange mix of titles it was. A schizoid combination. Sly's writing was already exhibiting a breadth of approach which later Soul groups—such as Earth Wind & Fire would strive to equal. And here were two diametrically opposed moods back-to-back on one two-pronged seven-inch vinyl. The first side to draw sales, 'Star' was a positive take in the common-man 'Everyday People' vein. To reviewer John Burks (writing in March 1970) 'it starts like a Jazz Crusaders vamp... you're halfway expecting a roaring trombone solo... and then chug-chug-chug the band starts swirling and churning and there's an incredibly sweet soul chick singer. Mavis Staples? No. Rosie Stone. She's overtaken by a mellow, mellow basso profundo/soul croon from Larry Graham, Sly's bassist. Then it unwinds into this sweet and pretty line, 'Everybody is a star... Everybody is a star...' and the word *star* is four separate drawn-out syllables, and they repeat the line over and again, deliciously over-lapping and repeating to the end'. This time there are clear strong vocals, a simple-song arrangement with Sly, Freddie, Rose and Larry trading lines over an uncluttered keyboard-led meditation. The lyric-idea is as equally simple, but affirmative in its inner-resources, 'when the system tries to bring you down' remember, you're a star 'so shine, shine, shine'. It's a tone that anticipates, but was stronger than the soon-come dilutions of Philly-Soul. And it rises above the facile celebrity day-dreaming of the songs scripted by Gamble & Huff for the insipid whine of the star-fixated

Stylistics. That *übermensch* 'celebrity' sense of the word is certainly present, but analyse the lyric closer and it's more to do with the inner-beacon of self-worth that's shining. Something more universal, and more valid. Every person, it says, is special in their own way.

To John Burks, this is Sly's "Hey Jude", 'with the same repetition-riffing ending effect'. But the racial sub-text was also relevant in the wake of segregation and the long-imposed second-class citizenship status. This was a simple affirmation that needed saying. Just as when Nina Simone wrote 'when you're young, gifted and black, your soul's intact'. A decade later producer Richard Perry would reinterpret the song through a version by Anita, Ruth, and June—The Pointer Sister, proving its enduring strength. Rose Stone would also later perform "Everybody Is A Star" as part of her brief solo career. The Jackson Five issued their version of the song. As would Gwen Stafani. Hip-Hop crew The Roots sample the Family Stone's original for their 2004 "Star" (on the album *'The Tipping Point'*), while Roots MC Black Thought raps about how people attempt to gain fame the wrong way for the Family Stone tribute album *'Different Strokes By Different Folks'* (July 2005).

But Sly's flipsides were always just as formidable, spin this single over, and you're drawn into the angry infectious stab of "Thank You (Falettinme Be Mice Elf Agin)". And to be sharply confronted by this more problematically complex track is a rhythmic and lyrical treat. There's a (coke?)-sniff, then—beneath the play-in, some barely audible spaced scat sub-verbals. Then, a sparse construction stripped down to a 4:48-minute rhythmic x-ray, a sound that takes Sly's sonic horizons outside the comfort-zone. And in doing so it marks the beginning of the Family Stone's second era, during which the music would take on a darker, more funk-based hue. Less intricately structured, less centred on dynamic interplay, Sly unhooks the taut groove and everything just falls into place. After a half-decade of fumbling proto-funk, this is the single considered by academics to constitute the first full embodiment—on 45rpm, of mature electronic-funk. With Larry Graham's startling first use of the fully-fledged thumb-plucked 'popping' slap-bass style marking the birth of the sound that would under-pin funk throughout the Seventies and Eighties—a staple of future-funk that would be subsumed into other genres too. It bounces like a 'Low Rider' car with its stereo on full blast. It future-recalls War's "Me And Baby Brother" with the same short stabbed vocal-lines powered on its repeated super-cool bass-figure, while its magical minimalist guitar-lick looks forward all the way to Prince, even the playful language-disruption will have its long-term effects in Prince's similar treatment of his song-titles.

And this is a record that shows an angry bitter face of the Family Stone that audiences had rarely glimpsed before. Its immaculate minimalism of jump-cuts and freeze-frames form an expression of the confusion in Sly's life, matched to that of the world he was being inundated by. Writing in *'The*

Observer Music Monthly' (March 2006) Barney Hoskyns claims to find a cut-up biopic 'evocation of Sly's teenage years in the gangs of his hometown Vallejo' in its lyric. Going on to observe that 'if the song's third verse expressed gratitude for survival, for the healing of wounds—'Mama's so happy / Mama starts to cry / Papa's still singin'/ you can make it if you try'—what stayed with the listener was the wired terror of its opening line: 'Lookin' at the devil, grinnin' at his gun...' It is 'perhaps the most savage chart-topper ever' adds Peter Shapiro 'the music was mean, but the lyrics were as caustic as anything the Sex Pistols ever conjured up. 'Dying young is hard to take, selling out is harder' croaks Sly, before proceeding to mock nearly all of his earlier hit singles' with sly lyric-references drawing listeners back to "Dance To The Music", "Everyday People", and "Sing A Simple Song".

'So, thank you for the party, but Sly could never stay'. No pretence, this single was a warning shot, declaring in tight altered-vocal harmonies that Sly would no longer pretend to be something he's not—as if he'd been faking-it or not being himself before? As if the 'Different Strokes' sentiment had been in some way insincere, and the 'blame the bite' was a phoney put-on? The band was more popular than they'd ever been, but Sly was dissatisfied. As an integrated band they'd strived to radiate the message of racial harmony, but the message was getting lost. He'd become tired of working for the values exalted by his more inspirational early-phase hits, when all the time the world was not *really* listening to what he was saying. With co-lead vocal contributions from Rose, Freddie and Larry, it seemed they were united in their frustration with the world, and with the failure of their power of affirmation to make a difference. But while the lyrics were scathing, they were as much directed at Sly himself, stating that the Family Stone were not always entirely peaceful, loving... or happy. Although, once again, this message was lost to most in the force of its powerful groove. So Sly was also (dis)respectfully thanking the audience for permitting this new honesty, for 'letting me be myself again'.

The song would be even more extremely reworked for the *'There's A Riot Going On'* album, but bizarrely it would also reap its own crop of pretender cover versions—including a stunningly compressed high-velocity version by Howard Dovoto's post-punk post-Buzzcocks Magazine. Van Morrison covers "Thank You..." and quotes from "Family Affair" on his *'A Night In San Francisco'* (1994) set. And a bewildering diversity of other versions exist from the likes of Victor Wooten, Merl Saunders & The Rainforest Band, Robert Randolph & The Family Band, Dave Matthews & Friends, and a version recorded by the Big Brovas Rap Crew for inclusion in the Warner Bros film *'Scooby-Doo 2: Monsters Unleashed'* (2004). Inevitably, a host of rap acts, from Arrested Development to the Bay Area's own Digital Underground would go on to lift samples from or cover Family Stone material. You don't have to delve *too* far into the rhythmic spine of Janet Jackson's 1990 hit single "Rhythm

Nation" to detect Freddie Stone's guitar riff from the bridging section of "Thank You". While musical magpie David Bowie surely had the same groove in mind when he conceived "Fame".

Two classic sides, their differences documenting the way the band's sound and dynamic were shifting drastically. Condensing those abstract ideas into back-to-back textures of sound. It earned them the cover-story of *'Rolling Stone no. 54'* (19th March 1970), with a big Stephen Paley photo. The revealing lavishly-illustrated feature within actually had its origins in the interview backstage at ABC's 'Music Scene' show in October '69 carried out with Ben Fong-Torres. It forms a rare, and valuable reference-source, because Sly distrusts the press. As a result, this is one of the few occasions when he's found in a one-to-one interview situation. We don't have much inkling about Sly's subjective inner-life, yet in this disjointed conversation he nevertheless opens up about aspects of his schooldays, his DJ-ing, and the 'Autumn' period. He seldom debates or verbalises his motivations. He has the illusionist's facility for not responding directly to questions. Not that he doesn't speak, because he does, but it's as though he's simultaneously engaged in some other conversation, one with himself. And it's too random to be eloquent. He can be tricky. His manner of communicating can be playfully confusing. His conversation comes in abrupt succinct bites, in the form of anecdotes and personally-slanted recollections. To him, they're probably the same thing. He's not rude, he just doesn't conform to what people generally regard as normal social behaviour. He's individualistic, different to most everyone else. In this interview—coming up to two in the morning, with Sly relaxing back into a big plush sofa distractedly fidgeting with his ornate silver bracelet, he provides teasing clues to his thought-processes. He boasts about how *his* band would never compromise by doing a cash-in 'Greatest Hits' package. 'We just want to do the right things' he explained, 'not for money… if it's the money that will satisfy you more than not doing something you don't want to do, then do it'. They'd never condone singing 'for Coca-Cola' either, 'we will never sell out. For any reason. To death. Anything like that. Anything like that, man'.

At a further point in the interview he expressed his dissatisfaction over unrealistic label expectations. 'The record company wants another LP by February' he protests, 'well, we could do some good songs—but that would be just another LP'. They 'expect a group to come out with another LP and another'. With dutiful journalistic powers of observation, Fong-Torres notes that Sly's head moves in a repetitive circular motion to illustrate the point, as he mused 'there's got to be more to it. But what else can you do? Maybe it's impossible.' For a moment his inventive imagination spins off on hypothetical tangents, 'what can you put on vinyl or acetate or plastic. Not just something like a funny-shaped LP cover. Gotta be something it says or does. Maybe melt the LP and turn it into something. Like hash you can smoke?' It's true that, after a long period of uniformity, record companies were experimenting with sleeve-formats, the Beatles had gatefolds with novelty inserts, the Rolling Stones with 3D art-work, the Small Faces with a circular boxed-sleeve, with scratch 'n' sniff innovations around the corner. But Sly had other options on his mind... a concept album with theatrical dimensions? 'The only thing that sounds interesting is something that ties in with a play that finishes what an LP starts to say, and the LP will be important on account of the play'. Something perhaps like *'Hair'*, a stage musical with an integral best-selling album, or, surely not... the Who's story-themed *'Tommy'*? So far, it could be argued that Sly Stone does not make great albums, only great tracks. Perhaps all he's talking about here is some unifying concept to make an album more than just an anthology of fine pieces? Something more than a sum of its parts...?

Meanwhile, 'Dance tracks are just nice, cool—but nothing.' He'd already proved that he could make a lot more than 'nothing' out of the dance format. 'Something should be done.' What Sly was saying was that he'd sensed that changes were needed to avoid lapsing into the kind of comfortable self-mimicry that afflicts bands when they get stuck in a moment that they can't get out of. A musician's reputation is rarely formed by their finest records, rather it is the image they project across a series of records that sticks in people's minds. The narrative those albums construct. And over the coming twelve months his answer to his own rhetorical question would shove the Family Stone, and music history, onto a completely new trajectory. If people thought they'd 'got' Sly & The Family Stone, then the changes, both internal to the band, and externally, meant that the next album would not be as immediately accessible as its predecessors. But—as the most challenging and rewarding of their albums, it would grow in critic's estimation over time. Writer John Burks agreed. Following "Thank You (Falettinme Be Mice Elf Agin)", he asserts 'when better records are made, Sly & The Family Stone will make them'.

But, in fact, throughout 1970, Pop music's most extrovert personality had released just one new seven-inch single—"Thank You" itself. During the previous eighteen-month period—the one between October 1967 and April 1969, the Family Stone had released no less than four full-length albums. As the sixties bled over into the seventies, every month seemed to count. And a near two-year silence could mean career-death. Now Epic was pestering for new material. Not only pestering, but withholding advances and freezing royalties in an attempt to pressure him to deliver new 'product'. Sly had already missed several deadlines. Although actually, by current standards, the gap between albums was not particularly significant. Certainly it was nothing as long-awaited as the five-years-in-the-making Stone Roses' *'Second Coming'* (1994), the decade wait for the third Portishead album (*'Third'* in 2008), and certainly nothing like the even longer wait for Guns 'n' Roses *'Chinese Democracy'* (2008). But over at CBS, Clive Davis was seriously concerned.

In the meantime, inbetweentime, on the back of the band's continuing high-status and the shattering effect of their blistering screen-presence in the *'Woodstock'* movie, a revitalised "I Want To Take You Higher" climbed to a US no. 38 in June. In fact, such was the song's popularity that the same year Ike & Tina Turner released their own cover, which also became a hit, peaking four slots higher than the Sly original, but one slot lower on the R&B chart! Many years later Marcella Detroit would do a respectable version of "I Want To Take You Higher" on her debut solo album. To fill the worrying twenty-month vacancy in the release schedule Epic resorted to repackaging *'A Whole New Thing'* in a new cover for re-release. Then, despite the bold manifesto Sly had proclaimed through *'Rolling Stone'*, in a further effort to disguise the gap, the three previously uncollected Family Stone tracks were gathered up onto the LP *'Greatest Hits'* which made it all the way up to no. 2 in *'Billboard'* in November, earning the group its second gold disk. A special remixed edition was issued in the new quadraphonic format. The gatefold sleeve playfully collages multiple images of the Family sitting, squatting, or even suspended in mid-air over the soft-top of a sports-car. Sly is both in the car grinning, symbolically sitting at the steering wheel, while he's there above it too. A teasing persistence of the fun wackiness image. And a schizoid metaphor of his role as both navigator, and participant in the apparently stalled Family Stone project. Reviewed positively by Charlie Gillett in *'Record Mirror'* at the time, now the hastily improvised album provides a time capsule spanning the first phase of the group's career. For this would be the final 'classic-era' Family Stone recording. To re-conjure them, all you have to do is slap the record down on the turn-table, drop the stylus onto the shiny black vinyl groove, and they're there, in your front room.

There's also a TV-clip of the Family Stone performing "Thank You (Falettinme Be Mice Elf Agin)". I don't even know where it's from. But it's cool as fuck. Remember Sly this way. He's predominantly in black, but being Sly there are fringes and silver edgings and a big floppy wink-hat that slouches down over his forehead. He plays guitar out-front. Freddie to his right, in a turban. Larry to his left. Forming a guitar triad. The groove is fluid, a thing of percussive overload, insistent electronic and vocal hooks. The band is impeccably on-message. Of course, in the UK, we never got to see it. Not until the internet. Rock TV back then didn't extend far beyond *'Top Of The Pops'*, and because it wasn't Top Thirty, it wasn't on there. So we didn't get to see Sly & The Family Stone at their finest. If we deliberately sought them out, we got to hear the records. If we bought the music press, we read the reviews and goggled at the photos. But the journalists were often confused and unsympathetic. And, in England, what live shows there were took the old showbiz adage of 'always leave the audience wanting more' and tested it to destruction. As audiences were soon to discover…

Chapter Eleven
'Different Strokes For Different Folks'

'Do you know what makes you tick?
Do you know how to avoid what makes you sick...'
("Colour Me True")

After their initial abortive UK trip, Sly finally got to play England. And nothing low-key either. The 'Isle of Wight Festival' was the closest most people here got to recreating their own 'Woodstock', a high-point of the national counter-culture on this side of the Atlantic. The other bands on the day-glo festival posters also mimic that earlier event—The Who, Jefferson Airplane, John Sebastian (joined on stage by former Lovin' Spoonful cohort Zal Yankovski), with additional impetus provided by the Doors. And Miles Davis, who comments that he, Sly and Hendrix and 'a whole bunch of white groups' arrived 'to play on this big farm off the southern coast of England'. It was the third festival to take place there, sprawling like a massive hit-and-run victim across the rolling fields of East Afton Farm, and it was the last—at least until its 1980s revival, with ferries from Portsmouth to Ryde trucking over 2000 refugees at a go. But by the time it was happening, the contrasting forces of the hippie scene were coming into stark opposition. With compére Ricky Farr hopelessly attempting to organise the chaos between the idealistic 'absolutely free' faction as they came up against the simple necessity of an entry fee to fund the increasingly extravagant price tags for the artists. The concept of serendipitous chaos, against the necessity for toilet facilities. The Isle of Wight even spawned its own outlaw free event outside the enclosure, its own 'Desolation Row', a stubborn out-of-bounds hillside community overlooking the stage that defied all incitements to move, with Hawkwind and Pink Fairies playing to the excluded.

In a glorious pyre of vanities, 'a rehearsal for World War III', both the straight press, and its underground counterparts conspired to savage the event from opposing directions. Conservative MP Mark Woodnutt was complaining indignantly that 'the law had been brought into contempt' at the festival, going on to explain that 'I am not a prude and I do not mind nude bathing at the right place at the right time, but I do not like fornicating on the beach, which is what we have been seeing'. Tut-tut. Reading about it now, the story carries all the immediacy of reportage from some distant war-zone. A visiting *'Oz'*-editor, Richard Neville, was producing an on-site fanzine called *'FREEk'*, Mick Farren was there representing the self-styled 'White Panther' faction, Caroline Coon was at the 'Release' enclosure tending to the drug casualties, while serialised dispatches in *'Friends'* were lamenting the creeping commercialisation and ego-tripping of its 'bread-headed sell-out' stars. Decades later, the Oasis track "Fuckin' In The Bushes" on their *'Standing On The Shoulder Of Giants'* (2000) album, samples comments made by members of the public—both pro and anti, as reported on a contemporary TV report on the festival.

In the seething midst of it all was Sly & The Family Stone, 'King of the Black Hippies'. But their eagerly-anticipated high-profile Saturday-night set failed to ignite (29th August 1970). *'Melody Maker'* kicked in first with an equivocal commentary on their slot. 'Eventually, those who had waited it out were rewarded by the appearance of Sly & The Family Stone, but what could and should have been the festival's real highlight ended with vague disappointment. Glistening under the hot stage-lights Sly stomped, bopped, and gurgled through a set which lasted only a couple of numbers, and not much more than half an hour. He was much appreciated, though, and promised to return on Sunday night. He didn't' (issue dated 5th September 1970). They failed to detail the set-list, which pretty much replicated what they'd already done in their now-mythic 'Woodstock' appearance—"Thank You (Falettinme Be Mice Elf Agin)" with Sly himself playing guitar, "M'Lady", "Sing A Simple Song", "Stand", "You Can Make It", "Dance To The Music", "Music Lover", building into the crescendo of "I Want To Take You Higher". But critical opinion seems unanimous. *'Friends'* agreed, with only the addition of a little more jive-talking, 'Sly & The Family Stone started out roughly but soon got down to the gut and began sending out some hefty, happy music and then prematurely left the stage for what looked like a short rap. When they returned, some cat was burbling nonsense over the PA, so they split, despite rumours to the contrary, never to return' (issue dated 2nd October). The 'burbling cat' was harried MC Jeff Dexter, appealing for calm. Whichever version of events you read, whatever the reasons, it's obvious that Sly had prematurely decided unilaterally to walk off stage. Loping into the wings as though he couldn't escape quickly enough, to snort whatever variety of white powder he was using that day. For some in the audience, thoughts went back to what they'd been led to expect by the legends of Woodstock, other's thoughts merely extended as far as their desperate need for the inadequate toilets.

Jimi Hendrix played, but seemed so stoned many didn't even bother to stay to watch through to the end of his set, instead traipsing back for the ferries trucking refugees over from Ryde to Portsmouth. A chastened 'Fiery Creations' never promoted another event. Leaving it to the fledgling low-key Glastonbury gathering to pick up the flame and fan it into a part of the national agenda. Nevertheless, there were final connections. Some time later, confirming rumours that had been in circulation for many years, Miles Davis' autobiography admits that he and Hendrix had finally agreed on a schedule to record together in the aftermath of the festival. An album that would never happen, because just eighteen days later, Jimi was dead. Hendrix—a star at twenty-four, was dead at twenty-seven. Perceptively Miles observes in retrospect that 'both (Hendrix) and Sly were great natural musicians, they played what they heard'. On the night before he died, Hendrix attended a Sly concert.

For the Family Stone, the Isle of Wight was only the jumping-off point for an extended tour that was intended to play to a capacity Albert Hall crowd (September 18th). As it turned out, the venue was switched last-minute to the 2,000-seater 'Lyceum Theatre' on Wellington Street, just off the Strand. The concert became the season's premier attraction, with a hipperati of stars and critics tripping between the pillars of the neo-classical portico to check it out. Emerging inside, there's a balcony overhanging the circle. Former Small Faces keyboardist Ian 'Mac' McLagan was in the audience, and his account captures something of both the excitement, and the unpredictability of the performance. 'The first time I saw Sly & The Family Stone was the first time they played in London. The show at the Lyceum Ballroom was rescheduled after their first appearance (the Albert Hall date) got cancelled. When they finally played, it was a magnificent show of just over an hour. He finished with "I Want To Take You Higher" repeating the chorus over and over. Abruptly they stopped the song and left the stage with the audience and me going crazy, hollering and screaming. I was up at the bar on the balcony, and it felt as if it was going to collapse with the people jumping up and down. We waited for a good five minutes before they came back on. Gregg Errico brought it in. 'Wacka Wacka Wacka Wacka, Wacka Wacka Wacka Wacka, Higher, I wanna take you higher…' We knew immediately we were only getting more of the same, and it was fine, as long as they didn't stop too soon. They played for at least ten minutes, Sly hollering, screaming and dancing. But when they finished, that was it, they weren't going to come back on. It was a final statement' (quoted from his book *'All The Rage'*, Sidgwick & Jackson, 1998).

In separate boxes Jimi Hendrix and Eric Clapton also watched the performance. There was talk that Sly and Jimi were to meet up and jam at the 'Speakeasy Club' afterwards. Neither of them showed. Clapton was carrying a left-handed Stratocaster he'd intended to gift Jimi with after the show. In the confusion they never actually got to meet up either. As it turns out, they would never meet again. Richard Williams was also there, writing for *'Melody Maker'* about how 'musically, the fascinating thing is the way Sly has adapted James Brown's rhythmic approach for all the band, so that the voices are jabbing and stuttering with the same driving insistence as the bass and drums'. He was less enthusiastic about the audience-crowding, and the relentless 'Woodstock'-style flashing of peace-signs 'reminiscent of a group of school-kids reciting something they're very proud they just learned'. Bram Stoker—creator of 'Dracula', had once been the theatre's business manager, promoting his friend Henry Irving there with Ellen Terry. What *they* would have thought of the concert is open to conjecture.

With Jimi's death, something of the hopes and excitement of the sixties were coming to an end. Love was turning to rage. But the summer was young. There were other festivals to come, with Family Stone dates spread elsewhere throughout the month. So it goes on. The rest of the tour took in additional appearances in Paris, Rome and at a German 'Love & Peace Festival' on Fehrman Island. McLagan reconnected with them as part of Rod Stewart & The Faces, who were also on the bill. 'It was a godforsaken, windy place in the Baltic Sea, but Canned Heat, Sly & The Family Stone, The Faces and a lot of other acts had come from around the world to play, or in Sly's case to collect his cash and leave. There was a Force Ten gale blowing straight towards the stage, and people in tents were huddled in front of bonfires to keep warm… Love and Peace in Germany 1970, was quite different to the American version in 1967, because somebody shot the promoter, burned his trailer to the ground and stole all the cash…'

There was one further knowing encounter when the Faces flew into Frankfurt for another stoned soul picnic where, again, 'it was one of those gigs where Sly & The Family Stone were supposed to play, but didn't. I caught sight of Sly walking past my open hotel-room door dressed for the gig and ready to play, but apparently after collecting his money he kept on walking. I suppose it was a case of gain stopped play'. For Sly, it had become a game, a power-trip, in which he was the controlling force. Their reputation meant that they had become an automatic go-see. The audience needed Sly more than he needed the audience. Lots of bands delay their arrival on stage, to extend anticipation, to raise tension, making their precisely-timed moment of appearance the signal for a mass orgasmic uproar. Sly took it further, testing the loyalty of even the most fervent Family Stone followers. Manipulating their already-suspended gratification, enjoying the whim of choice that was his to extend or withhold. Into the realm of will-they or won't-they. As he'd later write, it was 'no win, no place, no show' ("Remember Who You Are"). Each show for him was a theatre of power. The decision was his. To appear, or not to appear. They await his whim. He, alone, decides. Until the mere fact of their performance was in itself miraculous…

'His problem,' according to Bobby Womack, 'was he couldn't wait until the gig was over before doing the drugs. He didn't mess with nothing but cocaine, but when he found out you could cook it he became a chef'. Bobby advised him, 'don't go on stage with drugs in your system. Keep the performance clean. You can't go on stage loaded, tripping on a cocktail of drugs, and then stand backstage and get loaded again. After the show—that's different. That's your own time. Do whatever shit you choose to do. It doesn't matter.' Sly didn't agree, 'fuck that shit'. He'd joke about the appearance of the crowds turning up to witness the concert, ridiculing them as 'unhip'. As though they were unworthy of the privilege of watching the band. Then he'd start with a single line, just to sharpen the senses, to achieve the clear-headed invincibility that coke bestows. Then another. And another. First it was cool, then it got to be too much. Until Womack reports stoned conversations with Sly prior to shows, with the audience already impatiently waiting and him protesting 'I can't go on, man… it's hard enough for me to *talk*, let alone stand up and try to sing'. Yet in Sly's coke-raddled world it was never *he* who was at fault. He played gigs. It wasn't necessarily *always* him who arrived late—sure, he played the show-biz game of stoking anticipation, creating mystique. That's part of the strategy. But he was in control. Sure he was. It was a working method Sly was happy to advocate to what he considered his too-disciplined 'too square' companion. Explaining 'Bobby, if The Man told you to turn up at 9pm, you would be there at 8:30pm, but let me tell you a little something about show-business—it don't work like that. It's what you *don't* do that gives you mystique. Don't be available all the time, don't always be there.'

And Sly took advantage of not being there and not being available more often than was healthy for his career. If there was something—almost anything, more interesting to do. *'Rolling Stone'* reported that 'he cancelled twenty-six of the eighty engagements scheduled for him in 1970—twenty because his stomach was in convulsions and another six because of a clash with Kapralik. With "Everyday People" on the chart Cynthia underwent an emergency gall bladder operation, and Sly cancelled three months of bookings—including an Ed Sullivan show, while she recuperated. This year (1971) Sly has cancelled twelve shows out of forty—ten because of a legal battle with Kapralik, and two because his drummer quit.' The Family Stone were treating success in a very cavalier way. There was some biting the feeding hand. Some having cakes and eating them. Sly's tantrums and failures to show had become legendary to the extent that his contracts carried a penalty-clause for non-appearance. So that another aspect of missing gigs was the law suits that followed. And worse. A lot of times it seemed hardly worth going out on the road at all, because it was costing them so much. All the while, untroubled by the dialectics of materialism, the Family Stone were big spenders. There were people with them. The growing entourage, growing.

Safely back in the States, Sly reverted to the role he'd enjoyed with 'Autumn', but taking advantage of his new marketability to negotiate a production deal with Atlantic Records that guaranteed him his own imprint, 'Stone Flower'. 'A stone flower grows in a garden of truth' explained Kapralik helpfully. The project started off with high expectations—he had plush offices facing across from the circular Capitol Records tower at LA's 1750 Vine Street. Its reception-desk was covered full-length in violet fur. But his media mini-empire issued just four singles… before he lost interest. All of them feature a pseudonymous Sly himself with various other musicians, including Family Stone members. The Sly-discovered group 6IX was built around a harmonica-player he'd encountered some time before in Cleveland. Supposedly the inspiration for Sly's own forays into harmonica. Pronounced 'six', the group was made up of Charles Higgins, Gil Bottliglere, Paul Stallwell—plus Marvin Braxton who would later work with Attitudes, a group signed to George Harrison's Dark Horse Records. Their solitary release for Stone Flower was "I'm Just Like You", c/w the old Family Stone track "Dynamite". A further single emerged from white Californian R&B artist Joe Hicks—"Life And Death In G&A pts 1 & 2", recorded in New York with Hicks high voice—somewhat reminiscent of, say, Labi Siffre. Then there was a strong duo of singles by Little Sister—Vet, Mary and Elva, now looking like a foxy version of the Ronettes or Martha & The Vandellas. And both of their singles rapidly escalated into the Pop Top 40 and the R&B Top 10.

The first Little Sister single was "You're The One" (c/w "You're The One Part two")—written by the girls themselves and carried on a Sly-alike message of self-help positivity, the trio harmonising 'You're the one, / don't blame the neighbourhood. / You're the one, your Mama didn't make you good, / you're the one…' It reached no. 22, and no. 4 on the R&B chart, in the early months of 1970. It was followed by "Somebody's Watching You" c/w "Stanga", a solid re-tread of the *'Stand!'* track, which made no. 32 (and R&B no. 8) towards the end of the same year. This second single is significant for its innovative first-ever use of a Maestro Rhythm King (MRK-1) drum-machine to generate its rhythm track—so early the device hadn't even got more than a working name. It was simply referred to as a 'rhythm box' or 'funk box'. Sly was dissatisfied with its raw sound, he felt that when used according to the manual, its sound was unrealistic. Instead he resorted to holding down all five buttons simultaneously, running the tape, then rewinding, holding down a different sequence of five buttons, and overdubbing. The sound he contrived by such methods for the Stone Flower releases at the Sausalito Record Plant studios, formed a significant evolution on what had gone before. Sly played bass. And used electronic rhythms. Concepts that would be carried over onto, and anticipated something of the atmospheric edginess of *'There's A Riot Going On'*.

There were other potential recruits. A major *'Rolling Stone'* feature offers a unique glimpse into Sly-at-work at the time. Providing a unique insight, particularly in the light of his notorious inaccessibility. The revealing article opens with a glimpse of Sly checking out potential signings for his label. He'd advertised that he was looking for a guitarist, a bass-player, and a keyboardist. Stephanie was there, sitting to one side, taking notes and 'phone numbers. 'The first arrivals, a dozen or so young men, are standing around the foyer while Sly checks out the available amps and speakers… Sly calls the first guy into the small practice room, furnished with chairs, a huge speaker and an electric organ. He sets the pattern, showing right away not just who, but what he is. 'Okay, man' he says, his bassy radio-schooled voice smooth and soothing. 'This is like, not an audition, you know. Just play some stuff and let me hear you. Just do what you want and we'll join in and see how you sound. Know what I mean?' If the auditioner is an organist, Sly listens for a few bars, then slides in with a layer of bass… if it's a guitarist, or a bassist, Sly will jump behind the organ, pumping easily, happily behind the player.' He runs through a number of auditions, including a nervous straight-looking white kid who plays guitar and sings "Proud Mary". 'Sly perks up, big smile, listens a bit, and joins in, clapping his hands, rocking his purple body back and forth on his chair, singing out of harmony line on the chorus. '*Aw, yeah*!' he says at the end. 'Hey, man, that's great. Can you play another number?'

George Clinton was one of those who must have gone through a similar process. He claims 'we signed to Sly's Stoneflower label but never got a record out. We were signed to Stoneflower for a split second…' Sly goofed half-seriously about other artists he'd like to produce, Ray Charles, Aretha Franklin, Morgana King… Bob Dylan. This possibility, it seems, had even been suggested to Dylan by go-between Clive Davis, and Dylan was interested. But Sly also listed Ted Kennedy and Muhammad Ali as potential production-projects. He was casting his net wide. Yet despite such a promising launch Sly gradually withdrew his attention from 'Stone Flower'. He fell out with Joe Hicks over a shared girlfriend. And Little Sister's career ended in mid-air… either he lost interest, or he found their success in some way threatened, or distracted attention from himself. For Clinton, 'once I saw that he had to do his thing, and it was hard to keep in touch with him, I said, well, I just kept on going, doing it my way'. The label finally, quietly, winked into extinction in 1971, although the name was retained for Sly's publishing.

But there were other collaborations being forged. Bobby Womack 'stumbled in there with Sly'. Womack is now acknowledged as a true original and 'The Last Soul Man' genius in his own right. That wasn't always so. In his highly entertaining autobiography (*'Midnight Mover'*, 2007) he explains how 'Jim Ford, my writing partner, had a good idea. He came over to my place and told me that I needed to 'get something going—away from everything else that was going on'. He meant all the friction I had in my life. I didn't know it, but the friction was just about to be turned up—to way past full blast. Jim wanted to hook me up with Sly Stone'. Bobby was born 4th March 1944, a Pisces in Cleveland Ohio, one of five brothers so poor his steelworker father—Friendly Womack, declared 'fasting days' to disguise the fact that they had no food, and they grubbed through garbage cans for discarded pig's tails, pigs' snouts, ears and ox-tails to eat. The Womack brothers began singing by mimicking their father's inept 'Voices of Love' vocal group behind their backs. Until his father bartered himself a guitar in exchange for giving four free haircuts. Risking a beating, while Friendly was out, Bobby learned to play the instrument left-handed, with the guitar upside-down, igniting his style by listening to Floyd Cramer—a piano-player! Soon, the brothers were trying-out in local studios, but the results of their first-ever recording sessions were 'stolen' and released under a bogus name—'the record business started screwing me then and hasn't stopped screwing me since' he adds ruefully.

For a long time Bobby was known primarily in the UK as the originator of the Rolling Stones' "It's All Over Now" (later also covered by Rod Stewart)—which he had first recorded as part of the Womack brothers' group, The Valentinos. To deeper cognoscenti his name was familiar as a shadowy composer/session-guitarist behind countless better-known artists such as Joe Tex, Jackie Wilson, Ray Charles and King Curtis. At one point he'd even been thrown out for schmoozing his way into playing a Dean Martin session! He wound up being headhunted into Sam Cooke's band instead, and played on his 1962 hit "Twisting The Night Away". 'Sam Cooke had a helluva influence on me' he revealed, 'not only because he was a great singer but because he was a great person. Sam was the kind of person who made you feel like you were him and he was you. He did it so well.' It was Sam—himself originally the vocalist with the gospel Soul Stirrers, who first persuaded Bobby to graduate away from the pure gospel circuit towards the more lucrative secular market, in the face of threats of eternal damnation from Friendly. Emerging through Sam Cook's SAR indie-label, the second Valentinos single—"Lookin' For A Love", sold two million, rewritten by Bobby around an old gospel tune. His father promptly disowned his sons for selling out to the devil's music. Nevertheless, Womack's burgeoning new career ran aground when Cooke, the man he called 'my mentor, my second father' was shot dead in a sleazy Los Angeles Motel, 11th December 1964. Billy Preston played organ at Cooke's chaotic funeral in Chicago seven days later. Perhaps Bobby's closeness to his mentor explains how he came to marry Sam's widow—Barbara Campbell, only three months after the murder! He had just turned twenty-one, she was ten years older. The troubled marriage, entered more out of loyalty to Cooke than for any other reason, was violently resented by both families, by fans and record industry insiders.

Bobby began using coke to escape the pain. He got a call from Ray Charles, and toured with his band, but quit because he was terrified by Ray's habit of piloting the tour-plane himself. He did session-work at Chip Moman's 'American Studio' which brought him into contact with the greatest artists of the era. He played on Aretha's *'Lady Soul'* (1968), and *'Dusty In Memphis'* (1969). Previously unimpressed by Elvis, he found himself overawed by the King's charisma when he played the "Suspicious Minds" sessions. Dubious about the white boy Jerry Wexler called in for another date he found that Eric Clapton played more authentic Blues guitar than he did! Despite his growing reputation within the industry, his solo singles released on Checker (1965), Atlantic, and Keymen (1967) fared less well, going largely unnoticed. Oddly, the career turn-about happened during a tour supporting the violently confrontational Wilson Pickett. During the tour and the tie-in recording dates, Bobby generously gifted all of his own best songs to Pickett, then—because he had no originals left, he had to fill his own debut solo album—August 1968's *'Fly Me To The Moon'*, with covers! Yet a series of subsequent albums for Minit/Liberty through 1967-70 began attracting attention precisely because of this idiosyncratic melange of original compositions and rearrangements of odd MoR hits—such as the Frank Sinatra title-track, or his "Moonlight In Vermont", or the Mamas & Papas' "California Dreamin'". A further step forward was instigated by Sly Stone's sympathetic encouragement. Bobby could reach wider audiences, he urged, by adopting a looser more personalised format, playing to his raconteur strengths by involving direct raps around extended instrumental passages. A development that would earn him the nickname 'The Preacher'—witness the long rambling monologue about how he was being pressured to make his music sound more commercial, inserted incongruously into a lengthy 9:30-minute medley themed around his bluesy take on the Bacharach/David Carpenters' schmaltzer "(They Long To Be) Close To You". Consequently, signed to UA from 1971, he achieved a major breakthrough... a debt Bobby was to repay to Sly in years to come.

At Jim Ford's suggestion, the two artists first met on 'neutral' turf, in a booth at an Italian restaurant. Bobby came prepared as his 'mentor' Sam Cooke would have advised, wearing a suit and tie, carrying what was intended to be an appropriately businesslike briefcase. Sly's sartorial preparation was characteristically less formal, and he immediately called his bluff—'he say, hey, you're Bobby Womack, is this the guy that make all the funky music? You too funky to have a briefcase, you too funky to look like that. Pull that shit off. Take that goddam suit off and give me that fucking briefcase. You ain't got nothing in there anyway'. His appraisal was piercingly accurate. The briefcase contained nothing, other than a couple of sandwiches and a blueberry muffin. After that 'we got to hangin', we became very close, very quickly, because we had our music together'. When Womack subsequently arrived at the Family Stone's Bel Air mansion he was beckoned in by Sly with an inviting 'hey, you're a bad nigger, you're a bad motherfucker, here, have some coke'.

****

'Smelly, obnoxious…'
the definition of Funk,
according to 'Really the Blues' by
Mezz Mezzrow & Bernard Wolfe (1946)

What is this thing called 'Funk'…? We think we know it when we hear it.

Funk is a four-letter word. Funk? Why Funk? The dictionary defines 'funk' three ways. As 'a strong foul odour'. And as 'a type of polyrhythmic Black dance music with heavy syncopation'. We can effectively ignore the third meaning, 'blue funk'—a state of nervous fear. 'Funkster' is 'a performer or fan of Funk music'. And like Rock 'n' Roll before it, there are sexual connotations to the word. The dictionary entry goes on to explain 'Funky' as 'perhaps alluding to music that was smelly, that is, earthy (like the early Blues)'. But neglects to point out that it was also coarse slang for the musk of a sexually aroused woman. The smell of sex. Like much jive-talk, it has deep semantic roots. Buddy Bolden's "Funky Butt" dates as far back as 1907. Kenna's Hall, a New Orleans jazz hangout on Perdido Street was Bolden's favoured gig venue, known locally as 'Funky Butt Hall'—abbreviated to 'FB Hall'. Into 1950s jazz circles the word was by no means uncommon—as in King Pleasure's "Funk Junction", or "Crème De Funk" by Phil Woods and Gene Quill in 1957. There was an album the same year by Gene Ammons Allstars simply titled *Funky*. But it was sixty years after Buddy Bolden, in 1967, that Dyke & The Blazers released "Funky Broadway"—reputedly the first record title to carry the modern sense of the word. Around the same time, the west-coast Charles Wright & The Watts 103rd Street Rhythm Band were also issuing proto-funk sounds, although it would not be until 1970's "Express Yourself" that they took it nationwide.

By then, Funk—and the influence of Sly's Seven Funkateers, was very much in the air. If the planet of African-American music was spinning off its axis, Sylvester Stewart was in the cockpit, at the controls. What James Brown's funk machine had set in motion—freeing 'the groove' from song-structure and liberating R&B into long free-form work-outs, Sly Stone and his disparate hippie soulster Family were taking even further. He re-saw, re-thought, and reconstructed it. The 'New Breed' was playing the 'New Thang'. And some measure of just how effectively the virus it released had riddled music is the way it was already turning the rest of the industry in a new direction. For Sly, such collusions were more natural. Consumed by music, he'd always been drawn to its richest diversity. Although conforming at various stages of his career to the expectations of Doo-Wop, Soul, or grab-you-by-the-legs Funk, he'd never been limited by any one genre.

Motown bassist James Jamerson had pioneered the technique of bringing his instrument to the foreground of Soul records, a strategy Funk would build on, with his melodic bass-lines typically forming the core of the production. Funk took it further. The 'Mr Bassman'—according to teenybopper Johnny Cymbal, was 'the hidden king of Rock 'n' Roll'. And the hidden Funk king of the Family Stone was Larry Graham. He had taken out the patent on the 'slapping' technique of playing bass—and it had become the one element that had remained constant throughout Sly's recordings, one of the most widely imitated of his innovations. In fact—pretty soon it had become synonymous with funk itself. Funk's tricky riffs and rhythms tended to be more complex than what had come before, while its song-structures, melody and harmony, tended to be proportionally simpler, to the extent of de-emphasising the need for chord changes. Technically, Funk emphasised the first beat of the bar—'on the one', often employing the drums or a slap of the tonic. Funk could consist of a single riff, or two interlocking riffs, with the point of transition from one to the other forming its highpoint. But its most important defining characteristic was the generation of a signature groove, and the intensification thereof. What he had begun with "Dance To The Music" had become the industry's dominating vibe. 'There are two kinds of black music' announces the cover-blurb of Joel Selvin's *'Oral History'*. There was black music 'before Sly Stone, and after Sly Stone'.

Tony Hall, a 6ft tall Radio Luxembourg DJ used to contribute a weekly 'My Scene' column for *'Record Mirror'*. It was vitally useful for aspirant wannabe Mods in that it talked about the latest cultish American singles that qualified for in-crowd approval, those rare groove soul imports and credibly minor-label Tamla-Motown copyists. So it represented a seismic shift in 1966 when he abruptly proclaimed that the focus of hip had moved from black soul, which was no longer where it's at, to white west-coast bands. To some it was heresy, and he'd blown his authority. They stuck with what they knew, and they were still doing it into the Northern Soul 1970s all-nighters. Others were intrigued and hunted out the esoteric new sounds he quoted, the Seeds, Left Banke, and Sly-produced Beau Brummels.

He was right, to the extent that after a decade of phenomenal growth and innovation, black music had run itself into an impasse—what Jerry Wexler described as a 'wall', while simultaneously white Rock was stealing a move on it as the pulse of what was happening, man. The *'Otis Blue'* album of 1965 was recorded within weeks of Sam Cooke's murder. Yet incongruously, for an album that purported to cast Otis Redding as Cooke's successor as the embodiment of young black America, it used a beautiful white-model as its cover-girl. And for added white appeal, the track-listing lined up his idol's posthumously released "A Change Is Gonna Come" against a frantic cover of the Stones' "Satisfaction". Opportunistic covers of the Beatles or Rolling Stones, recorded as a commercial fillip to the white market, seldom proved convincing. Otis was always better working his own material than he was attempting "Day Tripper" or "Satisfaction", or Wilson Pickett doing "Hey Jude". When Fats Domino was cajoled into recording "Everybody's Got Something To Hide (Except Me & My Monkey)" he admitted he was totally baffled by the lyrics he was singing, and that he had no sense of emotional commitment to the song. Sure, Otis wowed the Love Generation crowd at Monterey. Yet he was never able to evolve far beyond that point, his performances becoming increasingly mannered, more stylised, and his career as 'an ambassador for us all'—in Joe Tex's phrase, would soon be brutally curtailed. Whatever he may have accomplished ended when his charted twin-engined plane went down in the icy waters of the Madison Lake Monoma on 10th December 1967.

Soul had to break away from previous formats, move on from the gospel passion of Stax/Atlantic artists. The streets were erupting in race riots, demanding a soundtrack to echo them. Black pride's mistrust of whitey meant it fostered a blacker, funkier, more ghetto-orientated soul sound. And it was Sly who offered the real viable route out of the Soul impasse by doing startling and innovatory things with R&B. His model of synthesis in production and composition showed how to transfigure black music into the new decade. David Henderson, writing in *'Crawdaddy'* (September 1968), identified what he termed an 'avant-garde of rhythm 'n' blues' which was bringing 'some black intelligence and variance to the dilemma in programming that the black stations have fallen under'. He listed Hendrix and Sly alongside the Chambers Brothers and Ritchie Havens. But neither of the latter would break as big as Sly did.

Purists might argue, and they did. But by taking it way off the mainstream radar, Sly opened a new era for Soul. Reviewing the Family Stone's *'Greatest Hits'* in February 1971, *'NME'* pointed out that the album formed more than just a collection, 'on reflection it can be said to represent the original blueprint which eventually helped to drastically change the stereotyped format of popular black music.' It continued, 'today, Sly's influence can be easily detected in the work of most top American soul acts… most notable being the Temptations, who re-channelled it to fit their own personal requirements.' Sly-style outlandish duds were triggering whole new trends in black fashion which overnight rendered the mohair brigade very passé. From the label that had once branded itself 'The Sound Of Young America', there were stories of Berry Gordy brandishing a copy of *'Stand!'* at Motown music staff meetings as an example of the direction he proposed the label should be aping. And what began within the swirling electro-effects and intrusive bleeps on the Supremes "Reflections" was taken to its most startling extremes when the Temptations divested themselves of their smart dinner-jackets, and began dressing down in a ghetto-chic of headbands, paisley muumuus and tough 'Stagger Lee' scowls for a magnificent run of 'relevant' singles. To *'Rolling Stone'* they 'began as one of Motown's funkiest and straightest R&B groups and have wound up the children of Sly Stone'. Not altogether comfortably, perhaps.

The Temptations had consistently proved to be Motown's top group, yet every stage of their career is defined by the production direction of backroom outsiders. Of course, the Temp's couldn't play with their voices, with instruments, with studio technology, and with musical theories as Sly did effortlessly in-house. No, they were the blank slate on which others wrote. When 'troubled' tenor David Ruffin was 'fired'—or quit the group in 1968 to go solo, he was replaced by husky-voiced Dennis Edwards from Birmingham Alabama (previously of the Contours). And twenty-six-year-old Motown writer/producer Norman Whitfield was quick to seize upon the shift to set about redesigning and toughening the group into its new high-concept 'heavier' phase. Whitfield later claimed Sly Stone showed him how record production could be 'the science of sound'. At one point Otis Williams claims to have brought the idea to Whitfield. Maybe he did, whatever, using a template co-opted from Sly Stone—taking Eddie Kendricks' existing high-range soaring falsetto but accentuating Melvin Franklin's booming deep bass voice in conscious imitation of the Family Stone's high (Rose)/ low (Larry) contrast, he took more rock-esque performances involving lead-vocal trading, and added complex orchestrated arrangements. With classic hit-maker Barrett Strong co-writing the songs with Whitfield, the Temptations entered the 'psychedelic soul' terrain by immediately riding their first 'Dance To The Music'-inspired single—"Cloud Nine", into a high Top Ten smash, and a 1968 Grammy-winner to boot. Reviewing the single, *'Rolling Stone'* detected a fade-out 'plainly imitative of Sly, with everyone 'boom-booming' for all they are worth'. It was followed by five more hits across the next two years, including their 1969 no. 1 "I Can't Get Next To You", and "Ball Of Confusion" no. 3 the following year. Here, each set of verses builds to a charged climax pitting a harmonica—again taken from Sly (as on "Higher"), against a brassy horn section. The best lines punch an escalating build of rap-style images snatched from the headlines—'suicide, too many bills, / hippies moving to the hills, / and people all over the world shouting 'end the war', / and the band played on' before returning to the deep-bass voice intoning 'that's what the world is today, a ball of confusion'. Yet despite further personnel changes, Eddie Kendricks quitting, Paul Williams leaving on medical grounds only to be found murdered in his car in Detroit, the Temptations hits continued with "Papa Was A Rolling Stone" making it as a 1972 chart-topper. And it remains a stunning record.

Still operating in the singles' zone, following the Temptations' successful rebranding, The Jackson Five were given the Motown Sly-makeover with the exhilarating "I Want You Back", and—take what you can gather from coincidence, but doesn't "ABC"—the Jackson Five's second American no. 1 in May 1970, bear an uncanny lyrical resemblance to Sly's "Harmony"? While the old Motown production-line system was already breaking down as its stars fought for greater creative autonomy. Marvin Gaye had spent long months reshaping his own career away from his catchy sweet-soul sixties teen-ballad hits, only to resurface in 1971 with his deeply introspective manifesto-album *'What's Going On'*. And things would never be quite the same again. Nothing in his earlier career as a tuxedo-clad heart-throb provided any hint he would cut a concept album dealing with civil rights, the Vietnam war and ghetto life. Led by the frequently-covered "Inner City Blues", it unleashed an era of socially aware soul. Equally startling was the music itself, softening and double-tracking Marvin's falsetto against a wash of bubbling percussion, swaying strings and chattering guitars. Berry Gordy was dubious, he thought it was doomed to fail, but its disillusioned nobility captured the public mood.

Stevie Wonder renegotiated his contract with Tamla and abruptly switched towards more progressive music, playing every instrument, perfecting the interplay between a variety of keyboard sounds, making extensive use of moog synthesiser and production techniques, writing more philosophical lyrics for his light, clear vocals on an innovative run of sublime albums beginning with *'Where I'm Coming From'* (1971), *'Music Of My Mind'* (1972), *'Talking Book'* (1972), *'Innervisions'* (1973) through to *'Fulfillingness First Finale'* (1974). Stevie's *'Songs In The Key Of Life'* (1976) influenced virtually every modern soul and R&B singer, brimming with timeless seductive killers such as "Isn't She Lovely", "As", and his Count Basie tribute "Sir Duke". Its twenty-one tracks encompass a vast range of life's issues—emotional, social, spiritual and environmental, all performed with bravado and lightness of touch in a soundscape that employs the shiniest synthesised studio toys the decade had to offer. No other R&B artist has sung about the quandaries of human existence with quite the same grace.

Former members of the Motown clan, the Isley Brothers, jumped labels into a new high-charting identity with "It's Your Thing", elevated by an awesome Funk-power that bridged Sly to Hendrix. While elsewhere, beyond Motown, the guilty-pleasure delights of Kool & The Gang, the Ohio Players, The Meters in New Orleans, Earth Wind & Fire, Undisputed Truth, and George Clinton /Bootsy Collins' extra-terrestrial Funkadelic/ Parliament were redefining the limits of everything that Soul had previously thought possible. In mid-1968 Curtis Mayfield took control of the means of production by shifting the Impressions from ABC to his own Curtom, and releasing a series of socially-aware gospel-political singles and albums. The Chi-Lites "Are You My Woman" is also a virtual Sly-alike, complete with a 'Larry' deep-voice 'boom-boom-boom'. Even jazz was melting in a smooth-flowing free-form 'Bitches Brew' of extended rhythms and endless improvisations. Simplifying from the dizzying rapid-fire structures of Bebop in favour of looser single-chord Jazz-Funk vamps. Sly's ingenuous street-wise sound spurred Miles to plug in and record such groundbreaking jazz-fusion works as *'On The Corner'* (1972).

After many years of hesitation and noncommittal silence, goaded by the frantic proddings of the zeitgeist, pushed this way and that by the rhythms of cool, the dam of lyrical restraint finally burst wide open too. Previously, it had been over-cautious. Before Sly very few soul or R&B artists ventured into political and social commentary. To Mike Marqusee, 'for the emerging black soul stars, authenticity came cheap; their struggle was for survival; they were avowedly and unashamedly commercial artists. For many, a hit record was the difference between penury and a modest degree of comfort. There were already so many barriers between themselves and the wider marketplace that the notion of erecting even more exercised little appeal. Politics was considered the kiss of death—far more risky for blacks than for whites'. Then Sam Cooke covered Dylan's "Blowin' In The Wind", and fashioned his own response directly inspired by it—"A Change Is Gonna Come" in late 1964. Soon after, Stevie Wonder charted with his own take on "Blowin' In The Wind", much to Motown's nervous uncertainties about their prodigy being tainted by political controversy. Sly accelerated the stalled snail-like evolution by rebuking their passivity on "Stand!" with 'you've been sitting much too long, / there's a permanent crease in your right and wrong'. After Sly it became expected—through soul, funk, and jazz into hip-hop too, to talk not only to the feet, but also ever so slightly, towards acerbic social observations on what the artist's inner feelings might be. The Temptations' "Message From A Black Man" warns that the civil rights struggle had turned a dark unsettling corner with 'no matter how hard you try / you can't stop me now'.

The Staple Singers revived the fortunes of Stax by reaching a US no. 12 with "Respect Yourself" (1971), a self-empowerment anthem of heavily-stated strength and considerable energy (written by Luther Ingram and Mack Rice). But even more defiantly, their 'B'-side "I Like The Things About Me", listed the Negroid featured they'd been conditioned to regard unfavourably—but no, not any more. No longer. Like James Brown, they were 'Saying It Loud, I'm Black And I'm Proud'. Between 1968 and 1973 James Brown, Marvin Gaye, Aretha Franklin, the Temptations, Bobby Womack, Stevie Wonder, and Edwin Starr produced a rich seam of socially-aware music. Surely, none of this could have happened without Sly & The Family Stone doing it first…? Providing a blueprint for everything that was to come. Taking it so far off the map it would never find its way back.

Effecting artists as diverse as Was (Not Was), as much as they did the George Clinton's and Santana's. At his not-inconsiderable peak, Sly had everything. There's a cliché about an artist 'defining their times'? Yeah—well, here is that artist. And so on, and so on, and scoobie-doobie-doo.

Perhaps he even supplied the answer to Marvin Gaye's rhetorical question? When Marvin asks 'What's Going On...?', Sly replies 'There's A Riot Goin' On...'

Yet the ensemble's organic weirdness was failing, even as Sly's influence continued to spread in tandem with their growing commercial heft. And from this point on, Family Stone recordings would be marked by Sly himself assuming even greater control of the creative process. With correspondingly diminishing input from his band-mates to the point where Sly would be playing most of the instruments on record himself. With "Thank You (Falettinme Be Mice Elf Agin)", in particular, as a harbinger of that next phase of the band's evolution. Moving it into a darker, more drug-hazed style of funk to reflect the incoming new decade. Gravitating towards something that better expressed its feelings of failed optimism. Sly worked harder than anyone he played with. And then played harder too. Rock mythology believes the party life-style to be integral to the job description, and Sly—the King of Funk-Rock, helped define that life-style. Weirdness? 'A freaky rival, never sing my freaky song' he points out (on "Say You Will"). True.

Chapter Twelve
'Revolution/Evolution'

'when I thought I was getting down that's when I start freaking out'
("L.O.V.I.N.U.")

'Don't Call Me Nigger, Whitey...'

In the fall of 1969, soon after 'Woodstock', the band moved en masse to Los Angeles, the 'City of Eternal Summer'. Into the Hollywood Hills. Into the exclusive Coldwater Canyon area. Into affluent Mulholland Drive. Into LA, choked on a banquet of frantic and unreal expectations. A place where movie fantasists mass-manufacture images for a living, where there are no cultural concepts that cannot be appropriated, neutered, used or abused. And it was a geographical switch that represented a total shift of scene in more ways than one. The relocation was a new start for every aspect of the Family Stone operation. A new year zero, a cultural revolution and a night of the long knives all rolled into one. It was a huge old house. A house with lots of rooms. Big enough to hide all manner of weirdness. And beneath those smog-orange skies the Family Stone partying-hard just got partying-harder. For—according to Bubba Banks, 'it all fell apart at Coldwater...'

Sly had met bi-racial Deborah Sara King—eighteen-year-old daughter of pioneering Oakland Blues guitarist Saunders King, in Frisco. She was with him at 'Woodstock'. And she was with him when they moved to LA. Debbie's sister, Kitsaun, worked there at the 'Stone Flower' recording base, in the production suite office. And there was Stephani Swanigan, well into her learning curve into strangeness. She was opinionated, and one of the few people strong enough to sometimes contradict Sly. 'People gave him stuff. Drugs were just there' she said, 'he didn't even have to ask for it. He didn't have to buy'. Coke provided the permanent high. While Sly maintained a locked back-up safe at Coldwater stocked to capacity with rows of bottles.

A labful of pharmaceuticals enabled by a psychologist in the hills who wrote the scripts. Each bottle crammed with half-a-thousand pills each— Seconal, Tuinals, reds, yellows and greens, 747s, the psychosedative Placidyls, and downers to control his colour-coded 'chemical cycle'. At one point Stephani even flushed Sly's stash down the toilet in an attempt to save him from himself. Sly had a sex-thing with Debbie, and occasionally slept with Stephani too, but she clarifies 'I was never his girlfriend… it would have made me less effective in the things that I was supposed to do'.

Freddie stayed over, when it suited him. Even sister Loretta stayed, until Sly fell out with her. She spooked him. Threatened his authority. She also tried to split Sly away from David Kapralik. She didn't trust him. Bubba Banks reappeared after a spell in jail. Sly trusted Bubba. Sly took Jerry Martini's room at the Coldwater spread, and gave it to Bubba. Jerry had no say in the matter. It was a done deal. Bubba, as Sly's aide-de-camp, brought James Vernon 'JB' Brown along into the clique. He'd previously been in the employ of Chevron Oil, in some vague capacity. There was also gangster Edward 'Eddie Chin' Elliott, a career criminal and long-time friend of Bubba. Together, they took over as Sly's personal security, 'controlling devils' according to Bobby Womack. 'I was his pit-bull' agreed Bubba. They scared and intimidated David Kapralik. And more. Sly used Bubba to wheedle Rose away from Larry. While recording the *'Stand!'* sessions Rose and Larry had shacked up together in Manhattan. She was a vibrant vivacious and vital part of the Family Stone. Sly didn't approve of their closeness, and schemed to bring her back on-side. And she had always been attracted to Bubba. At Bel Air, Sly used that renewed attraction as a weapon against Larry…

Goons, flunkies and junkies. In addition, Sly had Max, the English bulldog. He brought Stoner down from Frisco. Then acquired Gun, an intimidating uncontrollable pit-bull. Gun was a psycho dog. Inbred. Fuelled on the palpable pall of madness that hung on the air. Sly would use Gun for his own immense amusement. Wired, he'd stalk through the house goading Gun who was straining at the leash—or, as Womack remembers it, 'Gun trotted in, tugging Sly behind on that lead', shouting 'everybody hit the deck, the man is coming looking for you' and he'd laugh as they scattered, ran and hid from the snarling pit-bull. Sly could be a load of laughs when the devil-mood was on him. Never a dull moment. Sly briefly acquired a monkey. It would tease Gun, who was never quick enough to catch it. Sly would encourage their animosity, Gun would chase after the monkey, but it was always too fast. Until one day, the monkey jumped down and went 'heh, heh, heh' to attract Gun's attention but, when it went to run and jump back out of the way, its foot slipped. That was enough. Gun was on it in an instant, and ripped its chest out. Gun killed it. Gun attacked visitors. Especially male guests. Particularly male visitors if they wore a hat. Gun had a thing about men with hats. He also had a thing about chasing his own tail. He spent all day chasing his tail. Until Sly decided to do something about it. So he took Gun to the veterinary surgeon. The vet tried various curative methods. But Gun would not quit chasing his tail. So they amputated his tail. Sly took Gun home… where he chased his butt…!

It was Los Angels that proved to be the tipping point into badness. Drugs were part of its culture. That's what you do. 'If you get to laugh, and want to take a bath with someone you just got to know' Sly would later comment, 'it might be the season, or it could be the reason…' ("Who's To Say"). The season was New Year's Eve, from 1969 into the new decade. The reason, another instalment of the never-ending party going down at Coldwater Canyon. The party where Kitsaun King's boyfriend Jay called round with some 'Angel Dust'. The new wonder-drug. Like LSD, it was a synthetic hallucinogenic, originally manufactured in 1950 as phencyclidine—an intravenous veterinary anaesthetic, but inevitably by the 1970s it was being synthesised in illegal laboratories and had escalated to become a Class A street drug. Every room was full. And there were a lot of rooms. There were always people hanging, chopping out fat lines, doing blow. And this night, people from everywhere had dropped in. The whole scene devolving into one great party after another, where a gram of coke would never do, it had to be two-or-three ounces. Stoned people were sprawled around talking moonily in endlessly spaced tedium. At first Sly was a little scared of this new heavier PCP freak-shit. But Jerry and Jay sampled it. And almost died. Check out the symptoms, the drop in their respiration, their low pulse rate, nausea and blurred vision, their eyes flicking up and down. Its powerfully disturbing effects include sensory, temporal and mood distortions, catatonic dreamlike states, and extremes of both euphoria and depression. Hell, they're even drooling at the mouth. Ambulances had to be called. Discrete Hollywood clinics have an etiquette when it comes to OD's. But despite so dramatic an introduction, Sly's curiosity overcame caution. Soon he… and then Freddie had both graduated to this new, more potent, high.

Daddy KC was there. He knew what was going on. It was impossible for him not to. But he refused to believe in Sly's culpability. He blamed the bad guys, the dealers, the leechers. He blamed Bubba. But he could never bring himself to lay the blame on Sly or Freddie. They were always the victims.

****

'I hate to add to the heap of cultural mythology surrounding this done-to-death decade from said angle, but there's almost no other 'in' to begin explaining the downward spiral of Sly Stone, which is essential to understanding the genesis of 'There's A Riot Goin'' On'

(Miles Marshall Lewis)

Assembling the facts and sequencing the events is the easy part. Track-listing the albums, checking the chart-placings of the singles, the personnel involved, the dates and session details. Evaluating what they signify, gauging the motivations behind them, they are things not so easy to quantify. Yes, it's time for a little more cultural, and sub-cultural history. Again, if you just want the fun Pop-stuff you can skip the next few pages. But without all of *this*, there wouldn't be any of *that*. At surface level Pop music is disposable commercial ephemera. Something that fleetingly catches the public imagination for long enough to sell in economically viable units. Sometimes it can be more than that. Vinyl was the decade's CNN. It was a generational thing, it belonged— not only to the people, but to a mix of peoples, races, cultures. Even without consciously controlling the process, the producers and the consumers of Pop-culture were conspiring together to force the pace of aesthetic and social change. Forming and shifting opinion with each new record produced, each new record bought, each concert played, each concert attended. And certain records, certain artists, through a process of collision or collusion, attuned their work so finely to events that they time-fix it exactly. Consciously—or more frequently unconsciously, they conjured the ability to snare what was most intangible, most inexpressible about the moment.

Bob Dylan's lyrical imprecision was initially held against him by unsympathetic critics. 'The times they are a-changin''—isn't that a statement of the obvious? The times are always in a state of flux. Always have been. Others know better. It was exactly through what was suggested by that imprecision that his pulse so precisely coincided with the prevailing mood. But—reading his autobiographical *'Chronicles'* (2004), it becomes clear that he exerted only the most tenuous conscious control over what he was creating, that in a sense he was as perplexed, confused and amazed by the songs he was vomiting out as were his audience. The book reveals him as a less calculating and far more insecure person than his persona allows. Sly's creativity forms a more precise synchronicity to the shifting micro-moods of the time. Sharing a briefer, more concentrated period of years, but containing a contrastingly greater scattergun diversity of signifiers. Impinging on a range of different and often opposing factions, interpreting them in violently different ways. The simpler positivism of the cycle of records up to, and reaching their apotheosis with *'Stand!'*, coincide with a pervasive mood of optimism. Society was caught up in a process of being re-made, transfigured into a more caring more inclusively tolerant place. There were problems, there were lingering prejudices and injustices, but these could be surmounted. With "Dance To The Music" and—to an extent through *'Stand!'* too, Sly's populist instincts had played directly to the audience.

From now on, the more implosive energies of *'There's A Riot Goin' On'* would take it deeper, and he would no longer care to seek anyone's approval. In the same way that Dylan's articulate imprecision represents what reasoned dialogue could never do, *'There's A Riot Goin' On'* advances into the complex quagmire of any number of personal and societal failures. Not that any of this was necessarily uppermost in Sly's mind as he assembled the tracks that would make up the album. Or that he was even still conscious of their implications much beyond what was happening within his own immediate circle. Greil Marcus' fine essay 'The Myth Of Staggerlee' seems to assume a greater degree of conscious control on Sly's behalf than the evidence implies. Instead, so much of it lies in the exact elision between what he produced, and the way it was received. It was a two-way interaction to which his intensions were only ever incidental. That they bring together and seem to express so much is less evidence of the clear application of intellect, more of his intuitive responses to what is beyond expression in any other form.

Everywhere, the tone of the time was darkening. With splintering scenes replacing one another with the rapidity of the spin of vinyl slipping onto a jukebox turntable. For the white counter-culture it charts the fragmentation of idealism concurrent with the emergence of the dark side at its core. The resurgence of old power-structures, the inflexibility of tired intolerances, and the persistence of familiar corruptions even within its own supposed new beginnings. After 'Woodstock' there had been the toxic fall-out of its dark west-coast twin 'Altamont', which erupted into skirmish, brutality and murder as Jefferson Airplane, Ike & Tina Turner and their Satanic Majesties the Rolling Stones played beneath the blazing LA sun. After the first blossoming of day-glo idealism, it was becoming apparent that love was *not* all you need. By now, if Sly had been hung up on that same street corner, heat still bouncing down, melting the blacktop, he'd have sensed something different in the air. Something equally intangible, but less celebratory. The hippies and nubile flower-children were mostly gone from the Family Stone's original San Fran base. Haight-Ashbury itself, the epicentre of hippiedom, had lapsed back into ordinary ghetto-hood again, becoming a squalid mess of overcrowding, homelessness and crime, crawling with pushers and teenage runaways. Survivors creeping out of the wreckage like cockroaches after a nuclear attack. What Jim Morrison had once hymned as 'Love Street', and the Family Stone envisaged as "Love City"—Sly now transposed, and referred to obliquely as 'Luv 'n' Haight'. With no power left in the hippie flower, all that remained were the fading Rick Griffin posters, the Diggers' Free Store on Haight-Ashbury which was boarded over and closed, and paranoids prowling where placid peaceniks once paraded. Accompanied by the darkening narcotic pull of hangover. Of futility.

All the while, the underground press was functioning as its sensor, carrying the memetic message. 'If You're Not Part Of The Solution… You're Part Of The Problem'. Flicking through its pages you could watch the social landscape all around you heaving into new and more radical configurations.

Abbie Hoffman, in jail, wrote *'Steal This Book'* (1971), a 'manual of survival in the prison that is Amerika', gleefully dispensing advice on how to grow marijuana, how to beat the draft, obtain free land, set up guerrilla radio, and how to make Molotov cocktails. It lists free clinics, clothes outlets, food kitchens and draft counselling for the 'alternative society'. It also contains gems of wisdom such as 'avoid all needle drugs. The only dope worth shooting is Richard Nixon'. And even as the politics mutated, the *'S.F. Oracle'* began disseminating information less about free love, and more about sexually-transmitted diseases. As Greil Marcus says 'we had gone too far, really, without getting anywhere...'. Presidential hopeful Ronald Reagan was elected Governor of California on a platform that included the harassment of Hippies. 'A hippie is someone who looks like Tarzan, walks like Jane, and smells like cheetah' jibed the one-time 'B'-movie actor.

In the fall of 1972 Patty Hearst—heiress of media-magnate Randolph Hearst's Newspaper empire, grand-daughter of WR Hearst who was savaged by Orson Welles in *'Citizen Kane'* (1941), commenced studies at Berkeley. She was unwittingly destined to become a participant in the final absurdist theatre of Black Power. But for now, in the crucible of student radicalism, she discovered that 'almost all that had withered away. Only the dregs of the counter-culture movement—the hangers-on, the junkies, the derelicts, the freaks, the weirdos and the wasted warriors of the counterculture, were anywhere in evidence. The signs of residual hippiness could be seen entertaining the tourists on infamous Telegraph Avenue, which was outside the university campus, as they came in a variety of political persuasions and shocking attire. But for every political radical, you were just as likely to come on a Jesus freak or a macho tough leading a Doberman adorned with a thick collar of large spikes. Aggressive panhandlers swarm about coffeehouse entrances, physically accosting people, demanding 'spare change'. Punks loiter on street corners blatantly propositioning young girls in no uncertain terms' (*'Patty Hearst: Every Secret Thing'* by Patricia Campbell Hearst, Methuen 1982). There was even a brutal serial-killer known as The Zodiac spreading paranoia throughout the 'Frisco Bay Area by striking repeatedly during 1968. Among The Zodiac's victims were Michael Mageau (19) and Darlene Ferrin (22)—shot to death in a car park in Sly's home-town Vallejo. As the last confirmed killing happened on 11 October 1969, the 'Zodiac' was still taunting police attempts to track him down. A scare-scenario that provided the basis for two movies, firstly Clint Eastwood's breakthrough role as *'Dirty Harry'* (1971). Then, Sly & The Family Stone's "I Want To Take You Higher" can be heard on the soundtrack of David Fincher's *'Zodiac'* (2007). Simultaneously, Charles Manson's dune-buggy death-squad was ripping apart the benign face of the hippie dream. As he awaited the 'Helter Skelter' Race War that would transfigure Amerika, his acid-fried vision was uncomfortably closer to the truth than some might have imagined.

For black aspirations it was different again... The Last Poets rapped that 'The Revolution Will Not Be Televised...' But it was. On a nightly basis TV was screening black American soldiers in Vietnam. Black Moslems at the Olympics. Cassius Clay joining the 'Nation Of Islam' and becoming Muhammad Ali. While simultaneously, it was also screening the failures of the civil rights movement. The vicious backlash against the integrationist's most reasonable proposals. The commercial trivialisation of their cautious idealism. The public defeat and vilification of black leaders. The brutal extermination of others. Richard Nixon's illiberal clique was running the country, with J Edgar Hoover branding the Black Panthers 'the greatest threat to the internal security of the US'. He pledged to eliminate the party, and black activists came under close-FBI surveillance through the counter-intelligence COINTELPRO programme. Police were ceded more powers while the federal government seemed complicit in constitutional violations. Subsequently, over thirty Panthers died, mostly defending themselves from attack. Some, like Fred Hampton of Chicago, were killed in their beds. In April 1968 seventeen-year-old Panther Bobby Hutton was shot to death by Oakland police. Four months later, in LA, police killed another seventeen-year-old Panther, Tommy Lewis, alongside his colleagues Robert Lawrence and Steve Bartholomew. In January 1969 two party leaders of the Southern California Chapter—John Huggins and Alprentice 'Bunchy' Carter were murdered on the UCLA campus by FBI-sponsored assassins. The Panther's LA Minister of Defence—a former Vietnam GI called Geronimo Pratt, endured twenty-seven years in jail following his arrest in 1970. He was later awarded $4.5-million compensation when it emerged the evidence against him was fabricated—he'd been sentenced to life for a murder in LA that was committed while he was under FBI-surveillance in Oakland. As the FBI's own 'concealed' files proved.

Three-hundred more black leaders had charges pending. Militant Max Stanford and a dozen other RAM (Revolutionary Action Movement) cadres were arrested in 1967 on never-substantiated allegations of plots to assassinate mainstream civil rights leaders. A year later J Edgar Hoover personally testified before Congress on their ubiquitous agitational role in the urban ghetto insurrections. RAM was subsequently dissolved, its remaining members going underground. In the predawn hours of 28th October 1967 Huey Newton was badly wounded in a gun battle on a West Oakland street. A white police officer John Frey was shot four times and died within the hour. Newton was admitted into the nearby Kaiser Hospital, where he was chained to his bed. He spent over two years in prison for the murder, although charges were later reduced to 'voluntary manslaughter', then—after subsequent mistrials, dropped altogether, but only by July 1970. These incidents from black history would be commemorated by Public Enemy's "Party For Your Right To Fight" which brandished lyrics accusing 'J Edgar Hoover… he had King and X set up / also the party with Newton, Cleaver and Seale' (on their 1988 album *'It Takes A Nation Of Millions To Hold Us Back'*).

By the end of 1969 nearly every Panther office and party facility had been violently turned-over by police in league with the FBI, culminating in an FBI-orchestrated FBI-directed five-hour police assault on their LA office. But Panther cells had also been infiltrated by black under-cover cops and agent provocateurs creating splits by using 'black propaganda', exacerbating schisms, creating suspicions and inner rivalries with anonymous 'brown letters' carrying false accusations. Newton was accused of using drug and prostitution money to fund the party. At one point, even Bobby Seale himself seemed to believe the stories. They might have been brothers of the head, but theirs was never less than an acrimonious relationship. And—however provoked, there were other splits too. More moderate black leaders were critical of the Panthers for being too media-conscious, too suicidal in their tactics, too short term in their objectives. In a 1968 Oakland shoot-out—provoked by over-aggressive policing, one Panther was gunned-down and Eldridge Cleaver and a police officer were wounded. Rather than face charges complicated by pending parole violations, Cleaver jumped bail and fled—first to Cuba, then to Algeria, where he set up a Panthers-in-exile chapter which proposed a new terrorist agenda opposed to those of Huey Newton. It also—in a comic-absurdist episode that entered counter-culture mythology, briefly hosted runaway LSD-guru Timothy Leary. Soon, following further police pressure and gun-battles he fled for fear of his life, to commence a seven-year tour of communist and Muslim countries from Cuba and North Vietnam to the Soviet Union, where he was welcomed as a celebrity political prisoner.

Stokely Carmichael was no longer around either. He deliberately used the 'Black Power' slogan to distinguish his views from Newton and Seale's more inclusive 'Power to the People', which sought alliance with white sympathiser groups. They, in turn, took exception to Carmichael's frequently sexist and homophobic pronouncements—especially his attack on black author James Baldwin for his gay sexuality, and for the writer's relationships with white men. Frustrated by what he saw as the Panthers seeming acquiescence to white radicals, Carmichael resigned from the organisation in 1969 and left the country to live in Guinea, West Africa. On a diametrically contrasting political journey, by the early seventies Amiri Baraka's extremist attitudes softened as he recognised a mirror-image intolerance and racism in the radical advocacy of separatism, and his writing changed to reflect a newer perspective that sought to unite the races. Also adopting Islam, Max Stanford became Muhammad Ahmad, in which guise he went on to concentrate his attentions on the less-confrontational concept of 'reparations' to the descendants of slavery. While after his high-profile participation in the Chicago Conspiracy Trial, Bobby

Seale found himself facing fresh allegations in the 1970 New Haven Black Panther trials. Although resulting in acquittal by hung jury, the trials themselves were perceived as political repression, and provoked demonstrations and strike-action. Huey Newton—back on the street after jail and reimmersed in the struggle, realised that the Party would have to change as it emerged from its first phase of confrontation. That much was obvious. Newton's leadership was about to be severely tested as the Party consolidated, licked its wounds, and built its strengths and power for the new battles ahead. It was as though the Second American revolution was only just beginning, yet already it was blood-weary. And there were martyrs yet to be made. In July 1970 the arrest and trial of Alabama-born Marxist academic Angela Davis became a cause célèbre, followed by George Jackson's death in a hail of bullets in San Quentin on 21st August 1971.

All of this is relevant to Sly Stone's different—but related, kind of 'direct action'. To Greil Marcus *'There's A Riot Goin' On'* exists 'in the spirit of the death of George Jackson'. Born in Chicago in September 1941, Jackson spent the final twelve years of his life in prison, or—as Bob Dylan wrote it, 'they sent him off to prison for a seventy dollar robbery, / they closed the door behind him and they threw away the key'. To militants, prison provided a necessary blooding, a badge of honour. In its value-system, prisons were the birthplace of revolutionaries, especially black revolutionaries. To them, the capitalist establishment incarcerated black leaders on trumped-up charges of rape, robbery, or narcotic-trafficking in order to prevent them organising against the state. But it was in prison that they found time to study the cause of their oppression, and they emerged as revolutionaries. George Jackson was a near text-book example. It was in San Quentin in 1966 that he founded the Black Guerrilla Family pledged to eradicate racism, to maintain dignity in prison… and to overthrow the government! By 1970 he'd become a Black Panther field marshal. Awaiting trial for the revenge-killing of a guard in retaliation for the death of three jailed black activists—the guard's actions were dismissed as 'justifiable homicide', he was confined to solitary in the Soledad Prison maximum-security cellblock. It was here that he wrote his book of prison-letters, *'Soledad Brother'* (Bantam, New York 1970, ISBN 1-55652-230-4).

But there was more horror to come. George's seventeen-year-old brother Jonathan—who had written the foreword to the book, led a misconceived stunt designed to rouse publicity for what they termed this 'judicial malfunction'. They stormed a Marin County Hall of Justice and took the judge hostage (7th August 1970). In the confusion of their attempted escape, Judge Haley's head was literally blown off when a shotgun held under his chin was accidentally triggered. Jonathan was also gunned down. Only one of the combatants survived to reach prison. When ownership of the shotgun was traced back to activist Angela Davis, she immediately fled underground, becoming a fugitive and the subject of an intense manhunt for eighteen months. Sporting a huge afro, she was a formidable and charismatic intellectual, with a study-CV listing Brandeis, the Sorbonne and the University of Frankfurt. Her radical opinions had already attracted the unwelcome attentions of Governor Ronald Reagan, who got her fired from her position on the University of California. His decision was later overturned and she was reinstated, only for her to be charged with conspiracy, kidnapping and homicide. She then achieved the unique distinction of becoming the third woman ever to appear on the FBI's Ten Most Wanted list. The counter-culture was immediately rife with virally transmitted rumours, picked up and amplified by the underground papers, that, of course, the FBI had advance leaks of the Marin County scheme, but sat on them in order to force a confrontation, to discredit and exterminate the Panthers, and to implicate Davis. Just as George Jackson' brutal assassination—he was gunned down three days before his trial in what was described as a riot-hit escape attempt, was another FBI conspiracy specifically targeted at destroying the movement. The truth of such allegations is long time-lost, and will probably never be known. Few even care enough to ask the questions any more.

For black activism, the centre was not holding. The celebrity martyrs and radicals were leaving the moderate liberals behind, but where were they taking the struggle? In 1970, the man responsible from coining the 'Black Power' slogan—the exiled Robert Williams, returned to the US with the quiet acquiescence of none other than flint-hearted President Nixon. His freedom granted as a gesture towards cultivating goodwill with the Chinese leadership! But after assessing the state of the movement, with militant leaders in jail or in exile, the rest of the Panthers in disarray, rife with maddening internecine ideological divisions, debating the date of the coming 'revolution' like millenarianists awaiting Armageddon, Williams withdrew disillusioned from all but nominal leadership of the groups founded in his name. Had it all been in vain?

****

'This is precisely what the congregation of Sly's childhood church meant calling R&B the Devil's Music...'

'There's A Riot Goin' On' (Miles Marshall Lewis)

So was the music hijacked by the politics? In truth, no. The politics had been there from the moment the Family Stone coalesced into being. But Sylvester Stewart never really set out to be a spokesperson for change, never mind a radical political motivator on the advancing firing-line of cultural consciousness. That was never his bag. As Sidney Poitier phrased it, he 'didn't have the time, or the inclination'. Some people are nay-sayers. Sly Stone had always been a yea-sayer. Dancing, togetherness, love thy brother—the Gospel values, they were Sly's groove, expressed through the Family Stone's penchant for playful folly. Social polarisation had never quite figured in his credo. What unites people transcends what divides them. But it was never an intellectual thing. Not a reasoned thing. It's doubtful if Sly had ever preconceived or rationalised it down in any detailed way. Instead, it was there in attitude. He operated on gut-instinct. What felt good, felt right. He wanted to play his music with like-minded people who were open to its vibe. He wanted the career in music that his ambition and his work-rate carved out for him. But he seldom over-thinks things, that's not his style, and it's such a drag to even have to do that when there's so many better things to do with your time. Music. Getting high. Partying. Fuck all this segregationalist shit, let's just get together and party. Eminently sensible. And on one level—sure, Sly & The Family Stone *were* twenty-four hour party people. On overdrive, but seldom threatening. In fact, *un*-threatening in their glitter and wigged-out fun. Afro hair and stack-heel shoes. But Funky Positivism was always going to be a precarious place to be. As things polarised, shoving issues, and communities, further out to the extreme margins, the Stone Family found themselves walking a tightrope between the Pop-illusionary and the street-real. Between the posturing and the authentic. Yet somehow keeping to just the correct side of them all. But straddling the neutral centre-space of a high-speed two-way freeway, ripped by the contraflow slipstreams of both, was never gonna be a safe place to strut your stuff. And extremists with their own narrow agendas were intent on making that position more and more untenable.

There were those on both sides who found such simplicity unacceptable. White rednecks who felt threatened by the uppity ideas of egalitarianism. And black militants who considered Sly wasn't taking it far enough. On one side, the integrated black/white male/female 'family' membership could still be seen as constituting a full-bodied all-singing all-dancing provocation. Only more so. Meeting racial and gender divides, and dancing them away into irrelevancy. Where some found threat in otherness, Sly's first instinct was for the richness of difference. He'd never allowed colour to dictate his friendships, or define his music. Where some were so insecure or fearful of their cultural identity that they saw only the threat of dilution and loss in integration, Sly saw potential. Problems, restrictions, divisions were not so much evil or bad as just plain stupid, boring, dull—a drag. To have to deal with it was an annoying downside. Sure, 'in order to get to it, you've got to go through it' as Sly had told Dick Cavett, 'that's really the truth'. Of course there's shit to go through, but there's always shit to go through. And there's bad guys out there to get you. But that's just the way it is. So instead, he dealt by example. Look—this works. This is good. How can something this much fun be threatening? It's a way of reconciling two spheres of existence. Of uniting disparate audiences. A bridge spanning contradictory impulses. He never acknowledged the existence of social barriers, never mind accepted them as insurmountable. 'It's not segregated in Hollywood' he explained, adding 'well, it is… but I just never even look at that'. His songs treat the centrality of racial oppression—and how it was provoking mass radicalisation, head-on with ridiculing humour and sharp intelligence. Less as weapons of struggle, more as personal expressions created in response to the times. He was comfortable in his own skin. Racism was a hindrance. An irritation. A distraction. And sure, it kind-of makes sense to get together and fight back against all that badness. 'I can understand frustration' he wrote, 'I can understand how confusion creates back illusion'. How could it be any other way? Of course 'I understand the proclamation, we dig emancipation'. But he advocates caution, gradualism, he reverses the urgent sloganeering, cleverly turning it in on itself—'don't burn baby burn, you gotta learn baby learn, so that you can earn baby earn' ("Don't Burn Baby"). To a certain mindset, this elevated Sly into the most photogenic poster-boy for black aspirations. A vision so persuasive it mocked prejudice through its sheer euphoria. A vision that ridiculed theorists and moralists by its sheer relentless energies.

All of this, confronting—on the other side, a form of Black Fascism, to whom the Family Stone's stance was merely selling out by 'Uncle Tom'-ing. What if the militants were right? What if integration equated to nothing more than cultural dilution? Black Muslims rejected the 'oppressor' religion imposed on slaves to morally discipline and pacify them, in favour of an interpretation of what they saw as a non-white Islam. To Sly, that was another vexing step too far. A conscience dilemma too many. It's only now that Sly has to decide. When he's called to assume a position, to speak out, to make statements that don't come naturally to him. That go against his natural instincts. It's difficult for Sly. The Panthers had already called into question the Family Stone's racial 'compromise', demanding Sly replace Gregg Errico and Jerry Martini with black musicians. In Boston, Sly drew heat from Panther members urging him to drop Kapralik too—'get rid of whitey, get rid of the devil'. Sly stood out against them all. He held firm. Ben Fong-Torres quizzed Sly about his reaction to being caught between two such extreme positions, in which he found himself subject to attacks from both sides. 'It's so easy to say those words' he argued dismissively, 'it ain't nothing. I don't care. If anybody's hip at all, they know all you need in a flash to say those things. And so far in my life, anybody that's together hasn't said that about me. I believe a lot of people are misled by books. You could sit down at a typewriter and say the whole world's fucked up. So what? Or that it's beautiful… People I respect always say 'some asshole said this or that'. That cat doesn't know what he's writing about… it's stupid.' As a result, some activists simply denounced Sly's sell-out 'dope-infested lyrics' and called on the Black community to boycott his records. Others rationalised it this way. There was the set-listing that showcased titles such as "Don't Call Me Nigger, Whitey". Against a subtext of Watts in flames. Perhaps you *can* play it both ways? The bigger the star, the larger the target. Did the need to talk about the Black experience, and how it had impacted upon him, mean that Sly had changed his message? No, not exactly, but even those who now considered that everything *'Stand!'* stood for was no longer hip, the soundtrack for a world that no longer existed—were forced to concede he'd certainly expanded and opened up the dialogue. Sly's day-glo appeal helped bring black youth over into Rock, and white youth into Soul, just perhaps the black militants could utilise that to make him a subversive agent of their cause? Right on... Soul Brother!

Sly was far from the only musician called to the barricades. To stand up and be counted, against the forces of what Norman Mailer called 'The Armies Of The Night'. Celebrity provides instant access to the media. And Pop stars had suddenly assumed never-before levels of guru-like visibility. What they said mattered. For a generation who saw political significance in the extravagant afro's sported by Hendrix, Sly, and James Brown—to those early-primed by Leiber & Stoller's "Riot In Cell Block no. 9", Angela Davis and George Jackson were now readily adopted into the pantheon of heroic icons. And the Rock Tsar aristocracy conscientiously closed ranks around them, perhaps more concerned with burnishing their own radical-chic credentials, while preserving their rebel profile at a safe distance. A John & Yoko album-track hailed Davis as 'Angela, you're one of the millions of political prisoners in the world'. John 'Working-Class Hero' Lennon also recorded strident tributes to the victims of the Attica State Prison massacre, and even the IRA. But was careful to make his stance clear as early as the Beatles' "Revolution"—'if you want money for people with minds that hate / all I can tell you is brother you'll have to wait'. The Rolling Stones' "Sweet Black Angel" also relates the Angela Davis story—recorded December 1971 through March 1972. With just a hint of condescension it tells how 'for a judge they murdered and a judge they stole, / now de judge he gonna judge her... she's a sweet black angel / not a gun-toting teacher, not a Red-lovin' school mom, / ain't someone gonna free her, free de sweet black slave?' But as they were striking rebellious stances with an electrifying "Street Fighting Man", they were regretfully conceding there's nothing more a poor boy can do than play in a Rock 'n' Roll band. But Free Jazzer Archie Shepp recorded "Blues For Brother George Jackson" on his critically-praised *'Attica Blues'* (1972) album—which featured vocals by Joe Lee Wilson who'd once tied with the Family Stone on NBC-TV's 'Talent Search: Showcase '68'. And even Bob Dylan briefly re-energised his lapsed radicalism with a one-off non-album single expressing his shocked outrage—'they killed a man I really loved, they shot him through the head' ("George Jackson"). But while Rock stars struck insurrectionary poses for the titillation of record-buyers, the figures they hymned with their impeccable ghetto credentials, were genuinely and simply insurrectionary. They looked good on student posters. Good on T-shirts. They even looked impossibly good solarised into the distressed layout of the hippie press. A step more real than Hendrix. A frisson more committed. For this was liberation terrorism.

And beneath the rock star pantheon, the counter-culture was breeding its own celebrity insurgents. As anti-war protest escalated, and the National Guard were shooting demonstrating students dead on the Kent State campus, the SDS ('Students For A Democratic Society') reoriented itself more towards bringing an end to the Vietnam conflict. To Colonel Oliver North, the war for Vietnam was not lost in the killing-fields of SE Asia, but on the campuses of America. As King had more eloquently confirmed, 'the bombs in Vietnam explode at home. They destroy the hopes of a decent America. The promise of the Great Society have been shot down on the battlefields of Vietnam'. Although the SDS continued to be active on civil rights issues, it co-ordinated its activities with more radical groups, including those with more Marxist agendas. Among these were the Yippies, and the Weatherman Underground. Named for the supposedly prophetic metaphor in a Dylan song about 'you don't need a weatherman to known which way the wind blows', they were implicated in a number of bombings at colleges and federal institutions. Advocating violent revolution through acts of terrorism to achieve their goals. 'Yippie' was supposedly an acronym for Youth International Party, but it's more likely that such a rationalisation was an afterthought. For it took a more playfully Situationist approach to revolution. Co-ordinated by activists Abbie Hoffman and Jerry Rubin, they were too individualist and anarchic to ever conform enough to belong to the disciplined cadres of the radical left, preferring guerrilla street theatre designed to attract media attention to their grievances.

The Yippies became most visible when they won direct-action notoriety at the disruptions to the Democratic Party Convention in Chicago—30th August 1968. Much to their disapproval, the national convention nominated Vice President Humphrey in preference to their favoured anti-war candidate, Eugene McCarthy. So they ceremonially nominated their own presidential candidate instead—a pig called Pigasus. Chicago became a tribal gathering of some ten-thousand dissident and dissenting voices, a point of explosive convergence teeming and turbulent, frightening and electrifying, with those in attendance including William Burroughs, Allen Ginsberg and Terry Southern. Such writers contributed by documenting the pitched battles that erupted when hardline Mayor Richard Daley's storm-trooping police brutally assaulted draft-burning demonstrators, delegates, provocateurs, journalists, and unfortunate bystanders—apparently at random, in an attempt to clear Lincoln Park with tear-gas. Following the televised riots that rocked Chicago for three days with razor-wire barricades and running street battles,

Hoffman, Rubin, Bobby Seale, Tom Hayden and three others are arrested for conspiring to incite violence and crossing State lines with the intent to riot. The 'Chicago Seven' then proceeded to turn the protracted trial into a further act of absurdist theatre, until all charges were eventually dropped. But they were incidents that set up shock-waves of unease across the country. Simply for mouthily insisting on his constitutional rights to defend himself Seale was shackled and gagged. His autobiography includes a horrific description of the marshal's attempt to forcibly insert a plug of wadding into his mouth. But Judge Julius Hoffman's success in silencing Seale conversely became another bizarre Panther victory. The image of a chained black man in a court of law said more to the world about repression in a supposedly free society than a thousand manifestos. It was a disgusting scene, as commemorated by Graham Nash's song "Chicago" and Gil Scott-Heron's "H_2Ogate Blues". In a later BBC interview Defence lawyer Kunstler claimed that what the defence team *should* have done when Seale was gagged, was simply to all walk right out of that courtroom in protest, and not come back. It would have created an almost unprecedented situation because it meant the trial could then not have been able to continue. By sitting there and carrying on with the trial procedure they—all white men, were in a sense condoning the outrage. As it was, Seale was sentenced to four years for contempt of court. The *'Berkeley Barb'* front-page strip was reporting it all direct from Czechago USA, 'here in Chicago I know there will be a revolution, because it has begun and I am in the red and black center of it'. Graffiti in frame one says 'Destroy The Machinery Of The State'. Even the May *'Rolling Stone'*—with its more music-centred focus, ran a cover-photo of an armed cop kneeling over a half-dead, black and bleeding demonstrator, captioned 'American Revolution 1969'.

Those 'Off the Pigs' days are now as lost as the Jurassic, requiring a considerable brain-wrench to time-travel back there. It reads strangely now because we have the privilege of knowing what happened next. Back then, they didn't know. And although—for the radicals, the centre was not holding, Sly & The Family Stone had grown out of that same hippie consensus, and their albums serve as enlightening stops along the way. The tilt from *'Stand!'* into *'There's A Riot Goin' On'* charts the increments of all this progress precisely. Sly's music had been joyous, but as the sixties ended, so did the good times. As he peaked into his career apex, the simple notions of peace, community, and fellow-feeling which had formed his common-ground with the summer of love—the ideals he'd been advocating through his music, were becoming everywhere disillusioned. It was increasingly difficult to hang onto the shallow and now-tattered flower-child optimism, with its fragile ethic of spontaneous irresponsibility, and the hopes of imminent social transformation that they dared share with the angry radicals. That voice was being drowned out by a cacophony of unreason. Sly could no longer be the positivity-preaching visionary for that utopian multicultural future-world. But his defiant individualistic stance, his success, and the rapidly shifting political environment in which they unfolded, meant that he was never going to be able to step back either. He could never be a passive conduit for those social changes, or an impersonal conductor for the times. He had to learn how to navigate those currents. And the inner turmoil of his growing personal problems, as well as his dismay at the slow death of the civil rights movement tied in with all those other political causes, was to surface in the new music that was to come. From now on, his songs would carry a sense of resignation. The songs of a man at rest, but uneasily so. Critics tend to use the term 'darker' as a recommendation. When they're reviewing—say, the latest Harry Potter or James Bond, they say 'darker' meaning more real, more grounded, less fanciful. More mature in its outlook. As though 'I Wanna Take You Lower' is somehow intellectually superior to what preceded it. As though a deeper understanding of reality must by necessity involve a divesting of idealism, of optimism, of hope. That's not necessarily true. Just because it's harder to be positive does not mean it's any less real. And if experience was souring Sly's vision, that doesn't mean that what he'd already created is any less valuable. Or its message any less true.

For Sly & The Family itself, their newfound fame and success had come freighted with a deluge of problems, compounded by that added uncertainty concerning Sly's moral compass. With the group at the height of its popularity, they had become a repository for all that was strange, unbridled, creative, and tempestuous. All of which devolved most strongly down onto Sly himself. For the band was the band. But Sly was the star. If he'd ever had a clear idea of his life-goals and musical-ambitions he must have far exceeded them by now. He'd reached and surpassed the point where you achieve that dream, and into the point where you're living it. But he was simultaneously unravelling behind the scenes. The strain of pretending to be something he wasn't was taking him further past the tipping point into increasing unpredictability. And that thing lurking in his mind-basement was getting the upper hand. It was not the introvert-extrovert thing, because Sly was never the introvert. But it was one thing rapping about music with musicians, or cavorting and goofing with the band. It was one thing talking links between records over a DJ's radio-mike where they couldn't see you, and you can't see the people listening in. You knew the invisible audience was out there, but they didn't intrude too much into your own personal space. Then—at first, the concert audience-reactions were gratifying, their attention intoxicating, a narcotic hit to rate with the most powerful illegal street-highs. But their persistence could be a drag too. Sly was expected to produce wild rioting scenes of dancing and partying night after night. He'd become effectively enslaved to his own image. Living exclusively in the present tense. Until people came just to gawp at him, to see whatever craziness he was going to do, to see what he was wearing, whether he would say anything weird, as though he was some exhibit in a glass-cage.

He was under pressure. An imperfect hero for imperfect times. Yet in a bizarre way, Sly was also revelling in the sensation of power his position conferred on him. When Mr Stewart snaps his fingers, the whole damn world better get its ass in gear. During tours his behaviour was becoming more extreme, escalating into a need to control the members of an entourage that was multiplying proportionally, to thirty or more people. When the entire freakishly-garbed carnival booked into a hotel, distributed across some twenty suites, Sly would take possession of all the keys, he would instruct his security that no-one was allowed to eat until he did. Phone calls out were not permitted. A ration of coke could be a gift, or an instrument of control. Sly pushed, and pushed, and then pushed some more. Because when Mr Stewart gets up and does it, there's bound to be something worth doing. Bobby Womack told journalist Barney Hoskyns how Sly would be 'dressed all in red leather, he be handin' out the orders, like, hey, run Bobby a hot tub, give him a nice shave… Tiffany baby, come here, I want you to take Bobby to your room, y'know, fix him up, so I'm fuckin' some chick, and then I'm right back into the music agin'. Sly could use his charm strategically, deliberate and with purpose. Then switch just as smoothly into attack mode as lethal as a rabid dog savaging your ankle. It's said that a degree of single-minded ruthlessness can often polish a great talent. Even when it becomes nastiness. And the combination could be devilish. Enough to strike ice deep into the most resilient heart. Womack recalls an incident during a concert stop-over in New York when profligacy and extravagance resulted in the entire crew being marooned in a hotel without funds, and subject to increasing pressure from the front desk to settle the bill. As a last resort Bobby phoned Wilson Pickett to appeal for help, calling in on old loyalties, and although Pickett did not hold Sly in high regard he agreed to advance the outstanding cash. They waited. As promised, the Wicked Pickett eventually called round. Sly snatched the money from his hand with a terse 'you fucker, you should have been here with that fifteen minutes ago'.

Such behaviour seems symptomatic of the stoned megalomania that starts out with 'hey, I did all this, the Gold Discs, 'Woodstock', the hit records, I did all that, ain't I great?'—stoked by increasing dependence on recreational narcotics, especially cocaine. Only the fuzzy oblivion of white powders provided the ability to step back. To become the passive conduit amid changes he couldn't control. Gorging powerful pharmaceuticals enabled escapist relief from sensation-fatigue, it allowed him to look at the craziness from a safe distance—while remaining untouched by it. Anyone familiar with the potent magic of white-line fever knows the temporary rush of omnipotence it ignites in your head. The feelings of strength, power and invulnerability it induces, combined with a pleasing numbness. To John Phillips 'the sparkling crystals of pure coke focused and intensified it (your creativity), honed the inner edge until you felt, in a soaring nerve-pounding rush, that your creative blade could slice through anything'. For some, this narcotic trade-off is a kind of Faustian skulduggery, like the one that recruited Robert Johnson at the crossroads. You exchange your soul for nuggets of genius. But in that Blues' hellhound contract, those who consider themselves beneficiaries are more frequently the ones fate has cursed. Because there are bad reactions too. And by now Sylvester Stewart was single-nosedly supporting the Bolivian economy. A transition from Sly Stone… to Sly stoned. In a bizarre variant on the Mafiosi bullet-sharks' tale there were stories that Sly could be seen carrying a violin case loaded with coke wherever he went. On at least one occasion he even allowed an unwitting member of his police escort to carry it into the venue for him! A lot of people couldn't take what was happening, but they were too scared to tell Sly to his face.

Soon—following the Coldwater New Year's Eve party, there were even more powerful highs. The hypnotic sedative PCP—'angel dust' was stirred into the chemical cocktail. 'I switched from coke to pep, and I'm a connoisseur' Sly would write with bragging bravado (in "In Time"). Although it came in liquid form, as white crystalline powder or as pills or capsules, it could also be smoked like a joint—as 'killer joints' or 'supergrass', or injected, or shovelled into the nostrils like cocaine. As with other hallucinogenics it magnifies existing states, taking depression and instability into paranoia, and panic attacks into sometimes-violent behaviour. But 'once it got to the PCP part, it was over. That got pitiful… when Sly did the PCP he was just out of it' commented Hamp Banks (among the overlapping voices of the protagonists to Joel Selvin), '…all the way out. There wasn't anything happening no more. It wasn't about music. It was over. He was through. He was doing shit you would expect to see in some kind of institution for mentally retarded people. Sly had become a vegetable, and so had Freddie. He and Freddie walked around the house all day like zombies.' And while it was driving him deeper and deeper into ruin, Sly's vision, and his music were gradually growing slower and darker. People still respected Sly as a creative, innovative musician and artist, but maybe no longer as a person. The poignancy lies in the volte-face contrast between his now-subdued voice, and the energy and vitality of his earlier self, when he'd been so adept at charming so many people.

Drugs provided a further heat-shield against the critical friction their unreliability provoked as, after the stratospheric success, the Family Stone found itself re-entering a reality in which they were too wasted to show up at their own gigs. Sometimes—on the occasion when Sly's chemically snowblind condition allowed him to make it as far as the stage, the adrenalin of performance would act as a catalyst. And he'd rise, as mesmerising as he'd ever been. On other occasions it proved impossible to get Sly to stand for long enough to leave the dressing room, 'you can't stand long on wobbly knees' as he sang on "Only One Way Out Of this Mess" (on *'Life'*). A cancellation at the Trenton Armory in Newark, New Jersey led to an unpleasant confrontation with the understandably aggrieved promoter. Shades of the London Don Arden debacle. Only this time Sly ducked out of the repercussions, and let Bubba and JB handle the unpleasantness. They were less than pleased with the heavy flack they took on his behalf. But far from showing remorse, Sly's response was a jeering 'being sorry is for sorry people'.

The group were jetting to engagements on commercial flights. While Stephani laid on private 'planes—or sometimes a helicopter, for Sly and Freddie. Yet frequently the band was left waiting when the two main-man protagonists failed to show. There were times when the plane Stephani had organised for them wouldn't even get to lift off from the runway. With Sly and his crew inside too busy taking off into their own personal space, instructing the pilot they weren't ready to go. Hungry, they'd send out for a pizza delivery with the plane idling on the runway for four or five hours, burning up $8000 and more. Then there were tales circulating that once they'd made the venue Sly might refuse to take the stage until he'd finished watching the late-night movie. Or stories of Sly checking out to 'go shopping' while audiences waited. It even happened at the Oakland Coliseum, a hometown gig. They had a lot to prove. They wanted to make it good. Heavy-metal band Mountain were playing support as the Family Stone killed time waiting to go on. And waited. No Sly. He eventually arrived by 'copter, two hours too late, and in a physical state direct from Weird City—'too frazzled to go on'. 'Wrecked' might have been a polite euphemism. But stranger was yet to come...

27th July 1970 proved to be a controversial and highly publicised date. Events were solemnly recorded in the *'New York Times'* the following day, to the effect that Sly & The Family Stone had refused to play at a scheduled 16:30pm free concert at Grant Park in downtown Chicago, between the Loop district and the lakeside. That their refusal first provoked widespread restlessness, which then escalated into five hours of rioting. Kids went wild, mobs rampaged down Columbus Street south towards the Chicago River bridges or west down Munroe Street towards Michigan Avenue's Magnificent Mile, battling with ushers and police, torching buildings, and upending police cars. There were 150 arrests with twenty-five people—including ten cops, being treated in hospital. Three people were wounded in gunfire. The circumstances surrounding the event have since become mythic. 75,000 people turned up for the concert, sponsored by City Hall as an 'effort to reach out to young people'. Police claimed the violence was premeditated, that youths arrived tooled-up with baseball bats, sticks and guns. Sly's people claim the band were there, ready to play. Others that they were there, ready to play, but were actually turned back by the police because the riot had already begun. It was not Sly, but the heavy-handed policing and short-fuse troopers under the jittery control of Chicago's longest-serving Mayor, Richard J Daley—whose over-reactions had provoked the Democratic Convention riots on the same site, who were responsible for the violent confrontations. Not Sly. Thus does it ever run. Sure, the Family Stone had caused riots, of both the positive and negative kind, but Sly's music formed a more solipsistic riot of the mind, not just some Bacchic on-the-streets uprising. Nevertheless, it was Sly who got the blame. Some claim this debacle is the source of the irony behind the non-existent title-track on the *'There's A Riot Goin' On'* album. In a further cultural connection, that same 319-acre Grant Park became the site chosen by Barack Obama for his acceptance speech at his 4th November 2008 election night rally.

Meanwhile, Sly's reputation meant that it had become impossible to find promoters prepared to book the Family Stone. The demand was there. People wanted Sly & The Family Stone. But promoters had become wary, then avoided the risk of booking so unreliable an act at all. As *'Rolling Stone'* phrased it 'as the cancellations mounted Kapralik's slogan 'The Incredible & Unpredictable Sly Stone' gradually lost its bright, euphemistic ring'. It reached a point where no promoter would touch him… Then *'The New York Times'* dated 4th September 1971 carried a report that Sly's Hollywood landlord was suing him for $3 million, claiming Coldwater was inundated with 'loud, noisy and boisterous persons' and that he wanted Mr Stone to leave. The landlord objected to the fact that his property had degenerated into a 'psychedelic shack' where the Pusherman was a regular caller. Where demon hipsters prowled the zones where celebrity junkies gather, to feed and feed on their indulgences and appetite for (self) destruction, the loud, noisy and boisterous negative people who gave the place a bad name. Sly was forced to quit Coldwater, and move… elsewhere.

The Family Stone were standing on the rim of a precipice…

Chapter Thirteen
'The Revolution Will Be Televised'

'After all, crime is only a left-hand form of human endeavour…'
—suave lawyer Louis Calhern in John Huston's *The Asphalt Jungle*

'Everybody is a Star…'

So when did Sly & the Family Stone stop making sense…? Perhaps it was when they were scheduled to play the Dick Cavett Show on ABC-TV, 13th July 1970. A Family Stone performance-set would be broadcast from their Manhattan studios, linked to a brief televised chat between the guest—Sly, and their amiable host.

The Family Stone had done three shows at Cherry Hill, New Jersey, organised by Ken Roberts. After the last of them Kapralik whisked Sly away to visit Muhammad Ali in his New Jersey home. There was an existing connection between the two of them going back to records that the former-'Cassius Clay' had done for Columbia under David's auspices. After he'd embraced Sam Cooke in the ring, the ebulliently charismatic pugilist had cracked the US Top 50 with his own version of Ben E King's "Stand By Me". He'd also famously posed for a series of promotional photos with the Beatles in Miami, during their first US tour. But as a Pop-icon, like Sly, Ali's celebrity was fiercely divisive. He was smart. When knocked down by British boxer Henry Cooper, he quipped 'he hit me so hard my ancestors in Africa felt it'—a witty comment that also scored a political reminder of his racial slave-origins. He knew that by going around bragging 'I am the greatest' he offended white America. So he kept doing it. And they couldn't take it. He was equally notoriously reviled for his uncompromising espousal of the 'Nation of Islam', yet, transcending racial divides he numbered as many white admirers as black.

During the brief stopover, Sly was at his most charming. Ali's second wife—Khalilah (formerly Belinda Boyd), was suitably charmed. But immediately after the success of such a sociable evening, Sly lost his nerve and began having last-minute reservations about doing the TV show. Earlier he'd expressed his doubts about television in general, 'to even question that which can and can't be said, that what can't be televised, is ridiculous. The biggest problem with TV and the whole thing right now is the censorship. And as long as it goes on with as much force as it's got now, it's going to be hard for anybody to do anything like us would appreciate… I just want to be able to go on there and say what's on my mind' (to *'Rolling Stone'*). So he abruptly decided to pull out of the show, and declared he was flying back direct to LA instead. Valet, sidekick, and right-hand-man 'Bubba' Banks stopped him in his tracks, cajoling and threatening. He called in Bobby Womack for support to remonstrate with him. This date was an important opportunity to reach a wide TV-land audience. He'd signed on the line, he was booked to do it. He couldn't pull out. Apart from any other considerations of honour or obligation there were bound to be costly legal repercussions. But 'he just found every excuse to not go on that show' Womack later confided to Joel Selvin, author of the chilling *'Sly Stone: An Oral History'* (1998), 'he was petrified, now that I look back on it.'

Dick Cavett, a mild-mannered, impeccably liberal talk-show host had worked as a Magician and one-time 'talent co-ordinator' for Jack Paar's *'The Tonight Show'*, and for Paar's replacement, Johnny Carson. In 1968 he landed his own morning show, which transferred by 26th May the following year to prime-time, where it stayed through until 1974, initially through ABC, then through other networks. And he quickly specialised in engaging with risky subjects at some depth, the kind of edgy topics avoided by other presenters. With his literate and intelligent appraisals and quick humour, he was at his best interviewing the likes of Gore Vidal, Muhammad Ali, Salvador Dali—who appeared on-set with an anteater on a lead, Jimi Hendrix, Truman Capote, Timothy Leary, Isaac Asimov, Hugh Hefner, John Lennon and Yoko Ono. So he'd already debated with some pretty far-out guests. But no-one quite like Sly Stone.

Come show-time at the studio the following day, Sly was nowhere to be seen. In fact, he was still holed up in his hotel-room, nose-deep in toots of cocaine, busily deferring departure far as long as he possibly could. Every time Bobby or Bubba succeeded in wheedling him downstairs to the lobby, he promptly bolted back to his room to snook up another half-a-dozen fat killer lines. Eventually it got so crucial Bubba took the precaution of chartering a helicopter to chopper Sly off and carry him into Manhattan. When it arrived there was only passenger seating for two, so Womack opted to go with Sly. Breathing a sigh of considerable relief, Bubba watched the chopper suddenly pushing skywards with Sly and Womack aboard… but even then the crisis wasn't over. Heading back for the airport terminal in a state of some self-congratulation, Bubba couldn't help but notice that the 'copter was not thrashing its way across the sky, but circling back to land exactly where it had taken off. He doubled back to the helipad to investigate, what's the problem now? It turns out Sly insisted on changing seats with Womack. The intense rotor downdraft on Sly's side of the 'copter was blowing his cocaine around… that wind was a serious bummer!

The absurd awfulness extended interminably. Against all the odds, Sly finally found himself at the studio, barely on time. The next obstacle was to get him from the dressing room onto the set itself. Only now he'd begun complaining he was suffering from diarrhoea, and he vanished all over again. Perhaps he was caught up in Funk's third definition, 'blue funk'—a state of nervous fear? With the countdown ticking into its final seconds he got sidetracked into a toilet midway from the green room to the stage, for yet another dip into his coke-bag, dusting his nose and emerging with the residue glinting on his jacket like expensive dandruff. Cavett had already announced the Family Stone's play-in number, but cut prematurely to an ad break to cover. Eventually—despite everything, it all fell into place. At the sidelines just beyond the margin of audience-barriers and cables, technicians and production staff were agitated, but ready. The music-slot was scheduled to come first. Camera-cranes swooped up and arced in, deluging the monitors in colour. Framed there on-screen were the Family Stone, supercool and neon pimpadelic, with Sly the Showman looking every inch some exotic street-corner warlord. He was eye-twistingly suited and booted in a maroon jumpsuit slashed to the waist, and a flippety-floppety black hat resembling a tea-cosy-cum-turban, all elevated by skyscraper platforms. On cue they launched into a powerful version of "Thank You (Falettinme Be Mice Elf Agin)", and the Family Stone could still turn in a spectacular performance, the expertly-pitched electro-driven biorhythms sounding seriously unhinged, and quite wonderful, an hallucinatory bedlam of stasis and lurching gyrating momentum, slipping and slithering into each other. On TV the ensemble could colourise your monochrome, then turn up the colour contrast to maximum. A power-play it was impossible not to be moved by. As the number finished, Sly sauntered over for the chat with Cavett. During the transition from here to there, to plonk himself down in that fawn-coloured guest armchair, covered by the audience applause, he seemed to swagger a little, he lurched as he ambled, he swayed from side to side as he walked, as if metronomed to some inner rhythm. A metabolism thing. Or else tranquilised to the hilt.

Opening with 'You were almost late getting here' Dick Cavett mildly rebukes Sly, then politely enquires 'you cut yourself. Did you have trouble getting here?

Sly seems different now, smaller offstage than he'd seemed on. 'I got my house broken into,' he offers obliquely.

'It's an actual wound…?' Cavett persists sympathetically, 'a flesh wound, why are you injured there? Was it during performance?' This time Sly's response is a little more bizarre. He sprawls back into the chair. 'I broke into my house.' Then he corrects himself, no, he was 'trying to repair it'. Finally, as if running out of options, he turns it back on the host, challenging him 'if it was *your* house, *you'd* be a little late.'

Changing tack, Cavett points out 'You were going to be here one other time', referring to a previously blown-out booking. 'I was here…?' Sly queries guilessly, a foxy smile creeping up over his wide mobile mouth, as though deliberately misunderstanding.

'I mean *physically* here' from Cavett. 'I wasn't here, man' confirms Sly, laughing. By now he seems to be enjoying himself as a flummoxed Cavett strives to 'keep this conversational ball in the air'. Already this is less the usual interview mouth-to-mouth combat, less being 'able to go on there and say what's on my mind', and more a surrealist cut-up.

Sly breaks off whatever train of thought he's on, and shuffles up to sit forward in the chair to announce 'Dick, you're great. You are *great*. You know what I mean.' He beats his fist on his heart, slurring his deep nasal words, 'Booom! Right on. Sure thing. No, for real. For *real*, Dick. Hey Dick, Dick, Dick, you're great.' He reaches forward, takes the bemused host's hands in the long tapering fingers of his own hands, and makes him applaud. 'Well, you're not so bad yourself' concedes Dick. Sly leans back again, eyes rolling in contemplation. 'I'm kinda bad.' Then he reconsiders, 'I'm not so bad.' And sums up 'You're right. I'm not so bad, man.' He gleefully rolls the expression around his mouth and lets it out, slow and lascivious. His tired eyes rolling from side to side, down and skywards. Then he bares those big teeth in the wide mouth, and his long horse laughter rumbles deep and jarring.

There's more in a similar vein. Sly Stone's first language is believed to be English, but perhaps a 'Rosetta Stone'-program would help? It's not that he's being evasive, or even objectionable, it's not even that maybe he's being asked the wrong questions. More that he's lost in some private space where responses are being decided by the collision of chemicals in his brain. They move on. Cavett asks about his songwriting methods. 'I look in the mirror when I write', Sly drawled. 'The reason why I do that is because I can somehow be a great critique (sic) for myself, and I can react spontaneously before I realise that I'm going along with what I'm doing, and dislike it or like it before I realise that I'm doing it…'

Sly Stone had the talk-show host adrift somewhere between mystified and amused. But if Cavett didn't know what hit him, he couldn't have been aware at the time how close the whole thing had come to not happening at all. Later, a three-DVD set *'The Dick Cavett Show: Rock Icons'* collects the Sly & The Family Stone footage, alongside performances by David Crosby, the

Rolling Stones and Jefferson Airplane. There's also a revealing clip preserved at broadband speed on the iFILM.com website. So that now, viewers to U-Tube and related sites can watch the moment Sly Stone mutates into an absurdist laugh-out-loud comedy-turn right before their eyes…

****

There had been an overlong—near two-year, recording drought between "Everybody Is A Star" in December 1969… until "Family Affair" in October 1971. Then, just as Afro-American music was finally coming to terms with the seismic tremors set up by *'Stand!'*, and with deferred anticipations for more of the same, Sly & The Family Stone both consolidated it all, and set up new conundrums. "Family Affair" is a sexy, touching, eerily minimalist track, cantering on a soft-funk steady-as-a-metronome groove that Sly had programmed on a primitive drum-machine. Years later it would be listed in Dave Marsh's book *'1001 Greatest Songs'* (1999), and *'Rolling Stone'* magazine's '500 Greatest Songs'. Yet the title was initially released reluctantly, against Sly's wishes. It was Epic A&R-man Stephen Paley who laid the ground to out-manoeuvre Sly to have it issued as the new album's lead single. Paley had already functioned as a prime mover in overcoming label resistance to include a Columbia act—Sly & The Family Stone, on the Atlantic 'Woodstock' triple-set. Now, he began sending out advance acetates to strategic radio stations so that early DJ-play would determine its own inevitability.

His commercial instincts were immediately vindicated. The single climbed to the US no. 1 in just five weeks. Sly's fourth—and final no. 1 Pop hit, unseating Isaac Hayes "Theme From Shaft" from the pole chart position. And it was another seemingly effortless classic slice of seven-inch vinyl, but again—something that works on a number of levels, and it confounded every expectation. Sombre, at once mournful and playful, the voices are stripped plain to skeletal structures, etched out by Billy Preston's sombre Rhodes piano. Putting aside the earlier trademark dense play of voices, it left just Sly's lead laconic DJ-drone taken in a low too-stoned-to-care dark-bass, with Rose adding alternate refrain, pared of any quality of prettification. Delineating the good and bad aspects of family-life. 'One child grows up to be somebody that just loves to learn, / and another child grows up to be somebody you'd just love to burn', with Sly's delivery over-amped for emphasis, 'Mom loves the both of them, you see it's in the blood'. Are we talking Freddie and Sylvester here—one saint, one sinner? A dysfunctional family?—surely, we can all relate to that. The stress, compromise and despair in a nuclear family. But probably that's to simplify it too far. 'Family' can also mean peer group, as in 'Family Stone'. It can also be a generational 'family', or—perhaps, it's a nation, or when he stresses 'blood's thicker than mud' it's a racially-inclusive thing? there were already suggestions circulating that Sly had written the song in response to demands made on him by black nationalist groups who disapproved of his integrationist sensibilities. But no, to 'David R Kapralik'—who gets a 'special thanks' on the album sleeve for his services as 'Personal Manager', the song is about the fissures within the group itself. He told a *'Rolling Stone'* interviewer that it relates the story of Sly's own life, a life of stardom that was being cut up by the feuding factions surrounding him. Chief among those irritants, he hinted, was Sly's own family. Sly immediately retaliated with his denial. 'Song's not about that' he replied. 'Song's about a family affair, whether it's a result of genetic processes or a situation in the environment'. Sure, people disagree. There are rights and wrongs, but at the same time, when it all comes down to dust, we're on the same side, 'nobody wants to blow, nobody wants to be left out'. We're family, a family that claustrophobically takes care of its own. So keep out, meddle at your peril.

The consensus is that both interpretations are true, that Sly's strategy to avoid the star-as-victim syndrome was to link his personal pain to wider social issues. To Peter Shapiro 'he might have pissed off his fans', but this was his way of exacting 'retribution for the betrayal of both the civil rights movement and the sell-out of the counter-culture'. Prior to this, Sly's funk had celebrated dance, sex, life, good times... positive stuff like that. These sessions rarely happened that way, behind Sly's lopsided grin there were brooding and utterly compelling undercurrents, a tumour within its humour. 'When we made music it wasn't happy any more' agreed Womack, 'it had a dark side to it.' A sentiment that found its culmination when "Family Affair" was joined on the charts during that same December 1971 by the chart-topping psychodramas of *'There's A Riot Goin' On'*. As a taster for the black and paranoid gem it preceded, the single was only moderately representative of the intense density and stark darkness that lurked within the album's grooves. A mind-furnace of funk that conjures imagery intense enough to melt spines, then dip listener's brains in its flames. And this fifth 'Family Stone' album was one that actually *debuted* at no. 1. A Heartbreaking Work of Staggering Genius...? Well, a genius... staggering, certainly. A work of heartbreaking genius, without doubt. This was a work that formed a shattering 'new direction', one that stunned the critics, and the public—and just possibly endangered Epic's finances. The total project was rumoured to have cost them a cool million dollars! Across the build-up period before its delivery, Clive Davis was getting twitchy. It was he who'd inked the original contract back in 1967. Now he was worried that 'Sly was simply *not* producing albums at all. I heard stories that he was laying down hundreds of instrumental tracks in Southern California studios—without vocals. There was strong speculation that he would never sing again.' As leverage, he suspended Sly's contract, barring him from collecting back-catalogue royalties, then called a meeting with Sly himself, and was reassured by Mr Stewart at his most charmingly persuasive. Yet the label continued to wait, continued to allow him unprecedented license to produce himself, experiment and devise strategies, throwing himself into the pernickety sonic details involved in mastering the new album. In truth, it had run out of other options.

In the fall of 1971 Sly rented 783 Bel Air Road, a beautiful mansion with leaded windows, accessed through a cobbled drive lit by antique lanterns, set in five acres of surrounding grounds, with manicured lawns edged by landscaped terraced gardens. From its highest point, looking southwest, it was even possible to see the boats off the Santa Monica coast. It had formerly belonged to John and Michelle Phillips, the beautiful couple at the creative centre of the Mamas & the Papas. And to John Phillips it was 'a fairy-tale castle perched on a cliff high over Bel Air, a quaint but spacious monument to the grandeur of Hollywood's Golden Era'. Michelle—in her ghosted autobiography, romances giddily about how the English Tudor-style stately house had even earlier been home to Jeanette MacDonald during 'the first two decades of talking pictures'. How the MGM film star had lived there through the days of 1930's Tinsel-Town aristocracy, 'for all her long and happy marriage to (movie actor, director and businessman) Gene Raymond, through all those musicals with Nelson Eddy and Maurice Chevalier and Allan Jones, and through all those parties in the magical days of Hollywood's second golden age'. After thirty-two years there Jeanette MacDonald died of cancer in 1965, after which the property stood empty, until the former Mamas & Papas couple purchased it from her husband, and moved in.

Bel Air had always been a celebrity-studded community. Zsa Zsa Gabor was a near-neighbour. So was old-time actress Sandra 'Sandy' Duncan, the blonde singer and star of TV's *'The Sandy Duncan Show'*. Two other top TV shows used its winding road location for filming—ABC's proto-Buffy Gothic soap-opera *'Dark Shadows'* (which ran from 27th June 1966 to April 1971), and the sit-com *'The Beverly Hillbillies'* which used exterior shots of the mansion across the street. But in contrast to glitzy Jeanette MacDonald, the Phillips enjoyed a considerably less stable marital arrangement, and rapidly converted the mansion into a den of drug-fuelled bohemian debauchery. An overnight descent into an endless demimonde of opulence and junkie squalor. In the chaotic luxury they left in their wake, the in-coming Family Stone found traces of LSD and cocaine. Initially, conservative neighbourhood residents such as wealthy hotelier Arnold Kirkeby who lived opposite, strongly disapproved of the Phillips' flowing hippie kaftans and were overjoyed to see them leave. As Lou Adler recalled, 'they were pleased that a 'Mr Sylvester Stewart' was moving in'. Those 'uptight Bel Air snobs'—as Phillips called them, liked the sound of that. Little did they suspect that the house was to become an even more hair-raising twilight realm...

Coldwater was big. 783 Bel Air was even bigger. The living room ceiling must have risen some thirty feet, giving the space the impression of being the size of a basketball court, there was a ground floor formal dining room which the Phillips had converted into a Pool Room, and an English-style 'Pub' which had been 'brought over' and reassembled 'brick by brick'. They'd converted an east-wing library into an Indian-style hashish-den with paisley silks billowing from the ceiling, big Berber pillows designed by Toni at Profile de Monde, and a six-foot-high hand-tooled Indian hookah loaded with pot. According to Michelle 'there was a grape arbour outside the back door, and a path led from the house down to the pool… you went down stairs of slate, came through the grape arbour, and then, when you turned the corner in the rose arbour, you came upon a little water fountain halfway down to the pool. There was a love-seat by the fountain and then two more steps to more rose arbours and finally to the pool itself, built of slate. By the pool there was a small version of the main house, a pool-house with a large fireplace in the living room, a bedroom, a small stone-floored kitchen, a bathroom, a dressing room, and so on…' The gardens, avocado orchard, rose and grape bowers, were also home to a gorgeously-plumed peacock called Gideon, with two hens Sarah and Hannah, gifts from record-producer Lou Adler, which Sly inherited. The excitable peacocks formed the estate's first line of security. The second floor became Sly's master bedroom, where he installed his Jacuzzi and waterbed. He was also constantly buying and up-grading the latest stereo equipment.

Guns too. An arsenal of them. '(Sly's) goons were sullen, unfriendly and armed' wrote 'Papa' John in his own autobiography. There were financial catfights during negotiations, and defaulted payments. When Phillips attempted to redress the situation 'these people were rough. They laughed at me. There were lots of guns, rifles, machine guns, big dogs.' It was like the opening of "Thank You (Falettinme Be Mice Elf Agin)"—'looking at the devil, grinning at his gun…' As long ago as their first residency in the Las Vegas 'Pussycat á-Go-Go' the Family Stone would get bored during the extended periods of inactivity between rehearsals and performances, so they bought a clutch of cheap 22's and took the guns way out into the isolated wastes of the desert to shoot them until they became too hot to hold. Now there were more guns. More guns than anyone could reasonably justify. In a kind of attempted justification, there *had* been death threats, due to Sly's associations with radical political activists, so he took to hiring even more sinister bodyguards, including real former mafia hit-men associated with JR Vatrano. And they packed firepower. What was it Prince—a major Sly disciple, later wrote about 'high on crack, toting a machine-gun'?

Jerry Martini and his second wife—a Portuguese lady called Lynne, relocated from their home in Marin County, and moved into the pool-house guest bungalow. Freddie never lived at Bel Air. He stayed over. He played. But he maintained his own outpost of relative escapist sanity in the Oakland Hills. Poppa KC also maintained his own room. Every now and then he'd come down and cool things off. As best he could. Rose had a home in Oakland.

While Larry's behaviour was becoming erratic, exacerbated by the break-up of his marriage to Gloria. 'Everything was locked up, and no-one left until it was time to leave—and that was when Sly decided' Bobby Womack discovered. 'There were a lot of drugs around, and sometimes it seemed like everyone in LA was staying up there in Sly's house. He'd stay up six, seven days with the drugs, and with that kind of punishment you are going to hallucinate. We did that a lot of times. I stayed up maybe three or four days' straight. As Poppa Stewart himself would have attested after one of his periodic visits to the house, that was as close to reality as everyday life got at 783 Bel Air Road'.

A third floor studio had been installed and used by John Phillips for the final phase of the Mamas & the Papas career—and for the solo Scott MacKenzie album tied into his global hit "San Francisco (Be Sure To Wear Some Flowers In Your Hair)". The stables had also been 'torn apart' to convert them into an echo chamber. It was this hundred-grand eight-track studio that had been a major inducement in Sly's decision to take possession. After all, CBS had closed down their Hollywood studios. They had never been attuned to Sly's unique requirements anyway. The staff, technicians, even the equipment itself were fine for the old-fashioned MoR crooners and Swing Bands that had once formed the label's core roster of major star properties. They were fine for network TV and radio work. But when it came to funk—Sly was better off with his own studio, away from the 'white man's world of record companies and account execs.

To enter the home-studio there was a hidden staircase behind a sliding bookcase—like the access to Batman's TV Batcave, only this one led up to the attic. It was—according to Michelle 'also illegal, against the building codes. We had taken the fire loft to build it, and now had no third-floor exit'. There was, however, a lounge and reception area equipped with phones, couches and three banks of overlight lights with dimmers that could be used to fine-tune the ambience of the space. Vernon 'Moose' Constan—a high-school friend of Gregg Errico's and an electronics whiz-kid, further hot-wired the studio to Sly's demanding specifications, upgrading it to sixteen-track, while Sly's Winnebago motor-home was also rewired with recording equipment. Using these new techno-toys he continued working on the new album—what was provisionally titled 'The Incredible And Unpredictable Sly & The Family Stone'.

Perhaps the most unpredictable element about the extended sessions was whether they would ever be completed.

If the chemistry of the recording studio is good, it unfolds new potential for ideas, new techniques to enable new concepts. Studio costs had now become irrelevant. They were no longer a consideration. And, fully attuned to the infinite possibilities offered by his own studio, Sly was recording in bursts that went on and on. Sometimes the images ran into one another until he could no longer figure out which was which. Freed from the tight restrictions of studio-time, he unhooked the groove and let it flow where it would, too cool, or too stoned for verse-chorus-verse. For as long as the tapes spooled it all in. And sessions stretched on without end. They become recording marathons that rarely commenced earlier than midnight. At first, nobody got to go to bed until it was time to get up. Then overnight sessions would last for days. As long as five-days straight. Until they flowed over the course of several days, enabled by ingesting 'attitude adjusters'. Sly's night-owl ways forbade the presence of clocks. He always operated on a different time-zone to everyone else anyway. And for those caught up in it, the endless sessions at 783 Bel Air Road were vastly different to anything Sly had attempted before. 'We used to call it the prison because we couldn't get off the hill' Family Stone production manager and sound technician Robert Joyce said of the mansion. 'Sly's thing was no time. He made time, that was his thing. Now… we are doing it right now. That was the mentality'. Sleep only intervened when the physical state of those involved could stand no more cocaine. Track, track, and pass out. When Sly himself—recording in a horizontal pose, fell comatose into sleep it was literally impossible to rouse him.

Such spontaneous anthems as "Dance To The Music" or "Everyday People", had been recorded with the emphasis on live big-room ambience. Liberated from the necessity of that working method Sly was not only overdubbing instruments one at a time, but plugging them directly into the board to create a more parched, almost claustrophobic sound which coalesced into a shadowy force that just kept coming. Plugging into the mixing desk eliminates all extraneous sound. But it also meant that instruments were recorded separately, with artists seldom—if ever, physically playing all together in the studio at the same time. Sly was able to build tracks up though this greater reliance on multi-tracking, overdubbing most instruments himself, and eventually providing more of the lead vocal parts than before. The muddy, lurching recording style that resulted was partly due this incessant reliance on overdubs—as though endless re-recording had scraped off too much tape-oxide—a bit of technical malfeasance that serendipitously suited the album's spacey, mid-tempo songs, but is equally due to Sly's genuine search for a new form of expression. Tapes were then mixed and spliced into cohesion. Prior to digital sampling technology, that involved physically collaging lengths of analogue tape together with a razor-blade and adhesive-tape. Jimmy Conniff (son of Ray Conniff) was on hand to add technical expertise to this cutting and editing phase. It's a meticulous technique, and time-consuming. Another advantage of Sly's having his own studio.

For the band, the feeling of a shared sensibility was becoming less palpable, and this on-going break-up of the original Family Stone must also have been mother to much of its invention. As Kapralik opined in the *Rolling*

Stone' piece, "Family Affair" itself—one of the few pop-friendly spots on the album, might just have been an ironic comment on the rifts within the Family Stone itself. After all—apart from Rose, frequently there were no other group members present. Did Sly withdraw from them—the Family that had been his musical and spiritual mainstay? Or did they withdraw from each other? It's not even necessarily that Sly was excluding them, more that band members were frequently absenting themselves from recording sessions, leaving Sly alone with virtually unlimited studio-time on his hands. Although it's far from the *only* destabilising ingredient, Sly was also far from operating as the only group-member to be drug-addled and disillusioned. When you have talented, quality musicians who are working hard, playing hard, and doing it together, you have the makings of a great band. It's what the band does *together* that makes the music happen. But when those musicians cease playing together, and start playing for themselves, when that happens, the magic goes out of the band. People who used to love to play together start not caring anymore. That's when the band falls apart into rancour. In the loft studio Freddie would play, other times he 'would be too gone to play'. Cynthia and Jerry played on the sessions. But frequently—later on, it was difficult for them to relate their contributions to the track that eventually resulted. Once the group's in-house clown, Jerry had 'become a coke addict, drug addict, vegetable, idiot, zombie, sitting around waiting for my line like the rest of the ass-holes'. He and Sly had started out as friends together, on a mission. Now he had become a part of Sly's freak possessions. Sly's human zoo. There are stories of Sly sitting regally, with fine white lines of cocaine laid out in front of him. Another line, of people this time, with their nostrils extended out to the sacramental spoon he was offering. It conferred power. It was an instrument of status, and control.

  Gregg Errico was steadily phasing himself out of the band. The frustrating tedium of being peremptorily summoned to LA from his Bay Area base for promised sessions, only to be kept on hold on indefinite whim until Sly got around to using him, added to the accumulation of other irritant factors. He would be effectively gone by the date of the album's release. In his stead—at least in part, Sly set the crumpled percussive groove by employing the unconventional technique of mixing live drums with what were, at the time, primitive machine-made drum-tracks (especially apparent on the feed-in to "Africa Talks To You"). Here, the air of dislocation is enhanced by the cold, metronomic gallop of the 'rhythm box' which Sly programmed himself. Gregg plays on a few cuts (although he claims to hear himself on only one track), the majority of the live parts were played by Sly himself. He co-opted other Family Stone members for additional fills. But there's an impression they were treated as session musicians on what was, nominally at least, their own album. And in some sequences, there's input from a rotating cast of random unaccredited cronies, peers, sidemen and studio-visitors who were 'auditioned' directly onto the master-tapes. Sly took the opportunity of 'auditioning' girls for studio-sessions—in the sense that movie producers once used the 'casting couch', some of their voices may even have survived into the final edits. So, instead of his regular Family Stone crew, Sly was 'messing round with the best of them' as he'd write on "Sylvester", with session friends including such illustrious luminaries as Bobby Womack on guitar, Billy Preston adding keyboard, and Ike Turner—another West Coast R&B veteran with more than a taste for white powder.

Although the most obvious Sly Stone connection was that Ike had scored a considerable hit with his version of the Family Stone's "I Want To Take You Higher", Ike was the man who cut what respected authorities consider to be the first ever Rock 'n' Roll record—"Rocket 88" in March 1951. Little Richard cheerfully admits stealing the piano intro for "Good Golly Miss Molly" from "Rocket 88"—'the exact same, ain't nothing been changed'. Ike had then gone on to fire Jimi Hendrix for messing up the band's sound-balance with his effect-pedals, cut chart R&B hits which crossed-over to white audiences, and co-produced the quintessential 1960's black Pop *'River Deep Mountain High'* (1966) album with Phil Spector. He deserves recognition for his groundbreaking musical achievements. His Kings of Rhythm were touring and recording successfully long before Sly formed the Family Stone. And, for that matter, long before latecomer Annie Mae 'Tina' Bullock appeared. Ike had other protégés too, the Ikettes—for example, who scored a respectable run of delicious chart hits under his auspices, while Betty ("Shoop Shoop") Everett and Fontella ("Rescue Me") Bass both sang with Turner bands too. And even earlier than that—between 1951 and 1959, he A&R'd black or 'Race' artists from the same Memphis Sun studios that Sam Philips prospected white talent, playing as often-uncredited sideman for the likes of BB King, Johnny Ace, Elmore James, Otis Rush, and Buddy Guy. In fact, it was on his way to the Memphis Recording Service when a tyre blowout provided on-route writing time, which resulted in "Rocket 88". It debuted on Dewey Phillips 'Red Hot & Blue' radio-show on W-HBQ, and—leased to Chess records as a big 78rpm single, it charted. By 12th June 1951– while Sly was still in Vallejo barely just turned seven, it was no. 1 on the R&B and the jukebox charts. Three years later Dewey would break another local artist's debut hit, Elvis' "That's Alright Mama"!

Ike was born on 5th November 1931, literally on the wrong side of the tracks, on the black side of strictly segregated Clarksdale, Mississippi, deep in the Delta cotton belt. He was raised by his Mother, Beatrice Cushenberry, his early life shaped by strong and respected female figures. And psychologically—in a Southland where they still chained blacks to pick-ups and dragged them to death, a five-year-old Ike was traumatically witness to a Redneck lynch-mob smashing into his home, hauling his father away for an unprovoked beating—'he had holes in his stomach where he'd been kicked'. The white hospital turned him away, and he subsequently died from the long-term effects of the wounds. Later, thinking he'd murdered his stepfather, young Ike ran away to big-city racially segregated Memphis, where he lived out of trashcans while sleeping in alleys. This is not to excuse his later misogynist violence. But perhaps it goes some way to explaining it. Always sexually precocious, it was a Miss Boozie Owens who provided his initiation into rota-rooting before he'd even hit first grade. 'Sex' he explains, 'that's the dog in a man', and he was always voraciously drawn to what he terms 'the cat'. He was not yet twelve years old when middle-aged Miss Reeny became his third sexual partner! In such an erotically-charged atmosphere he was soon sharing girlfriends with pal Ernest, who's Daddy played ragtime piano and was a 'real whoring man'. When Ike heard Pinetop Perkins play boogie-woogie on his way home from school, 'it put a burn in my mind', and the connection was obvious. Musicians attract sex. Ike would go on to have numerous wives—eight or nine he says. Nigel Cawthorne—who ghostwrites his autobiography, puts the figure closer to ten, maybe twelve. But he was never, they both agree, legally married to Tina.

Meanwhile, Momma B had ambitions for her small-town fatherless black boy. And he had an eye to every hustle, already, while still at school he had graduated to DJ-ing at W-ROX. The school band called itself the Dukes of Swing, so Ike went one better, his own band became the Kings of Rhythm, and he was soon playing twelve-hour sets backing-up legendary Blues star Robert Nighthawk at local roadside joints. Playing West Memphis clubs a young Elvis came around to watch, and learn. Then, while writing, playing sessions and producing—as Sylvester Stewart would later do for 'Autumn', Ike contributed piano to BB King's first hit "Three O' Clock Blues", talent-scouted and produced Bobby 'Blue' Bland's debut studio-sessions, and worked on Howlin' Wolf's "Moanin' At Midnight"—all for one-off no-royalty fees! It was during a band residency in East St Louis that he 'became real, real whorish', with corrupt cop harassment, knife-fights, shoot-outs, and a roadie who got castrated and bled to death. But it was here that Ike met drummer Eugene Washington's girl Alline Bullock, and her sister 'Little Annie Mae', who was destined to become 'Tina Turner'. 'Tina' became pregnant by the tenor saxist Raymond Hill, and around the same time Ike wrote a song called "A Fool In Love". He originally intended it for vocalist Art Lassiter who 'sounded like the Ink Spots', but when he ran out owing Ike $80, Tina stepped in. Ike claims that he, himself, was never a natural performer, 'I built my career on standing in the background' he protests. 'I am an organiser. I ain't no goddamn artist.' Even "Rocket 88"—a celebration of a convertible Oldsmobile coupè, had been credited to 'Jackie Brenston & His Delta Cats'. But 'I wasn't going to have people running off with my shit again…!' And, learning from that name-theft, he deliberately issued "A Fool In Love" under the 'Ike & Tina Turner' dual-billing—allowing space for alternate 'Tina's as required, and patented it so that if Hill ran off with 'Little Annie' he could find himself another Tina, 'and keep on going'. No such problem arose. "A Fool In Love", issued on Sue records, was an instant hit, reaching no. 2 on the R&B chart and no. 27 on the Pop chart in August 1960. He then set about remoulding 'Tina' to become the raw visual focus of the band, modelling her style on movie jungle-girl Nyoka, and the Ikettes on the short-skirt majorettes who'd excited his prurient interest in Clarksdale parades. Inevitably, Ike and Tina became an item. For songwriting purposes, 'Tina was my Little Richard'—and for sex, Tina made 'my dick as hard as Chinese arithmetic'. How could they fail?

Soon there were more R&B hits, "It's Gonna Work Out Fine" (no. 14 for Sue, 1961) and "Poor Fool" (no. 38 for Sue, 1962) for Tina, and "I'm Blue" (no. 19 for Atco, 1962) and "Peaches 'n' Cream" for the Ikettes (no. 36 for Modern, 1965), but no significant cross-over sales into the white demographic until Ike bribed DJ's on K-FWB and K-RLA, white stations boasting twice the watt-output of their nearest black rival stations. They also got to play Jack Good's 'Shindig' TV show where they were advised to tone down the swaggering thrust of Tina and the Ikettes choreography, never to 'bump to the front… it was considered vulgar'. Nevertheless, their increasingly sexualised burlesque provoked network protests, and there was no return booking. The primitive up-front theatrics of the Ike & Tina Turner Revue 'invented' strobe and fire-extinguisher 'dry ice', while their screaming bravado was wilder and the Ikettes dynamic boogaloos more uninhibited than any other outfit on the touring circuit. Even Tina's subsequent solo career was based around what he termed 'the wedding' stage-routine he designed to gain sympathetic acceptance from female audiences. But oddly it was 'England that woke America up to the Blues'. The Turner Revue toured with the Rolling Stones, at the Stones invitation, playing the Albert Hall and even the infamous Altamont festival with them. With 'people like Janis (Joplin), the Rolling Stones, Clapton, and other groups, things changed. You had a younger generation that was not hooked on race'. The Phil Spector association propelled the cavernous reverberating "River Deep Mountain High" into the European chart, but ironically it was to be their throw-away cover of John Fogerty's "Proud Mary" that finally gave the Turners' their breakthrough American hit (no. 4 for Liberty in 1971). A track that even mistakenly includes Ike's voice prompting Tina, which was meant to be erased! With success, fame—and occasional infamy, came coke. 'As a producer' points out Jon Landau, in these latter years 'Ike Turner has been heavily influenced by Sly', and it was during those crucial months, that Ike Turner was guesting on Sly's sessions.

All-round good-guy Billy Preston was another favoured guest player—with his monster Afro hairstyle, his ever-present gap-toothed grin and his funky taste in clothes. His connection with Sly, of course, predated even the Family Stone. But since their Autumn days together he'd renewed another of his formative friendship—with George Harrison. George had drawn Billy into the fractious final Beatles recording sessions. He's there on the iconic *'Let It Be'* rooftop gig, qualifying as the only artist ever to get a joint credit on a Beatles record—he's there on the "Get Back" c/w "Don't Let Me Down" coupling. Billy's chirpy presence was enough to reinvigorate the group through the tense recording sessions of what would turn out to be their final album. Subsequently signed to the Beatles 'Apple' record label he hit no. 11 on the UK chart in his own right with the George Harrison-produced "That's The Way God Planned It", bringing its strong evidence of his enduring gospel roots direct onto *'Top Of The Pops'*. The 'B'-side of the single—"As I Get Older", was co-written with Sly. And his studio work with Sly at 783 Bel Air would soon prove to be equally as significant.

Strange to reflect that two of Sam Cooke's greatest protégés—Billy Preston and Bobby Womack, should both turn up on Sly's scary cocaine soundtrack (and they both made amends with gloriously deep versions of Sam's "A Change Is Gonna Come"). By now an industry veteran, Bobby had worked with the wicked wicked Wilson Pickett—writing his hits "I'm A Midnight Mover", "Ninety-Nine And A Half (Won't Do)", "I'm In Love" and other material. His personal involvement with Janis Joplin led to her recording his ballad composition "Trust Me" for *'Pearl'* (1971), her final album. Now, 'I played on *'Riot'*, I hear myself on that', comments Womack. 'I played wah-wah all over that album, and Sly just ran tapes the whole time, capturing the sound. I probably played on a lot of other things. But you would come back and tapes had moved and no one had seen them but him. There was some shit that never came out. There were many nights that I didn't want to go home. I was just there and we kept cutting.' His contribution to Sly's ongoing project was also a reciprocal two-way street. Much of the curious selection of material for his own album, *'Communication'* (1971), was recorded with Sly at his Bel Air studio, including his raspy vocal take on James Taylor's finest ever composition "Fire And Rain" and Ray Steven's jaunty happy-clappy "Everything Is Beautiful", alongside the straight gospel of "Yield Not To Temptation".

But his involvement with Sly did not come without a cost. 'It was so spacey' Bobby Womack confided to journalist Barney Hoskyns (*'Observer Music Monthly'* March 2006), 'I remember sittin' there in the dark in his studio, coked to the brain, tryin' to sing, staying up four, five, six days. That's just the way he was. You lookin' at his guy and thinkin', where in the fuck he come from?' Then, 'everybody in the house was high on weed and coke, and we would stay up night after night and play. Play, play some more and then play it again. One time Sly finally did get some sleep—on top of his piano, like a supine junkie lapsing into a coma. That's where I found him around five one morning. When I woke him gently, he looked up and started singing… 'one child grows up to be somebody that just loves to learn and another child grows up to be somebody you'd just love to burn…' it was from "Family Affair".' Bobby's guitar can be heard on the cut, he also harmonises on "Just Like A Baby". It was 'one of the greatest experiences of my life. In the end, it lasted too long'. 'Sly was crazy,' and afterwards 'I was too broke up to work, the drugs and partying at Sly's place had all taken their toll'. In the aftermath of the events he even went to the extreme of faking blindness as an avoidance strategy to get out of playing live. Telling the tale in his highly entertaining autobiography he relates how Stevie Wonder called round to offer his sympathies. With Bobby watching him through the fraying strands of his fake eye-bandages. Womack intended his next record project to be a country-music album he provisionally titled *'Step Aside Charley Pride Give Another Nigger A Try'*. A C&W album? The label 'thought I had been hanging with Sly too long'. United Artists, the distraught label, changed it to *'BW Goes C&W'* (April 1976), and then dropped him.

Meanwhile, other players are rumoured to have dipped in and out of what were still being termed the 'Incredible Unpredictable' sessions, as contributors, or merely adding presence. It's said that Herbie Hancock envisaged a whole new future for contemporary jazz after watching Sly first-hand. Fresh out of Miles Davis' experimental *'Bitches Brew'* (1970) line-ups Herbie picked up on elements of *'There's A Riot Goin' On'*, prompting him to move his own material towards this more electric sound. His *'Head Hunters'* (1973) nods most directly at "Just Like A Baby" on the side two track "Vein Melter", and as if to emphasise the connection there's another called simply "Sly". It was subsequently rated the highest-grossing jazz album of all time, much to the chagrin of Miles Davis himself. And Miles—the best, the greatest of jazz innovators dropped by too. When Miles calls round your session to check out what's going on, it doesn't come much better. Illinois-born Miles, a genre-defying direct link to the Bebop revolution of the late-'40's, doesn't dispense his approval lightly. Long before Sylvester Stewart was even born, and while Ike Turner was still a virgin, he'd been working with the best. Much of what is now considered edgily cutting, he was doing back then, clear down to the hip-hop vocabulary. Today, John Coltrane is seen as the most spiritual performer in jazz history, with his visionary *'A Love Supreme'* (1965) viewed as a transcendental vindication of the purest epiphany music can aspire to. Yet back then, Miles was forced to fire him from his group for nodding out between solos, picking his nose on stage and sometimes eating it! And to get a taste of the times—at the end of one Café Bohemia club set Miles allowed young gun Kenny Dorham up on stage to jam and was mortified when the guest's playing proceeded to blow the group to shreds. 'Man, was I pissed'. Fuming and nursing his hurt pride Miles schemed revenge. The following night he purposefully invited Dorham to join them *earlier* in the set, immediately following his solo by ramming into top gear, pulling every slick trick and maximising every technique from his not-inconsiderable resources of virtuosity, to wreak visceral havoc on the 'hippest audience in the city', and establish once and for all his supremacy in the pecking order.

Miles mistrusted and resented the white man, with good reason. In the southern states a form of 'racist to the bone' segregation was still enforced, with lynchings used as a means of control and intimidation, while even in more liberal NY whitey controlled every aspect of the music industry. They decided on arbitrary whim who would and would not achieve stardom through granting—or withholding access to radio, records, and touring. He respected and admired Louis Armstrong and Dizzy Gillespie, but despised what he saw as their wide-grin capitulation to minstrelsy white show-biz preconceptions. 'I wasn't about to kiss anybody's ass and do that grinning shit for nobody'. Yet, in a way unique to jazz, beyond wealth, popular status—or colour, cutting contests such as the one at the Café Bohemia, established respect. The one thing that set you apart was your improvisational skills. You could do it, or you were nowhere. When the more militant brothers protested to Miles—as they protested to Sly, why did he employ white musicians in his group when there were black players who needed the work?, his retaliation was instant, 'I'm hiring a motherfucker to play, not for what colour he is... if they're cool, they're cool, no matter what colour they are'. Miles could be considered arrogant. Part of that was defensive. The press branded him difficult, aloof. He refused to announce the titles of the numbers he played on-stage. If the people were hip to what he was doing, they knew the titles already, if they weren't hip to it, they didn't matter. He extended his silence to deleting liner notes from his albums. Miles Dewey Davis III never condescended to anyone, and 'didn't take no shit off nobody'.

He was not born poor-black. The son of a middle-class East St Louis dentist, he'd never come up through the impoverished blues tradition. He had absolute conviction in his ability, and that was enough. He knew his own value, and would accept nothing less. While he was supposedly studying at Julliard, he was taken in and adopted by the bop pantheon of 1940's New York, through whom he accelerated his chops, and picked up a heroin-habit. But neither drugs nor sex were as vital stimulants as music. The eighteen-year-old Miles was 'sucking in everything. Man, it was something', with 'music all up in my body'. Chief among those 'scientists of sound', Charlie 'Bird' Parker was a genius musician, but a failed human being. 'I loved Charlie Parker as a musician—maybe not as a person'. Sharing a downtown cab on 52nd Street, Miles protested that Bird's gargantuan fried-chicken eating habit—not to mention the white girl down there fellating him, were unsettling. Bird suggested Miles stick his head out the window if he was offended. He did, but could still hear every chomp and slurp. 'Bird did more weird shit than anybody I ever met'.

Later, dressed sharper than 'a broke-dick dog', Miles was hitting the first of his own multiple musical peaks with his 'classic sextet' (John Coltrane, Cannonball Adderley, drummer Philly Joe Jones, bassist Paul Chambers, with pianist Bill Evans replacing Red Garland). Each member playing 'above what he knows'. Marking a complete break with the prevalent 'hard bop' style, Miles stripped its complexities down into a new melodic simplicity named *'Birth Of The Cool'* (1957), while collaborating on the novelty LP 'long-playing format' with Canadian arranger Gil Evans for *'Sketches Of Spain'* (1960). August 1959's *'Kind Of Blue'* was the sound of an album whose time had come, its quintessential modalism an expression of musical genius to influence every subsequent generation. From the opening bars of "So What" its strength lies in its serene simplicity, a cool, spacey open-textured approach that takes the listener through a series of improvisations based around simple melody lines, as accessible for the novice as for the professional. But with a freshness that says it could have been recorded yesterday. A rare example of revolutionary music that almost everyone enjoyed from the moment they heard it, delicate, approachable but surprisingly expressive. *'Kind Of Blue'* is the definitive jazz album, which became the media's favourite source of brooding atmospheric mood music, a living musical history and a true American masterpiece. Yet the very month of its release Miles was arrested moments after playing a concert. Walking to a taxi with a white girlfriend a cop told him to move on. When Miles adopted a defensively aggressive stance, he was arrested. In memory of the harassment he later named one of his albums *'You're Under Arrest'* (1985). *'Kind Of Blue'* was followed by the quietist masterpiece *'In A Silent Way'* (1969), and the confrontational double-CD *'Bitches Brew'* which consists of long non-directed improvised interactions. Miles repeatedly reinvented himself and his music, he defied and despised all attempts to categorise or restrict his music. Yet by then, jazz was well into being relegated as the world's music of choice by crude upstarts Rock 'n' Roll and R&B. Miles never accepted such demotion. He evolved his clean unadorned style into the greatest jazz of the second half of the century through a series of audaciously inventive albums that did much to retain the profile and relevance of jazz itself. Within the restricted world of jazz, he was as big a star as it was possible to become. But he envied the greater success and commercial visibility of the less technically-proficient Rock Tsars he saw every time he turned on the TV. He was also there, watching ruefully from the sidelines, as the audience rioted for the Family Stone at the Newport Jazz Festival. And he saw access-points to their lucrative markets through the improvisational forays of Jimi Hendrix… and Sly Stone. Later, hanging out with Sly and Jimi, he was intrigued as much by their musical innovations as by their access to the kind of mass sales-figures he felt *he* deserved.

'I had met Sly and he had given me one of his albums' recalled the trumpeter, 'I liked it. When I first heard Sly, I almost wore out those first two or three records, "Dance To The Music", "Stand", and "Everybody Is A Star". I told (*'San Francisco Chronicle'* critic) Ralph Gleason, 'listen to this. Man, if you know a promoter you better get him to get Sly, because he's something else, Ralph'. This was before Sly got really big.' Later, he recalls how Clive Davis attempted to use him as a catalyst during the stalled 'Incredible and Unpredictable' sessions. 'The people at Columbia who own Epic—the label Sly was on, wanted to see if I could get Sly to record quicker. But Sly had his own way of writing music. He got his inspiration from the people in his group. When he wrote something he would write the music to be played live, rather than for a studio. Then after he got big he always had all these people around his house and at his recording sessions. I went to a couple and there were nothing but girls everywhere and coke, bodyguards with guns, looking all evil. I told them I couldn't do nothing with him—told Columbia I couldn't make him record any quicker. We snorted some coke together and that was it.' Miles judgement ends 'he wrote a couple of other great things, and then he didn't write nothing because the coke had fucked him up'. Yet it was 'with Sly Stone and James Brown in mind that I went into the studio in June 1972 to record *'On The Corner'*…' If *'On The Corner'*—Miles' own excursion into funk, subsequently failed to achieve the reception lavished on Herbie Hancock's *'Head Hunters'* (1973), he blamed what he perceived as inadequate promotion. He accused marketing preconceptions that still insisted on filing his records under the neglected 'jazz' category, despite Corky McCoy's cartoonish cover-art which shows at least three Sly-alike street-characters, one in a pink pimp-suit, one holding a big ghetto-blaster, and another in a 'Vote Miles' top.

Johnny 'Guitar' Watson also showed up at the sessions, and Sly's 'Stone Flower' protégé Joe Hicks. Another, more unlikely presence, was white southerner Jim Ford. 'Sly wasn't the easiest guy to hang around but he loved Jim Ford' recalls Bobby Womack. 'I think for Jimmy to be that close to Sly, he had to be doing something that was very important to the situation.' Sly himself had explained—if 'explain' is the appropriate term, to Dick Cavett about Jimmy Ford 'in LA beating up people'. He quickly corrected himself, 'no, not really'. Then elaborated helpfully how 'actually, he was writing beautiful songs, and he's destroying the minds of people who've been led to believe the world was flat'. 'Indeed?' deadpans Cavett. Originally from New Orleans, Jim Ford had dropped out of his academic pursuits in 1966, lured away to chase the California Dream. While passing through LA en route to Haight-Ashbury he encountered two Native American session players, Pat and Lolly 'Vegas' Vasquez. Future members of chart-group Redbone, they'd worked with the 'Shindig' house-band and had already cut their own album for Mercury. Using their industry contacts they brought Jim to Del-Fi Records where label-boss Bob Keane issued a pair of Ford singles through its Mustang subsidiary. There were other near-connections with fame. Ford co-wrote PJ Proby's hit "Niki Hoeky" with the two Vasquez brothers. His former girlfriend Bobbie Gentry did her own version. Nick Lowe recorded another of Ford's songs "Thirty-Six Inches High" during a UK sojourn, while Bobby Womack co-wrote and charted with Jim's "Harry Hippie"—written about Bobby's own brother (US no. 31 in January 1973). Sly himself slips a satiric reference to the hit in a later track, "In Time", teasing 'Harry Hippie is a waste'. Eventually Ford did get to record his own album— *'Harlan County'* (for Sundown in 1969, reissued by Edsel in 1997), a gritty stew of R&B-flavoured country-soul with a swampy Muscle Shoal-style rhythm section—closest in comparison to the likes of Tony Joe White, it includes Willie Dixon's "Spoonful", Delaney & Bonnie's "Long Road Ahead", "I'm Gonna Make Her Love Me", as well as his own lyrical narrative compositions. Sly was an enthusiastic champion of his talent, and although commercial success eluded him, Jim Ford even moved into Sly's West-LA Holmby Hills home for a while.

Buddy Miles also partied at Sly's Bel Air manse, the power-drummer fresh out of Mike Bloomfield's Electric Flag, but with a prior history stretching back to Ruby & The Romantics. Richard Pryor and Redd Foxx dropped by. Yet despite the eminence of such communal creativity, there's never a moment's doubt that the album-project underway was the purest distillation of Sly Stone. In fact, *'There's A Riot Goin' On'* is the closest to a solo project he'd yet produced. Perhaps that was, at least in part, forced on him by circumstances? Maybe he had no choice? Perhaps, in order to save the group, Sly was assuming an even greater part of it. Until it was only him. Multi-instrumentalist, lyricist, manager, strategist, visionary, spokesperson. Sly was the genius. The Family Stone his foil. Whatever it took to overcome those adverse factor, he took. A journalist asked Sly to comment on the rumour that he'd played all the instruments himself, 'I've forgotten, man' he explained. So—just how much had he played? a shrug 'whatever was left...'

Chapter Fourteen
'There's a Riot Goin' On'

'An exploration of and a pronouncement on the state of the nation, Sly's career, his audience, black music, black politics and a white world'

(*'There's A Riot Goin' On'* according to Greil Marcus)

In the fall of 1971, following final mix-downs at Sausalito's Record Plant studios—a location that was shaping up to become a favourite Sly-haunt over the troubled coming years, Sly personally chauffeured the final-edit spools down to the CBS Record offices. Much to the relief of Clive Davis. And the tormented album-sessions that had been Frankensteined together from all those multiple tapes—*'There's A Riot Goin' On'*, had somehow been transfigured into a masterpiece. Despite, or perhaps because of, all those seemingly disconnected, potentially disastrous fragmentations, it had become the soundtrack of a condition, the record of a state of being. Zeitgeist albums are, by definition, one-offs. Something owed to a unique configuration of circumstances. An artist's creativity is affected by all manner of influences, by altered states that might be called unbalanced, even pathological, just as it can be affected by numerous other involuntary factors. Nothing comes out of thin air. People have minds, bodies, cultures, which—to an extent, they can't do anything about. What the Delegate from Funk City USA had always excelled at was catalysing different factions, bringing contradictions together into a cohesive and funky whole. For this album those fundamental particles are just a little more dark-matter in nature. A little more opposed. It's only in the splicing, editing, and final mix-down that those opposing forces truculently elide into reconciliation.

The underground press had always liked the cooky-crazy cheerful wackiness of The Family Stone, while never investing them with quite the same seriousness it lavished on the Grateful Dead, Bob Dylan, or Jefferson

Airplane. With this album they were abruptly stunned into reconsidering that position. They were forced to accept that this was a psychedelic abattoir that perfectly caught the darkening mood of the moment. Vince Aletti, writing in *'Rolling Stone no. 98'*, admits that 'at first I hated it for its weakness and its lack of energy, and I still dislike these qualities.' Yet later 'I began to respect the album's honesty, 'cause in spite of the obvious deception of some cuts, Sly was laying himself out in all his fuck-ups. And at the same time holding a mirror up to all of us'. He grudgingly concludes that 'it's hard to take, but *'There's A Riot Goin' On'* is one of the most important fucking albums this year'. The late Timothy White, one-time *'Billboard'* editor and former *'Rolling Stone'* scribe, confirms this is 'a brooding, militant, savage, indictment of all the decayed determinism of the sixties'.

Taking another perspective, reviewer John Morthland writing in *'Creem'* (February 1972), pointed out that 'as many have noted, Sly Stone's style revolves around so many factors that it may, paradoxically enough, be as limited as it is ground-breaking'. And true, it's a dark, violent, hazy and paranoid album. With each track its strengths coalesce a little more. Tipping over the decade's event-horizon into a confused burnt-out hopelessness. This is an album ravaged by fall-out, from narcotic overindulgence, from the dream-deflation of black nationalism, from the bloated counterculture excesses all the way from the Haight to the Village and every other hippie ghetto in between, compounded by the strain of his own superstardom. It was the ageing of the dawn of Aquarius. And Sly was attempting to make sense of the bygone decade, the expectations surrounding him, black politics in a white world, the unwelcoming future, but most of all, himself. A dialogue between his inner, and outer realities. He was already in re-entry mode after the stellar ascent to fame during 1968-'69, where promise had proved itself a cruel illusion. And—as at certain rare moments before, and since, one man's nightmare took on a resonance for the times, in a haunting and prophetic portrait of desolation. The answers that the sixties provided, Sly is saying, do not compute. This was the definitive death-of-the-sixties artefact, an aural downer, in the aftermath of the decade that was supposed to change the world. There's a sense that if Sly & The Family Stone had won, we had all won. As Lillian Roxon observed, this unit 'demonstrate perfectly what will happen to music as old established groupings break down'. If they failed to reach that better future, we'd all failed. We win together, or we lose apart.

Within, and through the enclosed Family Stone worldlet, Sly had won his own personal revolution. While he'd discovered that the utopian worldview within the band, didn't necessarily work in everybody else's world. As a black artist, he still couldn't walk into a bar in Mobile, Alabama without getting into a fight. That realisation affects you. Ike Turner discovered the same thing when 'the whites accepted us as Ike & Tina, but at the Holiday Inn and the downtown hotels, they didn't give a fuck. I was just another nigger'. How far had things moved on from Cassius Clay returning from the September 1960 Rome Olympics, where he'd represented his country and won the Light Heavyweight Gold Medal, yet found himself refused admission to a segregated restaurant? In disgust he'd thrown his medal into the Ohio River. Sylvester Stewart was creating a vinyl metaphor of that moment. In that external reality, many chances had been taken, many chances blown. Now, it was all over. Perhaps that sounds pretentious. Is Sly being profound, or is he just full of shit? It's difficult to say with any degree of certainty. Fact is, a zeitgeist album reflects the spirit of the time in ways that its creator, and even those who respond by becoming purchasers, don't always themselves necessarily understand.

In the *'Observer Music Monthly'* (March 2006) Charlie Gillett called the album 'the diary of a man going through a lot of pain in an attempt to identify and define himself'. A disturbing but compelling album of sinister sound-plays and malevolent lyrics. Grittier, drug-laced, narcotically-hazed, filtered through drum-machine tracks. There are few escape routes. Once the listener is in, they are locked into its dark oppressiveness, its pained compromised-optimism and unrelenting self-examination. A watershed release for Sly's career, its right-on dramas still sound remarkable, different— ironically, in spite of the fact that the record has had such broad influence. Its intensity is almost unbearable even now. And it remains a critic's favourite, their estimation of its status has only grown with the passing years with an influence equal to, and surpassing the Family Stone's earlier work. This is the album that sets the pace for seventies funk with its louche elastic bass, slurred vocals, and more militant Black Power funk stance.

It starts from the cover on in. The McLuhan-smart media-saturation of consumerism meant that society's discontents instinctively knew the power of brands, symbols and images. And the vinyl album is confrontationally emblazoned with the American flag, the most powerful brand of them all. Sure, the British-invasion bands had used the Union Jack as an ironic Pop-Art logo, a Bridget Riley grid for a Carnaby Street take-away bag, something for the Who to flash across Pete Townshend's guitar, a design to splash across the roof of a mini. After all, it was the irrelevant symbol of a lost and largely despised imperialism. But the American stars-and-bars was—and is, different. Even with its fifty stars replaced by twenty-eight white-flower sunbursts… or were they bullet-holes? No, suns are used instead of stars, according to Sly, because 'stars to me imply searching… like you search for your star'. He adds that 'Betsy Ross did the best she could with what she had. I thought I could do better'. Betsy Ross was the Quaker woman who helped design and hand-sew the first, thirteen-starred American flag. By suggesting that his provocative tinkering was improving her patriotic design-classic, Sly was, to some, adding insult to injury. Just as insolently as the rioting long-hairs who were burning the flag outside draft stations in protests against Vietnam. Or 'Revolution for the Hell of It' activist Abbie Hoffman who created a TV uproar by producing a handkerchief using its design, and proceeding to buff his shoes with it. Sure, Jasper Johns had made Old Glory into a Pop Art icon. But wasn't Sly merely using its shock-value as a cynical inducement to consumerism… or, maybe he wasn't, perhaps—to put it another way, what those freaky drug-taking hippie longhairs were *really* doing, was reclaiming what that flag represents? Abraham Lincoln's inaugural address had spoken of looking to 'the better angels of our nature,' that's precisely what they were doing. Reclaiming those truths that the founding fathers had found so self-evident, that 'all men are born equal'. The declaration of the right to 'Life, Liberty, and the pursuit of happiness'—first declaimed beneath Betsy's own hand-stitched flag… isn't that what this whole generational party is really all about? Even though those founding fathers had owned their own slaves? The American flag as a symbol of national identity—and a growing imperial power, was—and still is something to be fought over. And here they were, using it for an album cover! Bruce Springsteen's ironic (and largely misinterpreted) 'Born In The USA' campaign some two decades away would, by comparison, be a far less dangerous statement to make.

It was Steve Paley who took the original photo for the album sleeve. He created three custom-flags—one for himself, one for Epic, and one for Sly who had it hung over the fireplace at 783 Bel Air. Once integrated into the LP art it featured a red, white and black design. To chat-show host Mike Douglas Sly explains he'd made the design amends, to 'change the colour of the flag'. Adding to the confusion by clarifying it further, the cover represents 'people of all colours', because black is the absence of all colour, white is the combination of all colours, and red represents blood, which all humans have in common. Well, that's alright then! Meanwhile, more practically concerned that no other defining text or titles appear, Epic took the precaution of stickering a 'Featuring the Hit Single "Family Affair"' strategically for identification purposes. They failed to realise that as you flip through the albums in the record store racks, the visual impact is already making statements, before the stylus hits the first groove. Hunt through the Polaroid-collage of images assembled by Lynn Ames on the inner gatefold and there's a jumbled selection of faces that might provide further clues. Or not. Various configurations of band-members, plus Bobby Womack and Buddy Miles (who had his own take on using ol' glory as a stage prop). Another US flag, this time with the stars replaced by a single CND symbol. Sly's dog, Gun. A statue-face of old Abe Lincoln. The Lincoln Memorial where Martin Luther King had delivered his 'dream' back in 28th August 1963. And a bit of the Gettysburg Address. The Marine Towers on the

Chicago skyline. The Capitol Building. Symbols of American power. And symbols of American opposition to that power. As some indication of Epic's continuing unease with the design, a later reissue would replace this cover with a less contentious shot of Sly in concert, facing a massed audience.

Issued on the 20th November 1971, it was a landmark album—as violent and disturbing as the world it was created in. *'There's A Riot Goin' On'* became a cultural juggernaut that developed a slow inexorable momentum, and was all the more powerful because of its total unexpectedness. Moody, disturbing and—perhaps, profound, it carried a seductive element of difficulty. Intimidating for the uninitiated. There's a sense that some effort on the part of the listener would not only be required—but that it would only reward repeated listens. The sound grabs from the opening moment, and is immediately peculiarly compelling, even addictive. After the fade-in wah-wha-ing guitars, the first vocal play-in line sets up the contradictions. 'Feels so good inside myself, don't wanna move...' ("Luv 'n' Haight")—the only lines Sly actually utters on the track. Slurred into 'feel sho good inshide myself' it's a clear statement of Sly's withdrawal into solipsism. That his relationship with the world outside had become marked by disinterested cynicism. An indication that if there *is* going to be a riot, it's one that's only taking place inside Sly's head. This is the steady retreat inwards that had been increasingly obvious to everyone around him, but had now become a condition that spreads throughout the album. Until you feel he's too fucked up to move even if he wanted to. Yet, if the warnings come from a personal interior, the effects are directed outwards. Here, after two long years between albums, Sly is back, but with a whole new definition of soul. He'd spent close on half-a-decade drawing up the blueprint for modern funk, now the dark struggles taking place within his psyche, presaged its dissolution. In moans of disquiet so visceral they transcend words, this is the sound that occurs at the point where the body truly meets the soul. You feel it first not in the head, but in the pit of your gut. And it's not difficult, even now, to imagine the confusion it inspired upon its release. Those involved in the album's gestation look back and tremble. Everyone was burned by it.

Progressing through the album track by track, from the Family Stone's Rose and Sly trading vocals on the first track, closing with an extended Rose and Lil Sis back-&-forth dialogue swapping the phrases 'feel so good' with 'wanna move' between them, into band two, "Just Like A Baby". Virtually a duet with Sly's spooky organ notes offset by Bobby Womack's 'oohs' and 'oh yeahs'. Feeding in with a chord progression vaguely reminiscent of Smokey Robinson's "You Really Got A Hold On Me", with Sly's off-kilter vocals so hoarse they're barely human, rasped out over the slow nod-out voodoo pulse, as he breathes 'just like a baby, sometimes I cry, / just like a baby, I can feel it when you lie to me' flowing into 'just like a baby, see the thing it's growin', / just like a baby, blowin''. Its 'druggy and exhausted' mood is enlivened by

Womack's biting guitar solo. So far in, and both tracks consist of half-vocals, drifting off into half extended-jams. Followed by the easy roll of "Poet", further reduced to a Sly solo—for the first time on a Family Stone album, infiltrated by stabbing keyboards reminiscent of Stevie Wonder's "Superstition" (which would follow in late 1972). The lyrics are stripped-down haiku-like, 'my only weapon is my pen, and the frame of mind I'm in, / I'm a songwriter, a poet'. The tones are deep, the words elide into each other, 'the things I flash on everyday, they all reflect in what I say…' But when he mouths 'I'm a schong-writer, oh yeh, a poet' it's as though he's taking a reality-check. Who am I? What do I do? This. I'm a songwriter. A Poet. Both an apology, and an explanation for opting out of other, more direct, forms of action.

The stuttered half-beats and compromised optimism that sugarcoats the bitterness in the next track—"Family Affair", snaps the album back into temporary focus. The percolating surge of the 'you'd love to burn' line slurring directly into your ear, coming clear at you from the speaker with enhanced clarity, and it feels to be the record's first pinnacle. In one sense, these tracks seem not to mix or share affinities, even though they meet. To Nick Kent, the contradiction of them co-existing on one piece of product sets up a frustrating blight on its overall cohesion as an audio-document. As though the one undermines the validity of the other. But to David Kamp, 'listen to his ghoulish, meandering delivery of the line 'newly wehhhdd a year ago / but you're still checkin' each other out / Yeahhh', it's like hearing a heat-warped 45 played at 33rpm'. In this sense, this already familiar track becomes a kind of go-between and mediator, a way of finding common ground between the material around it. Indicating that the album has other useful gears, with an intensity carried over into the fiery burn of the murky fog of its slower-paced songs. A reminder that Sly's extraordinary voice is an incredible instrument, full of howl and rasp, yet with just enough sensitivity to carry the album's quieter moments.

In the days before lasers replaced styli, albums had two sides. And closing side one—after "Africa Talks To You", there's the curious anomaly of calling attention to the cover-listed, but nonexistent title track. John Cage had 'written' a piece consisting of silence. Premiered in 1952, its title announced its duration—'4.33'. Now, Sly's silence is timed at precisely 0:00! So, a conceptual jibe it may be, but a pause for reflection it is not. Some claim it's a sardonic reference to the notorious Chicago 'Grant Park' no-show. With just a backward suggestion of Leiber & Stoller's "Riot In Cell Block No. 9". No, says Sly, "There's A Riot Goin' On" has no running time because 'I felt there should be no riots'. Whatever the devious motivation, following record-store returns due to complaints of 'incomplete' copies, the label took the precaution of adding a further explanatory front-cover stickers (and whereas Sly never wrote an actual song called "There's A Riot Goin' On" Mike Love rejigged new lyrics to Leiber & Stoller's song to create "Student Demonstration Time" for the Beach-Boys October 1971 album *'Surf's Up'* celebrating the Berkeley 'People's Park' riots, condemning the Kent State shootings, and attacking 'useless wars and racial strife' while retaining the 'there's a riot goin' on' chorus which Sly Stone disdained to use).

Detouring thematically, 'the songs seem to wander' writes Greil Marcus (in *'Mystery Train'*), 'to show up and disappear, ghostly, with no highs or lows'. 'Ghostly is right' confirms Barney Hoskyns, 'there's precious little warmth on this album. Even tracks as implicitly tender as the heavy-lidded "Just Like A Baby" and "(You Caught Me) Smilin'" sound diffuse, drifting'. If the humour is dark, shrouded in a veil of cynicism, then "(You Caught Me) Smilin'" can function both as Sly's twist on Smokey's "Tracks Of My Tears", and his contribution to the 'smiling faces' trope of seventies soul. From the strong ebony bass nudging the playful lyric into shape, 'you caught me smilin' again, hangin' loose / 'cause you ain't used to seeing me turnin' on...' to the more supportively inspirational 'I'll be around to carry on! / hey, you caught me smilin' again, in my pain, I'll be sane to take your hand'. A punching horn section frames both the beguiling Little Sister harmonies and Sly's impassioned vocal crack-up which catches a wistful flicker of the old optimism—recalling that, prior to 'Riot' there was never a problem catching Sly Stone smilin'. Technically, this is also the track that marks the first appearance of Gerry Gibson at the drum-chair. With Gregg Errico less frequently available, Sly resorted to using a stand-in replacement. And Gerry's contribution to this track also constituted his audition-tape for the band! While, legacy-wise, Coolio records his own version of "Smilin'" as a 'B'-side for his 1996 single "1,2,3,4 (Sumpin' New)".

Depressing? there's slighter evidence of that on "(You Caught Me) Smilin'". Nor on the dope-haze drug-sated surrealism of the next track, what Nick Kent terms the 'annoyingly cute tendencies' of "Spaced Cowboy" where Sly chuckles throughout. And you ain't heard nothing until you've heard Sly Stone yodel, etc etc. Sure, its deranged sardonic yodelling exhibits something of the impossible juxtapositions he'd contrived on *'Life'*, carried over into the new junk-heavy context. But with a new sense, less of controlled experiment, as of precarious disintegration shaped more by the various pharmaceuticals being ingested during the sessions. A perplexing sense that behind its stoned laughter, there's badness, even evil, a radical amputation from everything that had come before. But then there's the beautiful hot summer's day cool vocals and sub-Bacharach melody of "Running Away", with Cynthia's muted-Latin Tijuana-style trumpet fills, breaking into a solo that runs a feast of liquid Miles Davis-style squiggles. Virtually Rose's first full-length solo for a Family Stone album, sung in unison with Sly dancing and teasing the vocals, 'running away, to get away, Ha! Ha! Ha! Ha! / You're wearing out your shoes... Hee! Hee! Hee! Hee! / You're stretching out your dues, / ...the deeper in debt, the harder you bet, Hee! Hee! Hee! Hee…!!' Rose's saucy vocals mock and taunt its supposed victim even as he runs. These tighter tracks—with "Family Affair", tantalisingly reconnect to the *'Stand!'* economy. The melodies are as prettily beguiling as any pop tune, but Sly's lyrics and ironic vocals deliver reality like a brutal kick to the head, wrapping the same painful indecisions into deceptively bright packages. No—not everything's immediately depressive about them. Yet these tracks form the flip sides of the same coin.

It's *not* an album packed with obvious hits in the way that *'Stand!'* was, in fact it largely abandons the more radio-friendly hooks and lyrical themes he'd perfected on such prior releases. Instead, he'd alchemised his positives into negatives, with an album of shadows and omens. Beauty, dread, and psychedelic menace. If Sly had spoken earlier of evolving an album that was more than just a bunch of songs, a themed 'concept' album, this was it. On the track that *really* closes side one—"Africa Talks To You / The Asphalt Jungle", the man who once sang about 'hot fun in the summertime' now warns 'watch out 'cause the summer gets cold when today gets too old'. This is not about hot fun, dancing to the music, it's not about taking you higher, it's about disintegration. The sound of the century's biggest party turning sour from the inside. Down?—'in a way' Sly concedes to *'Melody Maker*'s Michael Watts, lowering his hand in a sort of elevator motion, 'not a down feeling, but down to earth'. Yes, the reek of the street. Police sirens and demonstrations. 'Flamin' eyes of people fear, burnin' into you, many men are missin' much, hatin' what they do'. Lynch-mob imagery and naked fear. And an overwhelming exhaustion. Where 'frightened faces to the wall, oh can't you hear your Mama call?'—where only the brave and strong survive. Yeah, Jones survives. Some music assails you, its very strangeness is what enraptures. This murky high-adrenaline riot-disco, restless and un-pretty, re-translates that language, reflecting the anxieties and ambiguities of living between a utopian ideal and the dystopian down-and-dirty reality in a place of collapsing time and space. Yet there are nagging problems, it could be argued that "Africa Talks To You / The Asphalt Jungle" is over-long, over-complex, jittery, more irritating and less accessible. Then again, what at first seems like an extended formless jam is rich with shuffling instrumental subtleties and depths, what Nick Kent calls 'fidgety coke-inspired embellishments twitching in and out of the mix'. Its second half drifts off as if dazed, mixed with ghostly voices warning 'Timber, all fall down' like the remnant from a diseased nursery-rhyme. The lyrics are broken and frequently puzzling (with this metaphor perhaps later clarified by Bob Marley's 'if you are the big tree, we are the small axe'). This is probably the only funk album that requires a lyric sheet, yet remains only partially understood even with one. And why is the track subtitled for the 1950 John Huston directed movie, the one with Sam Jaffe, Sterling Hayden, and a tantalising early glimpse of Marilyn

Monroe? It may be the film from which Quentin Tarantino derived many of his ideas for *'Reservoir Dogs'* (1992)—the master criminal, the million-dollar jewel heist, the individuals roped in to pull it off, but why should Sly feel the need to reference it? Because it's the story of a desperado's last-heist? Because, bucking the usual crime-thriller conventions of the time, it has the audience rooting for the bad guys, portraying the felons with all their human foibles, in a carefully delineated mirror-image of the supposedly respectable society they challenge? Because their dream goes tragically wrong…? Or the line of dialogue that argues 'after all, crime is only a left-handed form of human endeavour'.

Sequencing through side two—it might open with Sly's James Brown-imitation "Brave And Strong" ('Out and down / ain't got a friend…')—perhaps referencing Jerry Butler's hit "Only The Strong Survive", with Jerry and Cynthia's horns and Gerry Gibson's drums. It might continue through "(You Caught Me) Smilin'" and "Time", into the crazy "Space Cowboy"—with its growling talk-over vocal set to a busy clip-clop ('I can't say it more than once / 'cos I'm thinking twice as fast'). Yet even here there's an inescapable sense that the terrain depicted is also ominous, even toxic. The sense of tension gives its diverse images a striking visual and thematic dynamic. There's a dark sub-text that becomes discomfiting to decode, to decrypt. Foregrounding mood over Pop structures. As deeply as he'd believed in the promise of the counter-culture, the disillusionment here is equally extreme. Society now is a scary place, rife with betrayal and social paranoia, and the world doesn't seem safe ('you don't know who turned you in'). Instead, these are darkly hallucinatory apocalyptic dreamscapes. There's no letting up in its attack. Submerged anger and hypnotic bitterness are the watchwords for this unparalleled statement. "Time" slows down to barely perceptible life-signs that glitter with languorous beauty.

Sly concludes the album with the raging disdain of "Thank You For Talkin' To Me Africa"—arcing back to "Africa Talks To You" on side one, and a decelerated meaner near half-speed augmented-link back to "Thank You (Falettinme Be Mice Elf Agin)", but as radically different from its original as that had been from the Family Stone records that preceded it. Although the final track on the album, it was the first to be recorded, with the personnel (largely) unchanged from the template single, with Larry on bass and Gregg's drums. A cold groove. A dark groove. The genetic link to what had come before—'dance to the music, all night long / ev'ryday people, sing a simple song, Mama's so happy… Mama start to cry, Papa still singin'… you can make it if you try', points up the radical change Sly's music has undergone. With words replaced by strings of syllables that seem to have only a passing relationship to English. There's a poem, of sorts, on the gatefold sleeve which explains 'it's so complex, words get in the way…' As if it's describing something ultimately indecipherable, impossible to nail down in words. He can't express it. Language is too confining. That's why he'd become a musician in the first place. Because there is no other way he can express it. In ghetto vernacular, the original lyric had been a thanks for achieving creative freedom, for gaining acceptance on his own terms. Now 'many thangs is on my mind, words in the way'. The contrast can be frightening. From its painfully laboured intro and anguished vocals, its stoned slo-mo reversal, its self-indulgent transformation that drains the song of all its groove and spirit, as though its batteries are running down. A relentlessly leaden pattern of claustrophobic beats take it twisting and lurching into altogether darker terrain, varied only slightly throughout the track's seven long dead minutes. There's a slow stripped-down deep funk figure repeated three times before the vocal comes in, and when it does, it sounds agonised and weary, pulled up from out of the depths, struggling against an 'I'm so laid back I don't give a shit' inertia, to simply grind remorselessly on. A sloth-like riff-beast with vocals and muted trumpet buried deeper than a murder victim—its depressed tone and heavily reverberated vocals delivered over thick plodding bass, echoed by drums, with a sharp nervous guitar drowned in the backing track. 'Youth and Truth are makin' love, dig it for a starter./ I… want to thank you falettinme be mice elf… agin Thank you falettinme be mice elf… agin'. Meta-funk. A touchstone for all funk to come. Yet the ultimate disavowal of funk as party music. Constantly threatening its slide into final entropy. To Greil Marcus, it 'gathers up all the devastation of the rest of the album and slowly drives it home, grinds it in, and fades out…'

Whatever the final verdict, beneath what sometimes seems to be a dumb blathering incoherence, there's depth and detail here that *'Stand!'* never comes close to. Make no mistake, this could never be taken for the sound of a fresh young blood eager for combat, this is a beaten-up battle-weary veteran. And a veteran who holds only the most ironic prospects of triumph in a fight that can't be won. There are demons walking in these songs, just as surely as the demon-haunted blues originals of Robert Johnson thirty years previous. 'Lookin' at the devil, grinnin' at his gun. / Fingers start shakin', I begin to run, bullets start chasin' I begin to stop. / We begin to wrassle (wrestle), I was on the top'. So Sly has triumphed over the devil. This time. This is a disturbing masterpiece, a self-portrait of Sly Stone sorting through his own psychic detritus, as deeply personal an artistic event as Brian Wilson's *'Pet Sounds'* (1966), Bob Dylan's *'Blonde On Blonde'* (1966), or John Lennon's first *'Plastic Ono Band'* (1970) album. Marvin Gaye's *'What's Going On'* (1971) had come just six months earlier, around the time Stevie Wonder was making his own first forays away from the strict Motown machine with *'Where I'm Coming From'* (1971). And it was issued in direct chart competition with other bridge-burning artistic volt-faces. With *'John Wesley Harding'* (1967), and with that first *'Plastic Ono Band'* album, where both Bob Dylan and John Lennon were creating statements that form just as decisive denials of their own pasts. Like Sly they were rejecting musical styles they'd earlier originated. With reversals that call into question just about everything that had gone before, escaping their past by denying its value. Risking alienating and destroying their audiences by confronting and challenging them. In this sense it is not what *'Riot' is*, so much as the point at which it appears in the Sly Stone story. Its effect would not have been so resonant were it not for *'Stand!'*. And what *'Stand!'* stood for. It is the clear narrative that the relationship forms between the two statements. Even if that narrative is accidental.

A record of immense downered-out desperation, recorded under dire circumstances. Sly is all over the record, by turn whimsical, charming, narcissistic, sarcastic, evil, arrogant or truthful. What feels like pessimism, combined with a heavy dose of psychological self-torture, weighs heavily upon his natural talent, and then both ingredients become chemically accelerated…! Yet, even when he seems to be offering glimpses into his troubled state, it can be deceptive. He remains elusive, aloof. A man hung up in a mirror of his own construction, the drab deadened tonalities and dry unprocessed vocals create only illusions of heightened intimacy, in 'a deadening of all the senses'. Tracks are characterised by the strange brightly coloured loveliness of cocaine euphoria, strangely muted with crystal injections of electric piano, Sly's Fender Telecaster, the horniest of horns, clavinet, and soulful wah-wah'ed vocals.

If you listen to the album when you're high, in what you imagine to be the heightened perception in which it was created, you share a sense of delicious complicity with the artist. You are united by the ritual of its secret codes. You are granted insights into its hidden levels of meaning denied to the non-pharmaceutically initiated. What, to the un-stoned ear, is a mire of tediously meandering repetition, becomes—once herbally primed, a shifting oceanic mantra that ripples with delightfully erudite profundities, and ends way too soon. Both explanations are equally valid and are capable of being held by the same person at different times, in different states of consciousness. The Grateful Dead work this way. In a 'this is your brain on drugs' kind of half-awake half-asleep way. So does much of *'There's A Riot Goin' On'*… it becomes a tremendous machinery of colour and line, where figures gradually dissolve, space gets flatter, gets decoupled from their usual functions, veering into a powerful sense of darkness. It's impossible to navigate using the known constellations or fixed geographies of any existing musical value system. You put the album on—and can't bear to tear yourself away. There's work to do, things to accomplish, but all you're doing is trancing out to Sly. It's proof that Armageddon is at hand, an indisputable omen of end-of-times imminence. It's music to await the end of the world by. But it's also an album to reach for whenever the shit hits the fan. An album of star-studded doped-out damnation, a record of its time. What *'Melody Maker'* termed 'the most intense, emotionally troubled blues album in the history of modern black Pop'. Bobby

Womack told Barney Hoskyns 'Sly said to me, 'Bobby, you're one of the last gospel singers, and anything you do gonna be gospel. That's what you know, that's what you *bleeed*'. And he continues 'maaan, I'm comin' outta left field o' these motherfuckers'. He said 'Mah music is like the devil's music, it's got a little of yours in there (a little gospel), but you can't recognise it 'cause it's so loose and raw'.'

The record label press department were initially confused about to how best to promote their strange new vinyl property. After all, Sly's concerts were now as rare as Greta Garbo's press conferences. So the copywriters finally contrived a line about 'a new more mellow Sly has emerged from his musical exile to put together a very personal set of compositions, using his incredibly funky rhythm section and wah-wah guitar, but at a slower, more spaced-out pace'. Others knew better. David Kapralik suggested the marketing slogan 'Two Years is a Short Time to Wait for a Work of Genius'. Of course, it formed a dense not-easily-digestible sonic document lacking the immediacy of its predecessors, it needed time and familiarity to reveal its significance. It threw everything out of sync, demanding a context of its own. Although now it's regularly voted into the top albums of all time, back then the critics were less unanimous in their verdict. Reactions varied from disgust to disappointment to a wary enthusiasm. Phrases like 'blown it' tended to crop up in reviews. And it's hardly surprising that certain sections of the press—called upon to make snap-judgements after a few deadline-sensitive plays were more flummoxed, less charitable. *'Creem'*s John Morthland bemoaned 'the same plodding, lethargic beat that continues seemingly unabated for forty-five minutes', while Pete Wingfield writes in *'Let It Rock'*, decrying the album's 'sniffing self-pity'.

Over the years since, it's an album that has been picked over and decrypted by critics as comprehensibly as anything from the Dylan catalogue. For Sly uses the sorcery of language in a number of ways. And the listener can sense that sorcery, even if they don't get the literal meaning. The songs seem full to the brim with clues, connections and secrets, so the faith they place in the hidden significances of the lyrics is of the utmost importance. There are flashes of euphoria, ironic laughter, even some bright stretches, but clarity tend to be elusive. With the benefit of some hindsight Nick Kent recalled how 'Rock writers (particularly the self-consciously thinking man's breed) set about excavating their individual versions of 'Riot's true message. From amidst the enigmatic dope-haze of its home-base *'Rolling Stone'* naturally, was first in for the kill, their resident soul music correspondent dredging forth all manner of weighty conclusions about how Sly had, with this new direction of his, sculpted a total vision of current ghetto despair, a total aural documentary of what it was *really* like to be out there on the streets. How it goes further than any 'protest' record at the time, and perhaps further than any since. Only Robert Johnson's turbulent Delta blues can match it for sheer primal agony. Then *'Creem'* magazine came and set up a running dialectic with its most prominent spokesmen earnestly attempting to out-vie each other by extrapolating the record's true relevance on the grim light of the survival-obsessed 1970's'. About how Sly had received sharp lessons in the inflexibility of America's cultural divisions, and was expressing it all from beyond the one-dimensional perspective usually associated with such issues. While Nick Kent offered his own view of the album as 'high-grade speed-ball muzak' he nevertheless concedes that 'almost every one of these in-depth analyses possessed some degree of perspective about 'Riot's true worth'. Even later, and with the benefit of even greater hindsight, journalist Dave Rosen was able to detect in 'the introspective, yet political lyrics, the hard and dirty funk grooves, the inspirational, yet depressing songs—all of these elements would come to influence not only peers like Marvin Gaye and James Brown, but two generations of rappers and funkateers who paid homage to Sly's vision by making his samples and beats an essential backbone of their own innovations' (in *'Ink Blot Magazine'*). Obviously, he's right, but by limiting the album's influence to black music he's doing it a disservice. It's not difficult to see Bobby Gillespie using it to blueprint Primal Scream's *'Screamadelica'* (1991), to mention but one cross-genre example. Others who have directly covered or reworked its songs include Gwen Guthrie, the Beastie Boys, Lalah Hathaway, De La Soul, the Ultramagnetic MC's, and Iggy Pop.

With this album, was Sly writing his own career epitaph? Was he, with the compelling narrative of this determinedly contra-statement, taking fate into his own hands, ensuring that Rock history would remember him this way? It certainly forms the first real turning-point of the seventies, sending shock-waves through every avenue of music. Nothing would remain unaffected. Least of all Sly Stewart The Family Stone was heading towards one ineluctable ending, but he—its talisman, its architect, its mercurial genius would remain author of his own script. Compelled by the interaction between social upheavals, and his inner demons, he'd taken the new music he was creating to the absolute limit. Nothing could follow it, except silence. Perhaps it should have ended here? It was not so much his watershed, as the beginning of his decline. He would never get close to these heights again. From this point on, everything would be a retreat from this precipice, backing off from its grim truth. Sly Stone's whole tormented career seems to lead up to this point, and then back away from it…

Yet as late as the 2007 *'Vanity Fair'* interview, he was playing teasing games with the truth. Journalist David Kamp asks him if writing the album was impacted by the period's ugliness, the Kent State killings, the Attica prison riots, the Martin Luther King and Robert Kennedy slayings. 'Um, I paid attention to it' he concedes, 'but I didn't *count* on it. I wasn't going on any other program or agenda or philosophy. It was just what I observed, where

I was at'. Kamp persists, so it wasn't disillusionment with the sixties dream? 'I've never thought about it like that. I don't really feel like I'm disillusioned. Maybe I am. I don't think so, though'. Sly existed, like all eccentric geniuses, in a creative universe that functions according to its own rules, a world away from the dull conformity of the more mundane bands out there with their neat fringes and shiny guitars. *'There's A Riot Goin' On'* is one of those albums that seem to have arrived, fully formed, out of nowhere, with no precedent in popular music. Conclusions remain difficult to draw. Options remain open. Earlier he'd explained a little of his creative process. 'Tonight we're going into a recording session. That's right for now. The next night, something else. That's as far as I can see right now. That's as far as I need to see. But... as long as you see that you're going to do something, then there's nothing that can't be done...'

Chapter Fifteen
'Running Away Ha! Ha! Ha!'

'Sly Stone and the Devil. Hip mythology of three years past had that duo thick as thieves at one point—so tight you couldn't hardly tell the difference'

Nick Kent

'I'll be good… I wish I could… get the message over to you now…'

("Fresh")

Rock stars are forever doomed to play out their audience's fantasies and are, as a result, subject to their whims of childish cruelties. At the casual mercy of sales figures, chart positions, and the arbitrary ch-ch-changes of fashion, they are destined—for as long as their celebrity survives, to attempt to cheat fate on an album-by-album basis. At the moment, for Sly Stone, survival is placed on hold. Riding the success of the single "Family Affair", *'There's A Riot Goin' On'* effortlessly dominates the top of the American chart for a fortnight in November 1971, thereby financially underwriting Sly's narcotic extravagance and craziness for a further twelve months. And that craziness was becoming the stuff of legend.

Sly and Bobby Womack were being chauffeured down a ten-lane freeway in a limousine. The Arab driver sneaking glances in his rear-view mirror at the weird duo he was driving. Bobby snorting coke. A sexually ambiguous Sly in massive Afro beside him behind the glass, his face obscured by giant impenetrable aviator shades. When Bobby began to exhibit symptoms of being unwell—in an imminently up-chuck kind of way from a potent cocktail of narcotics and alcohol, Sly rapped sharply on the separating partition for the chauffeur to pull over. He indicated that 'no', you gotta wait till we hit the next gas-station. Too late, the projectile vomit erupts across leather upholstery and oriental fitted-carpeting. It's only now that the driver hauls in across lanes and up the verge, and in a comic-absurdist chase-sequence a vengeful Sly pursues him across all ten lanes dodging hurtling traffic, him in full glam regalia and knee-high boots with impossible stack-heels, him in full chauffeur uniform and peaked hat. Eventually Sly returned to the limo, satisfied, got in behind the wheel, and accelerated erratically into the high-speed lane, leaving the unfortunate chauffer stranded.

Compulsive, flawed, tragic, always a master of stylish perversity, Sly was further losing whatever sense of discipline still remained, whatever sense of control he still had over his life. And things were drifting. It wasn't as though he wasn't aware of what was happening. He was, just that he no longer cared. He had such confidence in himself, that even when he was losing control, he still felt he had everything together. The mind is well-capable of playing those tricks on itself. Especially when it's caught up in the unreality of success, and overheated by a coke c-jag, those tricks become amplified. If the alteration surprised those around him, they were going through their own similar changes, so that even those who caught fleeting glimpses of it were too into themselves to realise the full extent of what was really going down.

While behind the scenes there were other, more dramatic changes taking place. Watching through the car-crash visual experience of telegenic Sly stumble-bumming through his Dick Cavett TV-abattoir brought David Kapralik face-to-face with the realisation that he'd reached a point where he no longer had influence, let alone control over his wayward charge. Lines of communication had irretrievably broken down. It seems Sly had come to pretty much the same conclusion. In desperation, around late-July 1971, when there was no promoter in the country who would risk touching the Family Stone, Sly went through the intermediary of Al DeMarino of the William Morris Agency, who redirected him towards Ken Roberts. As an enabler. A fixer. To reduce the tension, to act as a fortuitous 'buffer zone' to reduce friction between himself and David. A former manager of Frankie Valli & The Four Seasons, Roberts had helped turn their troubled career around. Perhaps he could do the same for Sly? Ken Roberts… oh yeah! In a sense, he'd already begun the process, during the first weekend of January 1971, he was the guy responsible for putting the Family Stone on in West Virginia. He was there already.

Like Brian Epstein with the Beatles, David had been vitally instrumental in navigating the group's earliest success. As manager, on tour by Sly's side, he was constantly incessantly talking the group up to anyone prepared to listen. For one profile run in a national teen magazine the unfortunate journalist found himself trapped by Kapralik spieling relentlessly about what made Sly such a 'superterrific cat', to the extent that the story that eventually emerged ended up flooded by Kapralik quotes. But his usefulness diminished as the group's stature and independence grew. Was there a sexual element in David's relationship with Sly? The same kind of erotic frisson that attracted Brian Epstein to John Lennon? The crush that the Beatle found both flattering and amusing, which he used as a weapon to torment and tease the sensitive Epstein mercilessly? Certainly, by the time this 'Ken Roberts' element was introduced into the equation their relationship had deteriorated way beyond affectionate antagonism. Lurking within Sly's managerial situation there was a playful ingredient of closeness, and deliberate exclusion that went way above and beyond normal business practice. Spitefully, Sly was said to be purposely sabotaging concerts that would hurt David financially the most. While it was as if an infatuated Kapralik—rather than guiding and moderating, advising from a position of insider experience and rational judgement, was attempting to follow Sly into narcotic excesses to which his physical constitution and psychological mindset was ill-suited. Until it was taking him places he was no longer capable of going. When any 'great creator' reaches the top, David told *'Rolling Stone'*, 'the only thing to do is step back and lay back.' Yet he singularly failed to follow his own advice, until he was as 'blown away on cocaine' as the artist he represented, as strung-out as his client. Where Epstein had been a more cautious participant in the Beatles' chemical adventures, Kapralik had been less than reticent. And the situation only became more complicated as the dark indulgences of the Family Stone life-style reduced him to a snivelling, coked-out wreck. To David Kapralik 'the intensity of my relationship with Sylvester Stewart *and* Sly Stone was unbearable to me', stressing again his Jekyll & Hyde analysis of Sly's mindset. Later, Al Aronowitz delivered a verdict that 'David got very rich, but playing Jewish mother to a black pimp left him thinking about what every Jewish mother thinks about when her only son doesn't call her anymore. Suicide'. And it got to the point that on at least one occasion a distraught Kapralik, cut loose from his protégé, attempted to do just that. He tried to kill himself through a Nembutal OD in a Florida hotel room, the first of a number of failed suicide attempts.

Ken Roberts took a chance and took on Sly when no-one else would. Coming in clear-eyed, he was immediately able to make astute damage-limitation appraisals of the profit loss ratio, as well as the bewildering extent of the band's mismanagement. Despite their enormous success their finances were a mess, a short step from penury. So Roberts started in by applying a series of shock remedies. Taking advantage of the brief window between the success of "Family Affair", and the anticipation it built for *'There's A Riot Goin' On'*, he renegotiated Sly's finances by first extracting a hard-headed market-leading million-dollar advance per album (dependent on monitored continuing sales). Few other bands were in a position to demand such terms. Then he overhauled and rationalised the song-publishing rights, to Sly's advantage. At the same time, he was able to use the kudos this accrued as leverage to rein in Sly's worst intransigencies in ways that Kapralik was by now no longer capable of doing, and too compromised to even attempt. A new contractual arrangement helped ease David Kapralik out of his responsibilities, by gradually phasing his involvement out of the deal, thus tactfully maintaining a saving-face 'partnership' transition period. But the truth was that Roberts would eventually supplant David as the group's main facilitator.

The ace-in-the-hole that sealed the deal was the unprecedented coup of securing a three-night booking for Sly & The Family Stone to headline at Madison Square Garden, the giant sports and entertainment complex on New York's Pennsylvania Plaza—only recently reopened on the site since February 1968. Some 20,000 people turned out for the first triumphant performance, and the Family Stone played to sold-out capacity crowds for three successive nights—the Thursday, Friday and Saturday of the first week in September 1971. For the first time, they were using Gerry Gibson—the unsteady stand-in drummer to replace Gregg Errico. And the press was wary, running only mediocre or even damning reviews. Yet those three nights grossed $100,000, and proved that the band's incendiary choruses and its hands-on relationship with the audience were still more than capable of carrying the event. Then to the Philadelphia 'Spectrum' for a 2:30 Sunday afternoon concert with Earth Wind & Fire playing support. Both events sold out, and worked out……

****

This is the truth. Mainly. But these are stories that lurk in the haunting territory between memoir and fiction. The Family Stone were always a band mindful of the exquisite carnivalesque theatrics of Rock. The concert no-shows, the bust-ups, the gossip-garnering fables of excess. Sly was the star of his own inimitable show. He was also the glamorous protagonist of a doomed drama. With destructive forces both interior, and exterior. Touring is always stressful, on any band. They're living at a headlong pace, in free-for-all non-stop momentum. Coming off stage they have stretch limo's waiting to provide a rapid escape from lurking creditors with warrants or writs, and dealers with back-stage passes. All the 'people (who) offer you unnecessary strain…' (on "It Takes All Kinds"). They escape from venues in a welter of official and unofficial merchandising, the well-wishers, the narcotically well-endowed friends, visiting Rock legends, cocaine-cowboys, great-looking overnight party-girls offering sexual favours, regular girlfriends, touts, blaggers, record company people, publicists, the agent, the manager, the old friends, future friends, counterfeiters trading bootleg vinyl, those who've come to loot the rider, the odd journalist in a tour T-shirts chewing his pen. For longer-distance rapid-transfers there would be a private jet. But most times they travel cross-State in six limousines, three to a car. 'Every day's an endless stream of cigarettes and magazines' to Paul Simon, where 'each town looks the same to me, the movies and the factories'. It was a never-ending touring party lurching into menacing mauve sunsets, the pale glimmer of freeways unspooling through star-crazy nights, into strangely magical dawns. A tedium of ticket stubs, programmes, posters, comic-books, Dixie-cups and Cola cans, the debris of the road, the slur of exhaust fumes and stale bodies. It must have provoked odd introspections of those same four kids being trucked out across Vallejo to sing Gospel for strangers. The Stewart Four. Now this. Maybe the brakes will fail, their speed overcooking while cornering a bend on the Interstate? Down some terminal ravine. Detonating in the white-heat impact of igniting gasoline and a shrapnel of exploding auto-parts. How will that read in the press? How will they report that obit in *'Billboard'*, or *'Rolling Stone'*?

A band is uncompromising, and addictive in equal measure. A touring band is a pressure cooker of confined energies. The Family Stone was a large volatile unit of strong-willed individuals. Yet all the while, they're marooned in a desolation of beautiful boredom. Unhappy, and incredibly restless. Such a degree of stress and tedium was testing its irrepressible vitality to breaking point. By now, reading *'The Treasury Of Dogs'* or laughing along to Rudy Ray Moore stand-up scatology no longer worked. Instead, the tedium was first relieved—then exacerbated, by them all delving deeper into the alchemic synthesis of white powder, the novocaine for the soul, the escape clause. The first hit on the tongue that says 'yes' to another excess. But even those highs aren't as great as they used to be. It starts by making you calm. Then it starts making you not calm at all. It makes you edgy, and that's not so good. Bad vibes were poisoning Sly's party. It's becoming increasingly apparent there's a dark side to being spaced out. The come-down's are getting harder. There's paranoia lurking at the edges. Just a few years back it had all seemed so different. They'd been younger, fresher, keener. Now, perhaps comfortable numbness is a preferable option? Perhaps staying sat behind the KSOL DJ-console would have been a better career move? Building the city on Rock 'n' Roll…?

Behind it all, the growing tensions and seething ego-conflicts within the group were reaching breaking point. In the tangled yarn of their lives, micromotivations were leading to macrobehavior. If the band had become dysfunctional, it was because the power-structure within the group devolved primarily from Sly. He was in the loop for everything. He had to keep it going. Moving forward. Ensuring everyone got paid. Sly was the author of what happened, the guru and presiding genius. A wizard, a true star. That's a given. But if Sly had started out by aping Bubba's bad-attitude, now he'd become the real deal. No doubt about it. In his own mind, Sly thought of himself as the *baddest* dude around. Right on… so now, if you're fucked up, you might as well make it good. You might as well tick all the boxes. Sly, who once wanted to take you higher, was taking himself higher than just about anyone else. And that had led to a rift opening up between him and rest of the band. There was also friction between the two Stewart brothers, and another between them and their cousin Larry. First, Sly's cranky and quirky relationship with Freddie was deteriorating. Sure, 'Bro' Fred had his own ambitions. But, as with Art Garfunkel, there's no motivation to develop your own songwriting skills when your musical partner is bringing in compositions as crafted as "The Sounds Of Silence" or "Mrs Robinson"… or "Family Affair". Or—a closer analogy, brother Dave to Ray Davies of the Kinks. It was Dave who formulated the "You Really Got Me" riff which is one of the many candidates credited with originating Heavy Metal. It was Dave who lived the sixties life-style while brother Ray stayed at home and wrote about it. In any other group Dave would have been the acknowledged star. Yet in the Kinks he could only ever be the brother of the man who wrote "Waterloo Sunset" and "Autumn Almanac".

Same with Freddie Stewart. He was 'second in command'. But he was in Sly's shadow. He was a talented musician in his own right. A first-rate singer and guitarist. And a sweet guy. In any other band he'd have been a star. He *was* a star as an integral part of the Family Stone. But it was Sly who had the vision. Sly who had the creativity. And underlying their loving relationship there was part-jealousy. Part resentment. Part love and part-dependency. But Freddie… like Rosie and Vet, was family. Families tend to have issues. But they've already worked out ways of channelling those issues through the checks and balances of compensations and sublimations. They function as the family had always functioned. Even in extremis. When Bubba's growing influence over Rose led to her pulling out of engagements, Vet simply put on a blonde wig and stood in for her. Cynthia was not family, but even when she was emotionally entangled with Freddie, she was unwaveringly loyal to Sly. While Jerry and Gregg—while Gregg was still around, were happy just to smoke dope and drink Californian wine. It was a perfectly jig-sawed family, with each individual's own dysfunction fitting neatly into everyone else's. Yet there's something about the closeness of such a tight collaboration that becomes almost unhealthy. As if Sly had become vampiric, feeding off the faultlines of his group's skewed energies while at the same time choreographing them to enact his musical scenarios as his perfectly-tuned instrument. Sometimes, it's not wise to tamper too much with those internal stresses. Conflict within the group can be what gives it its edge. Conflict can sometimes feed creativity. By alleviating those tensions you might well lose the underlying creative element in the process…?

Only Larry constituted a genuinely comparable power-axis, an alternate pole. His was the fuzzed-up Fender that provided 'the bottom' from which the dancers just couldn't hide. But he had no close family connections, or long-term high-school friendship-relationships with the rest of the group. His contribution had never been less than significant. His bass-lines formed the vital foundation on which the collective sound was built, as clearly a defining identifier as Sly's compositions. But from the outset he'd never considered himself as anything other than a 'temporary' bass-player. In his own self-image he never saw himself restricted to just a rhythmically supportive role. He saw himself in a lead role… when the time was right. It was a situation that had been building, fuelled by the group's volatile sexual chemistry. Cynthia and Freddie were an on-going item, even though he was married to Sharon. Back when Larry had been into a relationship with sister Rose—he'd been simultaneously fleetingly involved with Sharon, behind Freddie's back! That resentment, that sense of betrayal still burned. Freddie and Larry had already got into a full-on fistfight. Barely months ago. Larry had even assembled his own 'crew', his own alternate entourage. Partly for protection from internal hostilities, partly as a gesture of independence.

This book is true, except for the bits that aren't. Truth is fluid. People remember it in different ways. And even when they remember it the same way they draw different conclusions, see different aspects and emphasises. But from whichever perspective you choose, 'Family' solidarity was splintering. Group biographies such as this relate to, and speak to something in all of us, something that is concerned with the ideas of belonging, and not belonging. The forming, rise, and fragmentation of a band allows us to compare and contrast, rehearse and recapitulate our own conflicts about friendship, loyalty, inclusion, and exclusion. The Family Stone—like any evolving organism, was never as coherent or static as their name implied. The Family that plays together was never destined to be the Family that stayed together. Where there had been chemistry, now there was a strong chemical imbalance. They lived in a constant muddle of alliances and counter-alliances, fallings-out and reconciliations. They lived—in short, pretty much like the rest of us. Only amplified to extremes. One of Sly's lackeys—JB Brown, recalls that 'The Family, to me, was one of the most hypocritical things that I had ever seen. I thought it was a sad situation because you respected them, thinking they are church and their religious thing was valid. But you watched them allow all this crap to take place… just the weirdest stuff you ever want to see.' But it happened. In a configuration without appropriate—or indeed, any boundaries, something beautiful had become irrevocably lost along the way. Tested, to destruction.

Gregg Errico had become the first of the original solid line-up to quit for other ventures. In the early months of 1971 he'd already psychologically 'severed the umbilical cord'. He'd reached the end of his tether. He knew it long before he did anything about it. It wasn't working. It was hurting. It was taking him nowhere. But it was his band. He'd been there at the beginning. He'd been part of its evolution, part of the struggle. How do you just walk away from all that? Until finally the negatives outweighed the positives, and he could take no more. He traded the rigours of the road, preferring to become producer and studio drummer, crafting albums by War's Lee Oskar and vocalist Betty Davis, while drumming for Carlos Santana, Peter Frampton, the Grateful Dead's Mickey Hart, David Bowie, and Weather Report. During the extended convoluted *'There's A Riot Goin' On'* sessions he'd been replaced by a succession of 'Funky Drummers'. And Gerry Gibson stood in at short notice. A Texan who'd drummed for Hanna-Barbera's cartoon band Banana Splits. He filled in... for a while. Meanwhile Sly auditioned, and passed over, a series of other drummers—including Buddy Miles, before eventually settling on full-time replacement Andy Newmark in 1973. Soon, there were other tremors of dissent. In early 1972—even as "Family Affair" reached a UK no. 15, Jerry Martini first enquired to Sly, then over Sly's head direct to the group's management, about royalties supposedly owed to him. Getting no result Jerry took it further, and initiated legal action against Sly in an attempt to get money he was owed, and to which he was entitled. Sensing trouble, Sly's reaction was to hastily draft in jazz saxophonist Pat Rizzo as a potential replacement should Jerry follow Gregg—with the implied threat that Jerry could very easily be replaced if he continued to display such disloyalty. Pat joined through a long-standing connection to JR Vatrano, in time to play the Madison Square Gardens' sets. As it was, the impending crisis was averted and Jerry stayed, with both Rizzo and Martini remaining in the line-up. Sly still knew how to be an artful user. A manipulator. If you could be useful to him, if you could help him, he knew how to be charming too. But all the while, incrementally, the background of negative vibrations was taking on more threateningly intense manifestations. Confrontations had become the order of the day, spilling over into more extreme incidents of vicious and random violence. Over what amounts to little more than a trivial misunderstanding, electro-boffin Vernon 'Moose' Constan quit after a beating administered by Bubba and Eddie 'Chin'. Sound technician Robert Joyce received another punishment beating after daring to contradict Sly. 'That was a terrible thing to happen because I loved Sly' he protested sadly, 'I would have done anything for him'. He left, to join David Bowie. On another occasion, back at a New York post-gig hotel party, Sly's crew sparked into a fist-fight with Three Dog Night—a band whose chart success was now eclipsing that of the Family Stone, on the back of their US no. 1 version of Randy Newman's "Mama Told Me Not To Come". Ken Roberts had to use all of his considerable diplomatic skills to smooth the situation sufficient to avoid punitive litigation.

    Whatever was left of the original group idealism limped falteringly into the new year. Despite the new managerial regime, the habit of no-shows continued. There was *supposed* to be a European trip for the 'Great Western Express Festival' in Bardney near Lincoln (28th May 1972), with Slade, Focus, Lindisfarne—and the Monty Python's Flying Circus team on the bill. Inevitably, it never happened, with *'Melody Maker'* reporting 'it became evident this week that Sly Stone will not be appearing, despite contracts having been exchanged.

The Beach Boys will take over Sly's bill-topping spot on Sunday'. Elsewhere, the seductively soft "Running Away" peaked at US no. 23 (in March), while the *'There's A Riot Going On'* album climbed the UK chart to no. 31 that same March (where it was issued with the added sales inducement of a free EP combining two hits with two previously unissued tracks), with "Running Away" following it into the UK charts, as high as no. 17 in May. A further single—"(You Caught Me) Smilin'", low-peaked no higher than a US no. 42, also in May. Such soft-core airplay album-extracts might have tempted wavering potential purchasers into misleading expectations of what to expect from the album. For there was precious little else by way of promotional activity.

Finally, by late 1972 all the badness came together, and the flashpoint tension between Sly and Larry Graham peaked over into critical mass. For Larry, it was already a case of—'when push comes to shoving', should he jump or wait to be putsched? It was Saturday, 25th November. The Family Stone played a poorly-received concert at the LA 'Coliseum'. Despite an impressive bill, fanfared by Los Angeles radio station K-ROQ as 'The Woodstock Of The West', it failed to draw upwards of 32,000 to a 100,000-seater stadium. The performance was tense with nervy equipment problems, part-imaginary—part edged by the tangibly hard narcotic force-field surrounding the band. To Greil Marcus, Sly's concerts had become his revenge-attack on an audience that had elevated him into self-loathing, observing 'Sly returned to the Pop arena at a time when black music had remade itself on terms he had defined, he damned those terms and invented new ones. He recognised the expectations of his audience, and moved to subvert them.'

Such head-games that had begun behind-the-scenes continued to simmer fractiously as they auto-piloted through the hits. But as ever, between this volatile group, the truth was never so simple. It was a band caught in several minds, which—given that most bands can barely muster evidence of one mind, must be considered an achievement in itself. Andy Newmark, by then replacing Gerry Gibson on the drum-riser, suggests that the only trigger it needed was that Larry had come onstage dressed up 'as flashily as Sly', distracting attention from the troubled troubadour himself. Maybe. Certainly, coming off-stage, the air between them was crackling with antagonism. Crisis. Suppressed hysteria. Blame for the poor show acted as detonator. And it briefly erupted into arms-flailing fists-flying violence. Later, surrounded by the multitude who piled into the dressing room after a show, Sly was at its epicentre flanked by the ever-protective Bubba and Eddie Chin. He was shaking hands, introduced to people he didn't really want to know, being congratulated and listening to their enthusiastic praise. While across its noisy, babbling crush of euphoria, was Larry's crowd. The two camps eyeing each other warily.

After the claustrophobic gig, it seemed good to be out of the venue. Now, while there's time to notice. The autumn breeze was almost warm. Fast-food night-cooking smells staining the air, tall shadows moving across the venue's canyon walls, the hiss of hydraulics as the tour-bus pulled away, into crawling lines of traffic. But back in the hotel foyer they found they'd brought the night back with them. Sly's entourage convened at the 'Wiltshire', with Jimmy Ford and Bobby Womack dropping around to join and 'party hearty'. Meanwhile, Larry's crew—with Vernon 'Moose' Constan and Robert Joyce, headed off for the 'Cavalier'. The elevator wouldn't come when it was called, they'd had little to eat since the last stop, the wired pall of knife-edged tension still palpable. By now, Bubba had convinced himself that Larry had contracted a hit-man to off Sly! It's some indication of the warped paranoia in the air that such an idea could even be seriously contemplated. And in the foyer the blame-game sporadically flared again. And a vicious fist-fight broke out between their rival factions, Bubba—brandishing a lethal walking cane, and Eddie 'Chin' Elliott's crew on one side, brawling with Graham's entourage on the other. It intensified. It got crazy, with no restraining crowd to intervene. It continued up the wide sweeping staircase and along the carpeted corridors. Larry and his new wife—Patryce, were seriously scared. He turned his head to left and right, wondering what the fuck to do next. It seemed there was less than zero chance of surviving this. Except to get the hell out of there! 'Running away, to get away, Ha! Ha! Ha! Ha!' According to some accounts, they were forced to scramble out of the hotel window to exit with their lives, clambering down into the lot beyond. From there Pat Rizzo was on hand to provide a high-speed get-away ride to safety. Larry had effectively quit. In fact it's difficult to imagine a more dramatic way of quitting a band, and—despite Ken Roberts' attempts to mediate, it was fairly obvious that this was the end of their road together. The rift was permanent. So Larry went on to form his own group, Graham Central Station… about whom there will be much more later.

The group's central cohesion, already irrevocably weakened, was terminally shattered. Unphased, Sly simply defined the abdication as 'the nicer the nice, the higher the price'. He merely seized the opportunity it presented for a line-up re-shuffle. Bobby Womack offered to step in as temporary replacement bassist. With cruel stoned-out humour, Sly told him he'd have to stand in line and audition with the rest. 'He was a trip' comments Bobby dryly, 'he was Sly'. After checking out Eddie Kendrick's bassist—Wornell Jones, Sly decided to recruit nineteen-year old Rusty Allen, who'd been working as Bobby Womack's stand-in bass-player. Rusty was auditioned live, in mid-concert, then toured intensively throughout 1973 with the Family Stone. Although nominally 'Family', these newcomers to the band—Rusty, Andy Newmark, Pat Rizzo, naturally saw things differently. Unlike those they replaced, they'd never experienced the co-operative fully-interactive phase of the Family Stone, they hadn't been there from the beginnings, so how could they? When they joined, when they became 'Family', Sly was already something elevated way above reality, he was already a star with an established back-catalogue of hits. He was less a fellow musician embarking in a mutual voyage of exploration, more an employer, an authority figure. From now on Sly would continue to tour and record under the 'Sly & The Family Stone' name, but each subsequent album would be made with a slightly different line-up, and would result in diminishing impact. The sporadic moments when the Family Stone managed to get their act together sufficient to play live, they remained a sweaty frenzy with a magic as potent as ever. But it was music torn from the warring bosom of a now terminally dysfunctional clan. And letdowns lurked around every corner…

It's 1973. The previous November Richard Nixon had won a second term, obliterating the liberal Rock star's choice, Democratic challenger Senator George McGovern with a huge majority. To Donald 'Field Marshal Cinque' DeFreeze of the Symbionese Liberation Army, it meant that 'a military-corporate coalition had taken over the United States in a silent coup'.

****

'The Family Stone' (2005—US. Director Thomas Bezucha)
>Nothing to do with Sly Stone, instead, this movie is a mawkish romantic meet-the-parents-style Christmas movie-comedy with uptight girlfriend Sarah Jessica Parker meeting Diane Keaton's New England family for the first time, with Claire Danes and Luke Wilson.

Sly Stone was Rock royalty. The Prince of Superfly. He was a star. He hung out with stars. Stars like Richard Pryor. Stars like Redd Foxx. And stars from other, higher constellations. Fortuitously, Pat Rizzo's uncle owned 'Jilly's Jazz Club' in New York. It was there, one night, that Rizzo was able to introduce Sly to Frank Sinatra. Posterity does not record what Ole Blue Eyes made of the encounter.

Terry Melcher was a young, hip, well-connected West Coast scenester, an industry apparatchik, a friend of Brian and Dennis Wilson, a colleague of the high-flying Byrds. As staff-producer for Columbia Records he—and his mother, were destined to be drawn into Sly's circle too. He was the son of fifties star Doris Day by her second husband—musician Al Jorden, although Terry took the surname of her third husband Martin Melcher. Terry was born 8th February 1942 in New York City, and made his debut as a singer, cutting several solo sides for Columbia as 'Terry Day'. When they failed to make waves, he moved behind the mixing desk instead, shifting his attentions to production with greater results, turning out a string of moderate hits in the sun-surf genre for artists as unlikely as Pat Boone and Wayne Newton, then for the Rip Chords, and—with future Beach Boy Bruce Johnston, as 'Bruce & Terry'. But it was his work buffing and tweaking eight best-selling albums for

Paul Revere & The Raiders, and then five for the Byrds, that established him as a name and a fixture in his own right.

Sly and Terry met through Kapralik's industry contacts. It was obvious. David had known Melcher, and stayed over at his Malibu home when he was in Hollywood. Sly and Melcher shared a mutual passion for autos, music, and hedonism. Sly had a collection of seventeen cars, including a low-slung one-seater yellow-and-black 1936 Cord, customised by the insertion of one huge fluffy pillow to serve as passenger-seating. He also had a Lamborghini—which was later confiscated by the IRS, and his big thirty-six-foot Winnebago motorhome. Even though whenever he did serious travelling he was chauffeured in stretch limousines! Terry lived in Beverly Hills, renting 10050 Cielo Drive, an enormous mansion with an immaculately manicured lawn. It was there he hosted A-List parties for the hippermost of the LA hip. And it was there, when mother Doris happened to be staying over, that the 'Last American Virgin' accidentally found herself in the same music-room as the notorious Sly Stone.

The one-time Doris von Kappelhoff, born in Cincinnati in 1924, had been a child star since the age of twelve, starting out as a dancer, until an autowreck forced her switch to singing. She'd then been a radio and dance-band singer during the forties, fending off the predatory advances of musicians while touring in the big-band era—and an American 'forces favourite' with her easy-listening 1945 record "Sentimental Journey". Her film debut came in 1948, replacing Betty Hutton who had pulled out of *'Romance On The High Seas'*, and from there she went on to star in a series of chirpy Warner Brothers movie musicals such as *'Lullaby Of Broadway'* (1951), the light comedy-Western *'Calamity Jane'* (1953), and as a strong independent shop steward in *'The Pyjama Game'* (1957), which all capitalised on the freckled peanut-butter girl-next-door cuteness she so effortlessly oozed. There was potent on-screen chemistry enlivening her romantic comedies with Rock Hudson too, their engaging arguments over sharing a telephone party-line lead to amorous entanglements in *'Pillow Talk'* in 1959, making her an even more massive star. Later, her 1964 success with *'Move Over Darling'* brought her back into the charts and renewed her celebrity for the new generation. But behind the image, all was less than sunshine. Her seventeen-year marriage to manager / agent Martin Melcher—credited as co-producer of *'Pillow Talk'*, among other of her movies, ended in tears. A strict Christain Scientist, he'd over-controlled and stymied her career, and when he died in 1968 she discovered he'd also mismanaged and embezzled some $20-million of her money. Also that he'd mistreated her son, Terry.

By 1973—when Funk briefly intersected her life, she'd quit movies after turning down the role of Mrs Robinson in *'The Graduate'* (1967), claiming 'I never retired, I just did something else'. But as she came down the sweeping stairs in her stretch-slacks and loose marine-blue blouse-top, and entered the music-lounge of Terry's lavish Hollywood mansion, there at the piano sat a star-struck Sly Stone. He instantly began picking out the tune of "Que Sera Sera" on the keyboard and—turning on his still finely-honed charm, told her how much he loved her recording of the song. 'I told her 'siddown girl'" explains Sly, 'I showed off, she liked that. Yeah, she's very aware. She's very wise'. She joined Sly, part-singing and part-humming along as he played, just as she'd shared a piano-stool duet with Frank Sinatra in their 'Young At Heart' movie. She was famously ungrand, and a natural comedienne, but knew how to play the star when it amused her to do so. For Sly, who was struggling with the same equation, her playful artifice amused him. Her conversation was littered with elements of her blonde ditzy screen persona, she'd use an affected 'darn it' or a tongue-in-cheek 'for gosh's sake'. She referred to herself as 'Dodo', while things she approved of tended to be 'darling'. Sly also saw himself as a mimic, affecting a posh English movie-accent when it amused him.

Although it went well, and both movie star and funk star were mutually charmed, the coincidental meeting only happened once. But as soon as word leaked out into the Hollywood community, ballooning rumours immediately exaggerated the unlikely encounter. Their meeting was soon hyper-inflated into an affair. Especially when it emerged that Sly was recording his own version of her most famous song. And he seemed to enjoy the mystification. At a time when Captain Kirk's interracial kiss with Uhuru on the bridge of the Starship Enterprise—in the 'Plato's Stepchildren' *Star Trek* episode, sent shockwaves through the television networks, Sly seemed amused by the very idea that such an outrageous liaison could have been consummated. Teasingly, although based on little evidence, and with no continuation, he refused to either confirm or deny the rumour. Even decades later, the question still surfaces in chat-room dialogue. Did they, or didn't they? While Doris would charismatically go on to enchant future generations, with even George Michael celebrating a love that 'shines brighter than Doris Day' on his Wham hit "Wake Me Up Before You Go-Go".

Even Melcher's mansion has achieved its own kind of gruesome notoriety through its unfortunate connection with another 'family'. On 9th August 1969 it had become the scene of the Manson Family's horrendous massacre of Sharon Tate, Jay Sebring, Abigail Folger, and Voytek Frykowsky. Although their *real* target is believed to have been Melcher himself. He had made the mistake of showing an early interest in Manson's audition demo's to the extent of visiting the strange tribe at their Spahn Movie Ranch to hear Charlie perform the songs in his natural setting. Manson sat on a rock and sang while strumming his guitar. The girls, all naked, sat in an admiring protective circle around him humming a background chorus. Before silicon breast-implants, before bikini-waxing, and probably without deodorant, that would still constitute a powerful inducement. Melcher became a target when he subsequently failed to follow through with a record deal, and was thereby considered to have betrayed Charlie's Rock star ambitions. His name appears prominently on their hit-list of targets. On the critical night the Mansonites were so stoned they failed to realise the switch, that it was Roman Polanski's entourage at Cielo Drive, not Melcher's. Nevertheless, Terry lived out the rest of his life in terror of retribution from the scattered members of Manson's family.

Chapter Sixteen
'Fresh'

'If you want me to stay...?'

Watching the final years of Sly's career is like watching a man fall from an extremely high building in very slow motion. Pop music is rarely built for posterity. But for some, history clings tight, and it can still kick loose. It's there on radio retro-spots. Movie soundtracks. TV-ads. It's downloaded as ring-tones. Alphabetically filed in the mega-store racks between 'Sam & Dave' and 'Supremes', or purchased through e-retailers, via what they term 'the long tail'. A back-catalogue shifting a hundred sales a week, a thousand a month—across years, across decades, eventually totals up to more than whatever happens to be the latest this-month's-big-thing. For Sly, that process continues. Hustler and dandy, urban outlaw and canny insider, self-promoter and self-destroyer, he has come to sum up the snarled values and skewed aesthetics of his time even as those origins become mythic, inaccessibly located in some increasingly frayed distance.

Sylvester Stewart—'this famous cat, this high-school gangleader-turned-whiz-kid, record-producer-turned-number-one-DJ, turned-gold-record-rock-and-roll-star' (according to *'Rolling Stone'*), his once-dream of wealth and celebrity had come truer than he could ever have imagined. And is there anything more corrosive than success? Socialist writer Irwin Silber observes that, 'unable to produce real art on its own, the Establishment breaks creativity and protest against and non-conformity to the system. And then, through notoriety, fast money and status, it makes it almost impossible for the artist to function and grow' (in *'Sing Out!'* magazine, November 1964). His open letter was addressed to Bob Dylan, but he's just as accurately identifying the cost that notoriety, fast money and status were extracting from Sly, and the impact it was having on his music. He was spending like crazy. The media gorged on its excesses. The Bel Air mansion had become a virtual prison for those holed up within. Sly even had rooms covered by a surveillance system of closed-circuit cameras. Throw in a pack of psychotic dogs compounded by a virtual arsenal of guns and it had become a scary place. But the devious deviant side of Sly retained a high threshold for horror, and for humiliation. With a control-freakiedom driven by paranoia, he'd traded his family for an entourage of acolytes. Using them as a buffer-zone against the increasingly clamorous demands of the outside world. Stephani, Sly's loyal secretary, later suggested that Sly was afraid of his own inner demons. Surrounding himself—first with the band, and later with his buddies, his version of Presley's 'Memphis Mafia'. All of it as a deliberate strategy to avoid ever having to be alone with his own noisy thoughts that refused to stay quiet. Who knows what monsters he was fighting? His coke-cocoon provided moments of dream-like isolation amid the aural carnage of distorted repetitive media-noise, as Sly retreated to an inner reality located somewhere several miles beneath its surface. The more his dependence became central, the more society receded until it reached that point, somewhere on the event horizon of reality, where it was completely eclipsed by what was taking place within the enclosed world of Bel Air. It had become society. Like Elvis holed up in Graceland. Like Jagger's 'Turner' in Powis Square. What went on behind its walls was something separate from the world. Like a dream come true…. or a nightmare.

Stephani recalls how she barely made it out of Bel Air Road alive. She called Ken Roberts—by then the band's acting manager (the 'Hobo Ken' who 'will be your friend, if you let him' according to Sly's later song), begging him to send a cab and $200. And she fled for her life. 'I had dissipated down to nothing, from no sleep, alcohol, and doing drugs. When I came home at the airport, my mother looked at me and started crying.' For Bobby Womack too, he told journalist Barney Hoskyns how 'as time progressed, I became paranoid at everything, I was always thinking I was going to get killed, that the Feds was gonna bust in on Sly. Later you give Sly one hit and he be lookin' around the room, *very* paranoid, you couldn't make no music with him. He be talkin' to you, but he ain't *there*. So I just said it aint no fun no more. I got to the point where I said 'I gotta get away from here'.'

There were still performances. Seldom tight. Always late. Time always a flexible concept. They showed up, and played the 'Frankfurt International Rock Festival' held at a German racing-circuit during a hot summer afternoon in 1973. Then journalist Rob Partridge reviewed their Sunday set at London's 'White City' in *'Melody Maker'* (15th July 1973), also described as a 'not-so-very-grand' night by rival music-paper *'Sounds'*. Then they performed a six-song set on 'Don Kirshner's Rock Concert'. But during a stopover back in Las Vegas, there are stories detailing Bob Marley & The Wailers getting thrown off a shared engagement. Booked to play the full seventeen dates of the Family Stone Spring tour, the Wailers—with Joe Higgs replacing Bunny Wailer, were dropped after playing only the first four shows. They went over so well that their applause and enthusiastic audience-calls continued well into Sly's set, upstaging the headliners. Left stranded in Vegas with no money, the Wailers nevertheless worked their way down to Frisco where they did a well-received live broadcast for KSAN-FM. The arc of their ascending star neatly intersecting, and in a direct relation to, Sly Stone's long diminuendo. At the LA 'Coliseum' Stevie Wonder opened the show for Sly, and kicked the Family Stone's collective ass. And the no-shows continued too. Soon after Pat Rizzo joined the line-up they were booked to play a return engagement at the Apollo. The legendary venue which had once been seen as so important to their status. But when Freddie failed to show up, Sly simply pulled out of the date rather than do it without him. Even the prestige and reputation of the Apollo by now failed to sufficiently impress him.

Towards the end of the year they were booked to play a sold-out Hollywood 'Palladium'. An audience of 5,000 had payed $7 each. Would they show? Won't they show? Would they show? Won't they show? Support act Papa John Creach of Jefferson Airplane's extended family plays for forty-five minutes. At around the 9:15 mark a Sly-influenced Kansas rock-soul band called Bloodstone turn in a torrid hour-long set, as tensions and uncertainties mounted. Until at eleven the house-lights went down—'yes, Sly is here' whooped the announcer, and the Family Stone troop on-stage. They began a little unsteadily, hit a groove with "Family Affair", then extended into a long unbroken piece that separated out into "Dance To The Music". Things were looking good. The audience were getting into it. Without warning Sly called a halt, told them he wanted to party, and they went into "I Want To Take You Higher". Much to the fans delight, they'd expected such a deluge of hits to come later in the set. They were wrong—it *was* later in the set. As the anthem peaked Sly promptly quit the stage. Only Andy Newmark remained going into an extended drum solo. Then he vanished too. There was some confusion, breaking out into the start of dissatisfied cat-calls, whistles, stomping and yelling... until Newmark returned, re-commenced the same solo a second time (exactly as Greg Errico used to do). After two minutes of it Sly and the band reappeared for two more choruses of "Higher". They waved the way artists wave after playing a full hard two hours. And vanished. They'd been on stage a little more than thirty minutes. There's a show-biz adage about 'always leave them wanting more', but surely that doesn't mean always giving them less? Less than either of the support acts? They'd showed. But only just. *'Melody Maker'* (November 1973) filed a review. Their writer called the event 'as big a rip-off as I've witnessed since I started reporting rock and roll'.

****

Yet Sly was still able to turn out one more funk classic. Buoyed by the critical and commercial wave established by *'There's A Riot Goin' On'*, the relatively lighter brighter *'Fresh'* album was never destined to sell in the same colossal proportions. In fact it back-pedalled a little, to climb no higher than US no. 7 in June 1973. The price of audacious early success is the heightened standard against which lesser achievements are judged a failure. And few careers illustrate this unforgiving principle more clearly than that of Sylvester Stewart. But while coolly received, *'Fresh'* was a leaner, warmer and more directly emotional collection that managed to pull off some amazing things. It represents something of an artistic, as well as a commercial step back from the edginess and self-indulgence of its predecessor. There's nothing here as viscerally raw as "Thank You (Falettinme Be Mice Elf Agin)". It's a more considered work. One in which new elements interact with glances back at what had gone before. It was the first record to be issued since the coup that had removed Kapralik, and—even as its name implies, *'Fresh'* also represented the start of a new recording regime. Yet the five-letter title apes *'Stand!'*, as though intent on rekindling something of those energies. Although unlike the collective gestation of that album, he'd begun by recording the songs with little input from anyone else—indeed, the first versions of "Skin I'm In" and "If You Want Me To Say" have their origins in the *'There's A Riot Goin' On'* sessions. And since those *'Riot'* tapes he'd been crafting material pretty much around his own needs. That the Family Stone were no longer the self-contained unit they had once been was obvious during those disjointed sessions. Now it was more formalised. 'He (Sly) played all the parts, except for the horns and stuff' session-engineer Tom 'Superflye' Flye told Joel Selvin. Tom—who had remixed the live Family Stone tracks for the *'Woodstock'* triple-set, as well as drumming for Don McLean and Lothar & The Hand People, explained elsewhere how 'Sly was kind-of the innovator of the track-by-track, build-your-record overdub style. When I was working with him, he almost never tracked more than one instrument at a time'. That way, 'he could play all the instruments himself, including drums… if somebody else could play it better, he would let them do it. If not, he just played it himself.' He would feel his way into a track by beginning with a basic metronomic rat-a-tat Funk-box rhythm, then build up from demo form to final version as instrumentations chimed together. Drums would go on last. Or sometimes not at all.

Many takes were wiped, re-recorded, or re-tooled. Certainly an earlier version of "If You Want Me To Stay"—as well as masters for much of the album, were completed in that way, before the maestro rejected them and re-recorded them completely with final mix-downs at the Sausalito Record Plant, blending in Cynthia's trumpet with Jerry and Pat Rizzo's saxes, Andy Newmark's live drums overdubbed last. At some point during those months Sly made enough alterations to change the entire tone of the record. However, the original tapes survived, and two versions of the album were soon circulating. There was some confusion. Sly delivered the finished tapes to Epic executives. Who were then astounded when he called in a second time with what he called the 'master tapes' of the same album. He didn't remember delivering the first set of mixes. By then, advance preview copies had already been distributed to journalists. Due to last-minute problems with the cover art-work they'd gone out in plain card covers, but these 'previous' takes differed in countless respects to the subsequently released official pressings. Those 'alternate' versions have since surfaced through bootleg channels. Everyone loves a little mystery, so why the wide variation here? Is it evidence of some sudden loss of self-confidence? A failure of his previously infallible commercial instinct, an uncharacteristic attack of nerves, uncertainty, indecision, loss of his intuitive compass? Perhaps, for the first time in a long long while, since before it had all begun, he'd started doubting himself, his own ability and discipline? But if it was greeted with some puzzlement on release, the album's stock has accumulated steadily over the years that followed, and across those years it has earned greater retro-approval.

Its seductively melodic 3:01-minute single "If You Want Me To Stay" became the last of Sly's run of Top Forty hits, making US no. 12 (and no. 3 on the R&B chart) in September. Music writer Miranda Sawyer goes so far as to call it 'one of the best songs ever recorded', before adding the qualifier that it 'manages to be funky, before trailing off into a jittery half finish'. The focus stays firmly on Sly, featuring him strongly on heavy-lidded vocals, his own layered backing tracks and drum-machine-generated rhythms, although Little Sister's background vocals are prominent. Sly also plays lead guitar—a Gibson Les Paul, keyboard and bass. The lyrics, delivered with a saturated intensity that's so cool it's almost-catatonic, are inevitably open to several interpretations. Most obviously, in the guise of an apology, he is persuasively arguing with his lover. She must allow him freedom to be himself, or he will be forced to leave her. It's a theme that supposedly had its origins as an explanation to his now-pregnant girlfriend—soon wife, 'Kathy' Silva after they'd had a spat. At the same time the message can equally be seen as a slap directed towards Sly's detractors. At those numberless writers and critics who were sensationalising his drug abuse and unreliability—he's saying, in paraphrase, stop all that press-sniping, or he'll be forced to quit making albums entirely. Sly's official 'Phattadatta' website adds a further layer of meaning. Sly wrote the lyric 'in which he asserted that he'd be gone for awhile', as a prediction he'd self-fulfil by withdrawing from music. The website claims that it was a deliberate part of his long-term strategy. Whatever, other versions of the song have since appeared by the likes of Red Hot Chilli Peppers, Etta James, and Eric Benet.

Carried by the guilty-pleasure pop-wise strengths of "If You Want Me To Stay", *'Fresh'* retains advocates who claim it to be Sly's last great album. Indeed, Miranda Sawyer lists it as one the 'Top 20 Cult LP's' in the *'Observer Music Monthly'* (21st April 1996). 'The cover shot alone justifies the price' she enthuses, 'exceptionally be-afroed Sly in skin-tight, studded, stitched leather two-piece and seven-storey knee-high stack-heels performing a flying karate kick... In the photo—taken by Richard Avedon, with Sly smirking like a lecherous Puck, he doesn't look like anybody's idea of the tortured artist.' Again, Stephen Paley was responsible for acquiring the celebrity photographer for the distinctive cover photo-shoot. A print priced as high as Sly's heels, at $2,500. Avedon, a former *'Harpers Bazaar'* and *'Vogue'* snapper, had built his reputation with portraiture of Marilyn Monroe in 1957 and President Dwight Eisenhower in 1964. He was there for Janis Joplin, Jimi Hendrix, Twiggy, a nude Aerosmith, and courtroom shots of the 'Chicago Seven' during the Conspiracy Trial. He was also the man responsible for the heavily solarised psychedelic Beatles poster photo-sequence, plus liner-inserts for their *'The White Album'* (1968). After the Sly sessions he would go on to snap Cher for the celebrated cover of *'Time'* (17 March 1975) and continued working right up to the brain haemorrhage that brought on his death 1 October 2004. Meanwhile, *'Rolling Stone'* debated the logistics of how the suspended mid-air action-shot of Sly Stone had been achieved. Wires perhaps? Or perspex sheeting? No—Sly was simply caught in mid-leap. After all—like Elvis, and attuned to the Bruce Lee martial arts fad, he had taken up karate!

There were vocal gymnastics too. After the sprawling tightness of *'There's A Riot Goin' On'*, *'Fresh'* might lack that unity—relying on some of the trappings rather than the substance, but as a result it can come over as charmingly disorganised. It might be no *'Riot'*, but it was his last serious attempt to create something genuinely subversive. His voice breaks up and out—more effectively than ever. He's seldom sounded in better vocal shape. Little Sister are strongly featured, adding flavour to the tracks. Dirty. Ravaged. Frisky. Wild. Happy Mondays learned everything they ever knew from this man. The lead-in track—and provisional album-title, "In Time" opens with programmed drums, before slipping smoothly into slow relentlessly syncopated Stevie Wonder overtones. A stalking teasing keyboard figure, a muted Pat Rizzo sax break and Sly's authoritative assured vocals, playfully dancing with shifting tone and emphasis, splitting 'procrasta' and 'nating' across two lines. "Babies Making Babies" manages to be both sorrowful, soul-searching... and yet still funky. Lecherous, but—Sly winks 'it's about grown-ups who are chronologically old enough to handle it'. With Larry not around (although his presence has been suggested, and he claims to hear himself on the album, perhaps by the incorporation of previously recorded backing tracks), the bass-line comes from Sly himself, or from Rusty Allen. 'Beneath the deceptively casual surface' notes Ian Cranna (reviewing the CD re-issue in *'Q'* August 1987), 'the record fairly teems with funky dynamics—especially Rusty Allen's busy bass, sneaking jazz and blues influences... all of which give the record precious personality and a curiously contemporary feel of purposeful street sensitivity.'

There's even the bizarre long-rumoured take on Doris Day's hoary old hit "Que Sera Sera (Whatever Will Be, Will Be)". Opening with the much-imitated Ketty Lester "Love Letters" piano figure, and carried by the clear heartfelt perfection of songstrel Rose at her finest, it's a polished diamond buried among the delicious junkyard arrangements elsewhere. Haunting, eerie—some might even say 'scary'. Originally written by Jay Livingston with lyricist Ray Evans for the 1956 Alfred Hitchcock remake of *The Man Who Knew Too Much* starring James Stewart and Sly's supposed amour Ms Day—she'd also used the song as the theme for her TV shows. Prior to Sly, the song *had* been covered in an October 1966 Soul context by UK-mod-clique favourites Geno Washington & The Ram-Jam Band—the hand-clappin' foot-stompin' funky-butt inspiration for Kevin Rowland's Dexy's hit. But those with an educated ear for the mouldiest of oldies would doubtless recall the High Keys tearing this sing-a-long relic to fast R&B shreds even before that—in 1963? Now Sly pours sulphuric acid over the fragments. So why "Que Sera Sera", what is the underlying wheeze behind Sly's first non-original recording since his 'Autumn' days? Some claim he's taking a secular song to church to benefit from Rose's deep gospel treatment, or that he's attempting to transfigure this most unlikely of vintage material in the same way that Ray Charles could alchemise show-biz dross into gold. Someone else suggests that because the good Lady Day had some claim to actually be a friend of Sly's, that this was done as a kind of jesting tribute? Don Was asserts that no, it's something entirely more personal. The lyric relates to Sly's own realisation that his career was out of control, so that what had been a song of youthful anticipation is now a song of bleak acceptance. There will be no future, but—hey, 'whatever will be will be'. It's acknowledging his surrender to destiny. But perhaps most simply and obviously, Sly recorded it because—as he told her in Terry Melcher's music-lounge, he remembered hearing Doris Day's transatlantic no. 1 hit version on the radio as a twelve-year-old kid in Vallejo, and he'd liked it…? Whatever, the Sly version could later be heard on the soundtrack of the Winona Ryder movie *'Heathers'* (1988).

Elsewhere, as a party album, *'Fresh'* might just about be one of the glummest party albums you'll ever encounter. There's a knowing self-awareness that runs like a thread throughout, with Sly dissecting his life with scary precision. Where previously he'd merged reality with the glammest fantasy to the point where it became difficult to tell whether or where he was being autobiographical, here he's self-observing each incision bare and unflinchingly. "Thankful 'n' Thoughtful" phrases it all with an explicitly confessional awareness of the precarious nature his day-to-day existence had assumed. Even the fact of waking up into a new day is, in itself, something of a source of wonder. A happy accident. He wakes Sunday morning and forgets to pray. Yet he should have been happy 'I still be there…'. Happy that, against the odds, to his own amazement, he's pulled out of his death-trip sojourn, and he's still alive. 'I've taken my chances—hah, I could have been dead', the threat of never waking up again is an ever-present possibility, 'something could have come and taken me away'. In the first line of *'Fresh'* ('there's a mickie in the tastin' of disaster'), Greil Marcus sees 'Sly's instinctive paraphrase of Nietzsche's belief that he who gazes into the abyss will find the abyss looking back, that he who looks too long at monsters may well become one.' And Sly Stone had done more abyss-gazing than most. 'But the mainman felt Sly should be here another day.' So the god he'd abandoned still had plans for him?—apparently. With only the deceptively sunny and melodic setting by way of contrast, and the gospel girl harmonies to hint at these more spiritual depths.

The next verse recalls how he'd 'started climbing from the bottom, oh yeah, all the way to the top'. And overnight—'before I knew it, I was up there'. But it's a high with a dangerous edge. A sentiment echoed on "Let Me Have It All" with 'closer to the top / looking down is quite a drop'. He'd lived the hippie dream, the showbiz dream, the revolutionary-liberation dream, the narcotic dream, and found them all wanting. Now, with every chord-change, he's staring into the bottomless void. As Greil Marcus observed, something is going on behind those eyes. Behind those obscuring shades. If you look carefully, deep in his eyes you can detect a much deeper damage than that self-inflicted by drugs. Something so tormented and helplessly frightened that he'd placed himself beyond reach. Yet despite being told 'I was dyin'', and he admits 'it ain't no joke…' he insists 'I don't want to go'. Music this confessional can be therapeutic, because it reveals its vulnerability. Because it is bare and unflinching, it motivates the strength to be strong. Until the very next track—the deterministic "Skin I'm in", opening with Sly using his larynx as an instrument to wail across a vocal range that defies most natural laws, and despite its neat strutting horn figure, it contradicts all of the previous thoughtful thankfulness for the fact of still being alive. 'If I could do it all over again / I'd be in the same skin I'm in'. Life is predetermined. So why waste time considering possible impossible alternatives? Whatever will be will be. The outcomes would be the same either way. Sly has shaped his own destiny. Others can only watch, dazzled by his virtuosity, yet baffled by his frailty. It's significant that it's only on these later 'back-from-the-abyss' albums, supposedly beyond the tipping-point of *'Riot'* and into his decline, that Sly's lyrics take on this unexpected maturity and personal depth. Nick Kent even asserts that three of these tracks— "In Time", "Thankful 'n' Thoughtful" and "If You Want Me To Stay", are 'arguably the best individual songs he's ever recorded, bursting with hip, sassy lyrical insights and cocksure musical savvy'. The early albums might deal with dance, fun, love, heartbreak, and a groupee, but only in the sense that Pop songs use such themes as subject matter. It's only now that he begins writing naked jive poetics and hip true confessions from his own perspective. Earning him his epithet 'Poet'.

Such a personal context invests substance in the other more brittle glimpses into his mental processes. The political soapboxing on "I Don't Know (Satisfaction)" loops back to the Rolling Stones' quote from "Run Run Run" on the first album (*'Whole New Thing'*). Over a mean surge of electro wah-wahing riff Little Sister chant a relentless nagging repetitive 'all we need is satisfaction, all we need is a little action, if it's only but a fraction'. They're even more strongly featured on the vaguely cornball "If It Were Left Up To Me". A track that almost amounts to the long-lost third Little Sister Stone Flower single. Its playful 'cha-cha-cha' and burlesque vaudevillian hi-hat flourish adding a touch of whimsy, as though the track had come adrift from some earlier career-phase, from *'Life'*. While "Keep On Dancin'" can only be an ironic self-referential comment echoing back to "Dance To The Music", the record that ignited his career, the song that none of the Family Stone had initially liked. But it's a more sinuously downbeat track than the kinetic explosion of its prototype, almost a recognition that you can't get back, irrespective of audience demands. And where the inspired original had been an egalitarian pass-around of vocal duties, this time there's only Sly. His exhortations to 'keep on dancin' seem a defiant denial of all the changes that had happened in the time-space since. Like the album cover-image, the Family Stone have been airbrush snowed into whiteness.

In total, there's a more sophisticated sound to *'Fresh'*, more concerned with the rich texture of the music than with catchy Pop hooks or choruses. Yet it can still be read as positioned to the correct side of introspection or self-indulgence, a bridge consciously uniting his two career-phases—or a 'hip limbo' between them. Taking the lyrical maturity and musical inventiveness of *'Riot'*, plus a measure of kick-ass funk from *'Stand!'*. John Ingham, writing in the *'NME'*, called the album 'one of the strongest and most positive musical statements of the year'. But is it the sound of a band waving, or drowning? Andrew Weiner, answering in *'Cream'*, attempts to have it both ways, this album, he opines, is not Sly attempting to fool the audience, but himself. It's his way to counteract the basic depression that still had a grip on his spirit. Certainly, this is bumpier funk, as nature intended, with album high points enough to fuel a dozen lesser careers. Wah-wah-funk pretenders like Jay Kay of Jamiroquai would drool over stuff like the impassioned vocal conversation of "Let Me Have It All". And ache to create something one-tenth as good as the nimble cocaine-tempos, frisky and playful vocal detours and voice-drops of "Frisky"- lifted as a single to peak at only US no. 79 in December. Sly's use of electronics, then in their infancy was equally impressive, for it vastly expanded the range of available textures, kick-starting the stylistic and ethnic fusions that have enlivened black music ever since.

But what of the earlier, rejected mixes? In what ways do they differ? The long groover "In Time" was added to the official release at a later stage. But the re-tracked "Let Me Have It All" lost its original wah-wah'd guitar and bass intro, while it gained new backing vocals and horns, and had the immediacy of the brilliant lead vocal reduced in the mix. The authorised "If You Want Me To Stay" had lost a bouncy guitar line, while gaining distant tinkling piano and behind-the-vocal organ chords. The re-tooled "Keep On Dancin'" had a new bass guitar intro, different keyboard parts, and an overall feeling totally unrelated to the rejected original. "Frisky" has its clever jigsaw intro toned down, a tricksy echo is added to the vocals, and it fades earlier. "Baby's Making Babies" has a new and inferior horn line and a stoned, stumbling feel that contrasts sharply with the crisp funkiness found on the bootleg edition. In its revised form "I Don't Know (Satisfaction)" similarly loses its sharpness and sense of space. "Que Sera Sera" has added extra Sly vocals with different emphases on the keyboards. The revised "Skin I'm In" no longer has a superb "High-Heel Sneakers" guitar towards the fade and the contrasting horn riffs are echoplexed with a mirror-like effect. "If It Were Left Up To Me" has extra horns, with Sly's vocal pushed up front. The original tapes feature a high rhythm guitar and no horns. They were 'up' and very optimistic in tone, all crisp funk, where the finished versions are muddier, more closely aligned to the soporific Sly of *'There's A Riot Goin' On'*.

Whichever version you prefer, but particularly on the original mixes, *'Fresh'* seems to be more engaged with the outside world, with a partial return to the buoyancy of sixties tunefulness. There were few artists as singular as Sly, and *'Fresh'* finds him as gloriously uncompromising as ever, with some of his best work at a time when it was least expected. To Miranda Sawyer, *'Fresh'* 'was the last good Sly Stone LP… sprawling, coke-raddled, spaced, suffocated, funked—the sound of a band imploding, unable to keep together when faced with Sly's 'problems'.' It's remarkable that even while running out of momentum he could still produce such a defiant swansong. If he could have maintained this standard for a couple more albums… but he didn't. If nothing else, this exercise was a strong intimation that the Family Stone would go down fighting, and—if necessary, in flames.

But that's far from an accurate reflection of the situation within the band. Andy Newmark had already ducked out—flying to London to sit in with Roy Wood, replaced in the Family Stone by Bill Lordan, who had some experience of drumming behind Jimi Hendrix. Yet—almost despite himself, Sly *was* still competing. Each album thus far had been packed with more ideas and original thought than most musicians assemble in an entire career. And each of them forms a significant contribution to how we got to where we are now. Flash forward, years later, and Simply Red cover "Let Me Have It All", while Andy Levine, singer with Maroon Five, who was only just *born* when Sly was hitting his commercial peak, happened upon "If You Want Me To Stay" when it was used on the movie soundtrack of *'Dead Presidents'* (1995). 'It introduced our generation to Sly' he admits, 'Sly's just the funkiest thing ever. He was completely unafraid to do whatever the hell he wanted.' The Maroon Five go on to record their own version of "Everyday People".

****

It's a weird contradiction. The early years of the seventies were already shaping it up to be a schizophrenic decade. The west was waking up from the hippie dream, so that—shadowed by the grey murk cast by the long comedown from the lofty expectations of the counter-culture, the vapid and sexless new decade was struggling to discover its own identity—which it wouldn't do fully until the advent of Punk. In the meantime, with the unitary force dissipating under the weight of money they were generating, the erstwhile-hippie bands were retreating into increasingly ridiculous postures, into roots country-rock, into tediously monotonous improvised dirges… or into rehab. In the meantime, inbetweentime, with the sharp end of Rock turning to albums, there were the un-pretty travesties of Glam and Glitter reverting Rock to monstrous cartoon 1950's satin-&-tat teenage moondreams. And the Revolution? it got wasted on the way. From the idealistic prequel that had begun with resistance to the uncomfortable truths of segregation and discrimination, it was undergoing a gradual, fitful death into a tawdry sequel of failure and delusion. Its long tail of righteous protest grinding down into a farce by now well-advanced into a final viciously blood-spattered grotesquery. Radical cells and their splintering factions were devoting more energy to hating, eye-gouging and outmanoeuvring each other than they did to waging war on the common enemy. As Francisco de Goya had termed it 'The Sleep Of Reason' is one that 'Produces Monsters'. The San Francisco-based Symbionese Liberation Army (the SLA) despised Huey Newton and the Black Panthers for having 'sold out'. They hated Angela Davis as a 'pig who had betrayed' her revolutionary comrade George Jackson. The Communist Party was 'all theory and no action'. They distrusted the left-wing counter-culture press, yet eagerly followed syndicated TV-bulletins for any updates on their own exploits, and were delighted when Walter Cronkite bestowed them a mention. White liberal sympathisers—such as Jane Fonda, who sought social change through legislative reform, were time-wasters postponing the revolution by dangling false hopes before the gullible masses. They dismissed the Weather Underground as 'phoney revolutionaries' because theirs were mere 'symbolic bombings' that killed no-one—apart from themselves (on 6th March 1970 an accidental blast tore apart a lower Manhattan townhouse they had turned into a bomb factory, killing three Weather Underground members!). While the NWFL—the New World Liberation Front, responsible for one-hundred bombings in the Frisco Bay Area between 1974 and September 1979, actually consisted of just two people, their campaign ending when their leader was arrested and charged with the axe-murder of his comrade/lover!

To distinguish itself from such lesser rivals, the SLA extended the middle finger of insurrection at all of the 'reactionary corporate-military pigs' of fascist Amerikkka—the three KKK's symbolising the Ku Klux Klan racism at the heart of its capitalist structure. They were led by ex-con Donald DeFreeze, who assumed the nom de guerre Field Marshal Cinque Mtume—which translates as 'fifth prophet'. And on Monday, 4th February 1974, eight of its mixed-race mixed-gender members abducted nineteen-year old Patty Hearst from the flat she shared with fiancé Steven Weed on the Berkeley campus. And the story broke big across the world. Held in a Daly City safe-house closet, Hearst was brainwashed—or, as they termed it, 're-educated' into joining their life of lawless danger. The actions she subsequently performed, the events she participated in—she later claimed, she did to survive. Even submitting to sex with two of the SLA 'soldiers'. Nevertheless, a series of powerful visual images define the brief arc of her terrorist career. Soon the poor little rich girl had become 'Tania'—a name adopted from Che Guevara's Bolivian comrade, and she was photographed brandishing a customised M1-carbine against the SLA flag, a seven-headed cobra. Feeding, and simultaneously inflated by the oxygen of publicity, she was coerced into taping demands, including the distribution of free food to the poor as a 'gesture of good faith'. A gesture that proved to be a disaster. In a West Oakland ghetto more than 5,000 people mobbed the distribution centre and stormed the trucks in a riot that left twenty hospitalised. California governor Ronald Reagan rejected further proposals. While 'Tania' was snapped again by the pre-CCTV security cameras in the act of what Trotsky called 'expropriation', robbing the Hibernia Bank in the Sunset District with a levelled carbine (on 15th April 1974).

With visceral inevitability, barely months into the campaign, Cinque and a clique of followers died in a bloodbath shoot-out, pitched against several-hundred surrounding CIA-directed Feds. Nine-thousand bullets were exchanged in an hour-long war before the stucco house on East Fifty-Fourth Street in LA's Compton ghetto was totally devoured in flame. On that same Friday 17th May 1974, Patty—with the bickering SLA duo Bill & Emily ('Teko & Yolanda') Harris fortuitously watched the unfolding incendiary drama on TV, in a motel adjacent to the Anaheim 'Disneyland'. By now, the underground press was careful to maintain a discrete distance from the SLA's horrific exploits. Their misconceived adventure was devouring lives, even as it was taking its heiress-victim's life and skewing it permanently out of shape. Yet the entire escapade, despite its terminal drama, was less a revolutionary insurrection than a media freak-show, a proto reality-TV event. If there was a point where the radical-chic separated from the radical, this was probably it. No Rock stars recorded tributes to the fallen SLA comrades. Dylan and Lennon had their own celebrity children uncomfortably closer, as potential kidnap-subjects, to Patty than they were to the terrorists. And the only SLA 'T'-shirts or posters were fun-ironic ones. The fully interactive link between Black Power and funk had been severed. There was no longer the necessity to 'Stand Up And Be Counted!' Muhammad Ali's grandstanding on 'The Mike Douglas Show' would prove less threatening 'Telling It Like It Is', and more endearing retro performance art. The social pressures, the angry psychological confusion and murky utopian dreams that had forced "Everyday People", "Don't Call Me Nigger, Whitey", "Don't Burn Baby"—and *'There's A Riot Goin' On'*, had evaporated.

Ultimately, Hearst was picked up by the FBI 19th September 1975—soon after her 21st birthday. Her arrest—at no. 625 Morse Street in Frisco's Outer Mission district, made the cover of *'Time'*—'APPREHENDED: Patricia Hearst alias Tania' (issue dated 29th September). She served two years of her sentence, before President Carter's act of clemency released her. By then, deeper in the weird symbiotic interplay between show-biz and terrorism, two dull movies were rushed out to fill the news-vacuum, recreating and packaging the escapade for its entertainment value. Paul Wedkos directed a TV-movie— *'The Ordeal Of Patty Hearst'* (1979) with Dennis Weaver, and Lisa Eibacher in the title-role. And Paul Schrader directed *'Patty Hearst'* (1988) with Natasha Richardson. In an even more disturbingly playful conflation of packaging and mass-marketing revolutionary-aspirations as consumer-entertainment, Hearst herself played a deranged terrorist in John Waters' *'Cecil B Demented'* (2000). While in a related dimension the legacy of the SLA combat unit became the template for new Euro urban guerrilla movements, in the dour shape of the kidnap-happy Red Brigades and the Baader-Meinhof Gruppe.

Strange and confused days indeed. As for Sly, his personal life was also in turmoil, with a gathering storm of dark arts and private pursuits hounding him, both personal and professional. He had always been more used to defining the times than he was simply moving with them. But ironically, at this point of his greatest influence-reach, he was scarcely in shape to make new music. With *'Fresh'* he had used a juggler's dexterity to keep the balls in the air, to demonstrate that he was still a player. But the album's success did little to staunch speculation that, for Sly Stone, the game was nearly up. Dogged with problems, lost in a cloud of clear white artificial energy, he no longer seemed in shape to even bother trying. The *'New York Times'* dated 28th September 1973 reports that he had been arraigned in Santa Monica for possession of drugs. It was the inevitable culmination of a long-drawn-out process. One that had begun on a farcical note, with an absurd incident in New York, prior to a Madison Square Gardens concert. Police were summoned to investigate reports of menacing behaviour involving Sly with a gun. He was arrested outside the

Harvey Radio Company off Fifth Avenue wearing his full Afronaut 'Space Cowboy' stage-outfit—only for charges to be dropped when the 'threatening weapon' in question turned out to be a cap pistol. 'If you gotta pistol' Sly explained dismissively, 'you gotta pull it out'. Adding more ominously that 'as soon as the white cats start winnin' all the fights with the Indians, then it'll be the black guys doin' somethin''. It escalated to more serious incidents, when the crew were arrested in Sly's Winnebago on the Santa Monica Boulevard. 'We used to ride around in his motorhome' Bobby Womack told *'NME'*, 'gettin' high and writing songs and making music. We would ride all up in the hills, and he wouldn't never stand still, he'd say, *'keep driving'*!' (October 1984). The police eventually took note, and pulled his Hippiemobile over. He bluffed, blustered, massaged the truth. On that occasion, he got away with it, it never came to court.

Later, the police went in mob-handed to raid the Bel Air mansion on the pretext of a (probably spurious) phoned-in report of a corpse being found on the property. It was a well-premeditated sting operation. Once there, with only Gideon and her peahens cackling a warning, the police were filing in beneath the hand-carved wooden gargoyles mounted over the doors, and beneath the spectacular French crystal chandalier that hung in the foyer with its dead bulbs no-one could be bothered to replace. Then they took full advantage of the opportunity to rip the place apart, with predictable results. Substances were discovered. This time there was no escaping the courtroom. But once there, the theatrics merely continued. Bubba claims that during a break in the hearing itself he escorted Sly to the 'shitter'. Returning moments later to check him out he found Sly in the cubicle snorting from a vial of cocaine. Bubba—a man not entirely unused to the hazards and consequences of bucking the legal system, was shaken. Sly's unperturbed response was that— 'hey, hang tough, I've employed a highly-paid legal team precisely to enable me to enjoy such indulgences—haven't I? Isn't that what I'm over-paying them to do? If that expensive lawyer is not the dude who can ensure that I can do this, then he's not the right guy for the job. So find me someone else, someone equal to the requirements of the task'. For anyone else, such a feeling that status purchased invulnerability might be seen as a symptom of increasing detachment from reality. Yet, in this instance, those highly-paid lawyers did the do. They were able to extricate him. Despite his openly irresponsible adventurism Sly got away with it. He was given a year's conditional probation, dependant on him attending a special detox programme which—according to California state law, was intended 'to give the experimental and accidental drug user a second chance'. Although his escalating drug use could neither be described as experimental nor accidental.

But worse was to come. While the band was away touring, they were unceremoniously evicted from 738 Bel Air. Rent had been set at $12,000 a month, plus $25,000 going into an escrow account every three months (a bond held by a third party, pending fulfilment of certain conditions). From the start there'd been problems, and payment defaults. Legal proceedings were lengthy and involved. Now it was over. Characteristically unphased, Sly and his party simply flipped cross-continent, into New York's high-rent Century Building. A big aerodynamically futuristic skyscraper with modified Art Deco twin towers, it was located on 25 Central Park West at the point where it intersects 62nd Street, overlooking the green luxurious expanse of the upper west side of Central Park in the city's most architecturally distinguished residential zone. The Dakota building is a near neighbour. Built on the site of the 'Century Theater' opera house where Isadora Duncan had danced and Sergei Diaghilev had showcased his fabulous Ballet Russe, the Century had opened in 1931— designed by developer Irwin S Chanin and Jacques Delamarre as a sister-building to the 'Majestic' which had opened the previous year. The wonderful Fay Wray—abducted Patty Hearst-style and carried up the Empire State Building by *'King Kong'* (1933), had been an earlier occupant. Now, in this latest chapter of its esteemed history, the Family Stone entourage colonised a ground-floor apartment complex.

They'd troop into a 'U'-shaped lobby set around a landscaped rear court, through the street-level retail space which lay beneath its towering 65-storeys. There, Rose and Bubba—by then an item, shared a suite next to Sly and Kathy's. Daddy KC also had his own apartment in the same building. Ken Roberts too. Yet Sly was unimpressed with the opulence, grandeur and history of his new abode. He immediately set about demolishing a dividing wall to create space sufficient to construct a new 16-track studio. Miles Davis became a frequent guest. There was a brief re-union with Viscayne Maria Boldway. Tom Donahue—from Sly's 'Autumn' days dropped by, and stayed over. He'd reappeared on the scene in time to suggest that Tom Flye would be a useful guy to have around the studio, and pointed Sly in his direction. Once the full crew were established there, things continued pretty much as they had done before, the apartment made claustrophobic with heavy wooden shutters over the windows, and Sly existing on a diet of pizza and sushi. He'd developed a passion for sushi. Although every now and again a concerned Daddy KC would come up to cook dinner for whoever happened to be there. In truth, Sly was already well into what has become his long disappearing act. As compelling a story as any from show-business Babylon. Others died and became martyrs, or got married and had kids, settled down into respectable acceptance, sort of… everyone but Sly, who simply detached from it all.

Conversely, by 1974, it was bass-man Larry making all the right commercial moves. Even prior to his edgy escape from the Stone Family he'd been knee-deep in dialogue with a band named Hot Chocolate. He'd already proposed himself for their album production job, so, once unleashed from Sly's dark dramarama, he found himself with a fully-rehearsed band at his disposal. He threw himself in with them full-time. Punningly retitled after Manhattan's Grand Central Station, the years of dancin' to Sly's music was rammed deep into their opening project—the eponymous album *'Graham Central Station'*. With a support roster numbering David 'Dynamite' Vega on guitar, ex-Billy Preston keyboardist Robert 'Butch' Sam, and Hershall 'Happiness' Kennedy, underscored by percussionist Patrice 'Chocolate' Banks—it was a propulsive aggregation of expertise and flashy Sly-alike funk. But there's an alternate interpretation. That Larry's input to the original Family Stone project had been so integral that their ideas had become inseparable. With Larry's throaty bass technique acknowledged as prototype by legions of bassists, and a quasi-'Little Sister' vocalist in Patryce, allied to the combination of Willie 'Wild' Sparks live drums with electronic 'funkbox' drum-machine, it could be argued that the album was less a new start, than a continuation of what Larry had been responsible for co-creating in the first place. Vernon Gibbs writing in *'Melody Maker'* noted that 'with his new album… and his first national tour, people are getting a chance to see just how essential Graham was to Sly's sound'. From the socially relevant "People" clear down to slurring the word 'standing' into 'shhtandin'' on Al Green's "It Ain't No Fun To Me"? But if the new band was a cloned extension of the Family Stone, it was a smoother Sly-lite, lacking the rough-edged unpredictability. While Gibbs conceded 'Graham has obviously learned much from his years with Sly' and 'the group demonstrate their affinity for the Sly sound', the end result was up-beat, 'his stage sound is razored sharp and equals the best rock bands.' Whatever the perplexing genealogy, in the conspicuous absence of new Sly material, the album quickly rose to a US no. 48 in February, while their single "Can You Handle It?" made a US 49 in May.

Chapter Seventeen
'Small Talk'

'Getting Down, Just For the Funk Of It...'
(Funkadelic/George Clinton)

Sly's private life was becoming increasingly frenetic, and publicly derailed. When he wrote 'things seem so hazy, and facts appear to glide'—in "Remember Who You Are", he was surely describing what it was like to be in the news more for his drug-busts than he was for his music. Jerry Rubin had finally decided that 'to live inside a media image is like a prison. Living for your image means sacrificing your true self.' Sly was discovering that too. Jerry died 28th November 1994—oddly, ironically hit by a car while jaywalking in a LA street. Transgressing to the end, yet so mundane an exit... while Sly merely messed up an appearance on Dick Clark's 'American Music Awards' show, incoherently doing his 'Sly Stone' impression on-stage, and then insulting Karen Carpenter backstage. When she tried to introduce herself as a fan of his music he tetchily responded 'Who is this bitch?'

He fared better when he co-hosted 'The Mike Douglas Show' (17th July 1974), where he found himself in an uncomfortably combative situation with Muhammad Ali. In the screen-shots Sly sits to the left of a smartly-suited Ali. He's wearing wide-flared trousers and a blouse decorated with astrological crescent moons, slashed to the waist. But despite such visual flamboyance it was Sly who found himself in the position of moderating figure in the fierce debate. In a deliberately provocative tirade on race and politics, quoting his Nation of Islam mentor Elijah Muhammad, Ali accused whites of the extermination of Native American Indians and racial-guilt for slavery. Sly scored a ripple of applause by interjecting that 'what Mike (Douglas) is trying to say' is that 'there's a way to say all of this without having any animosity'. Ali berates Sly for 'laughing and giggling' in his attempt to lighten the hostility, and accuses all who disagree with his point of view as 'you all hypocrites'. When Sly attempts to defuse hostility further by pointing out 'there's enough black people to help black people', Ali becomes by turn patronising, and teasing, accusing Sly of 'selling out'.

In a curious zigzag response to the way the new cultural wind was blowing, the liberal consensus was now embracing Ali. It was not so long since that Ali was provoking disapproval by deriding his one-time opponent—Joe Frazier, as a 'house-boy' and an 'Uncle Tom' for what he saw as Frazier's insufficient insolence towards the white elite. Whites had then looked to Frazier as the man to button the lip of the garrulous black braggart. Now, in an ersatz act of expiation those same racists who'd wanted the uppity Ali locked up as a traitor, rapidly discarded Frazier in favour of craving any opportunity to be seen simpering by Ali's side. Considering the strange circumstances, Sly acquitted himself well. Earning more applause by suggesting that Ali himself had benefited from white largesse, and chose to live in an opulent white enclave—gently goading 'where do you live my brother?' As a visitor to Ali's New Jersey home himself, he knew only too well. Yet the spectacle of two such gifted and iconic figures scoring points and tearing each other apart was less than edifying. An irony compounded by the fact that Sly had given his son the middle name Ali as a tribute to the boxer. Interestingly, a bewildered third corner of the heated four-way discussion was endured by Democrat politician Wayne L Hays, shortly before the Ohio Congressman was brought down by the revelation that he was retaining a former mistress on his payroll as his secretary.

Further revealing insights into Sly's mindset came through press interviews, which assumed the habit of devolving into theatre-of-the-absurd performances. There was a promotional visit to London, where Sly managed a 'lackadaisical' press conference the morning following his 'White City' concert. Held in a stuffy Kensington hotel-room with the curtains drawn to exclude daylight, it divulged little—'talking just is not his bag'. Even taking the initiative of visiting Sly in his New York den was little more rewarding. During a meeting with an Italian journalist Sly spent the entire time on his knees, scraping dog-shit off the carpet, to the utter distraction of the writer. Then he slapped a *Rolling Stone* interviewer around the face with a wet cloth. To Michael Watts 'he's a put-on artist', with 'a quick mind, twisting sentences and thoughts, and delighting in the aftermath of confusion, then slow recognition, that surrounds his audience'. To Nick Kent, 'if one ultimately got to him, the dialogue would invariably stay weighted down in a ditch of stoned jive gobbledegook... doped-out dada-speak, the kind of infuriating babble Sly Stone appears to consider an incredibly cool smokescreen device with which to thwart reporters and their penetrating questions'.

Michael Watts must have caught him on a good day, 'draped politely across the bed, answering questions with civility and genuine humour, saying 'pardon' a couple of times when he thinks he's mis-heard, asking courteously for a glass of iced water, cracking jokes with sure-fire disc-jockey laughter'. He asked Sly about his lyric-writing method, and he replies, very composedly, 'I get more thoughts sitting on the toilet'. Watts parries 'that's the best place to think', to which Sly continues 'well, it's the best place in the world to get rid of waste! And that undoubtedly gives you room to think'. In the ensuing laughter, someone comments 'that's life', which sets Sly off riffing a dialogue, careering impromptu into what Watts describes as a 'kind of dee-jay hipster rap, throwing rhetorical questions at himself'. It starts 'what's funny?' 'Life.' 'What's Life?' 'A Magazine.' 'Where'd you get it?' 'Round the corner' 'How much is it?' 'Fifteen cents.' 'That's funny.' 'What's funny?' 'Life.' (*'Melody Maker'* 5th May 1973). As the interview winds down Watts unwisely comments that he'd expected to find Sly more messed-up. In response 'his face bursts like an obscene sunflower into that wicked leer. 'I'm not fucked, man' he gasped in mock-pain. Then his eyes roll up into his head and he falls headlong on the bed, as if a half-dozen Quaaludes have just got to him. We all go along with the fun…till the next time…'

'Melody Maker' journalist Chris Charlesworth also endured the misfortune of being assigned an interview with Sly around the same time. An encounter that would provide an intriguingly darker glimpse into the state of Sly's head. Charlesworth recalls how a girl from the PR company took him to meet Sly at his Central Park West 'Century Building' apartment. He was told Sly 'didn't like hotels' but 'I strongly suspect that the reality of the situation was that 'hotels didn't like him'. They were met at the door of his apartment by a member of Sly's entourage, who informed them that his employer was 'getting ready'. They waited quite a long time, at least twenty minutes, and drank coffee. The living room of the apartment was airless, quite dark and very untidy, as was the adjoining kitchenette. Someone hadn't attended to the washing up. When Sly finally appeared he was dressed from head to toe in full stage regalia, a striking beanpole figure in a white leather outfit adorned with fringes and tassels, skin-tight pants and huge white boots with rhinestone studs everywhere, the whole ensemble topped off with a huge black aureole of Afro hair.

According to the published article, 'he extended a hand but looked elsewhere. Who could tell where his eyes focused beneath those silver shades?' ('Sly Stone: Super Sly', June 1974). He looked sullen, as if doing an interview with 'this white-boy limey' was not at the top of his priority list for that day. He was also, as Charlesworth now feels free to confide, 'high as a kite, by turns giggling, morose or tetchy, and he was constantly fooling around with this very beautiful, slightly Indian looking girl with incredibly long jet-black hair, almost down to her knees, who was also dressed in a white leather outfit. She sat next to him on the couch with her arm around his waist, and he was constantly touching her thigh. I was told she was his fiancée. They certainly made a handsome couple. Conversation was difficult. Sly either babbled unintelligently or answered in monosyllables. He was also very intimidating, deliberately so, antagonistic, trying to score points. Attempts by me to discover who played what on his records were treated as an insult—he played everything, drums, guitar, keyboards, brass, the lot. How dare I suggest otherwise? The 'Family Stone' were used solely for live work. He didn't want to discuss the reasons why so many of his shows had been cancelled in recent months, though he did mutter something about 'bad promoters'. He seemed to want to impress his girl, and she giggled a lot'.

But things rapidly developed from awkwardness into downright weirdness. 'After about fifteen minutes he stood up and said, 'I need to go to the toilet' and disappeared with the girl into another room for a full twenty minutes. I could hear a lot more giggling and what sounded suspiciously like her achieving orgasm. It sounds funny now but it was actually very embarrassing at the time. The girl from Sly's PR Company just didn't know what to say or do. She kept apologising to me and all we could hear was this giggling from the next room, and we both knew (or guessed) what was going on, but of course neither of us could bring ourselves to mention it. It didn't help that Sly's minder was sat with us, which made small talk even more difficult, so we sat in silence while I pretended to read a magazine. I should have written about all this in my story but I hadn't the nerve in those days, and in any case I didn't think *'Melody Maker'* would print it.'

Sly eventually re-appeared alone, looking rather pleased with himself but still unwilling or unable to communicate properly. When Charleworth asked him where he wrote his music, in the studio or at home, he repeated the joke he'd made to Michael Watts about writing 'on the toilet where you can't go'. In fact—from this point on, he managed to insinuate the word 'toilet' into replies several times, each time accompanied by a fit of giggles. The minder, sycophantic to a tee, joined in. Their behavior, to the journalist, seemed 'like a couple of five-year-old boys. I distinctly recall asking Sly what contribution bassist Larry Graham, then making a name for himself with Graham Central Station, had made to his records and he replied 'none'. As it happened I'd interviewed Graham fairly recently and he'd insisted he played bass on Sly's records. I thought it unwise to bring this up.'

At length the disjointed interview not so much drew to a close, as petered out. Monosyllabic, unintelligible answers, a contrary stance and uncontrollable fits of giggles were hardly the stuff to inspire interviewers. 'We left together, the PR girl and I, and if she apologised once she apologised a hundred times as we waited for a cab. It wasn't her fault that she was saddled with the rudest artist in the world.' Prior to meeting Sly Stone, Charlesworth had considered Neil Diamond 'the most disagreeable interviewee I ever had the misfortune to come across. Sly Stone was even ruder than Neil Diamond. What's more, I believe he *did* go and have a shag halfway through my interview with him. At least Diamond waited until after the interview was over...'

'He'd made some great music in his time' concedes Chris Charlesworth in retrospect, 'but I thought he was an asshole. That's why I wasn't surprised to read much later that Sly's career had gone down the pan. That he'd been jailed for drug offences and that he was broke.' Meanwhile, the beautiful 'fiancé' Sly was... intimate with, at the midpoint of Chris' interview turned out to be 'actress' Kathleen 'Kathy' Silva. Born Catalina Silva Morena she became Kathy, or sometimes Kathleen, for the sake of her acting career. She'd been cast as Ione in two 1970 episodes of CBS-TV's heart-warming show *'Family Affair'* (oddly enough). Then achieved her most high-profile role in *'Soylent Green'* (1973), the Charlton Heston action-movie based around SF-writer Harry Harrison's dystopian novel *'Make Room Make Room'* (1966). In the over-populated futuristic Manhattan of 2022 women came as part of a rented apartment's fixtures and fittings. But Kathy was not *the* furniture-girl who links up with Heston's Detective Thorn to discover the sinister secret of the food they eat ('Soylent Green is people!')—that part was taken by Leigh Taylor-Young. Kathy is merely credited as *a* furniture-girl, one of the decorative beauties in the group scenes. Nevertheless, appearing—even briefly, in a movie directed by Richard Fleischer, with Edward G Robinson there—who died just nine days after shooting completed, on 26th January 1973, adds a certain cachet to her admittedly slight CV. By the time of its drive-in screenings she was hooked into Sly's inner circle.

Sly met seventeen-year-old Kathy at a party at Billy Preston's spread. She was beautiful, open, with Hawaiian eyes. Sly and Billy jammed together, while Kathy half-imagined he was singing to her, until he swiftly... shyly? glanced away. He offered to arrange her a ride home, in his Winnebago, but the 'moveable feast' wound up back at 783 Bel Air, where Sly... ignored her. Going off to play music while she slept on the chaise longue. Soon, both Kathy and her sister April were vying for Sly's affections. And they were both recipients of his carnal attentions. Then Sly and Kathy were together in the swanky Century Building. When the Family Stone flew out to engagements Sly and Kathy travelled in first class elitist splendour, safely insulated from the world, while the band flew coach-class. Or they'd fly in helicopters or private jets, including an eleven-seater owned by Elizabeth Taylor. Kathy fell pregnant, and Sylvester Bubba Ali Stewart Jrn was born just two months before what was to become their garishly opulent Madison Square Gardens nuptials.

In the weird configuration of his brain, the 'Sly Stone' side was urging 'I ain't never gonna give no woman that much action'—as he'd confided to Bobby Womack, 'I'm nasty, I don't give a fuck'. While the 'Sylvester Stewart' hemisphere harboured a long-term admiration for Daddy KC and Momma

Alpha's enduring marriage, the fact that they'd stayed together for all those years. A part of him was inclined towards the same. Kathy preferred legitimacy for their son too. Sly had grown up as a component of a warm close family unit, and the part of him that wanted the same won out. So, at the start of a brief—if high-profile marital arc, on 5th June 1974, Sly and Kathy were married. They went down to the Manhattan City Hall to get the licence. In through the big columned archway, past the armed guards, up the wide marbleised staircase to the echoey corridors and office-space above to register. The next step was, the Family Stone were playing another New York concert. Why not combine the two occasions? Tie the knot on-stage at an opulent sell-out celebration in front of 21,000 paying guests! One could be forgiven for harbouring just the sneakingest suspicion that this most unhinged of public displays—kitsch myth-making worthy of Las Vegas cabaret, was more to do with a *'Hello'*-style PR-boosting exercise designed to counter all that bad-press than it was to do with the solemnity of marriage. But after all, Sister Rosetta Tharpe—of the Church Of God In Christ, had married her manager at the Washington DC baseball stadium in 1951, in the presence of 25,000 paying guests. More recently Tiny Tim married his 'Miss Vicki' Budinger, live on Johnny Carson's *'The Tonight Show'* in December 1969, and drew in some 45-million viewers! Even Sly's chosen venue was already ghosted with memory-echoes of the great and the good who had appeared there. While Sylvester Stewart was still an aspiring school-student in Vallejo, a flirtatious Marilyn Monroe oozed "Happy Birthday Mr President" to John Kennedy here on 19th May 1962, the Rolling Stones recorded their live *'Get Yer Ya-Ya's Out'* (1970) album on this stage 27th/28th November 1969, the famous Joe Frazier versus Muhammad Ali 'Fight Of The Century' took place here 8th March 1971, Billy Preston had joined George Harrison, Bob Dylan, Eric Clapton and Ringo Starr here for Rock's first great charity live-aid extravaganza—'The Concert For Bangladesh' on 1st August 1971, then Elvis broke the house attendance record by playing to 80,000 people here in June 1972. Now here was a spectacle to rival and out-shine them all.

As a 'Garden Party'—neither in Madison nor square… or a garden, there was magic in the air. An instrumental fanfare of "Family Affair" was played in place of the traditional 'Wedding March' as the event began. Prestigious fashion-design brand 'Halston' had been brought on board to provide the wardrobe. Synonymous with the hedonistic glamour of NY superclub 'Studio 54' Roy Halston Frowick's designs were chic clear across the social spectrum, all the way up to the pillbox-hat Jackie Kennedy wore to JFK's inauguration. Now the Halston tag was on the fifteen-hundred dollar outfits for each band member, and on the ostentatious Afro-gowns enveloping the willowy black-chic model brides-maids. Nothing was too much for Funk's own wedding of the year. As the fanfare ended, *'Soul Train'* host Don Cornelius—presiding as

MC, and TV-journalist Geraldo Rivera stepped forward in their role of ushers. Stephen Paley—Epic A&R man who did much of the wedding logistics, was best man, much to Freddie and Bubba's annoyance. With BR Stewart, Bishop of the Bay Area 'Church Of God In Christ' performing the service. After the wedding ceremony was complete, Sly joined the band at his Yamaha DX7 for the main performance. Then the 'Starlight Room' of the Waldorf-Astoria hosted the lavish reception. Daddy KC—wearing tuxedo and bow-tie, and Momma Alpha attended. Andy Warhol, who took meticulous care to be seen at all the right places, turned up with his 'Factory' crew. Lorna Luft—Judy Garland's daughter, was among the guests. And the event became the celebrity splash of the season. Sly's own Elvis and Priscilla moment. His own David and Victoria Beckham moment. Surviving film of the show provides irrefutable evidence of a gloriously surreal event. And it yielded the full anticipated publicity-deluge. *'The New Yorker'*, *'Time'*, and *'Newsweek'* all devoted breathless column-inches to the wedding. But it was to be the last high point of Sly's career arc. The final instalment of his American Dream turned sour.

And despite such lavish coast-to-coast exposure, the return-to-arms LP that should have been the recipient of all that gushing goodwill proved to be only a moderate success. Pete Wingfield suggests that 'by Sly's sluggish standards—it's not that long since the last album, *'Fresh'*, maybe married life has given him a creative surge...?' (*'Let It Rock'*, November 1974). But there's scant evidence of such a hoped-for creative resurgence. Issued in both standard stereo, and also the new wonder four-speaker quadraphonic format, *'Small Talk'*, in August, was an album for which the term 'lukewarm reception' might have been coined. It reached US no. 15, without generating a major hit. The first single to be spun off it, the obligatory 'Genius is Pain'-themed "Time For Livin'", peaked at a US no. 32, also in August. It might have served the purpose of injecting some much-needed energy—if only comparatively so, into the album, yet it became the Family Stone's final Top 40 single. For Sly, such underperformance only served to underline both a commercial and artistic decline. The second single, "Loose Booty" was even better, but fared worse. It got no higher than no. 84 in November. A blaring horn-driven workout, it was structured more the way you expect an up-tempo Family Stone track to be structured. It also benefited from an inspired deep-voice gospel-hook—'Shadrack Mesech Abednigo', a biblical chant playfully spliced into a call-and-response shout-back. To church-going families—like the Stewart's, who know their Bible, its recitation was a tongue-twister game. Brook Benton had already told the story in his early-sixties hit "Shadrack"—a tale from the Book of Moses about the trio who are cast into the fiery furnace, only to emerge unscathed due to the purity of their faith. Perhaps it's also a conscious reflection of Sly's childhood memories of Daddy KC putting Bible-verses to little improvised tunes for the amusement of his family?

For the album itself, Baby Sylvester Bubba burbles over the opening of the title track, a device Stevie Wonder would seize on to incorporate into "Isn't She Lovely" some two years later, as attentive Daddy Sylvester comforts 'shhh' in a touchingly sentimental vignette of paternal domesticity. The baby-sobs gurgle on, to form a motif, as Sly and Kathy's doting laughter and dialogue continues barely audible behind the minimalist lyric. The 2.01-minute "Mother Beautiful" has more play-in hints of contented domesticity, as strings (from Sid Page, formerly of Dan Hick's Hot Licks) seep in, drawing crazy spirals, to add saccharine. Sly oozes 'Who's the reason for my Daddy's grin', with the song-title providing the answer. There's a previously unsuspected tenderness here. Even the cover-shot seems to be a charming family-album shot with Sly—in a white rhinestone jacket, and baby Bubba cradled in the crook of his right arm, and Kathy's waist encircled by his left. Reinforcing the 'Wedding Album' tie-in. But examine the body-language signifiers more closely, and there are other interpretations to draw from it. Sly's joyous smile is directed upwards, away from them both. Baby Bubba's and Kathy's adoring attentions are both firmly focussed on him. Sly is the centre of attention, not the 'baby-makes-three'. Although—on face value, the album appears to be a homage to mellow family unity, and the lovey-dovey lyrics that hit you in the solar plexus seem to be delivered from his very core, it could equally be seen as subsuming those new elements in his life as raw material for his music. Unlike, say—John Lennon's own hymn to new fatherhood, "Beautiful Boy", or even Liam Gallagher's clumsy, if sincere "Little James", in such *'Small Talk'* tracks it's not the song's supposed subject—the baby, that you see, it's predominantly a reflection of Sly himself. Sly trying on paternity as his latest role. He is drawing them into himself. The focus, as on the cover, is most firmly on Sly. The reverse cover shows Sly narcissistically sprawled—presumably naked in a dishevelled bed, the sheet rumpled up around his waist. He sports an Afro which—unlike Billy Preston's touring version, is real.

No other personnel are pictured, despite sister Vet joining on keyboards and vocals. Andy Newmark was in the process of returning to session-work, so both he and Bill Lordan are on drums, laying a mellow funk groove. Rusty Allen provides bass. Sly himself is credited as songwriter, producer and arranger. But the lyrical content is slight, riddled with fragments of word-play that lack cohesion. "Say You Will" urges us to 'give a damn' around a dancing horn, then loses it as 'Jimmy cotton corn' is slur-pronounced 'chilli con carne', with the voice going where it pleases. Even when demonstrating he still possesses a voice that's all of itself, exhilarating in its wayward intensity, its focus tends towards the drowsily druggy, which makes it sound first breathless, then shrill, as if his mouth is intent on swallowing his own words. There's the line about 'a hippopotamus is way too fat for me', which seems to be there more for purposes of rhyme than reason. Elsewhere, "Can't Strain My Brain" has something of the unsettling creepiness and hip inertia of a *'There's A Riot Goin' On'* revenant, only for it to be sweetened with a dose of sawing strings. The second vinyl-side opens with Sly inviting the band to 'yo, punch in' on "Holding On", but it loses momentum through the turgidly dull "Wishful Thinkin'" and "Better Thee Than Me" which leads in with more laughter and tuning-up sounds. Although it soon hits a pleasing groove, it's a groove that doesn't really take it anywhere. And again Sly has scored string around the organ break. Finally, "This Is Love" is a brief oddity. Almost another Little Sister showcase, a Doo-wop track come adrift, a 'shuna-doo-wop' chorus... and little else. At least the Viscaynes could work a memorable melody around such a template.

Certainly it provides further evidence that no two Sly Stone albums—to date, are the same. And, as a celebration of love and laziness, *'Small Talk'* has its advocates for greatness. Reviewer Tom Nolan confusingly considers that 'this record is more to be appreciated in the mind than enjoyed by the ears' (in *'Phonograph Record'*, August 1974). It's possible to interpret the album as evidence of a more mature, more streamlined variety of funk. Or as the third part of a trilogy that had begun with *'There's A Riot Goin' On'*, reinforcing his dexterity with razor-creased electronics allied to caramel-smooth soul, songs sculpted from stone-cold funk that swerve into raw discoism, distinctly different from what had come before, yet in their way, just as influential. As such, typified by programmed drum-tracks set off by the mosquito-bites of highly syncopated electric piano, guitar and bass-lines, with lyrics that are wailed rather than sung, they set the bar for the popular funk outfits who would stake out the 1970's. And, as Sly battled to reinstate his credibility, the ripple-effect of this trilogy of albums would extend out beyond R&B.

****

'This is the End... Beautiful Friend...'

Soon after the Madison Square Garden event, Rose slipped away less conspicuously and married Bubba. While 'Newlywed' Sly and Kathy were 'still checking each other out' (according to "Family Affair"), but their happiness and domestic harmony were fated not to survive for long. For five months, in fact. The idyll they projected on *'Small Talk'* had the potential to be good for Sly, if not necessarily good for his music. Perhaps, if the scenario envisaged and projected by the album had been fully lived out, it could have saved him? Providing a much-needed 'time for giving... time for changing, rearranging...' Or perhaps it was already too late. Either way—despite his optimistic declaration that this was 'no time for breakin' our own fairy tale...' it was doomed not to persist. Instead, Kathy and baby Sly Jrn became part of his life-style, not an alternative to it.

And married life did little to interfere with his clubability, he was seen hanging out in New York's 'Mikell's, a club on Columbus Avenue and 97th Street where he jammed with Hugh Masekela. Bizarrely, he also guests on former-Byrd Gene Clark's underrated solo album *'No Other'* (Asylum/ Elektra, 1974). One of the principal songwriters on the first suite of Byrds albums Gene was also the first member of the group to bale out of the line-up, supposedly over his fear of flying. Since then his career had been only sporadically successful despite pioneering innovative moves into country-Rock with his Dillard & Clark Expeditions, a move that later reaped mega-millions for lesser practitioners such as the Eagles. Yet, signed by canny impresario David Geffen, there were high expectations for this album project. Johnny Rogan, author of the acclaimed Byrds biography *'Timeless Flight Revisited'* (1998) observes that 'Sly Stone was in attendance during part of the session (of title-track "No Other") and his presence seems to have permeated the music in subliminal fashion'. Gene Clark's own biographer John Einarson puts a slightly different spin on events, according to him Sly 'came in with an entourage of about forty people'. They brought in 'all kinds of cocaine' and took over the studio, ordered thousands of dollars worth of food from the restaurant next door—and charged it all to the A&M's tab. Whatever, it *is* an awesome track. But tales proliferate spontaneously around Sly Stone. He was a mythic figure. Even avant-folkie Tim Buckley enjoyed fabricating a story that he'd once disguised himself and worked as Sly's chauffeur. Of course, it wasn't true, but it made for a good story.

Perhaps Kathy failed to take notice of what was going on around her. Perhaps she hadn't read what was going on between Ike & Tina Turner, or Ronnie and Phil Spector? That when you're involved with a musical obsessive, you'll always come second to the music. That when you're hung up on a drug-user you'll always come a very poor second to the high. Perhaps she believed that things would work out differently for she and Sly. That she was bling-blinded by the intensity of it all. Caught up on a high of a different kind. Whatever she'd thought, whatever she'd anticipated, she was wrong. Hopefully, there was no physical abuse… although there are stories. And cocaine can induce uncharacteristically violent behaviour. Such actions might even be in keeping with Sly's pimp persona, but there's never any justification for it, not ever.

There were a series of shocks. First, soon after the mixed fortunes of *'Small Talk'*, there was another move west. Although he maintained the lease on the Century Building for occasional use, the extended Family Stone took up residence in Novato, in Marin County, on a hill on the west side of San Pablo Bay directly opposite Vallejo. This new control-central was an old-country mansion complete with circular staircase and adjoining stalls for the horses, all set in 43-acres of grounds. But for Kathy, it soon became a kind of gilded prison where she had everything she could possibly need, except a role. The second shock came when she discovered that Sly already had a daughter, Sylvetta Phunne Robinson, with Cynthia (a situation Sly might have been thinking of when he wrote 'a woman has a baby cute / illegitimate to boot, / who can say it isn't right?' on "Crossword Puzzle"). Of course, Kathy knew there had been other women. It's said that while still at High School Sly was heavy petting—and probably more, with fellow Viscayne Maria Boldway. That later he'd had a thing with Carol Doda, a white topless dancer in Frisco's North Beach. Then there had been Nita from the Vegas residency. Later there'd been Olenka Wallach, a Brazilian girlfriend out of Sausalito, with whom Sly had yet another daughter, Novena—from 'Novi' which means 'nine' in Portuguese. She was living in Mexico as what Bob Dylan called a 'mistreated mateless mother' (on his "Chimes Of Freedom"). But once Kathy knew about the situation with Cynthia—part of the Family, a constant component of the touring entourage, it was different.

Then Gun—the pit-bull that had been a fixture in Sly's life since the Bel Air days, attacked Sly Jrn. Gun had already attacked and killed Sly's pet monkey. Much to Sly's entertainment and amusement he'd also fought and seen off any other canine with the temerity to encroach on his territory. Now, when Gun noticed baby Sly toddling unsteadily across the hallway, he merely saw another potential rival. Think of the Stephen King novel/movie *'Cujo'* (1981/1983)—the lone woman battling the killer devil-dog. It was like that. Kathy faced off Gun, yelling her defiance, even when baby Sly's head was fast in its jaws. The nightmare incident resulted in the severely mauled infant needing 120 stitches. Half the skin was ripped off from his shoulder up to his left ear, which was nearly torn off. Kathy had been alone in the huge house. Sly—as always, was in the studio. In the Record Plant complex that he'd named 'The Pit'. Located at 2200 Bridgeway a little way from downtown Sausalito, north of San Fran, it officially opened October 1972—at $140 an hour, but within its wooden tree-shaded exterior he'd customised it to his own requirements, incorporating sleeping facilities so that he could stay over and never have to leave while working and reworking his endless never-completed sessions. It was even equipped with 'black lighting' to make the cocaine on the Flickinger mixing console more visible. Looking something like a mail-order warehouse located along a nondescript row of industrial buildings, it was the studio where the Grateful Dead recorded *'Wake Of The Flood'* (1973), and Fleetwood Mac' spread *'Rumours'* (1977).

But for Kathy, this final atrocity—compounded by Sly's absence at the studio, stressed to her the need to escape from an intolerable situation. On 30th October, she filed for divorce. What had started out in such a blaze of publicity, was dissolved in private, 'you can't leave, 'cause your heart is there, / but you can't stay, 'cause you been somewhere else!' Perhaps there was no room for a third party in the narcotically-bonded marriage of Sylvester Stewart to Sly Stone? Whatever, Kathy's career scarcely benefited from the publicity generated by her celebrity marriage either. The former Mrs 'Stone' picked up a role as Judy in a 1976 episode of James Garner's detective series *'The Rockford Files'*, then added her alluring beauty to a single 1982 episode of 'CHiPs', as Rhoda in the California motorcycle-cop series. To be generous, there may have been many other less well-documented appearances that diligent research has failed to uncover. Or perhaps that's it? Sly Junior was later reported to be living in Las Vegas, while Sylvetta Phunne would give Sly his first grandchild.

In the expanding ripples of other Sly-world connections, during the closing months of the same year Jerry Martini had begun hanging out with Carlos Santana. Also formed in San Francisco, bringing their fiery latin salsa percussions to the counter-culture stew, Santana's career had closely ghosted that of the Family Stone. They'd debuted at the Fillmore, signed to Columbia, and played the Woodstock Festival—their "Soul Sacrifice" collected onto the triple live album alongside the Family Stone's incendiary set. Their million-selling albums *'Abraxas'* (1970) and *'Santana III'* (1971) charted within the same time-space as *'Stand!'* and *'There's A Riot Goin' On'*, after which a similar loss of direction began to become apparent. Now Jerry and wife Lynne co-wrote "One With The Sun" for Santana's US Top 20 album *'Borbolleta'* (December 1974). Coincidentally Sly's former girlfriend Debbie Sara King was by then Mrs Santana, married to Carlos, thereby setting up a comeback connection for her father. Since his 1940's hits with material like "SK Blues", Saunders King had virtually retired from music following an early-sixties spell in San Quentin for heroin possession—in favour of church-work. Now he guested on Santana's *'Oneness'* (1979) album. And there were other successes from former members of the extended Stone Family, Graham Central Station's LP *'Release Yourself'* hit a US no. 51 in October (spawning another hit single with "Feel The Need"), while Sly & The Family Stone's own single—"Loose Booty", only managed a lowly crawl into the lower chart-zones, although it was able to claim some vindication when it was extensively sampled by the Beastie Boys on their "Shadrack" track for their *'Paul's Boutique'* CD (1989, an album that also sampled "Brave And Strong" for its "Three-Minute Rule").

To everyone capable of taking notice, not only had the Sly & The Family Stone project lost its once-irresistible magic, but Sly was so happily into snorting drugs he no longer seems to care. Everything was falling apart, as if he'd worked hard over the past four years to destroy everything he'd built up in the preceding two. The sets the band performed didn't vary as much as the audience might want or expect, barely altered from their 'Woodstock' highpoint. Following *'Fresh'*, the first full tour in two years included a homecoming gig at the 3,000-seater Berkeley Community Theatre—down from selling-out the Cow Palace. They played "Que Sera Sera", but scarcely touched on *'There's A Riot Goin' On'* or other more recent material, orientating instead towards familiar hits. As if *' 'Riot'* had been a bad dream best forgotten' muses Greil Marcus, who was there. Surely, since *'There's A Riot Goin' On'* scored so heavily in the charts, there must have been people who wanted to hear it live? Maybe it was too demanding to reproduce accurately on stage? Or maybe Sly was simply no longer much interested in performing, and it's easier to ignore rehearsing newer material with the band. And if audience expectations had been conditioned by what they'd seen in the 'Woodstock' movie, why disappoint those expectations? Far better to compress it all down to the minimum amount of time, for the maximum amount of money. So they wound up endlessly replicating—in concert, the set they'd done in the movie. Freezing the moment in time both on celluloid, and in performance, on stage each night. Their taste for presenting those hits in medley-form could also get a little tiresome when they'd already been seen several times before. The line-up changes had weakened group cohesion further. The sense of shared camaraderie that had powered them through the early days was nothing more than a memory. The expanded and altered personnel were technically faultless, but the original line-up had possessed a chemistry subsequent aggregations couldn't hope to match. By now there were mortuaries with a better record for live appearances than Sly & The Family Stone. And the concerts that did happen had more to do with economics than they did with music.

At last even Ken Roberts' patience had been stretched to breaking point. Although he lacked Kapralik's artistic vision, his hardheaded business instinct had created opportunities for Sly where all others had failed. There had been a brief trio of Spring concerts designed as a test run to work in new drummer Bill Lordan, including a concert at the Dallas 'Moody Coliseum' basket-ball arena, a mere twenty-five miles from Denton. Despite being attended by local family members, and with a fine mixed-race Swamp-rock Blues-band called Wet Willie playing support, the Family Stone set was poorly rehearsed, a show less about style and more about substance(-abuse), and it provoked a disappointing response. 'I wanna play right' Sly pleaded to the audience, 'or it's gonna be blamed on me tomorrow'. The situation was brought to a head in late 1974 by a projected concert at the 'Washington Capitol Center'—oddly with Graham Central Station playing support. When Sly didn't show, Larry took the stage, and—in the grand tradition of some Hollywood B-movie, he pacified and completely won over a 25,000-strong audience baying for Sly's blood.

For Roberts, it proved to be the final rift. The fan-base had eroded. Career-momentum had been blown. Live bookings had steadily plummeted since the turn of the decade. Promoters were increasingly wary of taking the chance of booking a band that might miss the gig entirely, turn up and refuse to play, or be incapable of playing by flaking out from drug-saturation. All three conditions were regular occurrences. Promoters demanded an up-front bond to cover no-shows, figures between $25,000 and as high as $50,000. In his own defence, Sly claimed his reputation for unpredictability was undeserved, that he'd been misrepresented by the press. That there was collusion between promoters and transportation operators, deliberately creating delays and obstructions so they could claim the bond. Whatever, concert takings bottomed. Apathy, and acute frustration fell like twin curses. Now Ken Roberts' relationship with the Family Stone had run aground too. Ken no longer wanted to be Sly's friend. Even Clive Davis was going through testing times, and was in no position to offer supportive advice. During 1973 he was subject to internal label investigations which accused him of appropriating $54,000 of Columbia's cash to decorate his apartment, another $13,000 to rent a Beverly Hills home, and $20,000 for his son's bar mitzvah! The charges led to litigious tax complications. Eventually the affair was settled on a plea basis, and he went on to greater successes as president of Arista, them BMG where he oversaw the development of Justin Timberlake and Christina Aguilera. His involvement with the 'American Idol' reality-TV phenomenon then found him instrumental in the irresistible rise of Kelly Clarkson.

Meanwhile, the syndicated newspaper 'Memo From Miller' column datelined 15th December 1974 carried a Sly-tale of such cartoon proportions you suspect... surely, it must be fiction? Bad, but not in a good way. The band were due to play a charity concert at the campus of New York's St John's University. Inevitably Sly showed up over an hour late, but worse was to follow. He'd only managed to stumble his way through the first three numbers when inexplicably he stopped, and walked off stage. No reason. No excuse. And once backstage he kept walking, heading for his limousine intending to execute a rapid getaway... only to find the car-pound so gridlocked it was impossible to move. By now the promoters—who were paying $16,000 for this single performance, were in hot pursuit to find out what the hell was going on. Discovering his escape route blocked Sly—in full concert regalia and stack-heel boots, began haring lickety-split up, out of the auto-park, with the gaggle of increasingly irate pursuers behind him—watch that Stone GO! Until they all wound up, strung out like some surreal 'Benny Hill' sketch, chasing around the college football field yelling and waving. Eventually Sly managed to re-connect with his car and make good his escape. For a band to have begun with such a bang, to end with such a whimper... to wind up in comic farce, is somewhere way-beyond irony.

Yet there were still reported sightings. Into 1975, Sly & The Family Stone began what was intended to be a residency at New York's Radio City Music Hall. Booked into the 6,000-seater venue for eight nights, opening Thursday 16th January with Kool & The Gang taking to the stage first, it drew an official audience-count of 1100, an attendance running from less than one-third to barely an eighth full. Lost in surrounding emptiness, those attendees looked to be even sparser. The atmosphere was grim, to Freddie there was 'no purpose, nothing happened, there was no magic'. The *'New York Times'* gloated 'we already have a candidate for 1975's Pop-music rip-off of the year' (18th June). They'd gone from audiences of 26,000 at their Madison Square Garden peak... to playing Radio City to a mere hundreds. Conclusive evidence to all concerned of the band's terminal deterioration. Following the disastrous engagement the outfit had difficulty even scraping together sufficient finance to get themselves home. Ken Roberts stumped up Jerry's fare back to California. There was nowhere else to go. It was their final concert. They'd collapsed in upon themselves like an imploding star, super-heavy with the weight of fame, drugs, and colliding ego's. When they separated, it was with the tacit agreement that the band was over. Sly & The Family Stone were dissolved. In fact, the *real* band, as such, had not existed for some time. During seven years they'd toured relentlessly, playing three tours through Europe, they'd sold out Madison Square Garden a record fourteen times, scored seven gold albums, two platinum, one double-platinum and one triple-platinum album, played every major TV show including Ed Sullivan twice. But as Sly writes (on "The Same Thing"), 'when you play, you pay...'

For this once-great band, it's all over, all their promise and thrill squandered. A poignant Cynthia Robinson later confided to Joel Selvin 'I never quit the band. I just stopped getting calls for gigs'. Seldom had a star departed the world-stage so abjectly, so diminished by a failure of self-control. If Robert Johnson—'King of the Delta Blues Singers', sold his soul to the devil at the crossroads in Mississippi in exchange for his finger-picking genius, Sylvester Stewart sold his soul to a different kind of demon, for a different kind of genius. And this was pay-back time. For The Family Stone, this was the end of history. There had been few precursors to Sly Stone and his band, now they had imploded in a trail of funk, drugs, and tears... Leaving just another messed-up Rock star in its wake.

In a kind of global symmetry, during the weeks that followed, the TV screens were documenting the final straggling pull-out of American personnel from Vietnam, the helicopters clattering up and away from the roof of the Saigon embassy building. Headlined in the *'Daily Mail'* (30th April 1975) as 'frightened, abandoned and waiting for its fate... this is Saigon as thirty years of war reach a climax with a Dunkirk in the sky'. As if quoting Jim Morrison the page bore, in huge bold black type—'THE END'. Within the week the South Vietnamese Government had announced its unconditional surrender to the Vietcong. And as the Family Stone set about reconciling themselves to living the aftermath of their Family-career, the war that had defined and shaped the sixties protest movement, its campaigns and set-backs, punctuating its growth and intensity, was also over, and the United States began the long trauma of adjusting to the humiliation of defeat.

****

'Now Do-U-Wanta Dance...?'

All of this was backgrounding and sharply delineating the months that, for the first time after his succession of successes, Sly Stone was tasting failure. The story of twentieth century music is the blackening of America, and then the world beyond. Sly's strengths had always been to universalise his music. To crossover stylistic, social and racial divides. From the day he was born, through the streets of San Francisco, out into the mean world of demanding predators and sinister places, he'd shape-shifted through a series of life-phases in which people had regarded him differently. With the Viscaynes—he and Frank Arleno had been the only non-whites in the line-up. As a DJ he'd spun records by English-invasion bands alongside the more regular play-listed R&B. With 'Autumn' he produced Pop-Folk and white proto-psychedelia as well as Soul-Dance. The Family Stone were as well-received at Woodstock as they were playing at 'The Apollo'. He'd mocked and effortlessly ridiculed the restrictions that sought to cage him. If there's a moral to the Sylvester Stewart story so far, it's that rules—social and musical, are there for the breaking. He'd more than just ridden the changes, he'd created them himself. To Richard Williams 'it's sometimes forgotten (but not by musicians) just what an effect Sly Stone has had on rock music since the appearance of "Dance To The Music" in 1968—in fact, his unique adaptation of the rhythmic techniques of James Brown now permeates every nook and cranny of rock, R&B and jazz. In the latter category, particularly, there are people playing licks he invented without even knowing his name. It's not too extreme to say that he redefined the concept of the rhythm section to include every instrument and voice in the band, and in the course of five years he's refined that approach to a very sophisticated degree' (*Melody Maker* 12th May 1973).

It had taken two years for black American soul to catch up with *'There's A Riot Goin' On'*. For a second time in his career, Sly had up-ended popular music, and the album's influence was just as widespread as *'Stand!'* had been before it. It represented the high-point of Sylvester as poet and innovator, upsetting audiences just as much as it had shocked other musicians into a revised awareness of what Sly was about. To Miles Marshall Lewis, 'the songs popular on black radio post-*'Riot'* had all become 'unsettling in their own way... by turns nervy and self-critical' in the same way that *'Riot'* was nervy and self-critical. Curtis Mayfield, the Staple Singers, the Temptations and War 'had turned away from mastering the pop (white) conventions of the day and set about getting their own houses in order by way of describing their own houses. And doing this in the early seventies was impossible without invoking no small degree of complete honesty, paranoia, and sombre introspection'. In other words, they had all incorporated *'Riot'*'s vocabulary into their soundscapes to craft their own responses to a confused and torn decade. It's just that these second-wave soul-brothers, those who took inspiration from *'There's A Riot Goin' On'*, were now eclipsing Sly himself as important funk artists. A route mapped out by Isaac Hayes, whose developing style couched his essential funk in swathes of rich strings, harp, voices, woodwinds and percussion. He also adapted the 'long form' to Soul, stretching songs out to ten minutes and more, and even when he was frittering that time away with repeated vamps and meandering monologues, it still seemed to work like a charm. Marvin Gaye and Curtis Mayfield rapidly picked up on the implications of what he was doing, and crafted their own albums drawing on similar styles, but with more expansive visions. Both stayed firmly ghetto-grounded, but were examining the problems to be found there. Marvin Gaye developed into the religious and ecological aspects of this 'new awareness' through a musical tapestry both deceptively easy to listen to, but ultimately disturbing, while Mayfield in particular began making uncompromising use of ghetto vernacular. His 1972 album *'Times Have Changed'* featured "Stop The War" as well as his cover of Marvin's "Inner City Blues". But while he performed at a Panther's rally in Oakland Auditorium in the company of Bobby Seale and Stokely Carmichael, he took care to also praise Martin Luther King's 'musical truth'.

So had Sly Stone's album been proved prophetic? probably not—not in the specific sense, but it was certainly viral. Its bubbling rhythmic cauldron radiated an uncanny funk currency that infected everything around it. It's impossible not to draw direct genealogical contour-lines from the metronomic drum-sound intro of "Africa Talks To You" all the way into the new-vogueish future-sound of synthesiser electro. They had all absorbed and digested the implications of *'There's A Riot Goin' On'*. But by doing that, Sly had taken black music to the extreme edge. And as TS Elliott wrote in his "Four Quartets", 'human-kind cannot bear too much reality'. So from there on—taking what innovations it found most malleable, it retreated, it took a step back, then another step back, step by step, into a safer black capitalism. After all, the music industry had always been as adept at castrating, parcelling and marketing dissent as TV-movies about Patty Hearst had been, no matter how awkward the content at first appeared. Soon, what had once seemed radical, had been replicated, copied, softened, and neutered into mainstream, converted into a marketable Blaxspoitation commodity. Artists striving to square the equation between funky-dude platinum mainstream sales, and an appearance of keeping it street street street, were adopting yet more extravagant ghetto-chic poses in futile attempts at illusory hyper-reality. It could be persuasively argued that the Temptations had begun the process by taking what had been volatile and spontaneous, and reducing it—in the label's 'factory' tradition, into marketable formula. By now it was all part of the weird contradiction that began with Disco overtaking Funk in marketing terms. And Sly Stone had practically invented all those tacky little fun-kee disco outfits that were now recycling his licks. So what happens next?

To John Phillips 'the Disco boom was peaking, but turning the pop-R&B sound into a mindless but simple formula that couldn't miss'. Although 'album sales were soaring. The logistics of the record industry during the mid-seventies determined that it had become a singles-orientated market dependent on strict radio formatting. The albums market was where the big profits lay, but they were accessed through singles-dominated playlists, so that 'having one dance hit on an album had made dozens of them rich', and 'the five-million (album) mark, once a virtual impossibility except for a handful of the very top artists, was broken over and over on the strength of one or two giant hits off an album—and sometimes a *debut* album…' Music 'had become a fast-buck business for a new rapidly growing class of slick one-hit wonders. New acts were signed up in great numbers.' If proof were needed, suddenly, on Sly's own label—Epic, Wild Cherry were urging 'Play that Funky music white boy' from the top of the charts. The white dopes were on funk. Initially at least, Disco had unassumingly fulfilled many of the social levelling aspirations that the post-'Woodstock' come-down had lost. It was open to working-class losers, and multi-cultural mixes of gays and straights, blacks and white, allowing them all their moment to strut—like Travolta, beneath the mirrorball on Saturday night, in a kind of classless equality drenched by the lasers and thudding bass-lines. And if Sly's intentions had always been to universalise his music, to leap racial divides, then—in a sense, wasn't this the perfect kind of 'post-racial' consensus he had always advocated? Well—maybe, but what conclusions was black music intended to draw from the fact that the biggest-selling Disco act of the late-1970's was the deracinated whine of the Bee-Gee's…? On the back of the movie, and with a string of video-led dance-singles, those high-falsetto poster-boys of *'Saturday Night Fever'* were selling albums by the millions (and "Boogie Child" from their *'Children Of The World'* is very much a Sly-alike). It meant that the black community had to evolve new signifiers.

And it was Earth, Wind & Fire, more than any other black outfit, who fulfilled the promise offered by jazz-funk fusion, adapting and developing Sly's clipped word-suggestion and nasal vocal affectations, to steal his hip young audience. But where they were adept at keeping it close to the dancefloor, with flash, glamour and immaculate choreography, there was little of Sly's menace or troubled political subtext. That was no longer part of the deal. Formed by singer/drummer Maurice White in Chicago in the mid-sixties—and recording for Capitol as the 'Salty Peppers', they were eventually picked up by Warners in 1971. Maurice had already played bass on the Fontella Bass hit "Rescue Me", but the experience of supporting Sly & The Family Stone at the Philadelphia 'Spectrum' made it apparent that more 'progressive black music' was even more of a commercial proposition. Their debut vinyl—"Love Is Life", became only a minor hit, and two Warner albums failed despite huge promotional campaigns. It was then that the band was reconfigured, Maurice and brother Verdine convening a new line-up around Phillip Bailey, Jessica Cleaves, Roland Battista, Larry Dunn, Ronald Wayne Laws and Ralph Johnson. Then—pulling free from their jazz elements in favour of wickedly electric rhythms, with shows defined by the visual pyrotechnics of magic, lasers, flying pyramids and levitating guitarists, the outfit's reputation took off stratospherically. Re-signed to Columbia in 1972 their *'Last Days Of Time'* album was followed by breakthrough hit singles "Shining Star" (no. 1 in May 1975), "Sing A Song" (no. 5 in December 1975), and a smooth cover of the Beatles "Got To Get You Into My Life" (no. 9 in August 1978), leading through an arc of hits into "After The Love Has Gone" (no. 2 in 1979). Soon, with eight double-platinum albums, two platinum and three boogie-dancing gold albums, Earth Wind & Fire had ensured they would remain a force to be reckoned with for some time to come.

The Ohio Players were an eight-piece Funk band almost as well known for their striking album covers as for their music. They first hit the big-time with the funky-riff based "Pain" on the Westbound label in 1971, but twelve years earlier the original members—from Dayton, Ohio, had come together as The Ohio Untouchables. They were the group who supplied the memorable backing for The Falcons searing R&B hit "I Found A Love"—with lead singer Wilson Pickett, for Lupine in 1962. Evolving through the usual innumerable line-up changes and name-switches they recorded several erratic sides for TRC (1967), Compass (1968) and Capitol (1969), before absorbing the lessons of James Brown and Sly Stone, to reach more contemporary audiences. In 1973 the Ohio Players opened a home-town show for the Family Stone, a lesson that was not lost on them. So that finally, "Pain" initiated a succession of throbbing chart variations—"Funky Worm" (no. 15 in April 1973), and "Ecstasy" (no. 31), into even biggest hits through a contract with Mercury. Subsequent releases—"Skin Tight" (no. 13 in November 1974), "Fire" (no. 1 in February 1975) and "Love Rollercoaster" (no. 1 in January 1976), consolidated their status as one of the tightest dance-machines on the scene…

Another name making Funk-waves… ironically, was original 'Family'-member Larry. It's not necessary here to detail it all. This is Sly's story. Larry Graham's is another book. Except at the points where the two lives intersect. But in a brief fly-through, the third Graham Central Station album, the breakthrough *'Ain't No 'Bout-A-Doubt It'*—climbed as high as US no. 22 and went gold in August 1975. Predominantly original compositions, but for Patryce's underwhelming vocals on Ann Peebles' hypnotic "I Can't Stand The Rain", it spawned no less than three chart-singles. "Your Love" ascended to no. 38, followed by the engaging riff-driven "It's Alright" which made it to no. 92

in November, then the sinuous instrumental "The Jam" which reached no. 63 (March 1976). It's unfair to make direct comparisons, and say the tracks may be slicker, while lacking Sly's indefinable spark, but such comparisons are inevitable too. Although Larry was never to hit the highs he had achieved with The Family Stone, he never quite experienced the lows either, and would remain a consistent presence. His Graham Central Station album 'Mirror' reached US no. 46 (June 1976). Into 1977 the success continued as the above-average April album 'Now Do-U-Wanta Dance' reached a US no. 67, with a synthesiser-swamped funk work-out called "Earthquake", an epic of over-production, phasing and murky echo—and the title-track itself which scored another R&B singles smash. Into July 1978, the now-credited 'Larry Graham & Grand Central Station' notched up a modest US no. 105 with LP 'My Radio Sure Sounds Good To Me'. As the group line-up lost cohesion, his wife Tina Graham was recruited as vocalist, but while the album fills the need for serviceable gut-level funk riffs, Pop-crossover status remained elusive. His bass was as elastic as ever—on "Pow", and the Doo-wop title track worked equally well, but melodically the album was weak. His final album of this Grand Central Station phase, the six over-long tracks that make up 'Star Walk', peaked as high as US no. 136 in July 1979.

A career-rethink came when Larry struck out as a solo act in June 1980, opting decisively away from pure funk and into the kind of chocolate-throated balladry he'd contributed to 'A Whole New Thing' with "Let Me Hear It From You", all those (short) years ago. He became a hot commercial property almost immediately. His album 'One In A Million' entered the US chart on its way to no. 27 and a gold certification, while the rich ballad title track written for him by Sam Dees was lifted as a single, elbowing its way past the opposition while streaking to a US no. 9, going gold in the process. In November his single "When We Get Married" climbed to US no. 76. With Sly now on what looked to be permanent vacation, Larry's August 1981 album 'Just Be My Lady' repeated the romantic ballad formula, its sleeve-art illustrating Larry dressed the part in a sharp purple suit and tie. Jesse & Jo-Ann Belvin wrote "Guess Who", while Tina's vocals and keyboard-player Eric Daniels were strongly featured. It provided yet another hit, all the way to a US no. 46, while its title-track made it to a US no. 67 in September, repeating the trick a third time with 'Sooner Or Later' which charted to US no. 142 as an album, and no. 54 as a single in July 1982. With the perhaps celebratorily-titled 'Victory' album making it to US no. 173 in August 1983. By then Larry was working with a new-Funk ikon, Prince…

While for Sly, his future albums would be critically mauled commercial disappointments. But better a diamond with a flaw, than a pebble without…

Chapter Eighteen
'Heard Ya Missed Me...?'

'You can't cry, 'cause you'll look broke down,
but you're cryin' anyway 'cause you're all broke down...!'
("Family Affair")

'The Cat That Walked By Himself...'

There's an intriguing cosmological theory that says the multiverse consists of an infinite number of parallel words. That there are alternate time-streams inhabited by variations of our own lives, acting out all the possibilities that might have resulted from our making different decisions, our choosing other forks in the life-path. It leads to an irresistible temptation to play the 'what if' game. What if things had worked out differently? What if, in one such alternate world Sylvester Stewart had scored a massive hit with one of his Viscaynes's-period singles—"Heavenly Angel" or "Long Time Alone". By 1970 he might have been reduced to touring the Golden Oldie circuit, still performing that same song. But there are other possible time-streams to speculate about, ones that might even tell us something about *this* reality. What if, for example, the arc of Sly Stone's career had peaked five years before... or five years after it did? If he'd happened when issues weren't quite so polarised, so forced into extremes? It's a fair guess that in either case Sly's natural talent and instrumental dexterity would guarantee him a solid career in music. Five years earlier and it's easy to imagine him building a reputation as either a writer/producer or a low-level artist himself churning out moderate Bobby Freeman-style dance hits. Or if he'd happened five years *later* than he did, he'd be leading a flash agile seventies Disco outfit through a career of catchy club anthems. What new angles might he have thrown onto that Disco era? Probably in both conjectural time-streams there'd be some elements of hearty partying, that seems to be hard-wired into the DNA. Only less dangerously so.

We'll never know, instead—in the real reality of the only time-steam we *do* know, the arc of his career was exactly synchronised to the zeitgeist of the moment that it *was* produced. And what gives Sly's greatest music its vitalities is that it was so precisely an integral part of its time. It could have happened no other way. At no other time. Like delivering the perfect punch-line, or like Jimmy Jones hit record, it's all down to timing, good ticka-ticka-ticka-timing. Although its applications have proved to be timeless, they could not have happened at any other time. Without the forceful provocation of extreme incidents things would have been different. Or might not have happened at all. Vitally, it was the precise moment that his career-arc *did* peak, caught up in its unique configuration of optimisms and betrayals, hopes and dreams—all those issues demanding his response, with his personae conflated by the dramas of his personal life, that provoked Sly into becoming more than that, into working—as Miles Davis phrases it, 'above himself', elevating him into creating work that was edgy, relevant and dangerous. That the same pressures that made him excel were the same that pressured him intolerably into extremes of excess, was part of the deal. If his life ended in failure—at least in long-duration career terms, his music could be interpreted as the better because of it. It was all part of the Robert Johnson crossroads contract with the devil. The ghouls he released were malign… bad, mad, and ultimately sad. They helped him create great music. But they also conspired to destroy him. Caught up in an immaculate cliché, he gained the world, only to lose his soul. But what if it had not all ended as it did, what if Sly had stayed actively involved in music…? What more was there to come?

Ultimately, in our familiar time-stream… there's only a long day's journey into night. Sly's is a story in which people experience things in extremes. And the narrative power of such a nightmare is hard to resist. He'd started out fearing the hit-magic could go away just as easily as it had happened. But that was before he'd succumbed to his addictions. Before he began lying to his body about the uncontrolled 'controlled substances' that were gradually sapping him of his once-prodigious talents. Sly's metabolism proved remarkably resilient to the substance-abuse to which it was relentlessly subjected. But those years of emotional, musical and chemical jousting eventually stripped its defences away to nothing. The old devil in him was finally taking its toll on his ability to continue working coherently. If you look for the earlier sweet sharp Sylvester of the radio-DJ days, you'll find he's left the building. By now this driven once-genius was regarded by everyone, even those closest to him, as a failure, and a liability. Where there had been joy and rebellion, there was resignation. He'd hit the pinnacle, and was free-falling. He'd gone from Funk to dysfunctional. Now, he was retreating further into a cocoon of cocaine and brooding introspection. Dissolving into Hollywood Babylon sleaze. He had everything, nothing, and all the space between. And if it seems that the story ends here, it doesn't. Sly was still only in his early thirties. As many decades of his life would follow as had already elapsed. It's just that they would not be as well-documented. Not as culturally prolific. Perhaps—not as eventful. Fact is—few know, and those who do know won't tell. Real, or made up? Biography or fiction? When you live out your life like fiction, some amount of imprecision can be anticipated, to bedevil those attempting to chart its details.

Yet the music still itches, and recording-work continues, even if—following the 'Radio City Hall' implosion, it drolly delivers doubt, and the futility of even trying. Assembling the next album involved a mysteriously haphazard alchemy. Sly trucked his tapes from one studio to another in his Toyota stationwagon, wary of leaving them where they could be lost or tampered with. Often there would be between forty-to-a-hundred reels of tape, none of which were documented or marked up. And he worked simultaneously, and apparently at random on any one, or on various combinations of tapes. Adding a bass part here, a guitar line there, doing a rough mix, endlessly tweaking or 'perfecting' material he considered inadequate—inbetween bouts of smoking, rapping, drug-necking and general hearty-partying. 'You see me at a party, and you know I party hearty' he reiterates, explaining 'I offer a joint to you, you can say yes or no' (on "So Good"). He enjoyed the comfortable familiarity of using the 'Pit' in Sausalito. 'It was a new concept in studio building at the time' comments engineer Chris Morris, 'the engineers, myself and Tom Flye, we would be down about eight feet, recessed from the main floor in a big hole, and in that hole were four speakers in a quad fashion, with a board in the middle. The musicians would play up above me on various levels'. Sly would stay locked in there for days on end, he'd installed his own bed, designed in the shape of big red Salvador Dali 'Mae West' lips, and—lying horizontally, radio-miked up, he'd even record from there. Every once in a while Sly would drive a portable rig out to the family home in Daly City—to where Freddie had retreated, and set up a makeshift studio in his mother's basement. On other occasions, rather than suffer dead studio time which he'd booked—then fail to turn up for, or which he'd snooze through, Columbia would truck equipment and technicians out to his apartment to work there.

Perhaps his ideas were filed away in some internal ordering system in his head. Or perhaps he reacted as the tapes were randomly cued in, picking up on a theme or a mood, a hook or a riff he'd improvised and then abandoned on some earlier date, often with Tom Flye shoving the faders. That must remain something known only to him. He also erased perfectly good material, only to record lesser work over it. He needed to consolidate through hard work, a feat still not beyond him, and he was working, even when drugs came equally high on his list of priorities. But there was more. Stephen Paley suggests that he'd lost his self-confidence and his sense of perspective, his ability to differentiate what was good, and what wasn't. A quandary complicated by 'a fear of completion'. His convoluted working method ensured that everything was in a constant state of adjustment, and forever incomplete.

Yet in November 1975, an album appeared attributed *not* to The Family Stone, but simply to 'Sly Stone'. Not that the sound was striking different. It wasn't. And if *'High On You'* was officially intended to snip the starting-tape on his solo career, it stalled no higher than an unpromising US no. 45. Its single "I Get High On You"—with Bobby Vega's nagging chugging deep-bass play-in, and high keening keyboard slivers of ice, packs as strong a character-payload as anything he'd ever done. With Sly slurring the lyric, after 'my temperature is rising' he avoids the obvious 'it's really not surprising', by substituting the flexible language invention of 'I hope you realising', while he's urging Little Sister's to 'shing it', and in response, their shrill harmonising adds sassy texture. It's no more than a straight no-nonsense sensual paean to the pleasures of the flesh set in a muscular danceable piece of disco, but the head-set stays right. As a single, it formed a buoyant 3.15 minutes of fun-funk with no sub-text and minimal lyrical import that nevertheless carried it into the R&B chart as high as no. 3. His power and popularity may have faded, but this was a result confirming that some elements of his genius remained intact, his instinct for a cool groove, his abilities as musician and arranger. It also forms a promising album side one opener. Unfortunately, what follows, despite its occasional funk strengths and high technical production values, makes less of a lasting impact.

"That's Lovin' You" is the first of the more experimental titles, a slow love ballad imaginatively arranged with Sly ascending into falsetto around jaunty instrumental breaks. It had started out as a backing-track created for Jimmy Gray Hall, an artist Stephen Paley was working with. When those sessions didn't work out, Sly took the tape back, and rejigged it for himself. Yet even with its lightweight repeated string motif allied to the regular rhythm section, it still gives the off-balance feel of an unfinished backing track, as if, with a little further development it might have become more than it is. Perhaps that's meant to be its geometry? On first impression, the remaining side one cuts can come over as even more crass and clichéd, although "Who Do You Love?" has a lot going on down in the mix which is dense with fuzz-guitar bass-lines and multi-layered horns. And for the intriguingly titled "Green Eyed Monster Girl" Sly comfortably reverts to Hammond organ for a perfect little Booker T/ Jimmy Smith instrumental hybrid. A hot and funky excursion by anyone's standards.

Flip the vinyl over, and side two wallows in the smug bubble-bath sentiments and sleepy pacing of "My World", transposing a cool Miles Davis-influenced horn solo with 'the reason for my smile / the mother of my child' glancing wistfully back at Kathy, via a Bobby Womack influence. Then, after the glib, avuncular politico outpourings of "Organize" (co-written with Freddie), there's a charming 'experimental' string-driven nonsense song "Le Lo Li", intercut with the girls chanting their enticingly pleasant backgrounds to Sly's simplistic ear-catchingly phrased message. There's a solution to the world's problems, he argues, a simple song might make it better for a little while, so sing *this* simple song, try a little doe-rey-me-fah, yet—for the 3.20-minute duration of the track, it almost seems to make sense. 'Different pills for different thrills' croons Sly, 'different days for different ways / different freaks for different weeks'. At the mid-point break he pauses to explain that the phrase 'Shakabra Shakadida' means 'right on brothers, and right on sisters', adding 'anyway, I learned it in Hawaii', followed by a teasing mocking laugh aimed at all such slogans, and at those who fall back on sloganeering. Finally, the ironic call-and-response piece "Greed" opens with a flourish—echoing "Stand!". At 4.13-minutes it forms the album's longest track, with horn charts lifted from James Brown, and as he repeats 'some of us will go astray' into the fade, with each repetition his voice is distorted in new and different electronic ways. As though he's exploring the various routes to do exactly that.

Although supposedly a solo album—produced by 'Sly Stone & Sylvester Stewart' with Sly credited as playing 'everything', and although Sly is alone on the sleeve, suspended in white space, lightly bearded, bare-chested, dressed-down in patched blue-jeans and baseball boots, he was still working through a mixed palette of interacting voices and a rich melange of jostling instrumentation. To this end it also lists contributions from Freddie, Jerry Martini, Rusty Allen, Cynthia, Bill Lordon, Cousin Gale, plus Tiny Melton, Vet and Dawn Silva. So—before you get into less familiar bullet-point accomplices, there's a Family Stone context. Then there's Rudy Love (vocals), Dennis Marcellino (sax), Bobby Vega (bass), Tricky Truman Governor (keyboards), Willie Wild Sparks (drums on "Le Lo Li"), 'Little Moses' (organ on "I Get High On You"), and others, with a 'special thanks' appendix taking in Mother & Father, David Froelich (his old Solano Community College Music Theory Instructor) and Ken Roberts.

Some vainly claim this is possibly his most underrated album. Defiantly arguing that, despite his unfortunate adventures with Bolivian marching powder, it's still possible to hear Sly's corroded genius at work. And certainly there's much to enjoy. It *is* intelligent funk. You dance to it. You listen to it as well. Unlike much else on the market, it constitutes multi-function dance music. Even if any measure of its 'greatness'—or lack of same, depends on how high you set the critical bar. Against Sly's earlier work? Or against the humdrum standard of his funk competitors? It rates much higher by the latter, than the former comparison. It could be read as the work of a witty satirist holding a pin to the inflated pretensions of his funk hipster rivals, bringing a refreshingly intelligent voice to their frequently vacuous dancefloor cavortings. But it's just as easy to detect the damage that lies beneath its dexterous rhythms. To interpret it as the sound of a machine coming to pieces, even though the engine is still running. The CD reissue insert point out Sly's triple role in music as predictor, innovator… and victim.

The press was losing its patience. Where once he'd stood alone in a field of one—*the* Mr Mysterioso Funkmeister, now there was strong-arm funk competition taking all the plaudits, while Sly—rather than taking the lead, seemed to be imitating his own former self. And the intensifying competition made it difficult for Sly's voice to be heard. To *'NME'*'s Pete Erskine it's simply 'the worst album Sly Stone has ever made'. He opens his review by stating that 'the consensus appears to be that the last Sly album of any real value was *'Fresh'*. To my mind, however, *'Fresh'* was only a simplified, laundered re-statement of *'There's A Riot Goin' On'*. To Erskine Sly's 'artistic impasse is all too evident. He has become tired-sounding, tiresome and self-indulgent simply because he really can't think of anything else to do. Sly's wit is negligible, his 'experimentation', in terms of his efforts to revitalise the over-familiar music-form he helped create, is only perfunctory. In this case he has tried to introduce a few subtle variants by way of occasional oblique string, horn and choral arrangements, but the resultant changes in tempo and atmosphere are only superficial'. His conclusion is that the album that constituted his greatest catharsis—*'There's A Riot Goin' On'*, had drained all the creative juices out of him and, by now, self-parody had settled there in its place. It was as though he'd thrown everything he had to give into *'There's A Riot Goin' On'*, and now nothing remained…

****

Rock 'n' Roll is tied into a traditional trinity alongside sex and drugs, because both of those peccadilloes and purgatories are distractions. While the artist's head is tuned elsewhere, while the mind is spinning, there will always be some freeloading lawyer or opportunistic junkie rummaging through the accounts, or raiding the stash. Despite Sly's intimidating musical gifts and awesome street savvy, fame, celebrity, and the industry had turned him over. And the following January, he filed for bankruptcy. The IRS took control of Novato as part of the settlement, as an epidemic of careerist accountant began circling. Temporarily Sly moved into a house owned by Ken Roberts in Mandeville Canyon. Was there a moment when he realised it had all gone wrong? Was this that moment? Or was it such a long slow gradual process that, almost imperceptibly, he'd collapsed over the tipping point into decline without being consciously aware of it? Perhaps, in a sense, he'd become immune from it all, so pleasingly numb that he'd disconnected from it? Until it was too late. How did it ever get to this?

By now his past triumphs and immense influence on just about every black band of the seventies had become a matter of history. But music has always to be in motion. Music is movement, music is never still. The 'genius' and the 'magic' of Sly Stone was—and still is a matter of record, whether that magic is found on the original black vinyl, or later on CD's or downloads. And those who delight in over-emphasising his flaws provide few clues as to why such an apparent master of folly managed to create such life-changing music in the first place. Music that beguiles for so long, and is still fresh and full of surprises four decades on. Certainly, Sly the monster can be held to account. But Sylvester the magus is an equal part of the equation—and that aspect still lurks within too. He'd opened the door to Soul's most creative artists by handing them the ability to stretch out their talent on albums that were not simply collections of singles-plus-fillers. He'd offered what Erskine calls 'a rhythmic prototype as influential as James Brown's in the spawning of future generations of upcoming black bands. The trouble is—as so often happens in the relationship between progenitor and copyist—those 'upcoming' black bands had begun to produce variations on the theme far more interesting than those put forward by its originators'. Industry insider-rumour portrayed Sly battling his demons until his studio-work had diminished to a trickle, hooked on the short-lived molecular dynamics of cocaine, unable to compose worthwhile new material, that he was in frequently poor health, often in trouble with the law, hounded by alimony and child-support charges.

Yet a further title—*'Heard Ya Missed Me, Well I'm Back'* (1976) arrived in the form of a rather simpler album compared to the richness of its predecessor. And despite the full 'Sly & The Family Stone' attribution being restored the sleeve-shot ironically portrays Sly as a one-man band. Or, as the *'NME'* review saw it, 'dressing up in one-man-band nigger minstrel drag, cocking his hat jauntily to one side, rolling his eyes'. Whichever way you look, the sleeve was pointing out the truth. Sly was now a self-sufficient operation. This was no Family Stone that anyone could recognise. It was *a* Family Stone, sure it was, albeit with several unfamiliar new Family-faces. On a track optimistically titled "Family Again" Sly adds insistent exhortations 'John and Sly gonna make ya high', then 'brother Joe gonna play some', or 'Hey Dwight get down tonight'. All of which only serves to demonstrate that it's a long way, but a short step from 'I'm gonna add some bottom, so the dancers just can't hide'. The 'John' is Johnny Colla then of Sound Hole, but destined to team up with Huey Lewis & The News a few years later. 'Brother Joe' is guitarist Joe Baker. But despite this pretence of 'Family', Sly plays pretty much everything on these last two Epic albums himself. He maintained a pick-up band he could draw on for occasional live dates. The loyal Cynthia Robinson—a constant since Sly & The Stoners, was still there among his main collaborators, as was Pat Rizzo. Back-up singers Lynn Mabry and Dawn Silva were also there (although they split away from Sly during 1976 to form the Brides of Funkenstein two years later—with George Clinton midwiving their 1979 Atlantic single "Never Buy Texas From A Cowboy").

Meanwhile, the title track opens unexpectedly with the kind of jaunty dancing flute you expect to frolic over the credits of a mildly amusing domestic sit-com. Or a Fifth Dimension record. It shows a Sly still capable of springing surprises. Then "Nothing Less Than Happiness" is a gooey love-duet as syrupy as anything Kapralik's Peaches & Herb ever produced. It almost sounds too easy. By this point, setting up a perfect studio groove had become second nature. Sly's experienced touch was such that he could conjure the alchemy almost intuitively, on autopilot. He knew how to work his sympathetic magic with musicians, he knew how to layer instruments, how to blend channels. It was not work. It was no longer even an intellectual thing. Merely a sensed thing. He turned it on, and elements just came together, until it felt correct, then it becomes corrector by degrees, then it was done. 'Zappity-zap and rata-tat-tat'. Once completed, it was no problem to throw a lyric repetition across it, a random phrase, a catchy title—such as 'what was I thinkin' in my head, what were you thinkin' in your head', 'sexy situation aaah-ha, sexy situation aaah-ha', or 'everything in you has to come out'—mostly meaningless, often nonsensical, but convenient hooks. Then edit the results down into the required album band-width. He knew how to contrive an adequate track, but what that working process could seldom achieve was to create a truly memorable song, or a hit single. With originality, and soul drained away, in its place there was only the slick efficiency of an advertising agency. Most of the remainder of the album had that same made-on automatic-pilot feel. "Let's Be Together" with—amazingly, Peter Frampton on guitar, envisages a playful seduction scenario of the kind Meatloaf would later construct around "Paradise By The Dashboard Light"—an escalating 'stop', 'don't stop', lapsing into a 'gimmie gimmie gimmie' lasciviousness. Or the catchy elliptical "What Was I Thinking In My Head"—built on a throbbing Philly rhythm, which received a modicum of dance-floor popularity. But despite such hopeful signs, few were fooled.

'Sly's been trying to get back up ever since' *'There's A Riot Goin' On'* wrote Neil Spencer, reviewing the album for *'NME'*. 'Each successive album proclaims his return to his former power and glory, then fails to supply the musical booty to back up the claims. None of the post-*'Riot'* albums (with the exception of the ambiguous *'Fresh'*) have been able to equal either the rippling energy and innovation of the Family Stone's early hits, or the slinking guile and seduction of *'Riot'* itself'. Despite the title claim, sales would indicate that few had actually missed Sly Stone at all. It's not as though the music is relentlessly poor, because its not. Many artists of the period would be proud to produce anything half as strong. It's just that there's little that's new or innovative, where Sly's own audacity had conditioned his audiences to expect more. This was the man once capable of raising the bar, switching musical trends around. Yet here he was repeating himself, re-covering familiar ground. He'd become a human chemistry set unable even to reinvigorate himself.

With the quality of his output diminishing in direct relation to his sales, and his increasing drug intake matching his intractability, Epic decided to sever their association with a contract-filling re-mix compilation titled *'Ten Years Too Soon'* (1979). It was an unstoppable chart-machine of familiar material redubbed with newer more Disco-friendly beats by DJ John 'TC' Luongo—without Sly's participation. The highly-regarded Luongo was also responsible for remixing Dan Hartman's "Relight My Fire" and "One Chain" by Santana, as well as tracks by The Real Thing, The Jacksons, and KC & The Sunshine Band. Luongo respected Sly. His intention, as the title implies, was to demonstrate by merely tilting the emphasis, that a decade previous Sly had been laying down the ground-rules for what had become 1979 dance-floor convention. Here was the proof. Across the period it samples from—with seven tracks taking in "Stand!" and "Everyday People" to "This Is Love" and "I Get High On You", Sly had been the leader of the pack, forging a path for others to follow. As Peter Shapiro phrases it 'this collects a body of music so brilliantly conceived that the seriousness of its politics never drags down the joy of the simple act of making music. As intelligent as Dylan, as fun as Motown…' Matched to strategic limited-edition 12" singles that got this reconfigured Family Stone back onto the dancefloor, the album served as a salient reminder that Sly had always been so much more than just an AM-radio hitmaker. Unfortunately, to those who remembered Sly's days in the vanguard of the movement this project represented a botched retrospective that only served to throw into sharper relief the paucity of what was on offer from the then-current 'Family Stone'. And by this late date, to the teen record-buyers who put singles into the soul charts, the album must have seemed uncomfortably out-of-step with the times. They no longer even considered Sly Stone a player, if they recognised his name at all. To them, it merely made it obvious that this one-time innovator had been left behind, to chase his own tail. Hot?—this was barely tepid. It also arrived with the impatient tick of the record company's biological clock as its click-track. Today, the Dance-Remix is a standard part of artistic expression—and of industry marketing. At the time, it seemed to arrive accompanied by the distinctive sound of cracked and broken fingernails scraping at the bottom of a very bare barrel. A contractual-obligation, running on empty.

****

Sometimes, even big bands get small. And the moralists were never far away when Sly slipped into one of his unintelligible darknesses. With his beautifully outrageous image, and his tight three-letter name, he'd been a gift to the press. Once, those u/g chroniclers had been fellow-travellers. Now, things had changed. Now they were finding it impossible to even find compassion, or resist the sneery quip. Preferring to sermonise, drawing conclusions on the wall. He'd wasted his genius. Lost his pride. His career and creativity had gone into unchoreographed breakdown, into free-fall. But there are other analogies worth considering. Bob Dylan was seriously unsettled by the messianic status bestowed upon him, and scared by the literary detectives rootling through his garbage-can for imagined clues to his inspiration. So much so that he 'retired' into self-imposed isolation on the other side of his 'motorpsycho nightmare', to reinvent himself through a series of deliberately flawed albums designed to disabuse them and shake them off his trail. Sly had reached a similar impasse. He was done in, and done down. Tired of words. The industry demanded hits. They were no longer forthcoming. He'd been swallowed-up and devoured by a terrifying situation from which there seemed no escape, one over which he'd only ever at best had partial control. There was no escape except further withdrawal into his own self-imposed isolation. Into night sweats and dreams of failure. So he took that step back from the precipice. He lit the touch-paper… and retired. But the legacy—for all his failings, was there for all to see.

Sly was every good thing gone wrong, a relic from the defining age of excess. Although it was only a few short years—but 10,000 light years on from hippie egalitarianism, or Black Power's Maoist cultural aspirations. These are days from a different world. The further we get from the time, the more difficult it becomes to make the leap of imagination necessary to inhabit them. Now, sex and drugs and rock 'n' roll is far more than just a cliché, it's a career expectation. It wasn't always so. Although, in another sense, it was ever so. Coke, purchased at around $30 a gram, tested for purity with a flame, or with Clorox, had become the 'national drug of the seventies'. From the poolside porn-shoots of LA—which were by now out-grossing the gross-out music industry, to the conspicuous star consumption of the 'Studio 54' superclub. Its effects were ravaging the corporate tempi and body fibres of Rock music. Just as the politics of HIV/AIDS were changing attitudes to promiscuity. Cocks had become dangerous, they were killing people. Roy Halston Frowick, the man who had designed the gowns for Sly's Madison Square Gardens wedding, died of AIDS in 1990.

And there are no rules to addiction. English 'Opium Eater' Thomas De Quincey was lost in awe at 'the apocalypse of the world inside me' induced by getting high. Artificial stimulants have always been part of bohemia, of art, of creativity. Ask the romantic poets, Coleridge, Baudelaire. Its subculture is a collective mythology that spans generations, languages, and continents. Every decade breathes new and vivid life into its familiar iconography, adding new realisms, while restoring its mythic allusions. Louis Armstrong, later seen as a reassuring family entertainer, spoke of smoking marijuana on the Mississippi riverboats. To Allen Ginsberg drugs were 'stimulators of perception'. Heroin may have fuelled Charlie 'Bird' Parker's startling Be-Bop innovations, but it also destroyed him and savagely abbreviated his life. Miles Davis and Ray Charles fought their own wars against addiction. Yet Ray seemed perfectly capable of producing work of genius, and of performing across a decade of addiction. Until, when finally faced with the full weight of legal repercussions, he was able to voluntarily impose a regime of cold turkey on himself and emerge free. Although—whisper it loud, wasn't it his period of dependence which produce his greatest work? Weren't some of his most powerful performances—"I Can't Stop Loving You", yearning paeans to junk?

People like to get high, they're hard-wired that way. It's a universal constant. The great Smokey Robinson makes a relevant point when he explains that 'a mistake is made about drugs. It's thought people get off into drugs for some deep-rooted psychological reason. Their Mom hated them when they were a kid, their Dad ran off, they lived in a real bad neighbourhood. This is bullshit. Ninety-nine percent who get off on drugs get off having *fun* with their friends. And I mean *fun*. Then, one day, they look up, and fun is killing them.' He's talking about cocaine. But those denied more exotic highs will experiment with airplane glue from Airfix box-kits. For Sylvester Stewart's generation teenage joints, passed around the ritual circle was already an integral part of San Francisco adolescence. Although those party smarties were made of less potent THC (tetrahydro-cannabinol) than modern strains, and diluted further by its circle-jerk pass-around etiquette. Acid-rock was different. And it was the same. LSD was not so much the catalyst as the ignition point of the psychedelic experience. After all, that's what the word means. It means the recreational re-creation of the lysergic-experience through a synthesis of sound and light distortions. At first LSD was not even illegal. During Sly's 'Autumn' years, it was still so new it escaped categorisation. More, prophets seers and sages such as Timothy Leary were openly advocating its use as a consciousness-expanding tool, a magic chemical bullet able to stimulate creativity and religious awareness. The downsides were conveniently back-pedalled. The drug culture was a positive thing. A bonding. A ritual. A tool. And naturally, irregular drug use was hardly something new to Sly or his 'Family' prior to the turn of the decade. Sly was always the first to pass the pipe around after a gig. Like the water-sharing metaphor in Robert Heinlein's cult-SF novel *'Stranger In A Strange Land'* (1961). It's a chemical romance that's good for creativity, isn't it? A road to excess that leads to the palace of wisdom. But *'There's A Riot Goin' On'* marked the subcultural switch from weed and acid, to heavier narcotics.

In the Chapare region of Bolivia, and across fellow coca-producing nations Columbia and Peru—but also into Ecuador, Venezuela, Brazil and Panama, the leaf has been cultivated for 3,500 years. It was used in everything from herbal tea to clothing. Since long before the time of the Incas, indigenous communities had been chewing the leaf, using its calcium, iron and vitamin-A-rich properties to boost strength and stave off hunger. But as in Paddy Chayefsky's *'Altered States'* (1978), as in Aldous Huxley's *'The Doors To Perception'* (1954), as in Timothy Leary's *'The Politics Of Ecstasy'* (1968), the plant-derived drug was more than just a high, it was an ancient tool to access mystical levels of awareness. Which is again to ignore the downsides. Although not physically addictive in exactly the same way as heroin, long-term high-dose dependency induces memory loss and behavioural disorders that persist long after cessation. Frequent coke-users start hearing things that aren't there, seeing weird shit that's not there. It produces paranoia. At its most extreme, deaths have been recorded from heart or lung failure. When a regular coke-user backs off and tries to break the habit, their temper gets short and easily stressed, things get on their nerves. It gets difficult to handle stuff. They no longer listen to music, read, or do anything. So they snort again.

Sly was far from the only celebrity with over-indulgence problems. Two of his disciples, George Clinton and Rick James endured their own battles. Richard Pryor transformed his cocaine excesses into a cutting comedy routine. While by contrast, the creative beauty of John Phillips—who wrote and directed the Mamas & Papas 'California Dream' from Sly's Bel Air mansion, became terminally disabled by what he calls the 'pure and deadly white powder'—never simply a physical thing, but also a sickness of the soul. Where once he'd rhapsodised the power of loving liberation, soon he was eulogising pure pharmaceutical coke manufactured by 'Merck Sharpe & Dohme' for clinical testing, until he endured the final decades of his life in squalidly pointless narcotic crisis. Ike Turner was another who knew all there was to know about the demon flake, he developed a nasal coke-hole he could 'put a pen through'. Throughout the years immediately before, and after his involvement in *'There's A Riot Goin' On'* he was living in a coke-blur. Initially he'd used its 'false energy' as a performance aid, something to help him stay awake and enable extended creative sessions at his own custom-built high-tech 'Bolic' studios. Then cocaine became an essential part of touring, hidden in the back of speakers, in wah-wah pedals, and even in the false heels of his platform shoes. The studio, which was 'like something out of a James Bond movie', had its own 'orgy quarters', and 'sometimes I would be sitting mixing at the board and two girls would be under the console sucking my dick'. In Tina's Feminist Survival-through-Strength bible *'I, Tina'* (1986) Ike was demonised as serial adulterer, drug addict and wife-beater. And not surprisingly, their relationship was in trouble, 'she was attractive, but not really sensuous in bed… to be honest, I felt that having sex with her was almost a duty'. Were there beatings? Yes. But it was cocaine, and Ike's sexually voracious promiscuity that Tina couldn't take. For years EMI's Ronald Bell toured Europe holding Tina's gown as she came offstage but—as Ike's ghost-writer Nigel Cawthorne points out, 'despite the repeated allegations that Ike beat Tina, Bell says, he never saw a mark on her'. And the volatile duo's final physical spat—in a limo on their way to dates in Dallas, was—according to Ike, deliberately provoked by her to supply the pretext for a split on the eve of signing a five-year record deal. Whatever the motives, the rift proved to be a major tipping point, and 'my life ain't been right since then'. His career had concentrated on assembling the Ike & Tina Turner Revue around Tina, not around himself, 'so I wasted my whole life building something, and then it got taken away from me'. Without its visual focus the Revue was 'a car with no motor'.

Ike was lost in a mess of washed-up sixties sexual liberation, and left stranded in the slipstream as Tina became an icon for seventies Feminism. As he relates, 'while I was hitting rock-bottom, Tina was becoming a star'. He was reduced to stealing silverware from hotels, while legal threats and counter-threats ricocheted around him. Stories of him hanging out around Brian Gibson's film-lot during the production of the slanted 1993 *'What's Love Got To Do With It?'* movie, signing autographs and grabbing some peripheral celebrity—even from a totally one-sided biopic in which Larry Fishburne and Angela Bassett's version of the Ike & Tina story vilifies him, are more grounded in reality. But he insisted that 'the movie confrontation at her comeback concert where I'm supposed to have threatened her with a gun—that never happened. I never went there'. It took a two-year two-month incarceration in California Men's Colony in St Luis Obispo—as convict No.E48678, to get him off dependency, 'the greatest thing that ever happened to me'. Yet he never managed to regain his career momentum, until a cocaine overdose finally contributed to his death in December 2007. In a final irony, announcing his death the BBC cited his most famous record as "River Deep, Mountain High"—a record created by Tina with Phil Spector, on which Ike played no part whatsoever. 'I don't give a damn who you are' he protested, 'cocaine is stronger than you are'. Smokey Robinson was more fortunate. For two-and-a-half years he was on cocaine. But the hits continued. And in 1986, he kicked the dependency through a combination of Motown Corporate discipline, and Jesus.

****

As a child, Sylvester Stewart was forever in church. 'His old man was a preacher, his old lady was an evangelist. It was church, church, church' according to Bobby Womack. As part of the congregation, he'd half-listen to preachers terrifying him with fire and brimstone images. He'd watch transfixing sermons threatening damnation and the devil. As an adult, he knew those who fear the devil most are those who know him most intimately. They understand, far better than any preacher ever can, why yielding to temptation is the original sin. And how sweetly tempting those temptations can be so, the temptations of ambition, fame, wealth, and numbing oblivion. If salvation depends on individuals living good and decent lives, that can be tricksy when you're leading a Rock 'n' Soul band. 'Sly was the little black sheep of the (Stewart) family' Womack concludes. The one 'who broke loose and, when he started to do something else, it wasn't nothing like church'.

The strict and inflexible doctrine of the Church of God in Christ determines that once you've crossed some unmarked border, there can be no going back. Damnation is nothing if not a total thing. Sin was ineradicably in his soul. Even when logic and reason tells you otherwise, what you learn as a child goes deep. It lies there, beneath all that is rational. Even as fame and narcotics take you higher, sin and damnation take you down. He was caught between god and Rock 'n' Roll, the sacred and the profane. Rusty Allen claims that Sly 'still had some of his religious values somewhere in there'. According to Rusty, Sly had confided 'I think I have done too much shit, too much wrong, and I don't think god will take me back'. Once, Sly and Womack had sat together, teasing out comparisons about each other's music. Bobby pointed out that rather than writing love songs, Sly's compositions were all about getting high. 'Yeah, because that's what I do' Sly reasoned, 'that's real. Real people who get high and come out bad.' When Greil Marcus suggested that Sly's problem lay with 'bad dope', writer Martha Bayles corrected him, 'Stone himself knew perfectly well that his problem was *good* dope'.

There's some degree of that self-awareness as Sly juggles the word-play of 'I know the feeling of being without, when deep within, you're deep without' ("Back On The Right Track"). It's a song from—against all expectations, yet another new 'Sly & The Family Stone' album. Timed to fortuitously coincide with a minor badass funk-thang revival, it arrived after three wasted years, with Sly newly signed to Warner Brothers following convoluted negotiations with label president Mo Ostin. Part of the new deal stipulated Sly vacate the producer's chair in favour of their 'black A&R' department's Mark Davis, newly recruited from MCA with his female trio Stargard. A stipulation that makes it the first and only time a nominally 'Family Stone' album would be—nominally, produced by anyone other than Sly. Together, they crafted another optimistically titled comeback effort with *'Back On The Right Track'* (October 1979). Some of the material—including "Sheer Energy" and "It Takes All Kinds", had begun as tapes salvaged from what had supposedly been Epic sessions at the Record Plant. Others started out from Sly's base-recordings layered instrument-by-instrument over a Maestro Rhythm King drum-track, at the Sound Factory studio on Ivar in Hollywood. There were token scatterings of original 'Family' members, with Cynthia and Pat Rizzo present. An estranged Freddie showed up adding his guitar to a nucleus augmented by tight bass grooves from Keni Burke and Alexander Doré, tied into drummer-percussionists Alvin Taylor and Ollie E Brown. They provided a strong rhythm section, but one conspicuously falling short of reliable former stalwarts such as Gregg Errico or Rusty Allen, and particularly the positive input of Larry Graham. Tom 'Super' Flyte was also there, along with engineer Chris Morris who'd worked on *'High On You'* with Sly for Epic, and who'd followed him to Warners.

Morris explained how 'a lot of times I would lay down a few measures from the Rhythm King and we would loop that, or maybe copy it twenty or thirty times and slice it all together in drum-time. We'd get three minutes or so of a locked-in drum beat and we'd go from there...' During the recording Sly lost his lyric-notes at one point, and had to rejig them from scratch. So the track that would eventually become "Who's To Say" begins with a wordless scat in the place of lyrics. Outtakes list it as 'Get Back', and there's some evidence of high spirits at the sessions. In the pre-recording banter for the same track Sly can be heard suggesting that 'Morgana King' should do this. He's referencing the jazz singer who was then enjoying a revived career-high due to her role in *'The Godfather'* (1972). Indeed, Steve Lake, writing in *'Melody Maker'* 4th May 1974 repeated earlier 'Stone Flower' suggestions that Sly had been 'casting his net for bigger fish' to produce, with Morgana King mentioned as a possible subject. So there was some continuity. But perhaps something else was lost, as well as lyric-notes... and time, in that bantering process? because there was frequent hard partying too. The slippery talent of the Lord of Misrule was still in thrall to false friends and vengeful drug dealers. LA is the West Coast centre of the music industry, so there were relentless visitor stop-overs at the studio. When Mo Ostin called by to check out progress, he found Maurice White, with other Earth Wind & Fire members there. As were some Temptations, with Lionel Richie and Stevie Wonder. While A&R man Lenny Waronker called by, along with former Harpers Bizarre drummer Ted Templeman—by then a Warners staff producer. After all, Sly's musical genius might be in eclipse, but his reputation for good times was still well-founded. During the final mix-downs for *'Back On The Right Track'* a newcomer called Prince Rogers Nelson was sequestered in an adjoining studio working on *his* debut album, *'For You'* (1978). Although neither album fared particularly well, the sessions formed a unique intersection in the career-trajectories of two singularly charismatic stars, one irresistibly rising, the other spectacularly declining.

For Sly Stone, even taking the album's poor-value running time into consideration, the results were painfully lacking in memorable moments. With an extreme brevity of 11.17-minute and 12.90-minute per side, even halfway in, the paucity of original ideas is getting problematic. The hardest of the cuts—"If It's Not Adding Up", is a tuneless clunker with Rose and Lisa Banks prominently featured. "Shine It On" is endlessly repetitive, but not in a good way, with Sly screaming in a-near James Brown style, as though the Founding Father of Seventies Funk is searching for the tune and the lyrics to match the funk signature-line. The closing surprise of the set is an instrumental cheekily titled "Sheer Energy", which features Sly up-front on harmonica. But for those who persist, and scratch deeper, there are some mitigating circumstances. The unfortunately titled "The Same Thing" is salvaged by its bracketed sub-title "Makes You Laugh, Makes You Cry", with its vocoder-scrambled vocals defining the moral ambiguity of the natural world—'the same food you eat to live, can make you die', and 'the same truth you thought you heard, can be a lie'. It's a theme recapitulating the line in "Remember Who You Are"—'somebody else's medicine could be poison to you…', connecting back to "Le Lo Li" on *'High On You'* with its 'different pills for different thrills'. It's easy to extend the duality into 'the chemicals you take to make you high, can destroy your creativity'.

"It Takes All Kinds"—written with some input from Alexander Doré, establishes a similar kind of moral relativism, perhaps an explanation—or self-justification, that falls way-short of outright apology. With a 'whatever-will-be will-be' shrug of stoic resignation he offers 'someone has got to win, someone loses', as though success-to-failure is a blameless up and down process. As though there are different strokes for different folks, but underneath it all, he persists 'everybody is a star', still. Again he recapitulates the title track, with a cautionary reminder that beyond the entire phoney façade of what the world judges as material success, what really matters is that you stay true to yourself, that 'all that you have got to do is remember who you are'. Then "Who's To Say?" takes it further. It fights back. In a line with a complex genealogy he poses the question 'what about the Joneses worried about the Stoneses?' Of course, it's the Family Stoneses who put the music to the dance, in opposition to the Bob Dylan everyman-square 'Mr Jones' who knows 'something is happening, but you don't know what it is, do you…?' Sly, by implication, is still on the side of the aware. As on *'Whole New Thing'* where he was exploiting the 'square' mindset versus the hippie-mentality, the 'we' in this instance, is still the cool, the hyper-aware. His is a 'we' still defined by attitude. But now he takes it further—as never before, and even levels an accusation at his faith when he demands to know why should the 'church decide how you should feel inside?' The implied answer is—no, it shouldn't.

Most critics failed to delve that deep. Despite Warner's claim that this 'is an album that is the beginning of the complete return of the Family Stone', what little critical attention it *did* receive resulted in nothing more than a consistent panning. Pete Wingfield's review in *'Melody Maker'* welcomed the 'down-home freshness' of opening track "Remember Who You Are" with its noodling bass-line and Rose's gospel-powered 'I believe… I believe, I'm back' as 'vintage Sly—it could have been made eight years ago, as a follow-up to "Family Affair" (8th December 1979). A hit-maker in his own right—"Eighteen With A Bullet" reached no. 7 in 1975!, Pete identified 'all the old quirky ingredients—skeletal rhythm track, wah-wah-guitar, and those stoned tones croaking their way through some typically telegrammatic, enigmatic, basically dumb lyrics, exhorting 'self-help' a la "Stand!", "Everyday People", and "You Can Make It If You Try".' With teasing irony he suggests that self-help is a commodity Sly could have used in recent times. However, while conceding that the track was benefiting from solid play on American radio—'which is more than any of his other records, over the last few years have managed', he dismisses the rest of the album—'what little there is of it', as serving only to reinforce the audience's direst pessimism.

'Back On The Right Track' failed commercially, peaking at a US no. 152 in November 1979. Its failure caused Sly to retreat even further. Into two decades of snow. In this book these albums have been detailed, or perhaps—to some taste, over-detailed. Because they are what remain. The albums, in their digital CD reincarnation are still there to be experienced, as fresh and sharp as the moment they were created… along with piles of cuttings from old music journals, a couple of books, some murky low-fi video on the internet. Their time has gone, and can never be reclaimed. The events can be described, pieced together from the accounts of participants or observers, but at best such virtual reconstructions can only provide an incomplete approximation. There's the movie sequence, and some TV-clips that give some visual idea of what it was like to be there. But for the essence of what Sly Stone did, there are the albums. And—although Sly's two Warner albums dropped out of sight for some two decades, until rediscovered on CD, it's within the albums that his truth remains.

To Simon Witter, profiling 'one of the first and greatest international black superstars', Sly Stone 'survived unimaginable amounts of sex and drugs' (in *'i-D'* magazine January 1988). He was spiritually tired of all the bullshit he'd lived through. He felt artistically drained, tired, with nothing new to say, unable to live with the weight of his gift. He'd lost the protective shield of his old band, he no longer had the self-assured professionalism that would have come from spending the previous years gigging and song-writing. Instead, that time had been devoured by a slurry of tattle-tales. He'd been involved with—and obsessed with, music continuously since he was a kid. It was all he'd thought about, all he'd lived for. But in describing Sly as a casualty, saying narcotics had ripped up his brain forever, Simon Witter was hardly alone. No better or more conveniently reliable diagnostic tools were available to advance the diagnosis further. So Sly provided that satisfyingly simple archetype, for forty years. Even as there were periodic speculations of a comeback, there was much more than just legend to live up to. The longer he stayed away, the more uncertain he became about coming back, or about the wisdom of even trying. The more he stayed away, the deeper he sank into some other dark world. He was the lonely long-distance muso. Operating at the limit of reason, he was peering into a void most of us are incapable of imagining, but which we experience by proxy, through Sly's tortured journey. Sly academic

Dave Marsh poses another question 'had Sly Stone been white, wouldn't he be as lionised today as rock musicians with whom his name was once spoken in a single breath—John Lennon, Jim Morrison, Bob Dylan? Despite his oh-so public dissipation and fall from grace, he does not even offer up a convenient corpse over which to lay hosannas. But time does not diminish his greatest work…' A lot had been wasted, but still the die-hards and fellow-travellers were left with the vague hope that all was not lost.

Chapter Nineteen
'Ain't But the One Way'

'One Nation Under A Groove...'

Although largely recorded through 1979, it was during March 1981 that Sly Stone's appearance as a supporting character on the Funkadelic LP *'The Electric Spanking Of War Babies'*—with its vivid collage cover, hit the stores. For funk pioneer Clinton, the brilliant mind behind Parliament and Funkadelic, it was to be his last project under the 'Funkadelic' title, and some see it as the final album of his golden era. Well, maybe. Originally intended as a double-set, there are nine tracks totalling 44:10-minutes playing time. Sly shares composer credits with Mr P-Funk himself on the fifth track—"Funk Gets Stronger (Killer Millimeter Longer Version)", he adds guitar and vocals too, produces the track and plays synth, keyboards and drums. 'Hey Sly' yells Clinton, 'funk gets stronger as it goes longer, silly silly really, killer-millimeter longer' (a reference back to 'beat is getting stronger, / music getting longer too' on "I Want To Take You Higher"), before they eventually break into a 'Sergeant Pepper' quote 'we'd love to take you home with us, we'd love to funk you home' closing with 'we love you yeah yeah yeah', melding into a bizarre re-take on the Beatles' "She Loves You". Just as Sly had quoted "Eleanor Rigby" all those years ago on the *'Life'* track "Plastic People". Although the album in total seldom reaches the epic heights of *'One Nation Under A Groove'* (1978), funk work-outs such as "Electro-Cuties", the reggae-infected "Shockwaves"—and "Funk Gets Stronger" itself, stand among its best cuts.

George Clinton's career closely parallels Sly's own. Although without Sly's innovations, there would likely have been no Funkadelic. But by the same token, it was through Clinton's inspired lunacy that the crazed Family Stone on-the-one chanting groove was taken to its (il)logical limit. It had all begun even earlier than that, in the 1950's. 'When I saw Frankie Lymon doing "Why Do Fools Fall In Love", that was it, pretty much everyone at school was in a group after that' he told the BBC4 documentary 'George Clinton:

Tales Of Dr Funkenstein' (October 2006). Not such an unlikely springboard perhaps—Frankie Lymon's precocious but ultimately tragic success inspired many imitators. But great things have to start somewhere, and in Clinton's case that was Plainfield, New Jersey, with the formation of a Teenagers-styled Doo-wop group called Parliament. A true barbershop outfit—they worked a salon straightening some hair, coiffing some others, and generally attending to customer's tonsorial needs while harmonising for them—and soon they'd become the hottest vocal quartet in town. With Motown on its mid-sixties rise, a record deal seemed the next obvious step. Unfortunately, the Motor City giant was less than sympathetic, so the group signed to a smaller Detroit label, Revilot instead. Then the band lost the rights to the Parliament name when Revilot was taken into receivership.

Undaunted, Clinton relegated the vocalists to secondary status, and put the group's backing band out front. The stage was set for a musical revolution. Clinton was exposed to more than just Motown at the time, and the new sounds he was alchemising began reflecting the increasingly vocal Vietnam War protests as well as the same black power pressures that had forged and stressed-out the Family Stone. Just as importantly, hippiedom was hip, and as Clinton puts it, when he heard the Beatles *'Sgt Peppers Lonely Hearts Club Band'* (1967) he 'lost it completely'. And soon, only a slight step behind Sly—Funkadelic had become more than just a band, it was a P-Funk conglomerate of identities in multiple guises. Footage of the group from the late sixties shows onstage freakery aplenty, beyond even the Family Stone's extravagance. Anyone wondering where *'The A-Team'*s Mr. T got the Mohawk idea for his hair need look no further than Clinton circa 1970! 'I want the bomb' he proclaimed, 'I want the P-Funk. I want my funk uncut'. With the Family Stone in temporary eclipse, and the group signed to Westbound, from *'Funkadelic'* in March 1970, to multi-talented Bernie Worrell's official debut with *'Free Your Mind... And Your Ass Will Follow'* (July 1970) later that same year, and Bootsy Collins joining for *'Maggot Brain'* (1971), the Funkadelic Mothership was in stratospheric ascent. Don Letts' film-documentary charts the next decade and beyond in fine detail, with mounds of footage and interviews with all the right people. It does two things in the process, first, it makes you want to hear the music again—including Eddie Hazel's amazing guitar solo on "Maggot Brain". Second, it makes explicit the link from Clinton and fellow passengers Bootsy Collins and Sly, to Prince and the hip-hop in the Eighties, through into urban music. From where Andre 3000 and Macy Gray got their sense of fun(k). As Dr Dre phrases it, 'back in the seventies that's all people were doing—getting high, wearing Afro's, bell-bottoms, and listening to Parliament-Funkadelic'.

But while George Clinton's outrageous creations conquered the Soul charts, they rarely crossed over onto the Pop listings—at least, not until the mid-seventies, unlike Sly's success which had always been equally divided between both markets. And while Sly had peaked early, only to suffer an extended decline, Clinton's star just kept growing. Clinton picked up the torch Sly had mislaid, maintaining his output and quality control, extending the sounds over ten years via an ever-changing family of bands. And where his message was blunter than Sly's had been, he nevertheless shoved the envelope too, into places where a humorous phrase might mean nothing more than playful tomfoolery, or might disguise some deeper political double-entendre. The apparently nonsensical title track of *'The Electric Spanking Of War Babies'* (1981) refers to what Clinton saw as the war department's manipulation of the media as a propaganda machine to promote its neo-imperialistic policies. Although it's not necessary to correctly decipher this subtext to enjoy its fun, and its occasionally surrealist groove. 'I, at the age of seventeen / was adopted by aliens' he announces. As with Sun Ra's extragalactic paraphernalia, these were aliens who supposedly 'programmed' him with a message for the world, the need to Get Funky. Yet from that point on the song then turns obliquely political with direct references to the Vietnam War—'you've seen the bomb (electric) / Vietnam (spanking of) / LSD (war babies)'. 'It's a bummer to find / that your mind / and your behind / gets exploded in time'.

At this stage Clinton was re-signed to Warner's Priority subsidiary, and found himself part of the label-structure within which Sly was languishing. And fortuitously, on the brink of sliding back into narcotic obscurity, Sly found he'd fallen into the safety-net of a supportive colleague. To tie in with the album Sly accepted an invitation to tour with Clinton's next post-Funkadelic project, the P-Funk All-Stars. He'd last been spotted at the Hawaii 'Sunshine Festival' in Diamond Head around Summer 1976. Now, relieved of the frontman responsibility, content to sit behind the keyboards and let Clinton carry the weight of being the show's focal-point, these ventures back into live-appearance gave Sly the renewed confidence and motivation to embark on his own brief solo 'Psychedelic Psoul' tour. For Sly, the culmination of this burst of activity was *'Ain't But The One Way'* (Warner Brothers)—Sly's eleventh and final album, recorded during 1981, but issued the following year. It's an album with a complex disrupted history, but to Clinton 'he's musical as hell, so he don't have no time limit on him', and the results are 'timeless'. George Clinton had started out enthusiastically collaborating on joint studio sessions with Sly, until the Stone-curse caught up with them. Some claim there was a joint-narcotics bust that actually happened in the studio itself, another that the arrest happened when they were caught freebasing on an LA freeway, although charges were dropped on a legal technicality. Whatever, Clinton fell out with Warners—his finances in chaos, complicated by legal problems compounded by copyright and trademark issues surrounding the multiple group-names under which he operated. The recordings were abruptly terminated and he acrimoniously took all his projects off the label. Some of the Funkadelic tapes which he took with him into his later incarnations included some with degrees of Sly input which would be leaked onto subsequent albums—including a powerful "Hydraulic Pump" listed as by 'George Stone and Sly Clinton' and featuring Bobby Womack.

While, disheartened, Sly vanished back into self-seclusion, and Warners called in Stewart Levine to salvage what he could from the remaining tapes. Credited as co-producer, Levine had already established his credentials by working with Hugh Masekela and the Jazz Crusaders, and would produce the *'Love Wars'* (1983) album for Womack & Womack—a duo consisting of Bobby's younger brother, and Sam Cooke's daughter. He was assisted in his Sly Stone reconstruction efforts by engineers Roger Dollarhide and Frank Nadasdy. Levine later told *'Record Collector'* magazine how 'Sly had already taken quite a long time to make the album, but it was unacceptable to Warners, and Sly was in no condition to work further on it. So I came into LA, and got the musicians together—some of the guys who had actually played with Sly, and who loved his music. We recreated the album. What you hear is a combination of what Sly started, and what we completed.' He later joked that Sly had told him, 'Man, this is how we have to work together in the future. I'll fuck it up, and you fix it!" But even considered as a flip self-deprecating jibe made about a comparatively modest proposition, coming from the man who had single-handedly fine-tuned the exacting specifications of *'Stand!'*, this was a revealing admission. On the sleeve 'special thanks' are, rather formally, extended to Frederick Stewart (no longer 'Stone'), Rose Banks (her married name), Cynthia Robinson, Pat Rizzo, Andrew Newmark, Kenneth Burke, Jerry Martini, Vaetta Stewart, and a list of others.

Notwithstanding Levine's tweaking, the album that resulted is virtually another one-man product, with Sly on guitar, keyboards and vocals, and—on "Hobo Ken", he announces 'I'm gonna play a little harmonica' too. It involves eight Sly originals. Plus the smooth easy groove and playful telephone overlays of "Ha Ha, Hee Hee", which is credited to Rizzo—with its laughter-echoes going back to "Running Away". Then there's a bizarre vocoder remake of the Kinks' "You Really Got Me", an echo yet further back to his KSOL radio playlist. At least Sly seems to be enjoying himself, burbling away around this funk workout of Dave Davies' classic riff with a pure flat-out muscular sax leading the charge. Elsewhere, the near four-letter euphemism that lurks playfully behind "Who In The Funk Do You Think You Are" runs a close approximation of the Beatles' "Get Back" backbeat (perhaps connected to the working title of "Who's To Say" on the previous album?), complete with little faux-Billy Preston keyboard runs. And a closer investigation of the lyrics reveal another Bible-questioning line—in the same vein that "Who's To Say" demanded to know why should the 'church decide how you should feel inside'. This time he's asking 'where in the funk is it in the book, what you should see and what to overlook?' Again, the implied answer is—no, 'the book' has no right to make such demands. Indeed, stripped of all frills and pretensions, it could be argued that much of this album constitutes perfectly enjoyable, perfectly competent funk. But while there are gems—the title track's keyboard trills, the neat organ-break and Rose's high vocal exchanges on "L.O.V.I.N.U", and even Sly's characteristic talent for coining bizarre lyrical image such as 'as tough as dehydrated rain'!, there are few moments quite quirky enough to match what had come before. There's the slyly inviting carnality that is "We Can Do It" suggestively oozing 'if you've got the glass / I've got the wine', a stab into the darker side of love and the seedier aspects of lust which is certain to provoke momentarily pleasing listener-reactions, although it's only necessary to flip back to the exuberant invention of the *'Life'* album to see what exactly has been lost along the way.

Closing enigmatically with another 'Shadrack Mesech Abednigo'-style kid's tongue-twister rhyme—'how could a would-not could-not, if a would-not could-not would', it's an album that forms a freakishly strange suicide note to mark the end of Sly's brief association with Warners. Odder still is the chilling stripped-back 0.44-minute "Sylvester". Sly slurs the words until they slide into each other, a wry phrasing peculiar to Sly and nobody else, recognisably the same streetwise style he'd once used to such devastating effect on "Family Affair". Autobiographically he admits 'his name is in the file of fame', yet behind the fame, he's a stranger. It's a track that provides a poignant glimpse into the mind-set of a man supposedly denied self-awareness by his own celebrity status. A protestation, and a reassertion, that somewhere within the long dark 'Sly Stone' shadow, there is still the same shy amiable Sylvester Stewart who'd come out of Vallejo, and Momma-dear still knows his name. Perhaps, lurking inside this brief vignette is Sylvester's final attempt to extricate himself from his monstrous out-of-control alter ego? But despite such promising moments, and despite Levine's best post-production efforts, the album was effectively ignored. Robbie Vincent's 'Radio London' show provided airplay support for "Ha Ha, Hee Hee", elsewhere the set was passed over.

And it seemed Sly was far too preoccupied, poised on a permanent event horizon of drug busts and legal manoeuvres, to even promotionally intervene in its fate. Later that same year (July) he was arrested in the LA Westwood Plaza Hotel for cocaine possession—giving his name to the arresting officers as 'Freddie Stewart'. And yet again in February 1983 in Illinois, where a firearms charge for possession of a sawn-off shotgun was added. More positive signs, whispers and mixed fortunes emerged during 1984. In an ironic turn-around, with George Clinton's sympathetic support stretched beyond all reasonable limits, Sly had resumed hanging out with Bobby Womack. And Bobby felt moved to intervene in the train-wreck drama that Sly had become. With or without a 'Family Stone', he no longer had the drawing power to headline a show. So instead, Womack honoured his debt to his former mentor by inviting *him* out on a two-month US tour, as part of his touring band. Bobby's fortunes had turned around dramatically following his work on *'There's A Riot Goin' On'*. He'd scored the movie theme for *'Across 110th Street'* (1972), later sequenced onto Quentin Tarantino's *'Jackie Brown'* movie in 1997. And his album *'The Poet'* (January 1982) provided his major break-through into the big-time. It was hailed as his masterpiece, even though record company politics ensured he would never receive his just rewards from its success. 'I'm a legend' he acknowledged wryly 'not a rich legend'. Now, with typically absurdist wit, Bobby—'The Last Soul Man', writes about touring with 'skinny old Sly sleeping in the corner of the living room—on his head'. Having successfully fought against his own chemical misadventures, Bobby also attempted to help Sly confront *his* drug nightmare. Following further arrests in June and August of 1983, and another in 1984 Sly acquiesced and entered rehab. Bobby provides an amusing account of what resulted. 'I heard he got a doctor or psychologist to cop for him while he was doing time. Sly's method was to challenge the guy, tell the doc that he would never be able to understand a guy like Sly unless he'd gone through some of the same stuff—and that meant taking the same drugs. 'How can you talk to me about drugs?' he demanded. 'You never saw a drug in your life. If you knew you'd try it'. He insisted on being treated by someone he could relate to. Before long, he had the doc under the desk doing a rock while Sly dished out the therapy. The doctor also switched testing bottles so that nothing showed up in Sly's piss when it came around to screening for pharmaceuticals'. These stories tally with Bubba's tales of his courtroom escapades. But following this programme of failed stabs of rehab for Sly, Bobby delivered on another promise, this time to his own late father—Friendly Womack, by returning to gospel for his *'Back To My Roots'* (1999) album. Although there was a remaining bond, it was Sly who suggested the name for Bobby's son Truth, in 1978, although the child didn't survive beyond four months. 'It's a sad thing, but I haven't heard from Sly in many years' admits Womack more recently. 'I don't know where Sly is at. I hear all kinds of stories, but I love him. If he made the turn I made, then we could talk. That would be beautiful, but it is what it is and life goes on. I just pray for him…'

Silences lengthened. To Sly, he was 'just travelling, going around, jumping in and out, and up and down'. During 1985 there were reports, following claims Sly had kicked his drug addiction, that several record labels were interested in signing him, including A&M. There was further talk of an album with George Clinton. Yet all that actually materialised from these eddies of rumour was that Sly managed a guest appearance on Jesse Johnson's major R&B hit "Crazay".

From Minneapolis, Johnson was a Prince protégé and former guitarist with Morris Day & The Time. Sly can be seen playing keyboards and singing in a curious mock-English accent on the video, which benefited from 'Video Soul' screentime on the BET (Black Entertainment Television) cable-network during 1986, although Sly dismissively shrugs off his involvement in the project as 'I just happened to go in the studio'. Then Sly successfully dueted with Martha Davis (of The Motels) on "Love And Affection" for the soundtrack of the mildly racist movie *'Soul Man'* (1986). It's tempting to speculate exactly how much Sly had researched the project he was contributing to. A white college student with bad grades exploits an affirmative action programme by pretending to be black, and colouring his skin to get into Harvard law school. For the man who'd once told it like it was with 'Don't Call Me Nigger, Whitey', surely Sly must have been aware of the powerful irony at work in supplying music for such a motion picture? A further film project foundered before even reaching that state of irony. There was a title-track intended for the light-hearted Whoopi Goldberg / Bob Goldthwait comedy romp *'Burglar'* (1987). A direct-to-video movie based around the Lawrence Block novel *'The Burglar In The Closet'* (1987). Listen to the soundtrack, and there are Sly-like punching horns melded to jerky eighties rhythms, but the history and authenticity of the track is dubious. And the screen credits for the 'original songs' list Bernard Edwards and Sylvester Levay, not Sly Stone. Yet among the unused session outtakes for *'Ain't But The One Way'* is a track given the title "You're The One" which resembles an instrumental theme for a 'Shaft'-style Blaxploitation movie. As though Sly—in an alternate lifetime, *might* have been scoring film soundtracks alongside the Isaac Hayes' or Curtis Mayfields'. Instead, during that same year, Sly got himself sufficiently together to record a one-off stand-alone non-chart single of his own—through the optimistic deal with A&M, but "Eek-A-Bo-Static" bombed, it failed to even register on the soul chart, and is now virtually impossible to find. It seems that around this time other musicians also reached out to induce this by-now near-mythic figure back into the studio with the offer of one project or another, because he crops up guesting on a bizarre miscellany of titles (listed in the 'Discography' section). But after a while he even stopped talking to people. He was still there, elusive, yet content to do without them. So they stopped asking. And history lurched on its haphazard way without him.

The rest of the decade is a pitiful postscript. A life gone bugshit. No longer even a theatre of the absurd, more a marginalised sideshow, with little that has anything to do with music. There's a confusing string of news clippings documenting minor brushes with the law. Just when it seems there was something positive on the horizon, fresh shit was heading fanwards. There's something infinitely depressing about watching some priceless elixir—compounded of promise, talent, and joy, swirling pathetically down some toxic drain. Again, in November and December 1986, he ran afoul of the law. There was an arrest, in Decatur, Illinois for cocaine use and possession. He missed several court dates. He'd no sooner informed the 'Los Angeles Times' that he was clean in a November 1987 feature, than he was charged days later for cocaine abuse. He was arrested after a two-night engagement at the LA Las Palmas Theatre, his last real gig for nearly twenty years. He disappeared, and there were stories circulating that he was declared a fugitive from justice in 1989, was arrested in Connecticut that same 14th November and extradited back to LA, where he admitted driving under the influence of cocaine. Pleading guilty to two counts of possession he was sent down for a nine-month sentence at a federal drug clinic.

Unnamed sources say he was never able to recover from that final arrest. But by now the world was no longer seeing Sylvester Stewart as flesh and blood, as a human being caught up in a human tragic-drama. They didn't even see him as a former funk-rock star. Mostly, they didn't see him at all. Somewhere, in semi-retirement, he continued to battle his sundry addictions with varying degrees of success. Reports of his mental and physical health were not encouraging. There was talk of him re-entering rehab facilities at the Lee Mental Health Clinic in Ft Myers, Florida, and later of a 45-day rehab at the LA Brotman Medical Center, elsewhere he was reportedly living in a homeless shelter, or in squalor in a sheltered-housing complex. George Clinton said he was living in Malibu. Or else he was living in splendour near Beverly Hills… or perhaps it was Napa Valley, with two female assistants, where he was recording demos in a home studio and riding his motorcycle. Or he was booked into the rubber-motel, all skulled-out and fucked-up. 'Seems to me its mystery, I cannot figure it out' he admits (on "L.O.V.I.N.U"), 'when I think I've got it down that's when I'm most in doubt… that's when your 'down' is out'…

****

'Thank you for the party, but I could never stay…'

("Thank You")

Arthur Lee had also slipped into drug-induced mental health problems. So much so that he ended up in prison serving a ten-stretch for fire-arms offences. All the while becoming—like Sly, even more legendary in his absence. They were both lost way out there in some spiritual desert, with no pretence they'd found the right answers. Their fade-away into limbo depressing for those who truly love their revolutionary music. But they'd taken the world on a hell of a journey. All the while, Sly remained inactive, falling deeper into an idiosyncrasy of despair and narcotic self-abuse, living in a series of apartments in the greater Los Angeles area haunted by legal battles, child-support issues, and medical ills. 'Time is passin', I grow older, things are happening fast.' He'd long since given up explaining himself. His final interviews consist of little more than monosyllabic denials of culpability. Until he eventually stopped talking altogether. Yet he's a musician, it's hot-wired into his DNA. As long ago as Vallejo he'd found something he was a natural at. Was empathically engaged with. And without which his life has no purpose. It's the one thing that justifies all the badness. Some stories claim Sly has hours of recorded material waiting to see the light of day. Fan and operator of the www.slyfamstone.com website, Jon Dakss, reports that he spoke to Sly on the phone, and was then flown out to Coldwater Canyon where Sly had a home. He stayed over the weekend during April 1997, and was treated to tapes of new music, 'it was very funky, with throbbing bass and pounding drums. It had a very tribal spirit, but it also seemed sort of evil'. They subsequently stayed in touch, until 'all of the sudden, I never heard from him again'. Meanwhile George Clinton talked of hearing a stash of thirty-seven new Sly Stone songs, three albums-full, awaiting release, 'and this time they don't have to worry about getting me to finish it for him'. And a few home-studio recordings—most probably dating from around the late 1980's or early 1990's, *have* surfaced as bootlegs, with Sly's voice and keyboards run over programmed drums. One song at least—"Coming Back For More", is reportedly excellent, with a hauntingly autobiographical narrative, 'been so high I touched the sky / and the sky says 'Sly, why you tryin' to get by?' …' Much later Sly himself, in conversation with David Kamp, talked of a huge backlog of new material, 'a library, like, a hundred-and-some songs, or maybe two-hundred'. He even starts rhyming lyric-extracts in 'an insistent cadence somewhere between a preacher's and a rapper's'—one called "We're Sick Like That" which goes 'Give a boy a flag and teach him to salute, / give the same boy a gun and teach him how to shoot. / And then one night, in the bushes, he starts to cry / 'cause nobody ever really taught him how to die'. Words as current as the latest CNN rolling news.

Yet they remain unheard. By way of explanation Freddie confided to *'Spin'* magazine that Sly 'didn't want to be out in front anymore. The glamour didn't mean anything anymore. He wanted to be normal'. Whatever 'normal' is. There's some irony to the fact that—after David Kapralik had sold the publishing rights of the Sly Stone catalogue to Warner Bros for around $400,000, that in 1984 when they re-sold it on to Michael Jackson's Mijac Music, their stock had risen dramatically, to the extent that they were priced at considerably more. Leaving the 'Prince Of Pop' in possession of both the Beatles—and The Family Stone legacy. Because by then, with the distanced past-tense perspective of hindsight, it was becoming increasingly obvious that historically, at least, Sly Stone had become a valuable resource. There was a ripple of favourable reviews when "Family Affair" was reissued on the CBS 'Upfront' dance label. In strictly commercial terms, "I Want To Take You Higher" was licensed for use in royalties-generating AT&T TV-adverts.

"Hot Fun In The Summertime" was used to promote Carnival Cruises. Then "Everyday People" was prominently featured by Toyota in its late-1990's series of prime-time TV-commercials, something that makes you want to rip out someone's windpipe.

More legitimately, Sly's well-sampled body of work, especially the impossibly bright early material, continued to provide the basic template for all forms of urban soul. Family Stone grooves persisted to haunt artists all the way from the Disco-era hits such as Chic's "Le Freak", into the smooth Glam-Funk of Prince. While those same Sly riffs and rhythms could be found lurking behind, and informing Hip-hop, into the nineties, and beyond. The Family Stone's "Trip To Your Heart" forms the basis for LL Cool J's 1990 hit "Mama Said Knock You Out". On the first wave of UK sample-based Acid House, the third hit from DJ Mark Moore's S' Express—"Hey Music Lover" in 1989, uses the 'I want to take you higher' refrain, then adds 'listen to the voices' sequences. Fatboy Slim and Kid Rock use Sly samples. Just as there are flashback style-reflections in up-front Outkast videos. Rap owes a debt to the lyrical honesty of *'There's A Riot Goin' On'* in describing the darker side of the black experience. Music journalist Miles Marshall Lewis points out that 'D'Angelo played *'There's A Riot Goin' On'* constantly in the studio while recording his masterpiece *'Voodoo'*. And if, for that first MTV generation weaned on "Beat It" and "Thriller", Michael Jackson represents the master of 'crossover', an ambiguous androgyny neither black nor white, male nor female, others with longer memory-reach already knew better. Sylvester Stewart had taken out that particular patent a full decade earlier. He'd got there first, and no-one has ever quite captured the sheer sense of joy that he once managed to get down on record. There were still few and infrequent Sly-snippets that surfaced every now and then in the press. On 29th January 1987 Sly reportedly helped launch the 'Fight For Literacy Day' in California. In 1991 he granted his permission to a cover of "Thank You (Falettinme Be Mice Elf Agin)" by a Japanese band called Thirteen Cats (13CATS), confirming his approval by playing guitar on the CD itself. And more obliquely, in his home-town Bay Area, Jody and Michael McFadin established a soul label called Luv 'n' Haight records in 1993, one of its projects involving singles by Oakland guitarist Eugene Blacknell, including his "Dance To The Rhythm". To Sheffield group ABC on their hit single "When Smokey Sings" 'Luther croons, James screams' but Sly Stone, he's 'the original, originator'. And 'the originator's work was still providing lessons for new musics.

Musicians come and go, but marketing is forever. And while Sly Stone was out of commission, Black music kept evolving. In Detroit, the onslaught of the late-1970's triggered a decline in the US auto-industry, and the city landscape of huge factories and skyscrapers rusted into an urban wasteland. Its music had been born from black workers flocking north into the city for the car assembly-line factory-jobs—Martha & The Vandellas could even be seen 'calling out around the world' in a promo film-clip dancing through the factory itself. Now the downtown home of Motown Records was finally bulldozed, so that simultaneously, both the Age of the American automobile, and its signifying musical expression, passed into nostalgia. And as the Motown decade closed, the contagion of cocaine and heroin insinuated even further through the black community, and the youth counterculture. The neural network of the 'underground press' disseminated viral-rumours of the CIA deliberately channelling mass narcotics into the ghettos, despite having signed up to the United Nations 1961 ruling that defined coca as a 'poisonous species' (due to its alkaloid content needed to refine cocaine). In 1971 Richard Nixon declared his 'war on drugs' in Latin and South America. Yet according to those same press sources, as GI's returned home from the war with big-time habits, and with nightmares that only heroin could numb, J Edgar Hoover and Nixon's Justice Department were busy looking the other way as CIA-backed warlords in Vietnam and Laos smuggled smack into American ghettos. Death-drugs were sold, and death-drugs were taken. After all, wasn't it preferable to have drug-gangs warring for turf and slaughtering each other, rather than that they become black-awareness advocates questioning the unopposed continuation of white power? Samuel L Jackson—a former black radical who served as an usher at Martin Luther King's funeral, and whose breakthrough role as a crack-addict in Spike Lee's *Jungle Fever* (1991) came directly after a rehab stint intended to cure his long-term addiction, spoke (on the Henry Rollins show) of how in summer 1969 all marijuana and hallucinogens vanished from the Atlanta streets, and the only available dope was heroin, resulting in widespread dependency and overdoses among young black males. Forget about the War on Drugs, this was a War *through* Drugs. 'That was the most effective defuser of the revolution that they came up with' Jackson argued, 'and it worked'. Better by far that the stench of burning tyres stay in the sink Housing Projects and wasteland apartments than in the white suburbs. Perhaps those proto-internet rumours were correct? Whatever, drug-consumption only escalated. And continues to escalate.

For a while—memories of the civil rights era enthused young African-Americans with something to believe in, now there was only a kind of blood-weary paralysis. And the main protagonists were either no longer around, or in no fit condition, to provide aspirational examples. Eldridge Cleaver, disenchanted by witnessing the actual workings of communism first hand, returned to Oakland in 1975 to face federal charges. By then, the Black Panthers were virtually over. He renounced what was left of the movement as part of his plea-bargaining. The most serious charges were dropped, and he did 1,200 hours of community service. But his series of bizarre metamorphoses had only just begun. He went on to tour the country giving rousing motivational lectures inspired by his switch to born-again Christianity. Then he became a Mormon convert, and a failed nominee for the Californian Senate as a conservative Republican candidate. Until his arc of celebrity finally hit bottom with a period of crack cocaine addiction aggravated by burglary and assault charges. He claimed to have kicked dependency, only to succumb to prostate cancer, of which he died in 1st May 1998, aged 62.

Elsewhere, rated high on the FBI's 'most wanted' list, Huey Newton spent three years of self-imposed exile in Cuba, assisted there by Bert Schneider—sympathetic creator of the Monkees and producer of *'Easy Rider'* (1969). Huey also returning to the US in July 1977 to surrender himself up. Acquitted after two deadlocked trials, he went on to earn a PhD from UC Santa Cruz in 1980. But recriminations and rumour continued to dog him and drag him down, with accusations of alcohol and narcotic dependency, small-scale Oakland protection rackets, charges of embezzling Panther funds, and even allegations of murdering a prostitute. Following a prison-spell for parole-violation, his story closed on an Oakland sidewalk where he died in a shoot-out with drugs rivals (22nd August 1989), or 'two shots in the dark, now Huey's dead' as Tupac Shakur eulogised it. And Bobby Seale? he was expelled from the party he'd helped build, after standing for public office in Oakland on a Panther party ticket. The 1973 campaign—part of an attempt to restructure the Panthers into a more conventional political machine, succeeded to the extent of promoting and coming within a few hundred votes of installing Lionel Wilson as the first-ever black mayor of Oakland. But by the end of the decade, with the Panthers in the final phase of terminal decline, Seale focussed his attentions on 'Reach', a youth education programme.

While Angela Davis—following her arrest, trial, and full-media acquittal, resumed her interrupted academe to become Professor of History of Consciousness at the University of California. But just as hip-hop uses historic samples from Sly and James Brown as an investment in the continuity of black culture, so references to the example of Black Power are punched deep into music and lyrics. The Game claims 'the dream of Huey Newton that's what I'm living through'. Tupac Shakur—whose mother Afeni was herself an active Panther, takes the legacy more literally with 'we gotta fight back / that's what Huey said'. Among many other Rap name-checks Public Enemy's Chuck D (Carlton Douglas Ridenhour) also defiantly refers to 'the shootin' of Huey Newton'. It could be counter-argued that the very need for that continuity to be restated implies that the radical's 'from the ghetto-up' struggle for pride and independence had failed. That racism is atavistic. That its eradication will not be achieved just by slogans and catchy anthems. Its attitudes are embedded in a collective reflex mindset.

Certainly, on the face of it, the rise of Thug-Gangsta Rap charts a long hard path from Sly's 'different strokes' to *'Get Rich Or Die Tryin'* (2003). The nine-piece (now eight-piece) Wu-Tang Clan—numbering Prince Rakeem 'RZA', Ghost-Face Killa (aka Tony Starks) and the late Ol' Dirty Bastard (aka Russell Jones), declared 'shame on a nigga who try to run game on a nigga. / Wu buck wild with the trigger, shame on a nigga who try to run game on a nigga. / We buck—I fuck yo' ass up!' This is the sound of black America turning in on itself, too caught up in its own internal rivalries to look outside itself. And such defensive-aggressive gun-totin' posturing tends to be a more common subject-matter than political involvement. Its 'keeping it real' religion of conspicuous bling materialism has more to do with the cult of capitalism than it has to do with the Panther's community ethos. Whatever was going on as the likes of P Diddy or Snoop Dogg flaunted their furs and gold, it wasn't the radical politicisation of the American black experience we'd been invited to expect from the likes of Public Enemy's *'It Takes A Nation Of Millions To Hold Us Back'* (1988). The slide from the socio-political concept album that Chuck D called a ' *'What's Going On'* for the hip-hop generation', a furious collision of Noam Chomsky-worthy agit-prop and the Bomb Squad's blitzkrieg beats representing the coming of age of hip-hop as an agent for social commentary—to the violence and misogyny to women 'ho's' that reduces the 'Sisterhood' to little more than pimp-token accessories of visible wealth, was all part of the Rap community's dismayingly reductive definition of success, as bitches and bling. But that's how the industry prefers it. After all, the media had grown far more ruthlessly expert at appropriating and marketing anger than it once was. Yet, rather than representing a 'Stagger-Lee' playful anti-hero, Curtis '50 Cents' Jackson's revealingly dark and unsettling autobiography is riddled with more fear, hurt and confusion than his image would seem to admit, taking the mythology of authenticity all the way to its illogical bullet-scarred conclusion. What had begun in The Game's 'Huey Newton'-dream had become a degraded self-perpetuating social currency. Rap had gone from Black CNN to the Shopping Channel.

And after all, Sly Stone—yeah, he was just a Pop Star who had some catchy hits, then blew it all up his nose when his career came adrift. That's certainly one spin you can put on it. But Sly was also the brother who always took for granted the sanity of an interracial America where justice was self-evident and people lived as one. His music had deliberately ignored the supposed conventions that divide skin-tones. His funky playful take on Rock had birthed itself in the Freedom Rides and the optimistic San Francisco counterculture. But like the streets of that city, the dream had temporarily turned sour. So why does it hurt so much? Look at where we are now. See how far we've come from the ideals that Sly was talking about. How much closer are we to the implementation of those ideas? 'One of the reasons why the philosophies within the songs of Sly & The Family Stone are so unpopular' explains Sly's official website, 'isn't because those philosophies aren't still valid. It's because in order to actually implement those philosophies it requires people to not only have faith in themselves, but also to have faith in other people.' One person can't change the world. But each, in their way, plays a part. So perhaps our collective fascination with that period of idealism has something to do with what might have been, with the notion of the unfinished, the unrealised? With potential derailed? That it all really *could* have happened, just like Sly envisaged, but instead we phucked it up… and somewhere, someplace, there's the suspicion that he was out there, maybe thinking about what could have been. Within that interpretation of events, the sad conclusion of Sly's active career implies a weary acknowledgement that the dream of justice in the republic founded on slavery may also have met its premature end. When now, on a small overcrowded globally interconnected planet it's more vital than ever to celebrate our differences, but recognise our common shared humanity more.

So had it all been in vain? Had it all just led to a new cul-de-sac, a new impasse? Did it all amount to nothing more than new commercial opportunities for merchandising? Not quite. As early as the high-gloss pages of the November 1969 issue of *'Playboy'* Jesse Jackson held forth on US race issues—'I hear that melting-pot stuff a lot, and all I can say is that we haven't melted…' Yet recent internet DNA research indicates that—contrary to this view, beneath superficial appearances, the American racial mix is more richly complex, multifaceted, and fluid than they could ever have supposed. Check back a couple of generations and there's black blood somewhere in the whitest family tree, and white blood in the blackest family. And there can have been no better example of the racial/gender melting pot than the Family Stone. They were the metaphor. And its most visible manifestation. So why—apart from the high-profile Condoleezza Rice, Oprah Winfrey, or Will Smith, are African-Americans still socially disadvantaged, in sinkholes of neglect and racial profiling, despite decades of civil rights and positive discrimination? Is it still 'simply a matter of white 'gots' abandoning black 'ain't-gots? Not quite. In the decades since the civil-rights movement, America has enmeshed itself in a cocoon of self-delusion and doubletalk where race is concerned'—according to Nik Cohn (writing in the wake of Hurricane Katerina), 'and many African-Americans, their own fortunes improving, have played along. The black middle-class has distanced itself from those left behind. Chris Rock, the black comedian, jokes that he loves black people—it's niggas he can't stand. For others, it isn't a joke… they are what's buried below. They are everything the American dream was supposed to wipe away. They aren't supposed to exist, yet here they are.' Perhaps by subsuming his own racial identity within the broad church of hardworking American idealism, Barack Obama (white Kansas mother, black Kenyan father) offers an almost Sly solution to the impasse? Perhaps what Obama calls the 'post-racial' settlement is a realisation of what Sly envisaged?

'There are a lot of black people who understand reality' Sly complained, 'but the ones who do all the talking are usually people like Leslie Uggams, who seems like a kind of white-black person. Or H Rap Brown, a black-black person.' He's contrasting the moderate singer and actress who played Kizzy in *'Roots'*, with the Black Power activist who declared 'violence is as American as cherry pie'. Figures who occupy the two extremist positions. 'All the people between, you never hear about them. I don't know what to call them. The majority, maybe they're not advertising themselves? Maybe they're not saying anything interesting?' Oddly enough, the tendency Sly was attempting to define *was* given a name—the 'silent majority', by Richard M Nixon (in his 3rd November 1969 speech). And perhaps there *is* somthing to be said for the mainstream, if only because that's where most humans choose to swim. And maybe events *had* forced a quantum-jump in small-town silent majority Yew-Nited States thinking. The Panther's blood-spattered history revealed complex new aspects on the race equation, similar to what happened following the London suicide bombings of 7/7 2005. On that occasion, Prime Minister Tony Blair was forced to make accommodation with and concessions to what were perceived as 'moderate' Muslim elements. But he was 'Engaging With The Islamic World', out of fear of their more extremist counterparts. So small-town main-street Yew-Nited States in the late sixties suddenly found itself nodding in agreement to the essentially pacifist and gradualist message of the likes of Martin Luther King, only when the perceived menace of the more militant armed Panther factions began to make their presence felt. 'Force' as James Baldwin perceptively observes, does not 'reveal to the victim the strength of his adversary. On the contrary, it reveals the weakness, even the panic of his adversary'. This revelation shoves things out to the margins, but 'invests the victim with patience'. To achieve change, it seems, both strategies—good cop, bad cop, are required. Fight fire with fire. A record by the Golliwogs. A strategy for confronting white racism.

So was there a revolution?—a political revolution, a revolution in consciousness, or was it merely down to revolutions-per-minute? just a marketing exercise for vinyl and 'Angela Davis' T-shirts? *Was* there a revolution? Obviously no—not in the sense of tumbrels rolling, the palaces of privilege burning, the proletariat taking over the means of production, distribution and exchange. But at the same time, taking the long view—yes, a seismic cultural shift had occurred, after which the world would never be quite the same again. 'Different strokes for different folks' seems a very modest proposal. As a revolutionary slogan it doesn't ask for very much. Live and let live. A tolerant multi-culturalism. An acceptance of eccentricities and non-conformity. Pretty much the stuff we take for granted. But not so then. The fifties, extending over into the early sixties were, despite the rose-tinted nostalgia for simpler times, fiercely and viciously intolerant. Even without bringing the Ku Klux Klan, segregated water-fountains and disgusting levels of racism into the equation, Eisenhower's white 'Great Society' was an intolerant and repressive place ready to ostracise and victimise the slightest signs of individualism. Film of DJ's vehemently smashing big shellac Rock 'n' Roll records on-air to prevent the virus of jungle rhythms from corrupting youth, the organised burning of Beatles records by the Christian Taliban, may all seem quaint now. At the time it formed the front-line in a vital war for the soul of America—and by extension, the planet.

San Francisco's collapse as a haven for runaway youth marked the end of an extraordinary decade. But its influence, for most people, had been a positive one. Hey, what's so funny 'bout love, peace and understanding? The movement it represented helped put Vietnam in perspective, preparing America for its 'retreat with honour' from an impossible political and military quagmire. The music may have been a distorted mirror of untold numbers of acid trips, but it survived to mark a time of liberated morality. Love-&-Marriage, back then, went together like a horse-and-carriage. And woe-betide anyone who took their loving outside that strictly heterosexual 'Stepford Wives' monogamy. Not only could it get you frowned on, it could get you socially ostracised in all manner of vindictively nasty ways. Gay sex or illegitimacy could earn you the 'morally insane' stigma. And that was no minor deal, it wasn't the celebrity 'rebel' status Rock bands strive to achieve now and gloatingly flourish, it could make your life exceedingly unpleasant. It could wreck your life. If the 'revolution' changed all that—which it did, then it succeeded. When the rednecks shoot the long-hair bikers in the final moments of *'Easy Rider'* the sequence represents uptight America striking back at the up-setters. The right to openly 'let me be me, and you be you' free love, is a hard-fought-for gift of the sixties. The underground press was the first place to champion 'different strokes for different folks', devoting space to black liberation groups, gay rights, the woman's movement, eco-consciousness, anti-censorship legislation, and openness to non-Christian religions. Baby steps perhaps, but with massive consequences that shape the world that would emerge in the decades that followed. The reverberations are still detectable. We might not exactly have achieved perfect Sly-world as he envisaged it, but flip back to chapter five and see how far we've come. When the racist assassins of Medgar Evers and James Chaney are finally brought to justice. It might have been a long time coming, but eventually the change did come. Without all of *that*, there wouldn't be any of *this*. Without Emmett Till, Florence Beaumont, Big Bill Broonzy, James Meredith, Malcolm X, the SNCC, NAACP, and the SDS, without Ike Turner's father, the Reverend George Lee, James Brown, Amiri Baraka, Andrew Anderson, George Jackson, Huey Newton... and yes, Martin Luther King.

And Sylvester Stewart. Their names are in the file of fame...

But wait, what was Michael Jackson's great contribution to music culture?

Perhaps it's so all-pervasive we no longer notice? Elvis' apocalyptical eruption altered what it meant to be a Pop Star forever. A year zero. He made Rock music global. The Beatles caused a paradigm shift that shook the music world on its axis. The next was probably Hendrix. Sure, the Beatles used feedback on "I Feel Fine", but the default guitar sound was clean and distortion-free until Jimi, then overnight, every guitarist was turning volume up to eleven, and playing long improvisations using every effects-pedal known to science. Punk was an anti-Hendrix, razing riffs down to short sharp shocks. And Michael Jackson? With his post-racial post-gender status he defined himself, not as King of Soul, or King of R&B, or even King of Rock 'n' Soul, but as King of Pop. No-one questioned it. When he recorded with Slash, or indeed with Paul McCartney, it wasn't cross-over. It was simply global-Pop. It was the condition that Sly had always aspired to, where race was not a consideration. Sure, Michael Jackson learned from James Brown, and evolved out of the old Motown machine, but those who bought *'Thriller'* (1982) or *'Bad'* (1987) weren't buying genre. The time was right. Sly had always thought that way. He was simply ahead of the social game. A generation too advanced for his time. That's his achievement. That's his tragedy too.

Chapter Twenty
'Thank You'

'Remember who you are… as I remember who I am…'
("Remember Who You Are")

Something is wrong…

    Some people can't bear to reflect on their past. Others are only too willing to dissect and seize the opportunity of rearranging it. Sly does neither. It's titillating when stars retreat into mystery. After all, it's the prerogative of mythic beings to do so, deities so concealed by their legend that their reality becomes lost behind the part-construct of image. Whether it's Greta Garbo, Syd Barrett, JD Salinger, or Bob Dylan. Steve Paley calls Sly Stone 'the Howard Hughes of his generation'. And despite everything, he retains that mystery. Myth—according to Jean Cocteau, is a lie that becomes the truth, whereas history is truth that becomes a lie. Both elements are present and correct in the Sylvester Stewart story. Mystery in Rock is hard to maintain, the press, the fan websites all conspire in revelation-games. If they're starved of truth, then myth and legend become perfectly acceptable alternatives. The stuff around the music becomes as fascinating as the music itself. Parties. Narcotic preferences. Sexual peccadilloes. Therapy. Lies that become truth. Truth exaggerated into fiction. So clamming up—if that's to be the chosen guise, doesn't necessarily ensure anonymity. Like Keith Richard, Shane MacGowan or Shaun Ryder, Sly Stone is held in high regard by those who consider Rock 'n' Roll something to be lived large, as well as something merely about virtuosity. His legend is that of the battle-hardened self-saboteur. The enigma who fell off the train. Secluded from the world, from reality. And despite—or perhaps because of his long vacation, Sly has kept that mythic aura, the kind usually awarded to Rock stars who die young. Indeed, at certain points in the tale he seemed destined to be racketed towards the pantheon of Jimi Hendrix, Sam Cooke… and Kurt

Cobain. Those who live furiously and die young. Part of the decline and free-fall career-path, from Rock 'n' Roll lifestyle to Rock 'n' Roll ending. Instead, he was alive, but deathly still. Un-dead. In an afterlife not so much out of the loop, as marooned in a loop he'd created all of his own. Until all that's left is the image of escape. With something almost appealing about such a symmetry. Some people have mystery written into their DNA. So alluring. So enticing. It stays that way all their lives.

A conventional music biography is not—on the face of it, the most efficacious tool for investigating such an elusive subject. The best attempts to write Sylvester Stewart's life necessarily run the risk of ending up with detailed accounts of concerts and vinyl, an arrangement of informational titbits, with a black hole at its core. A Sly Stone-shaped void. For the introduction of a biography about him written by Jeff Kaliss, Sly declares 'I don't know nobody, and nobody knows me, and they don't know what they're talking about.' Sly & The Family Stone were formed in San Francisco in 1967, and finally disbanded in 1975. Their perceived story is one that began as bright young things with sky-shooting promise, only to stutter along a precarious path that saw this vastly gifted ensemble, and its pilot forced into premature termination through the regular Rock malaise of overindulgence, intensified by pressures internal, and pressures external. What had begun with boundless talent, energy, joy and ambition, ended in desolation. Think of parallels with the doomed Space Shuttle carving a vivid incendiary display of re-entry across the clear blue skies as people watch in horrified fascination, until it detonates to extinction showering burned-out debris across counties and states. And even those relics hunted out by ghoulish souvenir-vultures for display on e-bay. Among whom must be counted the feeding-frenzy of journalists and writers determined to add their names to the Family Stone story by documenting its trajectory. Among whom must be counted books such as this one… And in the sense that Allen Ginsberg wrote 'I have seen the best minds of my generation destroyed by madness, screaming, hysterical, naked' exposure to such genius often wreaks collateral damage. We can at least count ourselves fortunate that all of the participants caught up in the cometary wake of Sly & The Family Stone survived to make it beyond the 1970's and '80's, and into the new century. Other narratives were not so fortunate.

Lives are too complicated and full of incident to do full justice to them. To detail all the various component-members of The Family Stone project as they spin off along their various tangents and life-paths would fill several books this size. Although strands of continuity go deeper. Some inexorable gravitational attraction seems to keep pulling them back in. They stay within orbit, and don't stray too far from the Mothership. After that fateful Radio City Music Hall break-up Freddie Stone linked with Larry Graham's Central Station for a while. He rejoined Sly for a brief collaboration on 1979's inaccurately-titled

'Back On The Right Track'. But something more than that was wrong. Maybe something that could only be corrected by taking a mortality check? For Freddie was in a place where it was necessary to reinvent his life for the sake of his own mental and physical health. Wiping the slate. Starting again. And he'd reached an age, and a place, where he was able to make that new existence happen. He determined to quit music entirely, and embrace a salvation that has both eluded, and been denied to his older brother. Re-confirming his Christianity in 1980 he took back his real surname and checked into rehab, drying out from the damaging effects of his ten-year cocaine binge. Many former junkies trade in a physical addictions for spiritual dependency by becoming born-again converts to rigid dogma. The reassuring moral framework of that old-time religion provides a refuge, a crash-pad of certainties. Especially if there's already a personal-faith background—as with Freddie Stewart. Ordained as a minister (in 1988) he found a new niche performing and preaching as Pastor Frederick Stewart of the Vallejo, California 'Evangelist Temple Fellowship Center' at 848 Sonoma Street. He drove a community coach for disabled children. And like others who survive autowrecks or near-death experiences, he came away with a renewed sense of urgency, and travelled throughout the States sharing his testimony. Telling the story of the deliverance he believes saved his life, in the hope that through talking of his experience, other lives might also be saved. His own radio-ministries included airtime slots for 'The Richard Roberts Program', 'PTL (Praise The Lord Show)', 'California Tonight Program', and the '700 Club'. Gradually, there was a cautious return to music too, but strictly on his own terms. During the years since, Freddie wrote songs for Rose and for Larry Graham, and was credited as song-arranger for the 1995 *'Promise Keepers'* album. While his own CD *'Everywhere You Are'*—released through Alexander Doré's C-MAD/ Geronimo Records in 2000, contains songs written, arranged and produced by Freddie. He announced it as a 'message of hope and encouragement'. Adding on his web-site 'I believe 'old fashioned' principles still work today… it's amazing what you can do with the Lord on your side'. In a collective movie-script with more than its fair share of stress and pain, Freddie at least seems to have emerged from the collateral damage as a happy man, living contentedly with his wife Melody, his children Casey, Stacey, Simon, Fred Jr, and his two youngest daughters, Joy and Kristi… and with his faith intact. Whether you subscribe to his belief-system or not, who can begrudge him that?

Meanwhile, Rose Stone was one of the first to be pulled out of the collapsing 'Family', by her husband—Hamp Banks. With 'Bubba' acting as her manager, and with stories rife of them initiating legal action against what remained of the Family Stone entity, she immediately commenced a solo career, cutting an eponymous album under her married name *'Rose Banks'* for Motown in 1976. The cover-shot pictures her in twenties flapper furs, a Billie

Holiday gardenia in the hair, and a suspiciously 'family'-looking entourage of five background guys. Co-produced by Bonnie Pointer's husband Jeffrey Bowen with Hamp and Berry Gordy himself on-team, there were two collectible spin-off singles, the fine easy-riding funk of "Whole New Thing" marred only by its excruciating synth (it's not the Sly original, but a Bowen, Jimmy Ford & Truman Thomas song), plus a sultry remake of the old Elgins hit "Darling Baby", featuring one-finger piano accompaniment and a lovely period sax break. The press-ad's provided a mini-biography to remind fans that 'her voice was heard loud and clear on such gold records as "Dance To The Music", "Family Affair", and "Sing A Simple Song", when she was an integral part of Sly And The Family Stone. Her debut album shows her dynamic vocal talents to the full'. Writing in 'NME', R&B authority Cliff White was not so sure. 'Sometimes singing like she suffers from inflamed adenoids, sometimes just quietly mellow, and occasionally breaking through the tonsular tissue with a wail or two' he nevertheless commended the Family's 'former first-lady's energetic reworking of Sly's "I Get High On You", while admitting 'she copes reasonably well with some gospel-soul ballads and a couple more funky ravers'. But to Cliff, the album was only 'an erratic but fairly original release' on which 'Rose makes an un-sensational debut on Tamla without actually disgracing herself' (24th July 1976).

Although the album fared better, and was well-received elsewhere, sales remained modest. She went on to sing in a back-up capacity for Michael Jackson, George Benson, Madonna, Phish... for Ringo Starr, and for teen-idols Hanson! But soon, separated from Hamp and reverting to her Rose Stewart maiden name, she determined to step back from secular music into the less frantic pacing of the music department of brother Freddie's 'Evangelist Temple Fellowship Center'. This allowed a gradual return to her gospel roots, by lending her voice to Sandra Crouch's Grammy-winning album 'We Sing Praises' in 1983—taking a solo on the old hymn "Power In The Blood". She extended the Crouch family association across years, while leading her own church choir in the San Fernando Valley, recording with the local choir and appearing on a weekly god-slot for national TV. She branched out further by guesting on the UPN-TV sitcom 'Good News'. But while she was building this new life, she maintained connections with the past by sharing guest vocals with Gwen Stefani on Fishbone's cover of "Everybody Is A Star", a track collected onto the 'Fishbone & The Familyhood Nextperience Present: The Psychotic Friends Nuttwerx' (March 2000). She even briefly returned to Motown, contributing her take on the Supremes' "You Keep Me Hangin' On" for UK Motorcity Records tribute to Holland-Dozier-Holland—'Shake Me, Wake Me' (1994). By then she claimed to be spending most of her time playing piano and writing songs 'with words that make a point'.

But there were further on-going continuities, for in truth, none of the apples fell too far from the Family tree. Rose's daughter, Lisa Stone, began singing with Cynthia Robinson and Vet Stewart. With the break-up of the original Family Stone, Little Sister had also disbanded. Vet's group-mate Mary McCreary married the mighty Leon Russell and worked with him on a spectrum of music projects (as Mary Rand and Mary Russell) and with Bob Dylan on his 'Saved' gospel tour. While Vet married Edward 'Eddie Chin' Elliott, and continued to perform solo, albeit in a low-key capacity. She conducted 'Vet's Music Ministry' as Choir Director of the 'Praise & Worship Team' in the same church Pastored by Elder Frederick Stewart, while singing informally with Cynthia and Lisa. Then, together, they assembled the 'Phunk Phamily Affair'—launched across the Easter weekend 2004 at the Frisco Broadway Studios. With Vet providing the momentum, they recruited vocalist Skyler Jett, with Tony Yates on guitar, Peter J Yates bass, Eric Moore (drums), and David Jackson who 'works his fingers' over the clavinet or Hammond organ. Others who drift around the periphery include Javance Butler & Aaron Patterson (keyboards), Johnnie Bamont & Shane Baird (saxes). Soon they renamed themselves 'Sly's Family Stone'—at Sly's instigation, and by 2005 there were excited internet rumours that they were working on tracks for an album with Sly himself. He was said to be contributing new material. As if. Other reports claimed Sly was invited to participate more directly, but declined. Yet rumours persisted. They played a 'Bringin' Da Phunk Into The New Millennium' tour with a ninety-minute set announced as being 'Endorsed & Produced by Sly Stone', and carrying 'the legacy of Sly Stone'. And—although there was significantly more to come from these developments, while James Brown was still saying it loud, clear through to his death on Christmas Day 2006, Vet Stone led her band in 'offering a salute' to the Godfather of Soul by playing a torrid version of his "Sex Machine" at the climax of their 'House of Blues' set.

Simultaneously—in further instalments of the catch-up game, the 'Family Stone Experience' included Gregg Errico, Jerry Martini and Gail Muldrow, while the 'Family Without Stone' also featured Gregg and Gail, with Alexander Doré. Although these were essentially little more than tribute bands from which nothing vital could be expected, by performing Sly material as part of their sets, even when sprinkled with original material, they served to keep the legacy alive. Gregg continued working as a respected Bay Area session drummer/producer in high demand. He played as a member of Gary Duncan's revived Quicksilver Messenger Service, worked with Santana and the Grateful Dead, and more recently produced an album for the Jamie Davis Big Band. Yet older affiliations persist. In an interview with *'Rolling Stone'* (March 2006) he confided that 'Sly's been calling two or three times a day lately, singing over the phone'. Andy Newmark also went on to become a sought-after super-session drummer, he sat in with Ronnie Wood on a Bobby Womack album, then played with Stevie Winwood, Roxy Music, and even BB King.

Larry Graham, meanwhile, had moved on from his Japan-only *'Fired Up'* album (1985), into a minor duet hit with Aretha Franklin—1987's "If You Need My Love Tonight". Then, after working as a sideman and songwriter, touring with the Crusaders and as part of Eddie Murphy's nine-piece Psychedelic Psoul (performing an extended "I Want To Take You Higher" as part of their set at the June 1993 'Montreux Jazz Festival'), the Family Stone reunion for the 'Rock 'n' Roll Hall Of Fame' seemed to act as a catalyst for him to reactivate the Graham Central Station logo. Miles Davis—as perceptive as ever, observed that '(Larry Blackmon and) Cameo reminds me of Sly Stone. But Prince got some Marvin Gaye and Jimi Hendrix and Sly in him, also even Little Richard'. And sure enough, Prince had modelled his Revolution by tipping a conscious nod towards the mixed-gender multi-race Family Stone, readily acknowledging not only the direct influence of their flamboyant stage-presentation but also of Larry's bass-playing in particular. Prince's 1987 *'Sign O' The Times'* album includes "Starfish And Coffee", which relates the story of 'Cynthia Rose'—surely a Family Stone namecheck? Now, throughout Larry's lean years, Prince remained one of Larry's most eloquent supporters, even drawing his "I Believe In You" into his live sets (Prince also extended his patronage to George Clinton's ailing career). By 1997 the new Central Station line-up had become the Purple One's regular support act, issuing another Japan-only CD—*'By Popular Demand'* (1997), and a studio set recorded at Prince's Minneapolis Paisley Park. With a revised line-up drawing Cynthia Robinson and Jerry Martini into the fold, with contributions from co-producer Prince himself, as well as Chaka Khan (guesting on "Free") and the Hornheadz section, adding to a retro-run-through of his earlier hits ("Intro" and an eight-minute remodelling of his earlier single "Just Be My Lady")—*'GSC 2000'* (1998) is a fairly satisfying set, with new Larry originals utilising the Prince—by way of Sly Stone, titles-device, "Love 4 1 Another", "I Just Found Somebody 2 Love" run over programmed drums and a return to the bass dexterity he'd neglected for the power-ballad albums. Even though there's more than an impression that he's marking time, rather than crafting anything vital or original.

By then the artist intermittently known as Prince was also going through his own period of confusion, in litigation with his label while assuming an increasingly strange series of escapist guises. Married to his dancer Mayte Garcia, tragically their child—Gregory, suffered from the rare skull affliction called Pfieffer's Syndrome. The baby's death in October 1996 marked the beginning of a profound shift in his worldview. Larry always claimed religious leanings, it's only necessary to check out the credits of any of his post-Family Stone albums to see that they all yield one for the 'Great Promoter In The Sky'. He laid thanks for his recovery from his life of drugs and violence through being born again as part of a Jehovah's Witness community in Jamaica. With

Prince's marriage to Mayte effectively over, it was Larry's turn to provide the strong bond of supportive friendship. 'Larry goes door-to-door to tell people the truth about god' Prince told the *'Observer Music Monthly'*, 'that's why I told myself, I need to know a man like him. He calls me his baby brother'. By 2001 Prince had also become a Jehovah's Witness, his new-found faith reflected in the arcane, for hardcore-fans-only album *'The Rainbow Children'* (2005), which goes some way towards laying the ghosts of his earlier contract-filling albums. And significantly, Prince's well-received series of UK concerts in 2007 included covers of Sly songs.

And David Kapralik? A present-tense profile by Al Aronowitz recounts how 'the day he gets out of hospital from his third suicide attempt, Dave Kapralik is ready to try to snuff himself again. He's got nothing' (*'The Blacklisted Masterpieces Of Al Aronowitz'*, 1988). The original Family Stone contractual arrangement entitled David to producer-royalties from all Sly's material, although he never actually produced a note of music. At one point he even sued his client for the $250,000 he felt Sly owed him under this agreement. Later, David took up residence on the Hawaiian island of Maui where—from 1997, he carried out a guerrilla campaign against the Columbia/Epic/Sony conglomerate aimed at correcting the confused royalty legacy from the Family Stone years. In a letter posted on the internet (dated 16th June 2005) he points out that 'Stoneflower Productions was owned 50-50 by Sylvester Stewart and myself. Throughout the intervening years (Stoneflower Productions delivered the first recordings to Epic in 1968) all the Statements I received showed the group and the production company deep, deep in the red. I had (practically) given up hope of ever being fully recouped and seeing some cash money.' However, 'many years later… I was told by Jerry Martini (with whom I stay in touch) that he and the group were starting to receive royalties. I then made an enquiry about receiving my share of production monies' but 'the Sony royalties people and legal eagles gave me the ol' 'razzle dazzle shuffle'. I then retained a local lawyer and we began to build our case'. The Hawaii State Court referred the case to a California court where Kapralik somehow lost his appeal, and, after considering the full cost of retaining an expensive LA law firm to pursue the grievance through the courts ('both financially and in terms of my health') he reluctantly 'cut bait' and ceased 'my pursuit of that which is rightfully due me'. At the time of writing, the situation remains unresolved. While oddly, David's *other* frequently overlooked clients saw an equally dramatic reversal of fortunes when Herb Fame lost one Peaches—Linda Greene, and acquired another in the shapely form of Francine Barker. They switched labels from Date to Polydor, only to score a US no. 1 with "Reunited" in March 1979.

Elsewhere, Billy Preston—one of the great collaborators, characterised by a huge smile and dazzling musicianship, followed his work with the Beatles and on *'There's A Riot Goin' On'* by making it to the next great pinnacle of Rock 'n' Roll by touring the States with the Rolling Stones through 1975. He contributed to many of their studio tracks too, including "Fool To Cry"—the disputed writing credits for which led to his acrimonious split with Mick & Keith. His own solo career, commenced in 1970, led to a Grammy award for his energetic participation in George Harrison's *'The Concert For Bangladesh'* benefit-album, and another for his instrumental "Outa-Space". He also wrote Joe Cocker's 1974 hit "You Are So Beautiful". Through a five-decade career he played with Aretha Franklin, Bob Dylan, Eric Clapton, the Jackson Five, Barbra Streisand, and Red Hot Chilli Peppers' massive *'Stadium Arcadium'* (2006). But he was also fighting the long-term legacy of drug-abuse. He was arrested and convicted for insurance fraud after setting fire to his own Los Angeles home, and was then sentenced to three years imprisonment in 1997 for violating the terms of probation for a cocaine possession conviction handed out earlier that year. Managed by Joyce Moore—wife of Sam Moore of Sam & Dave, one of Billy's final projects was contributing to Ray Charles' last album, *'Genius Loves Company'* (2004). Shortly afterwards he suffered chronic kidney failure, unsuccessfully received a transplant and was subsequently placed on dialysis. He fell into a coma on 21st November 2005 from which he never recovered. He died in the Scottsdale Healthcare, Shea Hospital in Arizona aged 59 on Tuesday the 6th June 2006.

All of those interacting lives are part of a long strange history that unwinds all the way from The Stewart Four rehearsing the gospel harmonies of "On The Battlefield For My Lord" in the family's front room. And despite the extended period of turbulent changes and personnel fall-outs, Sly's music has outlasted its era. There were various band relaunches in different guises with varying degrees of success. The 'Sinbad's Soul Music Festival' held in Aruba featured a 25th May 1997 one-off set from a reformed Family Stone, with Larry Graham rejoining a line-up numbering Rose, Cynthia and Jerry Martini. The show was subsequently screened on HBO, and led to Cynthia and Jerry joining Larry's revived Graham Central Station for its tour with Prince later that same year. During June of 2003 an even fuller band reunion took place, with extensive rehearsals 'in the back room of a music store in Vallejo'– missing only Larry and Sly. Freddie and Rose had written an album's-worth of new material together, with the intension of recording a sixteen-song studio set. Cynthia and Jerry were there, plus Gregg Errico who claimed that 'the keyboard is on the stage, the B3's running, and the seat is warm for him'. But 'him' didn't show, neither did the album. Of course, it's all based around supposition. But perhaps Gregg comes closest when he says about Sly that 'on one hand, he had the capabilities of handling all that attention, fame, big audiences. But on the other hand, there was another part of him that didn't want it, couldn't handle it, and wanted to be away from it. This fight always went on, where he wanted to be the biggest, the baddest, the best, and then, when he got it, he didn't want to be it. He was scared of it...'

'We could have been the black Beatles' adds Jerry Martini ruefully to *'Vibe'* magazine. Overlooking the fact that he, himself, was white.

But, despite appearances, the story was not yet quite over...

****

'The Long Journey Back...'

For Sly himself, these were still his 'buried' years. There are people who have bought every Sly record, who hunt out rarities, who spend their lives living in Sly-world in their heads. It's difficult to imagine today's iPod addicts indulging their generational artists to the same extent that their elder brothers or hip uncles suffered through ten years of buying poor disappointing dispiriting Bob Dylan, Lou Reed, Neil Young... or Sly Stone albums. Willing the next one to be the one that would justify the wait. Standing in line to buy that record, hurrying home once they'd bought it, slapping it on the turntable and listening to it over and over again, studying the artwork, hunting for details in its electric dreams, looking for clues, hints. Against the odds the baby-boomer generation, to which Sly's audience belongs, has not abandoned the music of its youth. It might have broadened its musical spectrum to include the likes of World Music, it might have acceded to more 'mature' forms like classical music or jazz. But it still buys the CD re-issues. And at the iPod Music store, the good people at Apple assembled what they term their 'Twenty-Five Bay Area Essentials' list for its download customers. Their list begins (1) "Truckin'" by The Grateful Dead, (2) "Somebody To Love" by Jefferson Airplane, (3) "Piece Of My Heart" by Big Brother & The Holding Company, and (4) "Thank You (Falettinme Be Mice Elf Agin)" by Sly & The Family Stone, plus the likes of Creedence Clearwater Revival, Tower Of Power, Blue Cheer, Quicksilver Messenger Service... and Graham Central Station ("Can You Handle That?"). The *'San Francisco Chronicle'* replied with its own download list, compiled by Joel Selvin and Aidin Vaziri, and published Friday 28th April 2006. Their list opens with (1) "I Want To Take You Higher" by Sly & The Family Stone, (2) "Dark Star" by The Grateful Dead, (3), "Slow Death" by the Flamin' Groovies, plus Jefferson Airplane ("The Ballad Of You And Me And Pooneil"), Moby Grape, and Tower of Power. Lists proving that in Rock, maybe everything's already been done, but it's seldom been done better.

By the time of the Family Stone's induction to the 1993 'Rock 'n' Roll Hall Of Fame' Sly had totally disappeared from public view, reportedly living in a large house in Southern California since the turn of the decade. All of the original six members of the Family Stone attended. But—as related in chapter one, at first, not Sly. One by one they took to the podium to accept the award with brief thanks, and just when it seemed it was all done—Sly himself suddenly materialised, much to everyone's surprise, including his former bandmates. The hall spontaneously erupted into thunderous applause. Wearing an electric-blue leather jumpsuit Sly went up to receive his award, delivered a hasty speech—promising 'see you soon', and vanished back to wherever he'd come from. At the time few took the promise seriously. They were wrong.

New York-based Avenue Records extended Sly a recording contract in 1995. It was enthusiastically talked-up by label manager Jerry Goldstein. Following in the uneasy steps of Kapralik and Ken Roberts, Goldstein—a former member of the Strangeloves group, the man who wrote "My Boyfriend's Back" for the Angels, was to become the new fixer managing Sly's affairs. What followed is mired, not only in obfuscation, but litigation. Goldstein cut off Sly's access to his royalties as part of a 'debt agreement' in return for a regular allowance. This is not an unprecedented of resolving financial problems. Except that Goldstein allegedly defaulted, causing Sly to quit his Napa Valley rented home in favour of a camper van. More positively, Goldstein spoke about an albums-worth of material dedicated to the memory of Miles Davis.

Miles had died 28th September 1991, aged 65, soon after taping his autobiography. There, in (largely) his own words Miles is every bit as confrontationally extreme as his music, and as his spikily bristling reputation would suggest—while he's sufficiently together to recall exact detailed personnel lists from obscure sessions he'd played even in the depths of addiction. The results of his interactions with Sly had led to the spacily electric million-selling psychedelia of 'Bitches Brew' (1970) and the ghetto-funkified 'On The Corner' (1972). Music that spun the genre almost single-handedly into what became known as 'fusion'. Herbie Hancock, Chick Corea, Billy Cobham, Jack DeJohnette, John McLaughlin, and Weather Reporters Wayne Shorter and Joe Zawinul all perfected their art as part of the Miles Davis group, through his inspired tutelage. For his later albums—'Tutu' (1987) and 'Amandla' (1989) recorded during the eighties, Miles' bassist Marcus Miller was a firm disciple of Larry Graham's slap-bass style.

But Sly's response—his reputed album of Miles-influenced funk, stayed in the realm of rumour. Jon Dakss spoke of hearing unreleased Sly music, 'the closest album I can use to describe what I heard was an album by Miles Davis, called 'On The Corner' (1972)'—which, significantly was the Miles Davis album most influenced by Sly. Sly's son, Sylvester Jr, added substance to the story in an interview with 'People Magazine', giving the project the title 'Miles And Miles'. But just because Sly's name was on a contract, didn't necessarily mean he'd honour it, or even show up. The Avenue production deal lapsed after producing precisely... nothing. Perhaps it was time to call closure?

Technically the contract with Goldstein survived for a decade, although it resulted in no new work, and predictably it ended in tears. With litigation and counter-litigation. And another long-term grudge. In January 2010 Sly launched a $50m lawsuit against Goldstein, alleging breach of contract, fraud, unjust enrichment and misappropriating artist royalties and assets. More damaging, amid reports that he was homeless and living on the dole, Sly played a set at the Coachella festival on 19th April 2010. It turned into a confused event, or—if you prefer, a 'sad spectacle' according to the *'LA Weekly'*, most noticeable for its rant against Goldstein. Billed to appear in the Majave Tent at seven, Sly was on-stage four hours late, at eleven, wearing a blonde-&-black streaked wig. The *'LA Weekly'* said the show proved to be 'truly awful on the part of the organisers (if they knew what they were getting), and especially awful on the part of Sly's current friends and handlers who let him go onstage like a ranting, raving shell of what he used to be'. He ran though a stop-start 36-minutes of "Stand!", "Family Affair" and "Higher" while berating his band, then stopped eighteen-minutes in to ask the audience 'how long I been on stage?' and how long he had to stay onstage to get paid. But then, most damagingly, he hit the self-destruct button and went into a mumbled vitriol directed at Goldstein, sharing a litany of his legal troubles at length. 'Fuck slander', he began, 'the white boy's name is Jerry Goldstein. He's part of it. What he did was he stole so much money. At the same time, I made so much money that I didn't know I was being stolen from' (according to the Associated Press). Inevitably, Goldstein responded by filing a countersuit for slander, alleging—with some justification, that his former client 'implied he was a thief'—to witness, Mr Stone's 'slanderous' comments from the Coachella stage. LA superior court judge Mark V Mooney allowed this case to go forward, while reassuring Sly's lawyers that 'you may... ultimately prevail'.

Meanwhile, even the original albums fell out of print and became increasingly difficult to obtain. Especially *'Whole New Thing'* and the original *'Dance To The Music'*. At a time when vinyl archaeology was unleashing lavishly remastered editions of the Kinks' back-catalogue, with The Who and the Byrds treated to luxurious academic collectors' digipacks rich with unreleased bonus alternate takes and rare 'b'-sides, such neglect was particularly irksome. Yet there was a growing 'Sly For Reappraisal' movement. The 2005 *'Different Strokes By Different Folks'* album seemed a token, if genuinely sincere gesture at confronting this neglect. Announced as 'created under the aegis of the reclusive Sly Stone' it claimed 'his approval of every aspect of the recording', resulting in 'a marriage of old school traditions and new school attitude'. The album 're-imagined' the hits of Sly & The Family Stone by utilising the original master tapes, personalised and updated by an impressive array of 'fiery all-star' contemporary artists. Originally trailered in the press as *'Sly 2k'*, and produced by Nile Rodgers, the project involved Beck, Maroon Five, Black-Eyed Peas, Lenny Kravitz, The Roots and Audioslave. Jerry Goldstein was listed as 'executive producer'.

While resurfacings persisted... and persist. Reported with the regularity of Elvis, or UFO activity over Area 51. They became mythic, the subject of internet-driven debate and analysis. One example, on Monday 15th August 2005 Sly was positively identified driving Vet from Beverly Hills on his custom four-wheel Harley motorcycle to the LA 'Knitting Factory', a club at 7021 Hollywood Blvd, where the ten-piece Phunk Phamily were performing a benefit for the LA Braille Institute. Advertised as an evening of 'Songs And Original Members Of Sly & The Family Stone', the bill also included Tyrone Wells & The Remedy and DJ Giancarlo. Although Sly declined to participate, he did hang around on the balcony long enough to watch the set open with "Sex Machine", "If You Want Me To Stay", a piano intro leading into Vet's lead vocals on "Somebody's Watching You" and "Everybody Is A Star", before closing with an extended "Thank You (Faletinme Be Mice Elf Agin)". A student film crew were there, coincidentally shooting footage for a projected band documentary ('On The Sly: In Search Of The Family Stone', One-Four Productions). They claimed to have captured fleeting glimpses of the rare sighting on film. He was described as resembling Bootsy Collins. A previous sighting—around the late 1990's, also claimed Sly was sporting an extravagantly-braided Bootsy-esque blonde Mohawk. But the 'Soul-Patrol' website disagreed, arguing he was wearing a white outfit, with hat and dark shades. Others insisted he'd kept his shiny biker helmet firmly in place throughout, like an astronaut. No-one provided absolute confirmation, and no-one's actually viewed the film.

When Warner Archives, through Rhino, issued a lavish CD—*'Who In The Funk Do You Think You Are'* (2001), anthologising all the existing issued and previously unissued material Sly had done for the label, the comprehensive sleeve-notes detail further histories. Credited to 'institute wordsmith' Bryan Thomas, the extensive text includes a quote from producer Mark Davis to the effect that he'd seen Sly in 1999, and heard forty uncompleted new tracks, 'but they were at the point where they were as good as they were going to be and he was looking to get past that'. To Davis, it appeared that Sly was 'still trying to figure out his puzzles'. Then the notes quote *'Rolling Stone'* critic Dave Marsh who considers '(Sly is) not merely a survivor but a winner and a star, a man who's seen the top and the bottom and almost all the places in between. If he's momentarily—or permanently—stranded somewhere in the middle, at least he's honest about it. I'll continue to listen to whatever Sly Stone sings, hoping he'll fight his way out, knowing he'll never stop trying. Because that's the lesson of his greatest music, and such a lesson must never be lost or forgotten. He hasn't. Don't you...'

That wait was rewarded when 'Reclusive legend Sly Stone' made a surprise showing at the '48th Grammy Awards' in LA on Wednesday 8th February 2006—his first genuinely authenticated public performance since the brief 'Rock 'n' Roll Hall Of Fame' debacle. Assembled as a full Family Stone reunion by Nile Rodgers—with five of the original six members, and Rusty Allen filling in for Larry—and, hope-against-hope, Sly himself, the appearance was preceded by weeks of conjecture. Nile Rodgers was a former member of the 'Apollo Theater' houseband where he'd played back-up to Ben E King, Aretha Franklin, and Funkadelic. He had also been an active member of the Black Panthers before teaming up with Bernard Edwards for the much-sampled slick-Disco mega-success of Chic. As a production team they'd also crafted hits for Sister Sledge, Diana Ross ("Upside Down" and "I'm Coming Out"), and Madonna. As such, he'd worked with divas and prima donnas. But never anything quite like this Family Stone. On his website Ron Jacobs (author of *The Way the Wind Blew: A History of The Weather Underground*', 1997, Verso) confided his pre-screening reservations about resurrecting Sly Stone. 'What song could possibly speak to the commercial nation of 2006 TV-land...? in a medium where everything becomes just another pose designed to sell a product, would Sly be able to make a point? Or would he even make it to the screen...? considering this, it didn't matter what he played, I guess, just that he would show up and play was enough...' 'Everybody was working hard to reunite the original band and get Sly's participation' a source working on the production side of the show told *'Observer Music Monthly'* (March 2006), 'but there was never any guarantee that he would actually surface, because he is so under the radar'. *'Rolling Stone'* circulated amusing gossip about security turning away this figure 'in a sort of Unabomber camouflage get-up that hid his face' because they assumed he was a homeless vagrant. So swaddled, layered, shaded, hatted and scarved as to be unrecognisable. In fact, when Sly did turn up, his right hand was encased in a cast, his damaged tendon the result of a motorcycle mishap. But the fact that he showed up for off-site rehearsals at all augured well. Sure, his attire—a tattered hoodie entirely obscuring his face, was the cause for some concern—as did the damaged infirmity of his rehearsal performance, the old swagger replaced by a fumbling vulnerability so vague that Rodgers decided to 'pre-record' a version of "I Want To Take You Higher" to cover anticipated imperfections.

On the night of gilt and mirrors, there was talk of severe stage-fright, and Sly's nervous vomiting. Ken Ehrlich elaborated to the *'Chicago Sun-Times'* about how he 'refused to leave his hotel room until he was given a police escort to the show and then waited in his car until the performance began'. Then, urban myth became public spectacle. As the cameras zoned in the band were lined up, and yes, Sly was there in an extravagant blonde hair-extension-enhanced Mohawk, opaque oversize Dior shades, a purple-lined silver lamé greatcoat, and pants cinched with the signature 'S-L-Y' belt-buckle. But he appeared stooped, head bowed, as though in pain. He barely managed eye contact with the audience—which included Aerosmith's Steve

Tyler and Joe Perry, John Legend, Van Hunt and Robert Randolph. They at first seemed unsure how to react as Sly began a faltering performance, his voice parched and wandering. His back seemed hunched, like a broken man betraying the legacy of the desperately poor nutrition that attends chronic cocaine use? But yes, against all expectations, his impressionistic vagueness still proved mesmerising. Just as they powered into the climax of "I Want To Take You Higher", Sly got up and sauntered to the front of the stage, rasped a verse, waved in the general direction of the audience, then wandered off-set before the last chorus was over. He kept walking, not stopping until he was outside the Staples Center building, where 'he went up the ramp, got on a motorcycle and took off', scorching tyre-rubber in his haste to escape. But after twenty years away from the stage, he'd shown up. And aged sixty-two, proved that he still had the necessary magic. Nile was reportedly 'disappointed', he'd hoped for more. But despite the odds, the majority of people around the show took a different take. Nile had got him on-stage. That was as much as anyone could reasonably have expected. Nile did everything he could to hold it together. But people had been trying to hold Sly Stone together for four decades, and what the Grammys got was probably all they were going to get... for now.

But at Vet Stewart's instigation, and a lot to do with her unstinting motivating efforts, there was more to come. Daddy KC and Momma Alpha died within eighteen months of each other, he in 2001, she following in 2003. Sly was at the funeral. Vet was there, 'they both died in my arms', and she 'promised her parents that she would once again make the rest of the world a safe place for her big brother to function in'. Her resolve to fulfil that promise never wavered, or for one moment weakened. 'I was persistent. I prayed a lot'. Then, on Sunday 13th January 2007 her 'Sly's Family Stone' appeared at the Anaheim CA 'House Of Blues'—adjacent to Disneyland, starting off the year with a celebration of Dr Martin Luther King's birthday. As the PhattaDatta website made clear, speculation about Sly actually performing with the band was to miss the point—'Sly is producing, writing for, and promoting his family now. That's his major focus'. Yet it proved to be a wonderfully surprising show, all the way from the opening blasts of "Dance To The Music". Vet took a commanding lead in a white leather outfit, alongside Lisa Stone. Skyler Jett was trading call-and-response vocals with guitarist Tony Yates, brother Pete Yates handling deep-bass. Stefon Dubose improvised his drumming duties into a powerful extended solo. Tony Stead took the Hammond B3 chair, once Sly's instrument of choice. While trombonist Mike Rinta and Johnnie Bamont's sax took their places beside founder horns Cynthia Robinson and Pat Rizzo. Eventually Sly himself briefly took the stage, at first a fragile and slouched figure, but his voice becoming stronger as he introduced his oldest daughter. Phunne stepped forward to rap her own 'Smooth Poet' lyric—'when I say Sly, you say Stone'. Then he announced daughter Novi who contributed some classical piano to the band's musical fusion—Claude Debussy's "Doctor Gradus Ad Parnassum", throwing in a Sly lyric as reference point. Finally, smiling like a doting father at a school concert, Sly introduced his niece Toddy—Vet's daughter, who ad-libbed around the music. They closed by rolling out "Thank You (Faletinme Be Mice Elf Agin)", Sly flashing peace-signs while stabbing keyboards, Lisa and Vet throwing in a hambone to evoke flashbacks to the earlier days of the 'Fillmore East' Hendrix gig, before a "I Want To Take You Higher" encore.

The only thing harder than quitting the limelight, is venturing back out into its glare. But, after staring so perilously into the abyss for so long, you either take that final plunge into oblivion… or you decide that life's maybe worth living after all, and shuffle a few steps back from the brink. It seems Sly was in the process of using this Family Stone vehicle as a kind of Trojan Virus to incrementally infiltrate gradual awareness of his renewed musical involvements. With a new booking agent in the shape of Steve Green, 31st March 2007 saw the group's return to Las Vegas, the city of their first eventful 'Pussycat á Go-Go' engagement all those long years ago. Since then, there'd been only a 1972 appearance at the 'Las Vegas Convention Center'. But—although deliberately low-key, the 'Flamingo Hotel Showroom' return was significant in that Sly himself was included as a named part of the package. As midnight gave way to morning, veteran black stand-up comedian George Wallace introduced the set to a 500-strong audience with the ironic quip 'April Fools! Sly Stone showed up!' But after the band led in with a four-song medley, Sly himself sauntered on stage to join them on Korg synth for a thirty-minute sequence of "Stand!", "Family Affair", "Thank You (Falettinme Be Mice Elf Again)", "If You Want Me To Stay" and the usual climax of "I Want To Take You Higher", during which he moved out to the edge of the stage to greet fans and shake hands. For the occasion he was sporting a black sequined jumpsuit with black patent platform shoes set off by red heels, a red sequined shirt, the black belt embellished with a huge 'S-L-Y' buckle—a neck brace, black knitted cap, and white Dolce & Gabbana shades. The spectacle was repeated when the band headlined the San Jose Arena Park's 'Back In The Day Summerfest'—a non-profit 'Benefit for Orphans', held late on the sunny Saturday of 7th July (7/7/07!) and sponsored by the indulgence-free 'Jubilee Christian Fellowship'. Following the Average White Band on-stage at 20:45, with huge video-screens streaming original 'Woodstock' Sly-footage, the band again jammed for some thirty minutes until Sly—head-down in a white-hooded sweat-shirt and radio-mic, baggy pants, gold chain statement jewellery and a baseball cap, positioned himself hunched behind the keyboard. Although initially flawed with unforgivable sound-problems—Cynthia's 'all squares go home' and much of Sly's first number got lost in the mix, the event proved a success, and it tied in with Sly's first major published interview in over twenty years.

For the prestigious spread in *'Vanity Fair'* (cover-dated August 2007), Sly was photographed riding his three-wheeled chopper in the extensive grounds of an impressive home in the country sparseness of Napa Valley. A property that, biographer Jeff Kayliss claims, was previously owned by Sharon Stone, he helpfully adds, in brackets (no relation), usefully clarifying that confusion, thanks Jeff. With an appointment to meet Sly at 'Chopper Guys Biker Products Inc', a Vallejo custom-motorcycle specialist, journalist David Kamp endured all the usual doubts about it ever taking place. Yet against the odds, Sly arrives a mere ten minutes late, on a flamboyantly customised banana-yellow trike, and in good shape, for 'a 64-year-old man'. Warily, elusively, he claims to have got serious about 'cleaning up' some fifteen years earlier. 'I just looked around one day, and it *was* cleaned up. Just hardly was nothing there. Just... certain people were not around'. And now 'I'm pretty cool. I drink now and then, a little bit—beer. And I smoke butts sometimes'. Is he indestructible?—no, only 'washable and rinseable'. When asked why he'd chosen to return now, he merely grins, 'cause it's kind of boring at home sometimes'. There's not, in truth, a great deal of dialogue. What little there is of it is generously inflated with exposition and recapitulated history. Kamp concludes that 'Sly relishes this sort of opaqueness—letting people in just enough to intrigue and confound them'. Yet it closes on an upbeat note. Throughout their face-to-facing, Sly had worn shades. Kamp asks 'can I see your eyes, Sly?' 'Yeah,' he says, pulling down the sunglasses, revealing healthily white whites and a remarkably unlined face, the same face from 'Woodstock', 'Cavett', and the cover of *'Fresh'*. It really is Sly Stone'. The interview also marked the kick-off point for a full ten-date European tour, including British dates—all performed under the full 'Sly & The Family Stone' heading.

Is it Sly & The Family Stone? Can it really be said to be Sly & The Family Stone? When that other glorious survivor—Brian Wilson, toured his triumphal 'Surf's Up', it wasn't the Beach Boys. When Arthur Lee played the final dates of his wonderful 'Forever Changes' tour, it wasn't with the original Love. Can it *really* be said to be the Who when Pete Townshend and Roger Daltrey headline at 'Live8' or Glastonbury without Keith Moon or John Entwhistle? I have my doubts. This chapter could be seen as a tack-on footnote to the main story. What they used to call the 'appendix'. The kind of bonus tracks you get on CD reissues of vinyl albums. The kind of bonus tracks added to the Sony Legacy remastered editions of Sly's 1967-to1974 albums, again crediting Jerry Goldstein as 'executive producer', but making the full catalogue available. But after all, what is gone forever can never be recreated. If you want the originals, buy those CDs or the DVD's. While at the same time, it's a cause for genuine joy that those artists—Brian Wilson, the Who, are not only still around, but retain the creative energies to put across often powerfully emotive performances.

Same with Sly & The Family Stone. Of course it can never be exactly what it was. People change, on both sides of the stagelights, times change, fracturing and disrupting meanings and relevancies. And it's obvious that in this confluence of ardour and damage there's more mutual warmth than there is radical confrontation. More blurry affection than excitation. As John Mulvey of *'Uncut'* magazine points out, 'the edge of those old records is missing, that precarious mix of tension and euphoria', instead, the pleasures of seeing Sly & The Family Stone now 'are less complicated, those of a party band, not a blazing collective with a revolutionary subtext'. Taking such vital songs out of their original social context inevitably casts them adrift as part of some 'oldies show'. It flies in the face of reason to hold any other expectations. Just enjoy what there is. And there's plenty to enjoy. Sly is back. Almost. Look closely, and you might just catch him 'Smilin' again. And to hear him sing 'Stand, in the end you'll still be you, / one that's done all the things you set out to do', and to know the things he went through, the things he set out to do, the things he achieved, and the things he threw away—and then to see him there, hunched and older but still standing, onstage, surrounded by his family… well, according to David Kamp, 'I got misted up'.

The tour commenced at the open-air 'Arena Santa Giuliana' in Perugia, Italy (Thursday, 12th July 2007) following a full-on Solomon Burke set. They crossed to the sold-out Montreaux Jazz Festival (13th), the Belgian 'Blue Note Jazz Festival' in Gent (14th), the 'North Sea Jazz Festival' in Rotterdam (15th), the 'Nice Jazz Festival' (19th), and the Finnish 'Pori Jazz Festival' (20th). Headlining at London's drizzling inner-city 'Love Box Weekender' (21st), the Family followed Blondie on-stage at around 21:50, with Sly wandering on to contribute two songs, then getting up for two more. Later—with Sly in an Afro and headband, they played what was reportedly the finest set of the tour at the Paris 'Olympia' (23rd), then the 'Jazz Aldea' in San Sebastian, Spain (27th), before finally climaxing at the modest Boscombe venue of the Bournemouth 'Opera House' (28th July).

By now the general shape of the events were refining into shape. With the band book-ending the set—starting off with "Dance To The Music", progressing through a varied mix of "Everyday People", "Hot Fun In The Summertime", taking in Vet's Little Sister "You're The One" or a slow sensual "Somebody's Watching You", and Sly joining for four or five mid-point numbers, usually soloing a strongly distinctive "If You Want Me To Stay", and closing with a rallying "I Want To Take You Higher". But although persistent promises of a 'new song' remained unconfirmed, as the tour progressed the presentation seemed to gain in confidence. Despite Sly's protestation that 'when waking up this morning he realised he was old, so he needed to take a break', the man who began the tour as a 'broken marionette, barely moving' was visibly loosening up, rocking to and fro behind keyboards he didn't actually play, dancing in a kind of shadowboxing slouch around the stage, yet showing more obvious pleasure both in the performance itself, and the reception he was receiving. Venturing out front, and finally—at the closing date in Bournemouth, leaping down off-stage to mingle with the audience as he chanted and danced to "I Want To Take You Higher". Sly's teasingly wicked humour was a constant too. Dedicated fan and potential biographer Willem Alkema relentlessly followed the tour, as he'd pursued Sly for many years. Sly finally consented to an interview, on condition that Alkema could ask just one question! As he relates (in *'Mojo 196'*, March 2010) a perplexed Alkema decided on an ice-breaker that might lead to more—'how does it feel to be back on-stage?' 'About five feet higher than I usually am' replied Sly, before laughing and walking off. 'After five years' writes Alkema 'this was my reward...'

Is this a postscript, a happy coda... or a new beginning? Whatever, shows continue. During the first week of December (2007) Sly played a series of dates at 'The BB King Blues Club & Grill' on New York's 42nd Street, with audiences stumping up $103.35 per ticket. Before taking the stage the atmosphere was hushed and weirdly nervy, so hushed Sly's voice could be detected croaking over the soundsystem 'Is the show starting? hold up, hold up'. Then, seemingly to an assistant, 'I don't want to fall'. And when he finally emerged he shuffled to the microphone, even if he later managed to throw in some playful choreography. During lulls in the show there was some dialogue. A shouted question from the crowd asked 'how you doing, Sly?' provoking the witty response 'eh...' Someone else enquired had Mr Stone ever been arrested? 'I've been arrested for armed robbery' he jibed back. The Family Stone—included Jerry Martini and Cynthia Robinson with Lisa Stone, meticulously ticked-off the roll-call of hits, continuing even when Sly momentarily vanished 'to take a piss'. He returned to deliver some tantalising unaccompanied rap verses—'you can't face a noun so you're straight adverbing it, / had an argument at home, and you had to have the last word in it.' Yet if there were those in the audience ghoulishly anticipating a 'train-wreck' performance, it's fair to say that few others were disappointed. Sly's 'one-world' concept of music still retains relevance, even if the more specific political references have become dulled. For after the show, the press reported that 'his best songs—exuberant and sometimes unsettling funk hits and experiments from the late 1960's and early '70's, haven't aged a day,' adding a barbed 'though the same can't quite be said of the guy who sang them'. Soon after, Sly, with George Clinton, was re-making another connection, joining the musicians on-stage for a brief and amazing appearance together at California's 'Voices Of Latin Rock' Show in January 2008. They ran through versions of "Thank You

(Falettinme Be Mice Elf Again)" and "I Want To Take You Higher" memorable more for their shambling joy than their technical perfection. The pair didn't stay long. Oddly, Sal Valentino was also there, performing his Beau Brummels' hit "Laugh Laugh". Another link in the story. But by the time he took to the stage, Sly was gone. Then there was Coachella festival on 19th April 2010, with Sly insisting—against the evidence, 'and everything is cool'.

Later, there was even a trickle of new material. August 2011 saw the release of *'I'm Back'*, credited to Sly Stone, Family & Friends. Of the fourteen tracks, eleven were various reworkings of old material, with an unpredictable array of guest 'friends'. Ray Manzarek of the Doors appears on "Dance To The Music"—with a bonus 'Extended Mix' and a 'Club Mix' of the same song. Ann Wilson of Heart joins Sly for "Everyday People" and Carmine Appice with Ernie Watts for "Stand!". Johnny Winter guests on "Thank You (Falettinme Be Mice Elf Agin)"—with an extra 'Electro Club Mix'. There's Jeff Beck on "(I Want To Take You Higher" and Bootsy Collins on "Hot Fun In The Summertime". And two versions of "Family Affair"—including a 'Dubstep Mix'. But drawing most of the limited attention the album received were the three new tracks, which prove that Sly has at least retained some of his quirky genius across the gulf of intervening years. "Plain Jane" and "Get Away" are Sly originals, while—check the credits of "His Eye Is On The Sparrow" and it says 'traditional', which indicates his reworking of a gospel source. Each of them could warrant a place on his earlier albums, while conceding style-innovations that invests them with some current relevance. 'Everybody plug your microphone in' he announces as "His Eye Is On The Sparrow" opens, and if the melody-line veers dangerously close to "You're All I Need To Get By" (the Ashford & Simpson hit for Marvin Gaye & Tammi Terrell) or "Someday We'll Be Together" (the Johnny Bristol & Harvey Fuqua hit for Diana Ross & The Supremes), then the gospel exhortations to 'change me, change me', erupting into falsetto squarks, come uncomfortably close to brother Freddie's faith. Low on lyrics the refrain 'his eye is on the sparrow, I know he watches me' indicates that he's found Jesus. While oddly, the title has already been worked by Lauren Hill. "Plain Jane" shows he can still get down deep and dirty with the party-girls, with vocoder-distortion and squechy bass-line. And "Get Away" is driven on a nice Prince-style drum-machine beat with Sly's oh-wow-oh-wow vocal-line and familiar slurred voice, buoyed by a strong sax break. But it's great to hear Sly announce 'I sing because I'm happy, I sing because I'm free'. Long may it be so.

The Family Stone. Like the great civilisations of the ancient world, all bands have a built-in creative arc, an often meteoric rise, a dazzling peak, followed by a long decline and fall. Oswald Spengler wrote about it. Some survive longer than others. Some self-destruct almost as soon as they've begun. It's counted out in their genetic code, the unique DNA-configuration that brings it all together in the first place. 'From the womb to the tomb' joked Sly, 'and that's it, baby. I checked it out'. Others hang on recycling tired licks long after they have any continuing justification to do so. The Rolling Stones become their own tribute band. The Who and the Pink Floyd persist beyond defections, feuds and deaths, yet still occasionally manage to recapture some shadow of what they once were. U2 and REM retain a currency value remarkable for their longevity. Yet they all leave, if they're fortunate, vinyl, film-clips, and memory-impressions that touch lives. One moment that impacts on the world is more than most of us will ever manage. To achieve more than that is a valuable thing. Sly & The Family Stone survive longer, and leave more of enduring value than most. Their legacy remains audible and visible. We should be grateful for that, rather than asking for more.

When things fall away, there are certain things that can never be lost. Time, and perspective eliminates Sylvester Stewart's latter-day failings. It releases him from fashion, and preserves him at his best. What Sly achieved, what he created, is substantial, and difficult to equal. A record of his life's work. In "Skin I'm In" he sings unequivocally 'if I could do it all over again / I'd be in the same skin I'm in'.

So, was he bigger or better than the others? No. He was an original. And you don't put originals on lists, in categories, or in comparison with others.

Chapter Twenty-One
Discography

Sly And The Family Stone: Discography
UK Singles

Sly & The Family Stone spend a total of only forty-two weeks on the UK chart

March 1968—Enters chart 10 July 1968 "Dance To The Music" c/w "Let Me Hear It From You" (issued March on Columbia DB 8369, re-issued June on Direction 58-3568,) reaches no. 7 (no. 10 on 'NME' chart 17th August), on charts 14 weeks. Re-issued c/w "Everyday People" in July 1982 as 'Epic Old Gold'

September 1968—Enters chart 2 October 1968 "M'Lady" c/w "Life" (Direction 58-3707) reaches no. 32, on charts 7 weeks

February 1969—Enters chart 19 March 1969 "Everyday People" c/w "Sing A Simple Song" (Direction 58-3938) reaches no. 36, on charts 5 weeks. Re-issued in 1975 on 'Epic'

August 1969—"Hot Fun In The Summertime" c/w "Fun" (Direction 58-4471)

October 1969—"I Want To Take You Higher" c/w "Stand" (Direction 58-4279)

February 1970—"Thank You (Faletinme be Mice Elf Agin)" c/w "Everybody Is A Star" (Direction 58-4782)

June 1970—"I Want To Take You Higher" c/w "You Can Make It If You Try" (CBS Epic 5054)

November 1971— Enters chart 8 January 1972 "Family Affair" c/w "Luv 'n' Haight" (Epic EPC 7632) reaches no. 15 (no. 14 on 'NME' chart 29th January), on charts 8 weeks

March 1972— Enters chart 15 April 1972 "Runnin' Away" c/w "Brave And Strong" (Epic EPC 7810) reaches no. 17 (no. 16 on 'NME' chart 13th May), on charts 8 weeks

March 1973—"Family Affair" c/w "Dance To The Music" (Epic EPC 1148)

August 1973—"If You Want Me To Stay" c/w "Thankful 'n' Thoughtful" (Epic EPC 1655)

January 1974—"Que Sera Sera" c/w "If It Were Left Up To Me" (Epic EPC 1981)

July 1974—"Time For Livin'" c/w "Small Talk" (Epic EPC 2530)

January 1975—"Loose Booty" c/w "Can't Strain My Brain" (Epic EPC 2882)

February 1975—"Dance To The Music" c/w "Colour Me True" + "Stand!" + "Ride The Rhythm" (Epic EPC 3048)

October 1975—"I Get High On You" c/w "That's Lovin' You" (Epic EPC 3596) as by Sly Stone

January 1977—"Dance To The Music" c/w "I Want To Take You Higher" (Epic EPC 4879, re-issued c/w "Stand!" EPC 7070 in Feb 1979)

September 1979—"Remember Who You Are" c/w "Sheer Energy" (Warner K17474)

November 1979—"Dance To The Music" c/w "Sing A Simple Song" (Epic EPC 8017/13)

August 1980—"Dance To The Music" c/w "Everyday People" (Epic EPC 8853, re-issued on Old Gold OG9188 in July 1982)

October 1986—"Crazay" with Jesse Johnson c/w "Be Your Man" (by Jesse Johnson only) (A&M AM360)

September 1987—"Dance To The Music" c/w "Family Affair" (Portrait SLY1)

September 1987—"Dance To The Music" c/w "Family Affair" + "Everyday People" + "Runnin' Away" (Portrait EPC SLYT1 12-inch)

US Singles

1966—"I Ain't Got Nobody" c/w "Can't Turn You Loose" (Loadstone 3951) 'B'-side is a cover of the Otis Redding song. No national chart placing. Since re-licensed by studio owner Leo Kulka through a number of labels (+ other tracks "Life Of Fortune And Fame" & "Take My Advice")

1967— "Underdog" c/w "I Want To Take You Higher" (Epic 10229) No chart placing

November 1967— "Dance To The Music" c/w "Let Me Hear It From You" (Epic 5-10256) Enters chart 2 March 1968, reaches no. 8, on chart 12 weeks

December 1967—"Dance A La Musique" (Epic) instrumental promo-only single as by The French Fries

June 1968— "Life" c/w "M'Lady" (Epic 10353)

November 1968—"Everyday People" c/w "Sing A Simple Song" (Epic 5-10407) Enters chart 4 January 1969, reaches no. 1 for 4 weeks, on chart 14 weeks

April 1969— "Stand" c/w "I Want To Take You Higher" (Epic 5-10450) Enters chart 26 April 1968 reaches no. 22, on chart 6 weeks. Re-issued in 1975.

Enters chart 30 August 1969— "Hot Fun In The Summertime" c/w "Fun" (US Epic 10497, UK Direction 58-4471) reaches no. 2 for two weeks, on chart 13 weeks (reissued Epic 50119) Enters chart 10 January 1970— "Thank You (Falettinme Be Mice Elf Agin)" c/w "Everybody Is A Star" (Epic 5-10555) reaches no. 1 for two weeks, on chart 12 weeks

Enters chart 20 June 1970— "I Want To Take You Higher" c/w "You Can Make It If You Try" (US Epic 10450, UK CBS 5054) re-entry of 1969 Hot 100 entry, reaches no. 38, on chart 3 weeks

Enters chart 13 November 1971— "Family Affair" c/w "Luv 'n' Haight" (Epic 5-10805) reaches no. 1 for three weeks, on chart 13 weeks

Enters chart 26 February 1972— "Runnin' Away" c/w "Brave And Strong" (Epic 10829) reaches no. 23, on chart 6 weeks

April 1972— "(You Caught Me) Smilin'" c/w "Luv 'n' Haight" (Epic 10850) reaches no. 42

Enters chart 14 July 1973— "If You Want Me To Stay" c/w "Thankful 'n' Thoughtful" (Epic 11017) reaches no. 12, on chart 13 weeks

October 1973—"Frisky" c/w "If It Were Left Up To Me" (Epic 11060) No chart place

November 1973— "Que Sera Sera" c/w "If It Were Left Up To Me" (Epic) No chart place

Enters chart 17 August 1974— "Time For Livin'" c/w "Small Talk" (Epic 11140) reaches no. 32, on chart 3 weeks

January 1974—"Loose Booty" c/w "Can't Strain My Brain" (Epic 50033) No chart place

August 1975—"I Get High On You" c/w "That's Lovin' You" (Epic 50135) as by Sly Stone

December 1975—"Le-Lo-Li" c/w "Who Do You Love" (Epic 501750) as by Sly Stone

February 1976—"Crossword Puzzle" c/w "Greed" (Epic 50201) as by Sly Stone

February 1977—"Family Again" c/w "Nothing Less Than Happiness" (Epic 50331)

1978—"Dance To The Music" c/w "Sing A Simple Song" (Epic 50795)

November 1979—"Remember Who You Are" c/w "Sheer Energy" (USA— Warner Bros. 49062, UK—WB K17474) no. 38 on US R&B chart, 104 on US Pop chart

1980—"Same Thing" c/w "Who's To Say" (Warner Bros. 49132)

October 1986—"Crazay" with Jesse Johnson c/w "Be Your Man" (by Jesse Johnson only) (A&M 2878) no. 2 on the US R&B chart, and no. 53 on the US Pop chart

1987—"Eek-A-Bo-Statik" c/w "Eek-A-Bo-Statik (instrumental)" (A&M 2890) no chart place

1988—"Ruby Shoes"

Albums

'**Whole New Thing**' by Sly & The Family Stone (US Epic 24324— October 1967, then Epic 30333, UK CD Epic EK 66424—July 1995) includes "Underdog", "If This Room Could Talk", "Run, Run, Run", "Turn Me Loose", "Let Me Hear It From You", "Advice", "I Cannot Make It", "Trip To Your Heart", "I Hate To Love Her", "Bad Risk", "That Kind Of Person", "Dog" + previously unissued track "What Would I Do" included on Sony's April 1995 CD re-issue (Musicians are Sly Stone, Freddie Stone, Rose Stone, Cynthia Robinson, Jerry Martini, Larry Graham and Greg Errico) 20th March 2007 40th-Anniversary Epic/Legacy digipak restored & expanded re-issue with bonus tracks "Underdog" (B-side version, mono), "Let Me Hear It From You" (B-side version, mono), "Only One Way Out Of This Mess", "What Would I Do", "You Better Help Yourself" (previously unreleased instrumental)

'**Dance To The Music**' (US Epic 26371— March 1968, UK debut album on Direction 8-63412—April 1968) includes "Dance To The Music", "Higher", "I Ain't Got Nobody (For Real)", "Ride The Rhythm", "Colour Me True", "Are You Ready", "Don't Burn Baby", "I'll Never Fall In Love Again", "Dance To The Medley: Music Is Alive/ Dance In/ Music Lover" + previously unissued track "Soul Clappin'" included on Sony's 1995 CD re-issue Epic 4809062. Reached no. 142 on US album chart. First re-issued October 1973 on 'CBS-Embassy EMB 31030' (Musicians as above) 20th March 2007 40th-Anniversary Epic/Legacy digipak restored & expanded re-issue with bonus tracks "Dance To The Music" (single version, mono), "Higher" (unissued single version, mono), "Soul Clappin'", "We Love All" (previously unreleased), "I Can't Turn You Loose" (previously unreleased), "Never Do Your Woman Wrong" (previously unreleased instrumental)

'**Life**' (Epic 26397—July 1968, originally titled 'M'Lady' for its UK release is CBS Direction 63461) includes "Dynamite", "Chicken", "Plastic Jim", "Fun", "Into My Own Thing", "Harmony", "Life", "Love City", "I'm An Animal", "M'Lady", "Jane In A Groupee" + previously unissued track "Only One Way Out Of This Mess" included on Sony's July 1995 CD re-issue Epic/Legacy 4809052. Reached no. 195 on US album chart. (Musicians as above) 20th March 2007 40th-Anniversary Epic/Legacy digipak restored & expanded re-issue with bonus tracks "Dynamite!" (single version, mono), "Seven More Days" (previously unreleased), "Pressure" (previously unreleased), "Sorrow" (previously unreleased instrumental)

'**Stand**' (Epic 26456— April 1969, UK Direction 8-63655/ CBS 63655—July 1969) includes "Stand!", "Don't Call Me Nigger, Whitey", "I Want To Take You Higher", "Somebody's Watching You", "Sing A Simple Song", "Everyday People", "Sex Machine", "You Can Make It If You Try" (Musicians as above). Reached no. 13 on US album chart. Listed at no. 118 in *'Rolling Stone'* magazine's 'The 500 Greatest Albums Of All Time'. Re-issued on CD Epic EK 64422 in February 1995. 20th March 2007 40th-Anniversary Epic/Legacy digipak restored & expanded re-issue with bonus tracks "Stand!" (single version, mono), "I Want To Take You Higher" (single version, mono), "You Can Make It If You Try" (unissued/cancelled single version, mono), "Soul Clappin' II" (previously unreleased), "My Brain (Zig-Zag)" (previously unreleased instrumental)

'**Greatest Hits**' (US Epic 30325, UK Epic EPC 7632/CBS 69002—1970) compilation, with "I Want To Take You Higher", "Everybody Is A Star", "Stand", "Life", "Fun", "You Can Make It If You Try", "Dance To The Music", "Everyday People", "Hot Fun In The Summertime", "M'Lady", "Sing A Simple Song", "Thank You (Falletinme Be Mice Elf Agin)". Reached no. 2 on US album chart. Listed at no. 60 in *'Rolling Stone'* magazine's 'The 500 Greatest Albums Of All Time'. Re-issued in various formats, as an expanded quadraphonic-LP in December 1975 (Epic E69002, and EQ30325), then in March 1981 (CBS 32029/40), and as a June 1990 CD (Sony 471-758-2 /CBS 4625241), March 1991 (CD 462542)

'**There's a Riot Goin' On**' (US Epic 30986, UK CBS 64613—January 1972) includes "Luv 'n' Haight", "Just Like A Baby", "Poet", "Family Affair", "Africa Talks To You/ The Asphalt Jungle", "Brave And Strong/ There's A Riot Going On", "(You Caught Me) Smilin'", "Time", "Spaced Cowboy", "Runnin' Away", "Thank You For Talkin' To Me Africa". First tranche issued with free limited edition 12" EP & fold-in newspaper. Re-issued February 1986 on Edsel XED 165, then CD April 1994 (Epic 4670632). (Musicians as above). Reached no. 1 on US album chart. Sly's only UK chart album it spends just two weeks listed, enters chart 5 February 1972, peaks at no. 31 the following week. Listed at no. 99 in *'Rolling Stone'* magazine's 'The 500 Greatest Albums Of All Time'. 20th March 2007 40th Anniversary Epic/Legacy digipak restored & expanded re-issue with bonus tracks "Runnin' Away" (single version, mono), "Instrumental Tracks #'s 1, 2 & 3—My Gorilla Is My Butler, Do You Know What? & That's Pretty Clean" (previously unreleased, mono tracks)

'**Fresh**' (US Epic 32134, UK CBS 69039—June 1973) includes "In Time", "If You Want Me To Stay", "Let Me Have It All", "Frisky", "Thankful 'n' Thoughtful", "The Skin I'm In", "I Don't Know (Satisfaction)", "Keep On Dancin'", "Que Sera, Sera (Whatever Will Be, Will Be)", "If It Were Left Up

To Me", "Babies Makin' Babies". Reached no. 7 on US album chart. Listed at no. 186 in *Rolling Stone* magazine's 'The 500 Greatest Albums Of All Time'. Re-issued on CD May 1987 on 'Edsel' (Musicians are Sly Stone, Freddie Stone, Rose Stone, Cynthia Robinson, Jerry Martini, Rusty Allen, Andy Newmark, Pat Rizzo, Little Sister) (Re-issued 1987 on CD Edsel XED 232). 20th March 2007 40th-Anniversary Epic/Legacy digipak restored & expanded re-issue with bonus tracks, all alternate mixes, previously unreleased album masters, "Let Me Have It All", "Frisky", "Skin I'm In", "Keep On Dancin'", "Babies Makin' Babies"

'**Small Talk**' (US Epic 32930, UK Epic 69070—August 1974) includes "Small Talk", "Say You Will", "Mother Beautiful", "Time For Livin'", "Can't Strain My Brain", "Loose Booty", "Holdin' On", "Wishful Thinkin'", "Better Thee Than Me", "Livin' While I'm Livin'", "This Is Love" (Musicians are Sly Stone, Rose Banks, Jerry Martini, Cynthia Robinson, Pat Rizzo). Reached no. 15 on US album chart. 20th March 2007 40th-Anniversary Epic/Legacy digipak restored & expanded re-issue with bonus tracks "Crossword Puzzle" (previously unreleased), "Time For Livin'" (previously unreleased alternate version), "Loose Booty" (previously unreleased alternate version), "Positive" (previously unreleased instrumental)

'**High Energy**' (US Epic 88124, also Epic 33462, UK Epic 80754— March 1975, and Epic EPC 22004) Double-LP 23-track combination of '**A Whole New Thing**' and '**Life**' 'as near faultless as funkadelic ever got' says 'NME'

'**High On You**' by Sly Stone (US Epic 33835—December 1975, UK Epic EPC 69165) includes "I Get High On You", "Crossword Puzzle", "That's Lovin' You", "Who Do You Love?", "Green-Eyed Monster Girl", "Organize", "Le Lo Li", "My World", "So Good To Me", "Greed". Reached no. 45 on US album chart, and spawns three US singles October 1975 "I Get High On You" c/w "That's Lovin' You", December "Le Lo Li" c/w "Who Do You Love", and March 1976 "Crossword Puzzle" c/w "Greed" (Musicians are Sly Stone, Freddie Stone, Cynthia Robinson, Jerry Martini, Vet Stewart, Rusty Allen, Dawn Silva, Tiny Melton, Rudy Love, Dennis Marcellino, Cousin Gale (Gail Muldrow), Bobby Vega, Michael Samuels, Willie Wild-Sparks, Little Moses, Bobby Lyles, Tricky Truman Governor, Bill Lordon)

'**Heard Ya Missed Me, Well I'm Back**' by Sly & The Family Stone (US Epic 34348, also Epic 33698, UK Epic EPC 81641—December 1976) includes "Heard Ya Missed Me, Well I'm Back", "What Was I Thinkin' In My Head", "Nothing Less Than Happiness", "Sexy Situation", "Blessing In Disguise", "Everything In You", "Mother Is A Hippie", "Let's Be Together", "The Thing", "Family Again" spawns February 1977 single "Family Again" c/w "Nothing Less Than Happiness" (Musicians are Sly Stone, Cynthia Robinson, Joe Baker, Dwight Hogan, Johnny Colla, Steve Schuster, John Farey, Dawn Weber, Virginia Ayers, Lady Bianca, Vicky Blackwell, + Ed Bogas, Armando Peraza, Peter Frampton, Sister Vet, Cousin Tiny)

'**Back On The Right Track**' (US Warner Brothers 3303, UK Warner K56640—October 1979) includes "Remember Who You Are" (co-writer credits Sly with Hamp Banks), "Back On The Right Track", "If It's Not Addin' Up", "The Same Thing (Makes You Laugh, Makes You Cry)", "Shine It On", "It Takes All Kinds", "Who's To Say?", "Sheer Energy". Reached no. 152 on US album chart, and spawns December 1979 single "The Same Thing (Makes You Laugh, Makes You Cry)" c/w "Who's To Say" (Musicians are Sly Stone, Freddie Stewart, Rose Banks, Cynthia Robinson, Pat Rizzo, Mark Davis, Joseph Baker, Keni Burke, Walter Downing, Gary Herbig, Steve Madaio, Fred Smith, Lisa Banks, Joe Baker, Hamp Banks, Alvin Taylor, Ollie E Brown). Reissued as '**Remember Who You Are**' (Charly, 2006) with eight original tracks plus two previously unreleased bonus studio jams, "Somebody To You" and "Lady Is A Champ"

'**Ten Years Too Soon**' by Sly & The Family Stone (Epic EPC 83640, and Epic 35974—January 1980) Dance compilation of eight tracks including "Dance To The Music", "Sing A Simple Song", "Family Affair", "You Can Make It If You Try", "Stand!", "Everyday People", "This Is Love", and "I Get High On You" remixed by John Luongo. Produces limited-edition singles 12" "Dance To The Music" (6:31mins) c/w "Everyday People" (5:58) (Epic 49II-08151) and 12" 33 1/3rpm promo "Dance To The Music" (6:31) c/w "Sing A Simple Song" (6:04) (Epic A5675)

'**Ain't But the One Way**' (Warner Brothers BSK3303/ WEA International 23700-1—1982, WB 923 7001) includes "L.O.V.I.N.U", "One Way", "Ha-Ha, Hee-Hee" (Rizzo), "Hobo Ken", "Who In The Funk Do You Think You Are", "You Really Got Me" (Ray Davies), "Sylvester", "We Can Do It", "High, Y'All". UK copies consist of those imported from the USA.

'**Who the Funk Do You Think You Are: the Warner Bros. Recordings**' (Rhino Records—1994) The two albums '**Back on the Right Track**' and '**Ain't But the One Way**' combined into a single package.

'**Sly & The Family Stone: Live at the Fillmore East**' (January 2003) Bootleg recording dated 1968, low-fi, but forming a valuable historical document

'**Sly & The Family Stone: the Woodstock Experience**' (June 2009) 2CD, with CD1 a compilation of single's versions of "Stand!", "Don't Call Me Nigger, Whitey", "I Want To Take You Higher", "Somebody's Watching You", "Sing A Simple Song", "Everyday People", "Sex Machine" and "You Can Make It If You Try" and CD2 the full live set from the 'Woodstock Music & Art Fair' 16 August 1969—"M'Lady", "Sing A Simple Song", "You Can Make It If You Try", "Everyday People", "Dance To The Music", "Medley: Higher-Music Lover", "I Want To Take You Higher", "Love City", "Stand"

'**I'm Back! Family & Friends**' by Sly Stone (August 2011, Cleopatra Records www.slystonemusic.com) announced as his first new record in three decades, this CD is largely made up of new versions of old hits—with celebrity guests,

"Dance To The Music" with The Doors Ray Manzarak (also in 'Extended Mix' and 'Club Mix'), "Everyday People" with Heart's Ann Wilson, "Family Affair" (also in 'Dubstep Mix'), "Stand" with Carmine Appice & Ernie Watts, "Thank You (Falettinme Be Mice Elf Agin)" with Johnny Winter (also in 'Electro Club Mix), "(I Want To Take You) Higher" with Jeff Beck, "Hot Fun In The Summertime" with Bootsy Collins, plus only three genuine new tracks— "Plain Jane", "His Eye Is On The Sparrow" and "Get Away".

Compilations

'**Dance to the Music**' (Epic 7" EP— February 1975) with "Dance To The Music", "Colour Me True", "Stand!", "Ride The Rhythm"

'**Sly Stone: Recorded in San Francisco 1964-67**' (Sculpture label US SCP 2001—issued circa 1972—1979) compilation of various solo rarities and oddities from the pre-Sly & The Family Stone period

'**Dance to the Music**' (various editions, Embassy EMB 31030—1973, Epic—April 1985) in LP and CD formats

'**Dance to the Music**' (Thunderbolt on vinyl THBL & CDTB1.029 —April 1987) First of two albums of early Sly Stone 'Danny Stewart', 'Viscaynes' and related material—"Yellow Moon", "Help Me With My Broken Heart", "Uncle Sam Needs You My Friend", "You're My Only Love", "Heavenly Angel", "Oh! What A Night", "You've Forgotten Me", "Honest", "Nerves" and "Long Time Alone"—with refreshing honesty the title read-out on my iTunes display says 'Bogus Bootleg Crap'! The second volume is '**Family Affair**' (Thunderbolt CDTB 119) in October 1987 & CD May 1991

'**The Collection**' (UK Castle CD CCSCD 307—November 1991) Hits compilation

'**In the Still of the Night**' (CBS/ Epic—December 1991, Magnum Collectors re-issue 1999) with "(I'll Remember) In The Still Of The Night" (written by Fredd Parris), "Ain't That Lovin' You Baby" (Jimmy Reed), "I Can't Turn You Loose" (Otis Redding), "Searchin'" (Leiber & Stoller), "Seventh Son" (Willie Dixon & Willie Mabon), "Watermelon Man" (Herbie Hancock & Jon Hendricks), 'fake' live tracks + Sly's "Don't Say I Didn't Warn You", "Swim", "Every Dog Has His Day", "Buttermilk Pts 1&2", "Take My Advice", "I Ain't Got Nobody", "If You Were Blue", "Rock Dirge", "Hi Love", "Life Of Fortune And Fame"

'**Takin' You Higher: the Best of Sly & The Family Stone**' (Sony CD Epic 4717582—June 1992, re-issued October 1994 on CD 4775062) with "Dance To The Music", "I Want To Take You Higher", "Family Affair", "Thank You (Falletinme Be Mice Elf Agin)", "I Get High On You", "Stand", "M'Lady", "Skin I'm In", "Everyday People", "Sing A Simple Song", "Hot Fun In The Summertime", "Don't Call Me Nigger", "Brave And Strong",

"Life", "Everybody Is A Star", "If You Want Me To Stay", "(You Caught Me) Smilin'", "Que Sera Sera", "Running Away", "Family Affair (Re-mix)"

'**Anthology**' (Double album Epic 37071—1981, Epic 22119/40—May 1982, re-issued June 1988 as Epic 4601751) also a revised track-list '**Greatest Hits**' (Epic EPC 32029—March 1981, then CD Epic EPC 462524-2—1990)

'**Spotlight on Sly & The Family Stone**' (February 1994—CD Javelin HAD CD119)

'**Masters**' (Cleopatra—1998) with "In The Still Of The Night", "Searchin'", "Don't Say I Didn't Warn You", Ain't That Lovin' You Baby", "Swim", "Every Dog Has His Day", "Buttermilk Pts 1&2", "The Seventh Son", "I Can't Turn You Loose", "Take My Advice", "Watermelon Man", "I Ain't got Nobody", "If You Were Blue", "Rock Dirge", "Hi Love", "Life Of Fortune & Fame", "You're My Only Love", "Heavenly Angel", "Oh What A Night", "You've Forgotten Me", "Yellow Moon", "Honest", "Nerves", "Help Me With My Broken Heart", "Long Time Alone", "Uncle Sam Needs You My Friend"

'**Rare Grooves**' (Classic World—2001) with "It Takes All Kinds", "Remember Who You Are", "Shine It On", "Back On The Right Track", "Who's To Say?", "Sheer Energy", "If It's Not Addin' Up", "The Same Thing (Makes You Laugh Makes You Cry)", "Somebody To You"

'**The Essential Sly & The Family Stone**' (Sony 510018-2—2003) 35-track Double-CD Hits compilation

'**Higher**' (Starbucks Hear Music—2005) with "Dance To The Music", "Everyday People", "Hot Fun In The Summertime", "Sing A Simple Song", "Thank You", "I Want To Take You Higher", "Family Affair", "You Can Make It If You Try, "(You Caught Me) Smilin", "Just Like A Baby", "In Time", "If You Want Me To Stay", "Time For Livin", "Que Sera Sera", "If It Were Left Up To Me"

'**Different Strokes by Different Folks**' (Starbucks' Hear Music label—12th July 2005) an album of cover versions, 're-imagining' the band's songs, other tracks that sample the original recordings, and some that do both. "Star" by The Roots (cover of "Everybody Is A Star", which it also samples), "Everyday People" by Maroon Five, "Family Affair" by John Legend with Joss Stone & Van Hunt, "Dance To The Music" by Will I. Am of the Black-Eyed Peas (track featured in movie *Stealth*), "I Want To take You Higher" by Steven Tyler & Robert Randolph. Also "Sing A Simple Song" by Chuck D, D'Angelo & Isaac Hayes, "You Can Make It If You Try" by Buddy Guy & John Mayer, "Runnin' Away" by Big Boi featuring Sleepy Brown & Killer Mike, "If You Want Me To Stay" by Devin Lima, "Love City" by Moby, "(You Caught Me) Smilin" by Scar, "I Get High On You" by The Wylde Bunch (Produced by Randy Jackson, Nile Rogers, Steve Jordan etc). Epic/Legacy release an expanded version in January 2006 with 're-funked' covers of "Don't Call Me Nigger, Whitey" by Nappy Roots & Martin Luther, and "Thank You Nation 1814" with Janet Jackson.

'**Seventh Son: the Soul of Funk Collection**' (San Juan Music Group—2006) with "Seventh Son", "Searchin'", "Swim", "Swim pt2", "In The Still Of The Night", "Ain't That Lovin' You", "Suki Suki"

'Higher' (Epic/Legacy 88697-53665-2, 2013) 4-CD box-set featuring 77 tracks, including 17 rarities and previously unissued material, going back to "Dance All Night" by Sly and Freddie (1965), "Silent Communication" (1967), "What's That Got To Do With Me" (1967), "Dynamite" with Johnny Robinson vocals (1968), four live tracks from the Isle of Wight Festival, plus "Hoboken" (1975-1977) and more, with lavish 104 page insert booklet.

Sly Stone Rarities

1952— "On The Battlefield For My Lord" c/w "Walking In Jesus' Name" (78rpm single Church Of God In Christ 78-101, Northern Sunday School Dept) by The Stewart Four (Sly, Freddie, Rose and Vaetta)

1959— "The Rat" c/w "Ra Ra Roo" (Ensign 7" single 4032) by The Stewart Brothers (Sly and Freddie)

1960—"Sleep On The Porch" c/w "Yum Yum Yum" (Keen 7" single 2113) by The Stewart Brothers

1961— "A Long Time Alone" c/w "I'm Just A Fool" (Luke 7" single 1008) by Danny Stewart (aka Sly)

1961—"Are You My Girlfriend" c/w "You've Forgotten Me" (Luke 7" single) as by Danny Stewart

1961— "A Long Time Alone" c/w "Help Me With My Broken Heart" (G&P single 901) as by Sly Stewart

1961—"Yellow Moon" c/w "Uncle Sam Needs You (My Friend)" (V.P. M. single 1006) by The Biscaynes

1961— "Yellow Moon" c/w "Heavenly Angel" (V.P.M. re-issue 1006) as by The Viscaynes

1961— "Stop What You Are Doing" c/w "I Guess I'll Be" (Tropo single 101) by The Viscaynes

1962— "Yellow Moon" c/w "Heavenly Angel" (V.P.M 7" single re-issue) by Sly Stewart

1964— "I Just Learned How To Swim" c/w "Scat Swim" (Autumn 3 single) by Sly Stewart

1965— "Buttermilk" c/w "Buttermilk Part 2" (Autumn 14 single) by Sly

1965— "Temptation Walk" c/w "Temptation Walk Part 2" (Autumn 26 single) by Sly

1971—"Rock Dirge" c/w "Rock Dirge Part 2" (Woodcock 001—bootleg of early demo session) by Sly Stone (with Freddie Stewart)

'**Precious Stone: in the Studio With Sly Stone 1963-1965**' (Ace compilation of Autumn Records tracks—CD Ace DCCHD 539—September 1994) Total playing time 72:37-minutes. With "The Swim" (by Sly & Rose), "I Taught Him" and "Don't Say I Didn't Warn You" (by Gloria Scott), "The Nerve Of You" and "Every Dog Has His Day" (by Emile O'Connor), "That Little Old Heartbreaker Me" and "I'll Never Fall In Love Again" (by Bobby Freeman), "Fake It" and "Laugh" (by George & Teddy), "Dance All Night" (by Sly & Freddie), "Little Latin Lupe Lu (Medley)" (Sly & Billy Preston), "Can't You Tell I Love Her", "Life Of Fortune And Fame", "Take My Advice" and "As I Get Older" (by Billy Preston, Sly Stone etc)—all plus Sly's "Scat Swim", "Help Me With My Broken Heart", "Out Of Sight", "On Broadway" (Jerry Leiber/Barry Mann/ Mike Stoller/Cynthia Weil composition), "Searchin'" (Leiber/Stoller composition), "Lord, Lord", "The Seventh Son" (Willie Dixon/ Willie Mabon composition), "The Jerk", "Ain't That Lovin' You Baby" (Jimmy Reed composition), "Buttermilk Pt.1", "Temptation Walk", "Underdog" + 1:32 Radio Spot (Liner notes: Alec Palao)

'**Listen to the Voices: Sly Stone in the Studio 1965-1970**' (Ace compilation, March 2010) with "Dance A La Musique" (by The French Fries), "I'm Going Home, Part 1" (by Joe Hicks), "For Real" (by Sly), "Life And Death In G & A" (by Abaco Dream), "I'm Just Like You" (by 6IX), "Man Does Not Live" (by Sly & The Family Stone), "Underdog" (by The Beau Brummels), "Can't She Tell" (by Billy Preston), "I Can't Turn You Loose" (by Sly & The Family Stone), "You're The One, Parts 1 & 2" (by Little Sister), "LSD" (by Freddie & The Stone Souls), "Life Of Fortune And Fame" (by Sly & The Family Stone), "Are You Sure" (by The Beau Brummels), "Dynamite" (by 6IX), "I Ain't Got Nobody aka Good For Real" (by Sly & The Family Stone), "You Really Got Me" (by Sly), "Stanga" (by Little Sister), "I Remember" (by Sly & Billy Preston), "Something About You" (by Freddie & The Stone Souls), "Take My Advice" (by Sly & The Family Stone), "Home Sweet Home, Part 2" (by Joe Hicks), "Somebody's Watching You" (by Little Sister), "Superfunk" (by Freddie & The Stone Souls), "Life And Death In G & A, Parts 1 & 2" (by Joe Hicks), "Small Fries" (by The French Fries). With new liner comments by Sly himself.

'**You Found My Only Love**' mostly previously-unreleased productions from Autumn 1963-1965, plus teen-pop "Help Me With My Broken Heart" and novelty songs "Uncle Sam Needs You My Friend"

'**Remember Who You Are**' (CD Charly CPCD 8033—March 1994)

'**Every Dog Has Its Day**' (December 1994—CD Prestige Elite CDGP 0125), includes tracks written by other artists with "(I'll Remember) In The Still Of The Night" (written by Fredd Parris), "Seventh Son" (Willie Dixon & Willie Mabon), "Ain't That Lovin' You Baby" (Jimmy Reed), "I Can't Turn You Loose" (Otis Redding), "Watermelon Man" (Herbie Hancock & Jon Hendricks), "Searchin'" (Leiber & Stoller), + Sly's "Don't Say I Didn't

Warn You", "Swim", "Every Dog Has His Day", "Suki Suki Pts 1&2", "Take My Advice", "I Ain't Got Nobody", "If You Were Blue", "Rock Dirge", "Hi Love", "Life Of Fortune And Fame"

'**Pearls of the Past**' (February 1995—CD West Coast Productions KLMCD 005, includes tracks by The Mojo Men)

Soundtracks

'**Woodstock**' (Atlantic 2663-001) movie/festival soundtrack triple-album features Sly & The Family Stone sequence of "Dance To The Music", "Music Lover", "I Want To Take You Higher"

'**Soul Man**' (A&M, 1986) movie soundtrack album featuring "Love & Affection" by Sly Stone with Martha Davis (of the Motels)

'**My Girl**' (1991, Epic) features "Hot Fun In The Summertime"

'**Dead Presidents**' (Capitol, 1995) movie soundtrack album features "If You Want Me To Stay"

'**Crooklyn**' Vol.1 (MCA, 1995) soundtrack album of Spike Lee directed movie includes "Everyday People", Volume 2 includes "Everybody Is A Star"

'**Patch Adams**' (1998) soundtrack album of Robin Williams' Tom Shadyac directed movie includes "Stand"

'**Living Out Loud**' (1998, RCA) features "Hot Fun In The Summertime"

'**A Knight's Tale**' (2001) movie soundtrack album includes "I Want To Take You Higher"

'**Moonlight Mile**' (2002, Sony) features "I Want To Take You Higher"

'**Stealth**' (2005, Epic) features the Sly & The Family Stone + Will.i.am "Dance To The Music"

DVD

Sly's the original "Thank You (Faletinme Be Mice Elf Agin)" from The Dick Cavett Show

'**Sly & The Family Stone: My Own Beliefs—Video Anthology 1968-1986**' (2-DVD set) Although the image-quality of this extraordinary bootleg set is uneven, no serious student of Sly-ology could fail to be impressed by this four hours of vintage live and TV-clips. From the earliest 'studio/promo' clip of "Dance To The Music", through the hits, the Dick Cavett and Mike Douglas talk shows, the Madison Square Garden wedding footage, and even an (unrevealing) 1980's TV interview

Stone Flower Label (Sly Stone Productions)

1969—"I'm Goin' Home Part 1" c/w "Home Sweet Home Part 2" by Joe Hicks (Scepter 12266)

1970— "You're The One" c/w "You're The One Part 2" by Little Sister (Stone Flower 9000) also available on one-sided white label promo

1970— "Somebody's Watching You" c/w "Stanga" by Little Sister (US Stone Flower 9001, UK Atlantic 2091-053) both sides also available as one-sided white label promo's

1970— "Just Like You" c/w "Dynamite" by 6IX (Stone Flower 9002)

1970— "Life And Death In G&A" c/w "Life And Death In G&A Part 2" by Joe Hicks (Stone Flower 9003)

Rosemary Stewart Solo—Rose Banks

'**Rose Banks**' by Rose Banks (Motown STML 12024—July 1976), with a version of "High On You", musicians include Freddie Stone, Rusty Allen, David T Walker, Pat Rizzo, Cynthia Robinson. Produced by Jeffrey Bowen

February 1976— "Whole New Thing" c/w "What Am I Gonna Do With My Life" (Electrola)

September 1976— "Right's Alright" c/w "Darling Baby" (Motown)

1977— "Darling Baby" c/w "Whole New Thing" (UK only—Tamla Motown)

1977—"You're Much Too Beautiful For Words" (UK only single)

1980— "Papa, Daddy Dear" c/w "Papa, Daddy Dear (Stone's Fusion)"

'**Already Motivated**' by Rose (Rose Stone: 2008) After a thirty-year gap, Rose Stone's returns with a laid-back but well considered set. Her work with Brother Freddie's church are apparent on the Christian concerns of "Higher Love"—although the sound is more an updated take on Sly's 'Riot' period—the slowly simmering title track, than it is gospel. In fact, a version of the Family Stone appears on "Sooner Or Later", while "Here I Go Again" includes a lengthy quote from "Thank You" and briefer interpolations from other hits. Despite the slightness of some of the tunes ("Love Is More Than Words") the confidence of her vocals and songwriting more than compensate. She adds a tasty organ solo to "Perfect Love"

Sly Stone Productions: 'Autumn Records'

1964—"I Taught Him Part 1" c/w "I Taught Him Part 2" (Warner Bros 5413) by Gloria Scott & The Tonettes

1964—"Let's Surf Again" c/w "Come To Me" (Autumn 1) by Bobby Freeman

1964—"C'mon And Swim Part 1" c/w "C'mon And Swim Part 2" (Autumn 2) by Bobby Freeman

1964—"S-W-I-M" c/w "That Little Old Heartbreaker Me" (Autumn 5) by Bobby Freeman

1964—"Little One" c/w "Jo-Ann" (Autumn 7) by The Spearmints

1965—"I'll Never Fall In Love Again" c/w "Friends" (Autumn 9) by Bobby Freeman

1965—"Off The Hook" c/w "Mama's Little Baby" (Autumn 11) by The Mojo Men

1965—"I Still Love You" c/w "Anything" (Autumn 15) by The Vejtables

1965—"Nobody But Me" c/w "I Think It's Time" (Autumn 17) by The Chosen Few

1965—"Dance With Me" c/w "Loneliest Boy In Town" (Autumn 19) by The Mojo Men

1965—"The Duck" c/w "Cross My Heart" (Autumn 25) by Bobby Freeman

1965—"She's My Baby" c/w "Fire In My Heart" (Autumn 27) by The Mojo Men

1966—"Somebody To Love" c/w "Free Advice" (Northbeach 1001) by The Great Society

+ LP 1964—'**C'mon and S-W-I-M**' (Autumn 102) by Bobby Freeman with "C'mon And Swim Pts 1&2", "Good Lovin'", "Ya Ya", "Walkin' The Dog", "Work Song", "Money", "S-W-I-M" + Sly compositions "Do The Monkey", "Speedo (The Monkey Man)", "I'll Never Fall In Love Again" and "That Little Old Heartbreaker Me". An expanded 2000 Ace CD re-issue adds five singles track including "Come To Me" and "Cross My Heart" + seven out-takes including Sly compositions "Friends", "Dance All Night", "Every Dog Has Its Day" and "Swing Me"

+ LP March 25 1966—'**The Wildest Organ in Town**' (Capitol 2532) by Billy Preston— his second album, arranged by Sly, and featuring three Billy Preston/Sly Stone compositions including one credited on the sleeve as "Advice", which will later evolve into "I Want To Take You Higher", "Midnight Hour" (Wilson Pickett & Steve Cropper), "Uptight" (May, Stevie Wonder, Cosby), "Hard Day's Night" (Lennon/McCartney), "Love Makes Me Do Foolish Things" (Holland/Dozier/Holland), "The Duck" (Smith/Nelson), + Preston's "Ain't Got No Time To Play", "Satisfaction", "I Got You", "It's Got To Happen", "Free Funk", "The In-Crowd", total 29:20-minutes. Producer: Steve Douglas

'Sly Stone & The Mojo Men' (San Juan Music Group—May 2006) deliberately misleading title as this album—with its blue cover-photo of a young Sly, is made up of the Mojo Men 'Autumn' sessions with Sly merely as producer and arranger, fourteen tracks are "My Woman's Head" (around the 'Dirty Water' riff), "The New Breed", "As I Get Older", "Something Bad", "Fire In My Heart", "She's My Baby", "Free As A Bird", "Girl Won't You Go", "Everything I Need", "Why Can't You Stay", "Off The Hook" (Rolling Stones' song), "Crazy Love Song", "Under The Influence (Of Love)", and "Dance Your Pants Off" (which features what sounds suspiciously like the 'Dance To The Music' horn arrangement)

Sly Stone Guest Sessions

1974—Reo Speedwagon album '**Lost in a Dream**', Sly plays guitar and keyboards on "You Can Fly"

1974—Elvin Bishop, Sly plays organ on album '**Let it Flow**'

1975—New Riders of the Purple Sage album '**Oh, What A Mighty Time**' Sly plays organ and piano on the title-track

1976—Temptations album '**Wings of Love**', writing, arrangements and instrumentation under the collective alias 'Truman Thomas'

1976—Bobby Womack album '**Don't Know What the World is Coming To**', background vocals on title-track. Sly also shares vocals on track "When The Weekend Comes" on his 1987 album '**The Last Soul Man**' (also included on the 1993 album '**I Still Love You**')

1978—Bonnie Pointer album '**Bonnie Pointer**', writing and instrumentation as 'Truman Thomas', also on her 1979 album

1981—Funkadelic album '**The Electric Spanking of War Babies**', writing and instrumentation on "Funk Gets Stronger Parts 1 & 2"

1982—Godmoma album '**Godmoma Here**', writing and instrumentation on "Be All You Can Be"

1983—P-funk All-Stars writing and instrumentation on the album '**Urban Dancefloor Guerillas**' (CBS) including "Catch A Keeper", a 5:46-minute co-composition from Sly with Donnie Sterling and George Clinton and Sly background vocals with Dawn Silva, also the P-funk All-Stars 1992 compilation album '**Go For Yer Funk (Clinton Family Series Volume 1)**' which includes a 1981 demo version of "Who In The Funk Do You Think You Are" (Sly's track from '**Ain't But the One Way**'), and he plays bass on the 1980 track "Superstar Madness" on their 1994 album '**Testing Positive For the Funk (Clinton Family Series Volume 4)**'. 'Hydraulic Pump'—featuring Bobby Womack, was reissued in expanded form by Westbound as '**Hydraulic Funk**' (1995) with Sly co-writer credits on "Pump Up & Down", "Hydraulic Pump Pts 1&2", "Throw Your Hands Up In The Air", "Catch A Keeper", "Pumpin' You Is So Easy".

1983—Gene Page Headliners featuring Sly Stone & Danny Pearson, guest leads on the album '**Chasing the Rock**'

1986— Jesse Johnson album '**Shockadelia**' (A&M) features Sly Stone guest vocals on "Crazay"

1989—The Bar-Kays album '**Animal**', Sly co-wrote and co-produces the track "Just like A Teeter-Totter"

1990—Maceo Parker album '**For All the King's Men**', Sly guest lead on "Tell The World"

1990—Earth Wind & Fire album '**Heritage**', Sly guest lead vocal on "Good Time"

1991—13Cats album '**March of the 13Cats**', Sly plays guitar on their version of "Thank You (Falletinme Be Mice Elf Agin)"

Beau Brummels: the Vinyl-Ology

"I Wanna Twist" by Sal Valentino & The Valentines (1962 Independent single)

"Laugh Laugh"/ "Still In Love With You Baby" by Beau Brummels (Sly Stone production—Autumn single 8—December 1964/ UK— Pye 7N-25295)

"Just A Little"/ "They'll Make You Cry" (Sly Stone production—Autumn single 10—1965/ UK Pye Int 7N-25306)

"You Tell Me Why"/ "I Want You" (Sly Stone production—Autumn Single 16—1965/UK 7N-25318)

"Don't Talk To Strangers"/ "In Good Time" (Sly Stone production—Autumn single 20—1965/ UK 7N-25333)

"Good Time Music"/ "Sad Little Girl" (Autumn single 24—1965)

'**Introducing the Beau Brummels**' (Sly Stone production— Autumn LP 103—1965) with Laugh Laugh/ Still In Love With You Baby/ Just A Little/ Just Wait And See/ Oh Lonesome Me/ Ain't That Loving You Baby/ Stick Like Glue/ They'll Make You Cry/ That's If You Want Me To/ I Want More Loving/ I Would Be Happy/ Not Too Long Ago (issued October '65 on Pye NPL28062 in the UK when *Record Mirror* opines 'their sound is early Liverpudlian with a touch of the San Francisco'. They award it just two stars. A 1995 CD re-issue from Sundazed SC6039 adds bonus tracks 'Good Time Music' + a demo of 'Just A Little')

'**Volume Two**' (Sly Stone production— Autumn LP 104—1965) with You Tell Me Why/ I Want You/ Doesn't Matter/ That's Alright/ Sometime At Night/ Can It Be/ Sad Little Girl/ Woman (instrumental)/ Don't Talk To Strangers/ I've Never Known/ When It Comes To Your love/ In Good Time (1995 re-issue from Sundazed SC6040 includes an alternate take of 'Woman' + instrumental 'When It Comes To Your Love')

Related memorabilia includes Ron Elliott's solo album '**The Candlestickman**', plus '**Autumn in San Francisco**' (Edsel ED141) and '**The Autumn**

Records Story' (Rhino/Edsel ED145) which includes rare version of "The Jerk" recorded with The Bobby Freeman Band, and an early demo of "Sad Little Girl", more demos and rarities appear on '**San Fran Sessions: the Beau Brummels**' (Sundazed SC 103) a richly documented 46-track three-CD set. Also recommended is compilation '**Autumn of Their Years**' (Big Beat CDWIKD 127)

Dramatis Personnae

Sly Stone (Sylvester Stewart, born 15th March 1944 in Denton, Texas) 1967-1975, vocals, organ, guitar, bass, piano, harmonica, etc. Official website http://www.phattadatta.com/

Freddie Stone (Frederick Stewart, born 5th June 1946, Vallejo) 1967-1975, vocals, guitar. Official website http://www.stonecisum.com/

Larry Graham (Born 14th August 1946 in Beaumont, Texas) 1967-1972, vocals, bass guitar

Rose Stone (Rosemary Stewart, born 21st March 1945 in Vallejo, California) 1968-1975, vocals, piano, electric piano Rosiecrans@aol.com

Cynthia Robinson (Born 12th January 1946 in Sacramento, California) 1967-1975, trumpet, vocal ad-libs. Has two daughters, and six grandchildren.

Jerry Martini (Born 1st October 1943 in Boulder, Colorado) 1967-1975, saxophone. After Sly he joined Larry Graham's Central Station in 1997, and moved to Waikiki Beach in Honolulu with his fifth wife.

Gregg Errico (Born 1st September 1946 in San Francisco) 1967-1971, drums. Later produced '**Nasty Gal**', the first of three funk albums recorded by Betty (Mabry) Davis, ex-wife of Miles

Vet Stone (Vaetta Stewart, Sly's 'little sister') Stephen & Vaetta Reese

Little Sister consisting of Vet Stone plus Mary McCreary and Elva Mouton, backing vocals Official Little Sister/Stone Family website http://www.slyslilsis.com/

Gerry Gibson 1971-1972, one of several interim drummers replacing Gregg Errico. Later plays on John Lennon's '**Double Fantasy**' album

Andy Newmark 1973-1974, drums, replaces Gerry Gibson, and is in turn replaced by Bill Lordan

Bill Lordan drums for the 1974 '**Small Talk**' album, later hooks up with Robin Trower's band

Pat Rizzo 1972-1975, saxophone

Rusty Allen 1972-1975, bass, replaces Larry Graham. Has worked with the Edwin Hawkins Singers

Skyler Jett—becomes vocalist/percussionist with 'Sly's Family Stone', after he's already replaced Lionel Richie in The Commodores. Also has credits for "My Heart Will Go On" (in 'Titanic') as well as soundtrack contributions to 'The Bodyguard' and 'License To Kill'.

Books & Other Reference Works Consulted

For the Record: Sly & The Family Stone—an Oral History by Joel Selvin (Quill Publications 1998, New York, ISBN 038-079377-6) plus 'Sly & The Family Stone: Lucifer Rising' by Joel Selvin, feature in Mojo magazine (August 2001)

I Want to Take You Higher: the Life and Times of Sly & The Family Stone by Jeff Kaliss (Backbeat Books 2008, ISBN 978-0-87930-934-3)

Midnight Mover: My Autobiography by Bobby Womack (John Blake 2006, ISBN 1-84454-148-7)

Miles: the Autobiography by Miles Davis with Quincy Troupe (Simon & Schuster 1989, ISBN 0-330-31382-7)

Mystery Train by Greil Marcus (Faber, 1975, ISBN 0-571-22721-X)

Takin' Back My Name: the Confessions of Ike Turner by Ike Turner (with Nigel Cawthorne) (Virgin Books—£16.99—ISBN 1-85227-850-1)

There's a Riot Goin' On by Miles Marshall Lewis (Continuum $33^{1}/_{3}$ Paperback 2006 ISBN 0-8264-1744-2)

'Rolling Stone no. 54' (19 March 1970) 'Everybody Is A Star: The Travels Of Sylvester' by Ben Fong-Torres

'Melody Maker' (5th May 1973) 'Sly Stone Interview' by Michael Watts

'New Musical Express' (19th June 1976) 'Sly And The Devil: Was Walkin' Side By Side' by Nick Kent

'Spin' (1985) 'Sly Stone's Heart Of Darkness' by Edward Kiersh

'i-D' magazine' (January 1988) 'Stone Free: Sly Stone' profile by Simon Witter

'Record Collector No. 164' (April 1993) 'Sly & The Family Stone: Funky People' by Peter Doggett

'Observer Music Monthly no. 31' (March 2006) 'Looking At The Devil: Sly Stone' by Barney Hoskyns

'Vanity Fair' (August 2007) 'Sly Stone's Higher Power' interview by David Kamp

Mojo (March 2010) 'Sly Stone: On The Edge' interview by Willem Alkema

www.phattadatta.com named by Sly himself, and Sly's own site 'Phattadatta is the next step in the revolution evolution of Sly'

http://en.wikipedia.org/wiki/Sly_%26_the_Family_Stone

http:www.slyandthefamilystone.net

http://sly-and-the-family-stone.com

Family Stone Official website http://www.familystoneband.com/

Family Stone Experience website http://www.familystoneexperience.com/

Official Epic Records Sly & The Family Stone website http://slystonemusic.com/

www.phunkphamilyaffair.com

www.stonecisum.com Pastor Fred Stewart 'Freddie Stone' website

Steve Reese, Sly historian (and Vet's husband), appears at the 2004 Soul-Patrol East Coast Convention with 'History Of Sly & The Family Stone' presentation, from www.slyslilsis.com T. Watts, writer and researcher

www.ingramcontent.com/pod-product-compliance
Lightning Source LLC
Chambersburg PA
CBHW032147080426
42735CB00008B/613